ELECTRONIC MEDIA MANAGEMENT

Fifth Edition

ELECTRONIC MEDIA MANAGEMENT

Fifth Edition

PETER K. PRINGLE

MICHAEL F. STARR

ELSEVIER

AMSTERDAM • BOSTON • HEIDELBERG • LONDON
NEW YORK • OXFORD • PARIS • SAN DIEGO
SAN FRANCISCO • SINGAPORE • SYDNEY • TOKYO
Focal Press is an imprint of Elsevier

Focal
Press

Acquisitions Editor: Amy Eden Jollymore
Assistant Editor: Cara B. Anderson
Publishing Services Manager: Simon Crump
Marketing Manager: Christine Degon
Interior Design: Jennifer Plumley

Focal Press is an imprint of Elsevier
30 Corporate Drive, Suite 400, Burlington, MA 01803, USA
Linacre House, Jordan Hill, Oxford OX2 8DP, UK

∞ Recognizing the importance of preserving what has been written, Elsevier prints its books on acid-free paper whenever possible.

Library of Congress Cataloging-in-Publication Data Application Submitted

British Library Cataloguing-in-Publication Data
A catalogue record for this book is available from the British Library.

ISBN 13: 978-0-240-80639-6
ISBN 10: 0-240-80639-5

For information on all Focal Press publications
visit our website at www.books.elsevier.com

05 06 07 08 09 10   10 9 8 7 6 5 4 3 2 1

Printed in the United States of America

Table of Contents

V

vi

vii

X

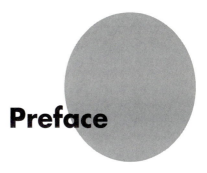

Preface

Every generation probably would claim that it lived in changing times. What distinguishes this generation is the pace of change. The rapidity with which advances occur quickly renders obsolete traditional methods of doing things.

With their reliance on technology, the media—especially electronic media—are particularly susceptible to change. Proof lies in the confused reactions of many executives to the results of Roper's latest quinquennial Media Comparison Study. One of its findings is that television viewing has increased since 2000. But that conclusion may suggest more about consumers' video consumption than about the television medium in an age of mushrooming growth in the number and variety of video distribution methods.

Confusion about the transformation we are witnessing is not limited to TV executives. Decision makers in all media face the task of trying to identify trends and understand their possible implications so that they may take actions deemed appropriate at the time. In the pages that follow, the authors have attempted to prepare prospective managers to handle the complexities that characterize today's electronic media environment.

The organization of the book remains unchanged from the fourth edition. However, all chapters have been updated. New case studies reflecting contemporary challenges accompany each. Similarly, the glossary and the bibliography include the language and the literature of this new era.

The authors have been assisted in their efforts by reviewers and users of the fourth edition, to whom they offer thanks.

They are also appreciative of the support they have received from the staff at Focal Press. And they are especially indebted to their editor, Amy Jollymore. Her insights, guidance, and suggestions have made the writing of this edition instructive and rewarding.

Acknowledgments

Terry Bonvillain, CPA

Dan Brown, Vice-President and General Manager, Citadel Broadcasting, Chattanooga

Duane Bryan, Advertising and Promotion Manager, WRCB-TV, Chattanooga

J. Y. Elliott, III, Miller & Martin, Chattanooga, Nashville, and Atlanta

Randy Feldman, WYES-TV, New Orleans

Ralph Flynn, Local Sales Manager, WRCB-TV, Chattanooga

Mark Fratrick, Broadcast Investment Analysts

David Freeman, WWOZ-FM, New Orleans

Deborah S. Grugen

Greg Guy, Patrick Communications

Richard Helmick, Cohn and Marks, LLP

Steven Mitchel, National Association of Broadcasters

Larry Patrick, Patrick Communications

Susan Patrick, Patrick Communications

James Starr, LaTerr Broadcasting Corporation

Tom Taylor, *Inside Radio*

Tom Tolar, President, Sarkes Tarzian Television

Chuck Wilkins, Director of Sales, Citadel Broadcasting, Chattanooga

Kennard Yamada, Local Sales Manager, WGOW AM/FM, Citadel Broadcasting, Chattanooga

Broadcast Station Management

This chapter examines broadcast station management by

- defining management and tracing the roots of today's management thought and practice

- identifying the functions and roles of the broadcast station general manager and the skills necessary to carry them out

- discussing the major influences on the general manager's decisions and actions

As the year 2000 approached, many Americans were preoccupied with the projected havoc that the so-called "millennium bug" would inflict. They were flooded with predictions that the computer, the revolutionary technology that controls the nation's transportation, utilities, banking, and many other institutions, would plunge society into chaos. And all because programmers had failed to anticipate the consequences—when a new century began—of identifying years only by their last two digits. In the event, of course, the new millennium began as the old one had ended, with only isolated problems.

That the dire predictions proved to be unfounded may be attributed to the fact that decision makers throughout the country acted. They digested the facts, contemplated the alternatives, formulated plans, and implemented them. In other words, they managed change.

Managing change is a way of life for broadcast station managers, who have to contend routinely with a shifting public policy climate and accelerating technological innovation. But that is only one of the challenges they confront. Like any other business, the station must be operated profitably if it is to survive and satisfy the financial expectations of its owners. At the same time, it must respond to the interests of the community it is licensed to serve by the Federal Communications Commission (FCC). Balancing the private interests of owners and the public interest of listeners or viewers is a continuing challenge.

A broadcast station engages in many functions. It is an advertising medium, an entertainment medium, an information medium, and a service medium. To discharge those functions in a way that satisfies advertisers, audiences, and employees is an additional challenge. Another challenge grows out of the increasingly competitive environment in which broadcast stations operate.

Internet and satellite radio are alternatives to radio stations, whose average weekly listenership is down two hours from the late 1990s.

Television station managers face continuing competition from wired cable, which added more than five million subscribers between 2000 and 2005.[1] In the same period, direct broadcast satellite (DBS) services more than doubled their penetration of TV households to 19 percent.[2] Add to the mix digital video recorders (DVRs), videocassette recorders (VCRs), digital video disk (DVD) players, the Internet, and other content-reception devices, and it is easy to understand why managers conclude that they face unprecedented competition.

Responsibility for a station's operation is entrusted by the owners to a chief executive, usually called the *general manager*. As a result of the explosion in in-market consolidation of radio stations in the 1990s, many general managers found themselves running multiple stations or "clusters." Typically, they are called *market managers*. This chapter will look at the functions and roles of the person charged with ultimate responsibility for the fate of a broadcast operation, be it a stand-alone or part of a cluster.

First, however, it will be helpful to consider what management is, as well as the evolution of management thought and practice during the lifetime of broadcasting.

2

MANAGEMENT DEFINED

If you were to ask a group of people what management means, chances are that each would offer a different definition. That is not surprising, given the diversity and complexity of a manager's responsibilities.

Schoderbek, Cosier, and Aplin define it as "a process of achieving organizational goals through others."[3] Resource acquisition and coordination are emphasized by Pringle, Jennings, and Longenecker: "Management is the process of acquiring and combining human, financial, informational, and physical resources to attain the organization's primary goal of producing a product or service desired by some segment of society."[4] Others view it from the perspective of the functions that managers perform. For example, Carlisle speaks of "directing, coordinating, and influencing the operation of an organization so as to obtain desired results and enhance total performance."[5]

Mondy, Holmes, and Flippo expand those functions and underline the importance of people, as well as materials: "Management may be defined as the process of planning, organizing, influencing, and controlling to accomplish organizational goals through the coordinated use of human and material resources."[6] That is the definition that will be used in this book.

EVOLUTION OF MANAGEMENT THOUGHT

It is tempting to think of management as a comparatively modern practice, necessitated by the emergence of large business organizations. However, as early as 6000 B.C., groups of people were organized to engage in undertakings of giant proportions. The Egyptians built huge pyramids. The Hebrews carried out an exodus from Egyptian bondage. The Romans constructed roads and aqueducts, and the Chinese built a 1500-mile wall. It is difficult to believe that any of these tasks could have been accomplished without the application of many of today's management techniques.

To understand current management concepts and practices requires familiarity with the evolution of management thought. It traces its start to the dawn of the twentieth century, when the foundations of what later would be called *broadcasting* were being laid. Just as broadcasting has evolved, so has systematic analysis of management. The dominant traits of different managerial approaches have been identified and grouped into so-called schools. The first was the classical school of management.

THE CLASSICAL SCHOOL

Classical management thought embraces three separate but related approaches to management: (1) scientific management, (2) administrative management, and (3) bureaucratic management.

Scientific Management   At its origin, scientific management focused on increasing employee productivity and rested on four basic principles:

- systematic analysis of each job to find the most effective and efficient way of performing it (the "one best way")
- use of scientific methods to select employees best suited to do a particular job
- appropriate employee education, training, and development
- responsibility apportioned almost equally between managers and workers, with decision-making duties falling on the managers

The person associated most closely with this school is Frederick W. Taylor (1856–1915), a mechanical engineer, who questioned the traditional, rule-of-thumb approach to managing work and who earned the title "father of scientific management."

Taylor believed that economic incentives were the best motivators. Workers would cooperate if higher wages accompanied higher productivity, and management would be assured of higher productivity in return for paying higher wages. Not surprisingly, he was criticized for viewing people as machines.

However, his contributions were significant. Management scholar Peter Drucker attributes to Taylor "the tremendous surge of affluence . . . which has lifted the working masses in the developed countries well above any level recorded before."[7] Job analysis, methods of employee selection, and their training and development are examples of ways in which principles of scientific management are practiced today.

Administrative Management   If Taylor was the father of scientific thought, the French mining and steel executive Henri Fayol (1841–1925) can lay claim to being the father of management thought. While Taylor looked at workers and ways of improving their productivity, Fayol considered the total organization with a view to making it more effective and efficient. In so doing, he developed a comprehensive theory of management and demonstrated its universal nature.

His major contributions to administrative theory came in a book, *General and Industrial Management*, in which he became the first person to set forth the functions of management or, as he called them, "managerial activities":

Planning: Contemplating the future and drawing up a plan to deal with it, which includes actions to be taken, methods to be used, stages to go through, and the results envisaged.

Organizing: Acquiring and structuring the human and material resources necessary for the functioning of the organization.

Commanding: Setting each unit of the organization into motion so that it can make its contribution toward the accomplishment of the plan.

Coordinating: Unifying and harmonizing all activities to permit the organization to operate and succeed.

Controlling: Monitoring the execution of the plan and taking actions to correct errors or weaknesses and to prevent their recurrence.[8]

To assist managers in carrying out these functions, Fayol developed a list of 14 principles (Figure 1.1). He did not suggest that the list was exhaustive, merely that the principles were those that he had needed to apply most frequently. He warned that such guidelines had to be flexible and adaptable to changing circumstances.

Principle	Explanation
1. Division of work	Specialization of work results in higher and better productivity.
2. Authority and responsibility	The right of the manager to give orders and to demand conformity, accompanied by appropriate responsibility.
3. Discipline	Obedience and respect for agreements between the firm and its employees.
4. Unity of command	An employee should receive orders from only one superior.
5. Unity of direction	Each group of activities having the same objective should have only one plan and one head.
6. Subordination of individual interest to general interest	The interest of one employee or group of employees should not prevail over that of the concern.
7. Remuneration of personnel	Payment should be fair and, as far as possible, satisfactory to both employer and employee.
8. Centralization	Each firm must find the optimum degree of centralization to permit maximum utilization of employee abilities.
9. Scalar chain	The line of authority, from top to bottom, through which all communications pass.
10. Order	Materials and employees in their appropriate places to facilitate the smooth running of the business.
11. Equity	Kindness, fairness, and justice in the treatment of employees.
12. Stability of tenure of personnel	Employees must be given time to get used to new work and to succeed in doing it well.
13. Initiative	The freedom and power to think out and execute a plan.
14. Esprit de corps	Establishing harmony and unity among the personnel.

5

FIGURE 1.1 Fayol's 14 principles of management. (Source: Henri Fayol, *General and Industrial Management.* Translated by Constance Storrs. London: Sir Isaac Pitman and Sons, 1965, pp. 19–42. The explanations have been paraphrased.)

Fayol's contributions may appear to be merely common sense in today's business environment. However, the functions of planning, organizing, and controlling that he identified are still considered fundamental to management success. Many of his principles are incorporated in business organization charts and, in the case of equity, are enshrined in law.

Bureaucratic Management   At the same time that Taylor and Fayol were developing their thoughts, Max Weber (1864–1920), a German sociologist, was contemplating the kind of structure that would enable an organization to perform at the highest efficiency. He called the result a *bureaucracy* and listed several elements for its success. They included:

- division of labor
- a clearly defined hierarchy of authority
- selection of members on the basis of their technical qualifications
- promotion based on seniority or achievement
- strict and systematic discipline and control
- separation of ownership and management[9]

It is unfortunate that contemporary society associates the word bureaucracy with incompetence and inefficiency. While it is true that a bureaucracy can become mired in rigid rules and procedures, Weber's ideas have proved useful to many large companies that need a rational organizational system to function effectively, and they have earned him a berth in the annals of management thought as "the father of organizational theory."

Contributors to the classical school of management concerned themselves with efforts to make employees and organizations more productive. Their work revealed several of their assumptions about the nature of human beings, among them the notion that workers are motivated chiefly by money and require a clear delineation of their job responsibilities and close supervision if work is to be accomplished satisfactorily. Such assumptions would not withstand the scrutiny of the school that followed.

THE BEHAVIORAL SCHOOL

The trend away from classical assumptions began with the human relations movement, which dominated during radio's heyday in the 1930s and 1940s. Among the greatest contributors to the movement were Mary Parker Follett (1868–1933) and Chester I. Barnard (1886–1961), both of whom rejected the view of the "economic man" held by the classical theorists.

Follett, a philosopher, argued in her writings that workers can reach their full potential only as members of a group, which she characterized as the foundation of an organization. In reality, managers and workers are members of the same group and, thus, share a common interest in the success of the enterprise.

Barnard, the president of New Jersey Bell Telephone Company, conceived of an organization as a "system of consciously coordinated activities or forces of two or more persons." As employees work toward the accomplishment of the organization's objectives, they have to be able to satisfy their own needs. Identifying ways of meeting those needs and, simultaneously, enhancing the effectiveness and efficiency of the organization, are the principal challenges facing managers.

However, the most far-reaching contributions to the human relations movement were made by Elton Mayo (1880–1949), a Harvard University psychologist. Between 1927 and 1932, Mayo and Fritz J. Roethlisberger (1898–1974) led a Harvard research team at Western Electric's Hawthorne plant in Illinois. The research focused on ways of improving worker efficiency by evaluating the factors that influence productivity. Its results redirected the course of management thought and practice.

What was observed in only one of the experiments gives a clue to the importance of the Hawthorne studies. To determine the effect on productivity of lighting levels, illumination remained constant among one group of workers (control group) and was systematically increased and decreased among another (experimental group). Contrary to expectations, productivity in both groups rose, even when the lighting in the experimental group was decreased.

The result of this and other experiments, combined with observation and interviews, convinced Mayo and his team that factors other than the purely physical have an effect on productivity. They realized that the one constant factor was the degree of attention paid to workers in the experimental groups. Thus was born the *Hawthorne Effect*, which states that when managers pay special attention to employees, productivity is likely to increase, despite a deterioration in working conditions.

The recognition that social as well as physical influences play a role in worker productivity marked an important milestone. Henceforth, greater attention would have to be paid to the needs of employees, who were now perceived as something other than mechanical, interchangeable parts in the organization.

The human relations movement evolved into the behavioral management school. It assumed dominance in the 1950s and 1960s, as the new medium of television was establishing its popularity in American households. Among this school's major contributions were new insights into the needs of individuals and their role in motivating workers.

In an attempt to formulate a positive theory of motivation, Abraham Maslow (1908–1970), a psychologist, asserted that human beings have certain basic needs and that each serves as a motivator. He identified five such needs and organized them in a hierarchy, starting with the most basic:

- *Physiological:* Food, water, sex, and other physiological satisfiers
- *Safety:* Protection from threat, danger, and illness; a safe, orderly, predictable, organized world
- *Love:* Affection and belongingness
- *Esteem:* Self-esteem and the esteem of others
- *Self-actualization:* Self-fulfillment; to become everything one is capable of becoming[10]

7

The physiological and safety needs are seen as primary needs, and the remainder, dealing with the psychological aspects of existence, as secondary. Maslow theorized that when one need is fairly well satisfied, it no longer serves as a motivator. Instead, attention turns to the next level on the hierarchy. However, he recognized that the order is not rigid, especially at the higher levels. For example, some people may value self-esteem more than love, and others may never aspire to self-actualization.

There is little empirical data available to support Maslow's theory.[11] Nonetheless, it led to the realization that satisfied needs might have little value in motivating employees and that different techniques might have to be used to motivate different people, according to their particular needs.

While Maslow considered all needs to be motivators, Frederick Herzberg (1923–2000), another psychologist, proposed that employee attitudes and behaviors are influenced by two different sets of considerations. He called them *hygiene factors* and *motivators*.[12]

Hygiene factors[13] are those associated with conditions that surround the performing of the job and include the following: supervision; interpersonal relations with superiors, peers, and subordinates; physical working conditions; salary; company policies and administrative practices; benefits; and job security.

Responding to employees' hygiene needs, concluded Herzberg, will eliminate dissatisfaction and poor job performance but will not lead to positive attitudes and more productive behaviors. Those are accomplished by meeting the second set of considerations, the motivators, or factors associated with the job content. They include achievement, recognition, the work itself, responsibility, and advancement.

Interestingly, there is a close relationship between Herzberg's hygiene factors and the lower-level needs identified by Maslow, and between the motivators and Maslow's self-esteem and self-actualization needs.

The implications of this two-factor theory of motivation are clear. Employees have certain expectations about elements in the environment in which they work. When they are satisfactory, workers are reassured that things are as they ought to be, even though those feelings may not encourage them to greater productivity. However, when environmental expectations are not met, dissatisfaction ensues. An employer must provide for both the hygiene needs and the motivators to achieve a motivated work force. The critical task, therefore, lies in satisfying employees' needs for self-actualization by giving them more responsibility, providing opportunities for advancement, and recognizing their achievement.

Studies appear to show that Herzberg's theory is applicable more to professional and managerial-level employees than to manual workers. Nonetheless, his contributions provided a better understanding of motivation and have had significant effects on job design.

Influenced by the theorists of self-actualization, and especially Maslow, Douglas McGregor (1906–1964), an industrial psychologist, underscored the importance of assumptions about human nature and their effects on motivational methods used by managers. He argued that, despite important advances in the management of human resources, most managers clung to traditional assumptions, which he labeled *Theory* X (Figure 1.2). Managers who saw their employees as having a dislike of work, lacking ambition, and requiring direction were likely to rely on coercion, control, and even threats as motivational tools.

McGregor offered *Theory* Y (Figure 1.2), which took an entirely different view of human nature. Managers who adopted these assumptions considered employees capable of seeking and accepting responsibility, and of exercising self-direction in furtherance of organizational goals—without control and the threat of punishment.

McGregor summarized the difference between the two theories in this way:

> The central principle of organization which derives from Theory X is that of direction and control through the exercise of authority—what has been called the "scalar principle." The central principle which derives from Theory Y is that of integration: the creation of conditions such that the members of the organization can achieve their own goals best by directing their efforts toward the success of the enterprise.[14]

Theory X

1. The average human being has an inherent dislike of work and will avoid it if he can.
2. Because of this human characteristic of dislike of work, most people must be coerced, controlled, directed, or threatened with punishment to get them to put forth adequate effort toward the achievement of organizational objectives.
3. The average human being prefers to be directed, wishes to avoid responsibility, has relatively little ambition, and wants security above all.

Theory Y

1. The expenditure of physical and mental effort in work is as natural as play or rest.
2. External control and the threat of punishment are not the only means for bringing about effort toward organizational objectives. Man will exercise self-direction and self-control in the service of objectives to which he is committed.
3. Commitment to objectives is a function of the rewards associated with their achievement.
4. The average human being learns, under proper conditions, not only to accept but to seek responsibility.
5. The capacity to exercise a relatively high degree of imagination, ingenuity, and creativity in the solution of organizational problems is widely, not narrowly, distributed in the population.
6. Under the conditions of modern industrial life, the intellectual potentialities of the average human being are only partially utilized.

FIGURE 1.2 Theory X and Theory Y. (Source: Douglas McGregor, *The Human Side of Enterprise.* New York: McGraw-Hill, 1960, pp. 33–34, 47–48. Reprinted with permission of McGraw-Hill, Inc.)

By drawing attention to the key role played by employees in the attainment of organizational goals, and the importance of recognizing and striving to satisfy their needs, the behavioral school has had a lasting impact on management. In particular, it has resulted in greater attention to the work environment and on-the-job training for employees, and in a realization that people-management skills are a fundamental management attribute.

MANAGEMENT SCIENCE

This school of management thought had its origins during World War II and was known, in the beginning, as operations research. In some respects, it represented a reemergence of the quantitative approach favored by Taylor. However, advances in management technology, especially the computer, rendered it much more sophisticated.

Basically, management science involves construction of a mathematical model to simulate a situation. All variables bearing on the situation and their relationships are noted. By changing the values of the variables, the outcomes of different decisions can be projected.

By replacing descriptive analyses with quantitative data, this approach has been useful in management decision-making on matters that can be quantified, such as financial planning. A major shortcoming is its inability to predict the behavior of an organization's human resources.

MODERN MANAGEMENT THOUGHT

By the 1960s, management theory incorporated elements of the classical, behavioral, and management science schools. However, theorists could not agree on a single body of knowledge that constituted the field of management. Indeed, one writer likened the situation to a jungle.[15]

Since then, steps have been taken toward clearing the jungle with the adoption of approaches aimed at integrating some of the divergent views of disciples of the earlier schools. Three of those approaches are *systems theory*, *contingency theory*, and *total quality management*.

Systems Theory   According to the systems theory, an enterprise is seen as a system, "a set of objects with a given set of relationships between the objects and their attributes, connected or related to each other and to their environment in such a way as to form a whole or entirety."[16]

An organizational system is composed of people, money, materials, equipment, and data, all of which are combined in the accomplishment of some purpose. The subsystems typically are identified as divisions or departments whose activities aid the larger system in reaching its goals.

Certain elements are common to all organizational systems (Figure 1.3). They are *inputs* (e.g., labor, equipment, and capital) and *processes*, that is, methods whereby inputs are converted into *outputs* (e.g., goods and services). *Feedback* is information about the outputs or processes and serves as an input to help determine whether changes are necessary to attain the goals.

10

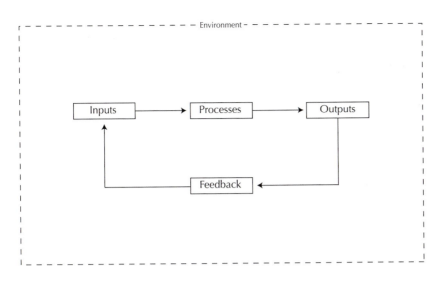

FIGURE 1.3 **Systems approach to organizational management.**

11

Management's role is to coordinate the input, process, and output factors and to analyze and respond to feedback.

The systems approach emphasizes the relationship between the organization and its external environment. Environmental factors are outside the organization and beyond its control. But they have an impact on its operations. Accordingly, management must monitor environmental trends and events and make changes deemed necessary to ensure the organization's success.

Contingency Theory The contingency, or situational, approach to management traces its current origins to systems theory and the desire to identify universal principles of management. It recognizes that principles advanced by earlier schools may be applicable in some situations, but not in others, and seeks an understanding of those circumstances in which certain managerial actions will bring about the desired results.

It is ironic that this line of thought did not emerge as a major force until the mid-1960s, since its significance in the study of leadership was recognized in the 1920s by Follett. She noted that "there are different types of leadership" and that "different situations require different kinds of knowledge, and the man possessing the knowledge demanded by a certain situation tends in the best managed businesses, other things being equal, to become the leader of the moment."[17]

The recent study of contingency principles has been relatively sparse, focusing mostly on organizational structure and decision making. Finally, however, this approach has attracted the attention of theorists to functions other than leadership and has impressed on the field the realization that management is much more complex than earlier theorists imagined.

It is this complexity that makes it impossible to suggest a style for all managers, including those who manage broadcast stations. What is appropriate for one manager in one circumstance with one group of employees may be quite inappropriate for another manager in another circumstance with a different group.

Total Quality Management (TQM)   Revolutionary developments in the world and in the workplace triggered changes in management thought and practice in the last decade or so of the twentieth century. The end of communism's dominance in the former Soviet Union and Eastern Europe created new opportunities in a world already characterized by the growing internationalization of business. An era of global interdependence was ushered in by the formation of a single trading bloc among European countries and by ratification of the North American Free Trade Agreement (NAFTA) by the United States, Canada, and Mexico. Technical innovation and the growing heterogeneity of the American work force rendered the organizational world of the 1990s strikingly different from that in which early theorists operated.

Accompanying these developments was a focus on customers' needs and, especially, on their expectations of quality in the products they purchase and the services they use. This gave rise to a new approach to management, total quality management. The approach may have been new in the United States, but its underpinnings were not. In fact, it drew elements from management science, scientific management, and the behavioral approach, and it may be characterized as another attempt to clear the jungle. Nor was its practice new. It was introduced in Japan in the aftermath of World War II by several Americans, the most prominent of whom was W. Edwards Deming (1900–1993), a statistician.

The foundation of Deming's approach to TQM is the conviction that uniform product quality can be ensured through statistical analysis and control of variables in the production process. As the philosophy evolved and technological change became commonplace, his insistence that employees be trained to understand statistical methods and their application and to master new skills assumed greater significance. So, too, did awareness that employees are an integral part of the quality revolution and that, without their total commitment to continuous product or service improvement, any attempt to practice this management philosophy will be doomed.

MANAGEMENT THOUGHT IN THE TWENTY-FIRST CENTURY

Recognition of the importance of individuals and their commitment to organizational improvement are fundamental characteristics of the latest approach to management. It is called *the learning organization*.

Management thinking and practices described so far reflect responses to the challenges of the times. Proponents of the new approach have concluded that new challenges—including the accelerating pace of technological change, increased consumer choice and sophistication, and globalization—demand a new perspective.

The learning organization had its origins with the 1990 publication of Peter Senge's book *The Fifth Discipline: The Art & Practice of The Learning*

Organization. In the intervening years, Senge, his colleagues at MIT, and others have developed the concept and witnessed its adoption in organizations of different types and sizes.

In contrast to the traditional focus on organizational efficiency, the principal distinguishing feature of the learning organization is systematic problem solving. But that is not a job for managers and supervisors alone. Indeed, all members of the organization are expected to challenge the way business is done and to question the thought processes typically used to solve problems. Together, they work to identify new problems, develop solutions to them, and apply the solutions. That requires the free flow of information throughout the organization. It requires, also, that all organization members understand their job and how it relates to the jobs of others, share a vision of the organization's purpose, and display a commitment to accomplish the purpose.

In large measure, the success of the learning organization hinges on management's willingness to facilitate the exchange of information and to establish an environment conducive to continuous learning. Encouraging employees to use their creativity and providing them with the freedom and resources to engage fully in problem solving are additional requirements.

The contributions to management thought and practice described in this chapter provide some guidelines for the manager. However, pending the development of a set of universal management principles, the style of most managers probably is summarized best by business mogul T. Boone Pickens, Jr.: "A management style is an amalgamation of the best of other people you have known and respected, and eventually you develop your own style."[18]

13

MANAGEMENT LEVELS

It is often assumed that management is concentrated at the top of an organization. In reality, anyone who directs the efforts of others in the attainment of goals is a manager. In most companies, including broadcast stations, managers are found at three levels:

Lower: Managers at this level closely supervise the routine work of employees under their charge and are accountable to the next level of management. A radio station local sales manager who reports to the general sales manager is an example. So is a television control room supervisor who answers to the production manager.

Middle: Managers who are responsible for carrying out particular activities in furtherance of the overall goals of the company are in this category. In broadcast stations, the heads of the sales, program, news, promotion and marketing, production, engineering, and business departments are middle managers.

Top: Managers who coordinate the company's activities and provide the overall direction for the accomplishment of its goals operate at this level. The general manager of a broadcast station is a top manager.

Even though the contents of the remainder of this chapter apply in varying degrees to all three levels, the focus will be on the top level, that occupied by the general manager.

MANAGEMENT FUNCTIONS

The general manager (GM) is responsible to the station's owners for coordinating human and physical resources in such a way that the station's objectives are accomplished. Accordingly, the GM is concerned with, and accountable for, every aspect of the station and its operation. In discharging the management responsibility, the GM carries out four basic functions: planning, organizing, influencing or directing, and controlling.

PLANNING

Planning involves the determination of the station's objectives and the plans or strategies by which those objectives are to be accomplished. Through the planning process, many objectives may be identified. Usually, they can be placed in one of the following categories:

Economic: Objectives related to the financial position of the station and focusing on revenues, expenses, and profits.

Service: Programming that will appeal to audiences and be responsive to their interests and needs; the contribution of the station to the life of the community.

Personal: Objectives of individuals employed by the station.

A major purpose of objective-setting is to permit the coordination of departmental and individual activity with the station's objectives. Once the station's objectives have been formulated, those of the different departments and employees within those departments can be developed. Individual objectives must contribute to the accomplishment of departmental objectives. In turn, they must be compatible with those of other departments and of the station. In addition, all objectives must be attainable, measurable, set against deadlines, and controllable.

Once agreement on objectives has been reached, plans or strategies are developed to meet them. Planning provides directions for the future. However, it does not require the abandonment of plans that contribute to the achievement of the station's current objectives and that are likely to be instrumental in enabling the station to accomplish its future objectives.

Planning cannot anticipate or control events. However, it has many benefits since it

- compels the GM to think about and prepare for the future
- provides a framework for decision making
- permits an orderly approach to problem solving
- encourages team effort
- provides a climate for individual career development and job satisfaction

14

ORGANIZING

Organizing is the process whereby human and physical resources are arranged in a formal structure and responsibilities are assigned to specific units, positions, and personnel. It permits the concentration and coordination of activities and management control of efforts to attain the station's objectives.

In the typical broadcast station, organizing involves the division of work into specialties and the grouping of employees with specialized responsibilities into departments. The following departments are found most frequently in commercial broadcast stations.

Sales Department

The sale of time to advertisers is the principal source of revenue for commercial radio and television stations and is the responsibility of a sales department, headed by a sales manager. Many stations subdivide the department into national sales and local/regional sales. Sales to national advertisers are entrusted to the national sales manager and the station's sales representative company, or station rep. Local and regional sales are the responsibility of the station's salespersons, typically called account executives.

Program Department

Under the direction of a program manager or director, the program department plans, selects, schedules, and monitors programs. The department also provides relevant content for the station's Web site.

Promotion and Marketing Department

This function involves both program and sales promotion. The former seeks to attract and maintain audiences, while the latter is aimed at attracting advertisers. Both functions may be the responsibility of a promotion and marketing department. Some stations assign program promotion to the program department and sales promotion to the sales department.

News Department

In many stations, the information function is kept separate from the entertainment function and is supervised by a news director. The department is responsible for regularly scheduled newscasts, news and sports specials, documentary and public affairs programs, and for Web site news content.

Production Department

In radio, this department is headed by a production director or creative director and is charged with writing and producing commercials. Commercial production is a responsibility of its television counterpart. In many TV stations, the department also includes technical support personnel for newscast production and for master control operations. A production manager supervises the department's activities.

15

Engineering Department

A chief engineer or technical manager heads this department. It selects, operates, and maintains studio, control room, and transmitting equipment, and often oversees the station's computers. Engineering staff are also responsible for technical monitoring in accordance with the requirements of the FCC. In some stations, studio production personnel are located in the deparment.

Business Department

The business department carries out a variety of tasks necessary to the functioning of the station as a business. They include secretarial, billing, bookkeeping, payrol,l and, in many stations, personnel responsibilities.

Broadcast stations engage in other functions, which may be assigned to separate departments or subdepartments, or may be included in the duties of departments already identified. The following additional functions are among the most common:

Traffic

Traffic often is carried out by a subdepartment of the sales department. It is called the traffic department and is headed by a traffic manager. The function includes the daily scheduling on a program log of all content to be aired by the station, the compilation of an availabilities sheet showing times available for purchase by advertisers, and the monitoring of all advertising content to ensure compliance with commercial contracts.

Continuity

Continuity is concerned chiefly with the writing of commercial copy and, in many stations, constitutes a subdepartment within the sales department. The continuity director supervises its work and reports to the sales manager. In stations where the writing of program material and public service announcements is included, the continuity director may answer to the heads of both the sales and program departments.

The general manager's success in organizing rests heavily on the selection of employees. Of particular importance is the selection of department heads, to whom the GM delegates responsibility for the conduct and accomplishments of the various departments.

The GM also must strive to ensure that the organizational structure enables the station to meet its objectives, and that problems arising from overlapping or nonexistent responsibility are corrected. The structure is influenced by many factors. They include the number of employees, the size of the market, and the preferences of the GM. As a result, there is no "typical" organization. Figure 1.4 contains an example of the structure of a medium-market television station. Figure 1.5 reflects the organization of three commonly owned radio stations in a market of similar size.

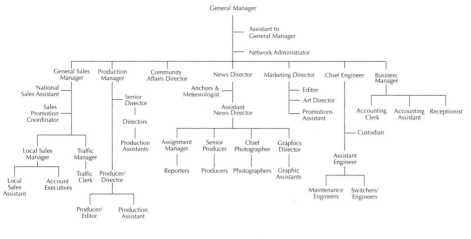

FIGURE 1.4 Organization of a commercial television station in a medium market.

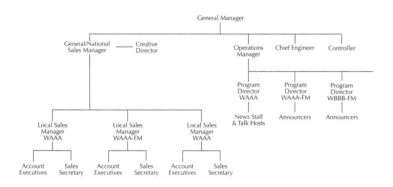

FIGURE 1.5 Organization of three radio stations operating under the same owner and general manager.

INFLUENCING OR DIRECTING

The influencing or directing function centers on the stimulation of employees to carry out their responsibilities with enthusiasm and effectiveness. It involves *motivation, communication, training,* and *personal influence.*

Motivation   The major theories of motivation were discussed earlier in this chapter. For the general manager, motivation is a practical issue, since the success of the station is tied closely to the degree to which employees are able to satisfy their needs. The greater their satisfaction, the more likely it is that they will contribute fully to the attainment of the station's objectives. Accordingly, the GM must be aware of the needs of individual employees and must create an environment in which they want to be productive.

Basic needs include adequate compensation and fringe benefit programs, safe and healthy working conditions, friendly colleagues, and competent and fair supervision. For most employees, such needs are met adequately and do not serve as powerful motivators.

Satisfaction of other needs may have a more significant impact on how employees feel about themselves and the station and on their efforts to contribute to the station's success. Included in these higher-level needs are factors such as job title and responsibility, praise and recognition for accomplishments, opportunities for promotion, and the challenge of the job. Once basic needs are satisfied, therefore, the GM must respond to those higher-level needs if motivation is to be successful.

Communication   Communication is vital to the effective discharge of the management function. It is the means by which employees are made aware of the station's objectives and plans and are encouraged to play a full and effective part in their attainment.

As a result, the general manager must communicate to employees information they need and want. They need information on what is expected of them. The job description sets forth general guidelines, but they must have specifics on their role in carrying out current plans. If they are to shoulder their duties willingly and effectively, they want to know about matters influencing their economic status and their authority to carry out responsibilities.

This downward flow of communication is important, but it must be accompanied by management's willingness to listen to and understand employees. Accordingly, it is necessary to provide mechanisms for an upward flow of communication from employees to supervisors, department heads, and the GM. Departmental or staff meetings, suggestion boxes, and an open-door policy by management permit such a flow.

Lateral flow, or communication among individuals on the same organizational level, also is important in coordinating the activities of the various departments in pursuit of the station's plans and objectives. A method used by many stations to ensure such a flow is the establishment of a management team that meets on a regular basis. Usually, it comprises the general manager and all department heads.

Training   Most employees are selected because they possess the background and skills necessary to carry out specific responsibilities. However, they may have to be trained in the use of new equipment or the application of new procedures. Occasionally, employees are hired with little experience and have to be trained on the job. Whenever training is necessary, the general manager must make certain that it is provided and that it is supervised by competent personnel.

One of the major benefits of training programs is the provision of opportunities for existing employees to prepare themselves for advancement in the station. As a result, employee morale is heightened, and the station enjoys the advantage of creating its own pool of qualified personnel.

Some stations encourage employees to advance their knowledge and skills by paying for their participation in workshops, seminars, and college courses, as well as their attendance at meetings of state and national broadcasting associations. In all such cases, the general manager should be sure that the experiences will contribute to the employee's ability to carry out responsibilities more effectively, thereby assisting the station in meeting its objectives.

Personal Influence   Stimulating employees to produce their best efforts requires that the general manager and others in managerial or supervisory positions command respect, loyalty, and cooperation. Among the factors that contribute to such a climate are management competence, fairness in dealings with employees, willingness to listen to and act on employee observations and complaints, honesty, integrity, and similar personal characteristics. In effect, personal influence includes all those behaviors and attitudes that contribute to employees' perceptions of their importance in the station's efforts and achievements and the worthiness of the enterprise of which they are a part.

CONTROLLING

19

Through planning, the station establishes its objectives and plans for accomplishing them. The control process determines the degree to which objectives and plans are being realized by the station, departments, and employees.

Periodic evaluation of individuals and departments allows the general manager to compare actual performance to planned performance. If the two do not coincide, corrective action may be necessary.

To be effective, controlling must be based on measurable performance. The size and composition of the station's audience can be measured through ratings. If the audience attracted to the station or to certain programs does not match projections, the control process permits the recognition of that fact and leads to discussions about possible solutions. The result may be a change in the plan, such as a revision downward of expectations, or actions to try to attain the original objectives.

Similarly, sales revenues can be measured. An analysis may reveal that projected revenues were unrealistic and that an adjustment is necessary. On the other hand, if the projections are realizable, discussions may lead to a decision to hire additional account executives, make changes in the rate card, or adjust commission levels.

The costs of operation are measurable too. They are discussed in Chapter 2, "Financial Management," along with methods of controlling them.

MANAGEMENT ROLES

Management functions reflect the major responsibilities of the general manager. However, they provide little insight into the diverse and complex activities the general manager undertakes on a daily basis.

Henry Mintzberg found that managerial activity is characterized by brevity, variety, and fragmentation.[19] Managers spend short periods of time attending to different tasks and are interrupted frequently before a specific task is accomplished. Writing memoranda, reading and writing letters, faxes, and email messages, receiving and making telephone calls, attending meetings, and visiting employees and persons outside the organization are examples of activities that consume a great deal of a manager's time and energy. There are others as well.

Mintzberg identified ten roles and grouped them in three categories: (1) interpersonal, (2) informational, and (3) decisional.[20]

INTERPERSONAL ROLES

As the symbolic head of the organization, the manager serves as a

Figurehead: The manager carries out duties of a legal or ceremonial nature. For the broadcast station general manager, this role is discharged through the signing of documents for submission to the FCC and by representing the station at community events, for instance.

Leader: Establishing the workplace atmosphere and guiding and motivating employees are examples of ways in which the general manager carries out the leadership role.

Liaison: The general manager is the liaison between the station's owners and its employees. Dealings with peers and other individuals and groups outside the station link the organization with the environment. Accordingly, the GM's relationships with other general managers, program suppliers, and community groups reflect this role.

INFORMATIONAL ROLES

The manager is the organization's "nerve center" and, as such, seeks and receives a large volume of internal and external information, both oral and written. In these roles, the manager acts as a

Monitor: Information permits the manager to understand what is happening in the organization and its environment. Receipt of the latest sales report or threats of a demonstration to protest the planned airing of a program enable the GM to exercise this role.

Disseminator: The manager distributes external information to members of the organization and internal information from one subordinate to another.

Spokesperson: In this role, the manager speaks on behalf of the organization. An example would be a news conference at which the GM reveals plans for a new broadcast facility.

DECISIONAL ROLES

These roles grow out of the manager's responsibility for the organization's strategy-making process and involve the manager as

Entrepreneur: The manager is the initiator and designer of controlled change. For example, the GM of a TV station may set in motion procedures aimed at attaining first place in local news ratings.

Disturbance handler: In this role, managers deal with involuntary situations and change that is partially beyond their control. An example would be resolving a dispute between the program manager and the sales manager on the advisability of carrying a particular program.

Resource allocator: The manager determines priorities for the expenditure of money and employee effort.

Negotiator: The manager represents the organization in negotiating activity. Working out a contract with a program supplier or union would place the GM in this role.

MANAGEMENT SKILLS 21

To carry out their functions and roles effectively, managers require many skills. Robert L. Katz identifies three basic skills that every manager must have in varying degrees, according to the managerial level.[21] For the general manager of a broadcast station, all are important:

Technical: Knowledge, analytical ability, and facility in the use of the tools and techniques of a specific kind of activity. For the general manager, that activity is managing. While it does not demand the ability to perform all the tasks that characterize a broadcast station, it does require sufficient knowledge to ask pertinent questions and evaluate the worth of the responses. Accordingly, the GM should have knowledge of

- the objectives of the station's owners
- management and the management functions of planning, organizing, influencing or directing, and controlling
- business practices, especially sales and marketing, budgeting, cost controls, and public relations
- the market, including the interests and needs of the audience and the business potential afforded by area retail and service establishments
- competing media, the sources and amounts of their revenues
- broadcasting and allied professions, including advertising agencies, station representative companies, and program and news services
- the station and the activities of its departments and personnel
- broadcast laws, rules, and regulations, and other applicable laws, rules, and regulations

- contracts, particularly those dealing with network affiliation, station representation, programming, talent, music licensing, and labor unions

Human: The ability to work with people and to build a cooperative effort. The general manager should have the capacity to influence the behavior of employees toward the accomplishment of the station's objectives by motivating them, creating job satisfaction, and encouraging loyalty and mutual respect. An appreciation of the differing skills and aspirations of employees and departments also is essential if the station's activities are to be combined in a successful team effort.

Conceptual: The ability to see the enterprise as a whole and the dependence of one part on the others. To coordinate successfully the station's efforts, the GM must recognize the interdependence of programming and promotion, sales and programming, and production and engineering, for example. Equally important is the ability to comprehend the relationship of the station to the rest of the broadcast industry, to the community, and to prevailing economic, political, and social forces, all of which contribute to decisions on directions that the station will take and the subsequent formulation of objectives and policies.

22

To these skills, the successful general manager should add desirable personal qualities. They include:

- *Foresight,* the ability to anticipate events and make appropriate preparations
- *wisdom* in choosing among alternative courses of action and *courage* in carrying out the selected action
- *flexibility* in adapting to change
- *honesty* and *integrity* in dealings with employees and persons outside the station
- *responsiveness* and *responsibility* to the station's owners, employees, and advertisers

The GM also must be responsive and display responsibility to the community by leading the station in its community relations endeavors and by setting an example for other employees to follow.

INFLUENCES ON MANAGEMENT

The degree to which the general manager possesses and uses the skills described will play an important part in determining the station's fortunes. But there are other forces that contribute to the GM's decisions and actions and that influence the effectiveness with which the management responsibility is discharged. The most significant influences are described in this section.

THE LICENSEE

Ultimate responsibility for the operation of a radio or television station rests with the licensee, the person or persons who have made a financial investment in the enterprise and enjoy an ownership interest. Like all investors, they expect that they will reap annual profits from the station's operation and that the financial worth of their investment will increase in time. As a result, the general manager must seek to satisfy their expectations and weigh the financial impact of all actions.

THE COMPETITION

Radio and television stations compete against each other and against other media in the market for advertising dollars. That translates into competition for audiences. A station gains audience from, or loses audience to, other stations, and few significant management actions will pass without producing a reaction among competitors. Similarly, many of the general manager's actions will be influenced by those of competing stations.

THE GOVERNMENT

23

As detailed in Chapter 7, "Broadcast Regulations," the federal government is a major force in broadcast station operation. It exerts its influence through its three branches—executive, legislative, and judicial—and through independent regulatory agencies, chiefly the Federal Communications Commission.

Executive Branch   Broadcast stations are affected by the actions of several executive branch departments, notably the Executive Office of the President, the Department of Justice, the Food and Drug Administration (FDA), and the National Telecommunications and Information Administration (NTIA).

EXECUTIVE OFFICE OF THE PRESIDENT   The President influences broadcast policy and regulation in numerous ways. He can recommend legislation; he nominates members for, and appoints the chairperson of, regulatory agencies whose policies, rules, and regulations apply to radio and television stations; and he can exert influence through the annual federal budget process.

DEPARTMENT OF JUSTICE   This department prosecutes violators of the Communications Act and of rules and regulations applicable to broadcast station operation. The department's antitrust division is concerned with station ownership and may take action when it believes that ownership or other circumstances are resulting in a restraint of trade.

FOOD AND DRUG ADMINISTRATION   A division of the Department of Health and Human Services, the FDA regulates mislabeling and misbranding of advertised products.

NATIONAL TELECOMMUNICATIONS AND INFORMATION ADMINISTRATION   Part of the Department of Commerce, the NTIA advises the President on telecommunications policy issues.

Legislative Branch   The House of Representatives and the Senate enact broadcast legislation and approve the budgets of the regulatory agencies. In addition, the Senate has the power of approval of presidential nominees for regulatory agencies. Both the Senate and the House may influence broadcast policy and regulation through congressional hearings on issues of controversy or concern.

Judicial Branch   Federal courts try cases against violators of laws, rules, and regulations, and hear appeals against decisions and orders handed down by regulatory agencies.

Regulatory Agencies   Federal regulatory agencies operate like a fourth branch of government and enjoy executive, legislative, and judicial powers. The agency with the greatest influence on broadcast operations is the FCC, whose role is described later. The commission regulates radio and television stations in accordance with the terms of the Communications Act of 1934, as amended. For the general manager, its most significant and awesome power is that of renewing or revoking the station's license to operate.

Other regulatory agencies that influence the broadcast media are the Federal Trade Commission (FTC), which polices unfair trade practices and false or deceptive advertising, and the Federal Aviation Administration (FAA), whose concerns include the placement and maintenance of broadcast towers.

Broadcasters are engaged in interstate commerce and, for the most part, are subject to federal authority. However, state and local governments may also have an impact on stations through laws on matters such as business incorporation, taxes, advertising practices, individual rights, and zoning and safety ordinances.

THE LABOR FORCE

The number of people available for work, and their skills, have a direct influence on the success of all businesses, including broadcasting. The station's ability to hire and retain qualified and productive employees is a major determinant of the station's performance.

LABOR UNIONS

The general manager of a station in which personnel are represented by one or more unions is required to abide by the terms of a union contract governing, among other items, wages and fringe benefits, job jurisdiction, and working conditions (for details, refer to Chapter 3, "Human Resource Management"). In nonunionized stations, the general manager must be

24

attentive to the treatment of employees, not only for reasons of morale or competitiveness, but to guard against the threat of unionization.

THE PUBLIC

To generate advertising revenue, the station must attract an audience for its programming. Accordingly, as noted in Chapter 4, "Broadcast Programming," the public is a major force in program decision making. Organized publics, also known as citizen or pressure groups, attempt to influence decisions on a wide range of actions. Among the causes undertaken by different groups have been improvement in employment opportunities for minorities, the elimination of violent and sexual content, and the promotion of programming for children.

ADVERTISERS

The financial fate of commercial broadcast stations rests on their appeal to advertisers. Attracting audiences sought by advertisers and enabling advertisers to reach them at an acceptable cost are major factors in program and sales decisions.

ECONOMIC ACTIVITY

25

The state of the local and national economy determines the amount of money people have to spend on advertised products and their spending priorities. When the economy is sluggish, businesses pay more attention than usual to their advertising expenditures and may be tempted to reduce them, thereby posing a challenge for broadcast stations and other advertiser-supported media.

THE BROADCAST INDUSTRY

Standards of professional performance and content are set forth in a station's policy book or employee handbook. Individual employees subscribe to industrywide standards formulated by broadcast organizations or associations in which they hold membership. The National Association of Broadcasters (NAB) in 2004 announced plans for a task force on "responsible programming" that would consider adoption of an industry code of conduct.

SOCIAL FACTORS

Since broadcast stations must be responsive to the interests of their communities, social factors play an important role in program decisions. Stations must analyze, interpret, and respond to trends in the size and composition of the local population, employment practices, income, and spending habits.

TECHNOLOGY

Advances in technology resulted in the emergence of radio and television broadcasting and continue to play a major part in station practices. Today, the general manager experiences, and must respond to, the influence of new broadcast technologies, as well as those technologies that provide alternative means of accessing entertainment and information content.

WHAT'S AHEAD?

In an era of dramatic change and accompanying uncertainty, it appears that TV station general managers can prepare for one event with some certainty: the end of analog and the switch to all-digital broadcasting in 2009.

The prospect of Congressional legislation establishing that year as the "hard date" became real when NAB President Eddie Fritts told the Senate Commerce Committee in July 2005 that the organization would support such a law. Now, the planning can begin in earnest to capitalize on the opportunities that digital affords.

As they prepare for the all-digital age, general managers face many challenges. One of the most significant will be the decision on how to use the newly available channels. It will have to take into account factors such as the sources and availability of content, its appeal to targeted audiences, and the recruiting of suitably skilled employees. Probably the most important consideration will be the revenue-generation potential of the decision. Already, the industry has spent an estimated $3.5 billion on the digital build-out and additional expenditures lie ahead.

As noted in Chapter 4, "Broadcast Programming," the general manager may find partnerships with telephone companies appealing. Even alliances with competing stations are a possibility. One group CEO has proposed that broadcasters pool their capital and their digital channels to offer wireless cable in markets across the country.[22]

Expanding and diversifying program distribution methods will be important keys to success in the future. Increasingly, viewers are growing accustomed to "on-demand" media. In other words, they want to control what they use and when they use it. One 2005 study found that heavy and medium on-demand consumers account for more than one-third of Americans.[23] Their number will continue to grow and managers must strive to respond to their desires.

The challenges posed by changing technologies and lifestyles will confront radio station general managers, too. Internet radio, satellite radio, iPods, and other audio sources provide listeners with an array of attractive alternatives. Again, consumer control is a major determinant of their choices. For example, the study cited earlier found that the top two reasons for using Internet radio are the ability to listen to content not found elsewhere and to control/choose the music played.[24] At the same time, radio managers may find comfort in another of the study's conclusions: more than 80 percent of Americans say that they will listen to terrestrial radio in the future as much as they do now, despite advancements in technology.[25] Time will tell!

SUMMARY

Management is defined as the process of planning, organizing, influencing, and controlling to accomplish organizational goals through the coordinated use of human and material resources.

The current practice of management has been influenced by several schools. The first was the classical school, which focused on the productivity of organizations and their employees. It was followed by the behavioral school, which drew attention to the importance of satisfied employees to successful operation. Management science was characterized by attempts to quantify the likely outcomes of different managerial decisions. Modern management thought strives to integrate the various perspectives of earlier schools by concentrating on systems theory, contingency theory, and total quality management. The newest practice is the learning organization, which emphasizes systematic problem solving through the participation of all organizational members.

The general manager of a broadcast station has four major functions: (1) planning, or the determination of the station's objectives and the plans or strategies to accomplish them; (2) organizing personnel into a formal structure, usually departments, and assigning specialized duties to persons and units; (3) influencing or directing, that is, stimulating employees to carry out their responsibilities enthusiastically and effectively; (4) controlling, or developing criteria to measure the performance of individuals, departments, and the station and taking corrective action when necessary.

On a day-to-day basis, the GM carries out several roles—interpersonal, informational, and decisional. Technical, human, and conceptual skills are required, together with personal attributes.

Among the significant influences on the GM's decisions and actions are the licensee, competing media, the government, the labor force, labor unions, the public, and advertisers. Economic activity, the broadcast industry, social factors, and technology also are influential.

Technological advancements, and the changing consumer expectations they permit, will present both opportunities and challenges. Managers' ability to respond effectively to the demands of the new environment will be vital to success.

27

CASE STUDY

You are the GM of a talk radio station. You have just arrived home after eating out with your wife. It's about 11:15 P.M.

The telephone rings and you answer. Your program director is on the line. He wants to know if you have seen the late-night TV newscast. You haven't. He tells you that the popular host of your midday program has been arrested for DUI. The newscast included footage of the host being led to a police car in handcuffs.

Next morning, you call the program director and the local sales manager to your office. You want to hear their thoughts on an appropriate course of action.

You begin by quoting from the station's policy book. It states that employees convicted on alcohol or drug charges may be terminated.

The program director argues that—even if convicted—the host should be given a second chance. He has increased the numbers for the time period and his "loose cannon" style generates lots of controversy and calls.

The sales manager concurs. She says that advertiser demand for the program is growing and clients are pleased with the results of their buys.

EXERCISES

1. What factors will you weigh in determining how to deal with the host?

2. Do the arguments of the program director and the local sales manager have merit? Explain.

3. If you decide to go along with their recommendation, will you allow the host to remain on the air or remove him pending further legal proceedings? Justify your response.

4. If you decide not to dismiss him, will you attach conditions to his continued employment? If so, describe them.

28

NOTES

[1] http://www.tvb.org/rcentral/mediatrendstrack/tvbasics/04.

[2] *Ibid.*

[3] Peter P. Schoderbek, Richard A. Cosier, and John C. Aplin, *Management*, p. 8.

[4] Charles D. Pringle, Daniel F. Jennings, and Justin G. Longenecker, *Managing Organizations: Functions and Behaviors*, p. 4.

[5] Howard M. Carlisle, *Management Essentials: Concepts for Productivity and Innovation*, p. 10.

[6] R. Wayne Mondy, Robert E. Holmes, and Edwin B. Flippo, *Management: Concepts and Practices*, p. 6.

[7] Peter F. Drucker, *Management: Tasks, Responsibilities, Practices*, p. 181.

[8] Henri Fayol, *General and Industrial Management*, pp. 43–107. Explanations of the functions have been paraphrased.

[9] Max Weber, *The Theory of Social and Economic Organization*, pp. 329–334.

[10] A. H. Maslow, "A Theory of Human Motivation," *Psychological Review*, 50:4 (July 1943), pp. 370–396.

[11] For an example, see Geert H. Hofstede, "The Colors of Collars," *Columbia Journal of World Business* (September–October 1972), pp. 72–80. After studying job-related goals of more than 18,000 employees of one company with offices in 16 countries, Hofstede concluded that there was a high correlation with Maslow's theory. The goals of professionals related to the higher needs, of clerks to the middle-range needs, and of unskilled workers to the primary needs.

[12] Frederick Herzberg, Bernard Mausner, and Barbara Bloch Snyderman, *The Motivation to Work*, pp. 113–119.

[13] Herzberg, Mausner, and Snyderman, *op. cit.*, p. 113. Herzberg explained his use of the term *hygiene* as follows: "Hygiene operates to remove health hazards from the environment of man. It is not a curative; it is, rather, a preventive. . . . Similarly, when there are deleterious factors in the context of the job, they serve to bring about poor job attitudes. Improvement in these factors of hygiene will serve to remove the impediments to positive job attitudes."

[14] Douglas McGregor, *The Human Side of Enterprise*, p. 49.

[15] Harold Koontz, "The Management Theory Jungle," *Academy of Management Journal*, 4:3 (December 1961), pp. 174–186.

[16] Peter P. Schoderbek, Charles D. Schoderbek, and Asterios G. Kefalas, *Management Systems: Conceptual Considerations*, p. 260.

[17] Henry C. Metcalf and L. Urwick (eds.), *Dynamic Administration: The Collected Papers of Mary Parker Follett*, p. 277.

[18] T. Boone Pickens, Jr., "Pickens on Leadership," *Hyatt Magazine*, Fall/Winter 1988, p. 21.

[19] Henry Mintzberg, *The Nature of Managerial Work*, pp. 31–35.

[20] Mintzberg, *op. cit.*, pp. 54–94.

[21] Robert L. Katz, "Skills of an Effective Administrator," *Harvard Business Review*, 52:5 (September–October 1974), pp. 90–102.

[22] Harry A. Jessell, "Marshaling the Troops," *Broadcasting & Cable*, April 26, 2004, p. 9.

[23] *Internet and Multimedia 2005: The On-Demand Media Consumer*, p. 4.

[24] *Ibid.*, p. 20.

[25] *Ibid.*, p. 26.

29

ADDITIONAL READINGS

Brown, James A., and Ward L. Quaal. *Radio-Television-Cable Management*, 3rd ed. New York: McGraw-Hill, 1998.

Buckingham, Marcus, and Curt Coffman. *First, Break All the Rules: What the World's Greatest Managers Do Differently*. New York: Simon and Schuster, 1999.

Certo, Samuel C., and S. Trevis Certo. *Modern Management*, 10th ed. Upper Saddle River, NJ: Prentice Hall, 2006.

Covington, William G., Jr. *Systems Theory Applied to Television Station Management in the Competitive Marketplace*. Lanham, MD: University Press of America, 1997.

Daft, Richard L. *Management*, 7th ed. Mason, OH: South-Western, 2004.

Drucker, Peter F. *Management Challenges for the 21st Century*. New York: HarperBusiness, 2001.

Drucker, Peter F. *Managing in a Time of Great Change*. New York: Truman Talley Books/Dutton, 1995.

Herzberg, Frederick. *Work and the Nature of Man*. Cleveland, OH: World, 1967.

Maslow, Abraham H. *Motivation and Personality*, 2nd ed. New York: Harper and Row, 1970.

Robbins, Stephen P., and Mary Coulter. *Management*, 8th ed. Upper Saddle River, NJ: Prentice Hall, 2005.

Sashkin, Marshall, and Kenneth J. Kiser. *Putting Total Quality Management to Work: What TQM Means, How to Use It and How to Sustain It Over the Long Run.* San Francisco: Berrett-Koehler, 1993.

Wicks, Jan LeBlanc, George Sylvie, C. Ann Hollifield, Stephen Lacy, Ardyth Broadrick Sohn, and Angela Powers. *Media Management: A Casebook Approach*, 3rd ed. Hillsdale, NJ: Lawrence Erlbaum, 2004.

30

Financial Management 2

This chapter reviews the increasingly important area of financial management and examines

- the two major forms of financial statements used in the industry
- basic accounting terminology employed by electronic media managers
- methods used to produce good financial performance and to monitor financial progress

For years, electronic media education has focused on the operating skills thought to be necessary for a successful career in the industry. Traditionally, the major topics studied have been sales, programming, production, and management. Massive changes triggered by the deregulatory climate of the 1980s catapulted another subject to prominence in the curriculum. That subject is financial management.

Deregulation brought financial speculators into the electronic media business. The prevailing wisdom of the mid-to-late 1980s was the "greater fool" theory. Under this concept, money was made by selling a broadcast license or cable franchise to another at a profit. Operational performance was de-emphasized in favor of appreciation potential.

All that changed around 1989. Prices had risen to the point that operations could no longer retire the massive debt run up by speculators. Numerous electronic media companies went into default, and prices dropped.

By the early 1990s, broadcast stations and many cable systems were valued on a multiple of the cash flow they generate. Operational financial performance was the new coin of the realm.

Then, in 1996, everything changed again with the passage of the Telecommunications Act. Gone were the national ownership limits on radio. Those for television were relaxed. In-market ownership combinations of up to eight radio stations were permitted, depending on market size.

The adoption of the new law set off another round of speculative buying and consolidation, almost without regard to financial performance.

The radio consolidation was largely completed by late 2001. Today, operators are returning to the basics of producing operating results and return on investments for public and private investors. Clearly, into the new century, operational financial performance is to be the coin of the realm once again.

This switch has been prompted by the fact that, by the middle of 2004, the post-1996 consolidated operators were receiving negative reviews from financial analysts and were being characterized as market underperformers. Now, more than ever, management personnel must be well versed in understanding and achieving financial results.[1]

Pressure to acquire basic financing and accounting knowledge is coming from other sources, too. In the technology-driven decade of the 1990s, lines of distinction between traditional forms of electronic media became blurred or nonexistent. This development spawned a need for a new breed of communication manager—one with both a traditional background and basic accounting and financial skills.[2] As the industry has progressed since the Telecommunications Act of 1996, the financial management element of the managerial equation has assumed even greater significance. Today's manager is concerned more about sales and making and meeting budget forecasts, and less about programming.

It is not possible in the pages of this chapter to make anyone a financial expert. The goal here is to acquaint the reader with financial terms and concepts and with the typical financial reports used. It is recommended strongly that today's electronic media student pursue a more detailed examination of these matters through finance and accounting courses.

THE ACCOUNTING FUNCTION

The accounting function in the electronic media is performed using specialized computer software developed by various companies. The leading television traffic and accounting systems are provided by Columbine. Radio software companies include Computer Concepts and Wicks Broadcast Solutions/CBSI. Some of these systems are integrated or interfaced with digital audio systems. Examples include Digilink by Arrakis and Audio Vault by Broadcast Electronics.

Even with computerized systems, mistakes often are made. Ad agencies report that there is a 70 to 80 percent discrepancy between invoices and what actually aired.[3] As a result, stations and agencies are moving to a new form of electronic invoicing—electronic data interchange (EDI). As of this writing, 50 to 90 percent of stations use EDI in some form. Traffic system vendors are testing such systems. Eventually, paper orders will be eliminated.[4]

Whether computerized or manual, certain accounting concepts and terminology are basic. Any person with serious management ambition must master them.

Effective financial management requires detailed planning and control. Planning expresses in dollar terms the plans and objectives of the enterprise. Control involves the comparison of projected and actual revenues and expenses. The basic planning and control mechanism is the *budget*.

To prepare the budget, management collects from department heads financial data and reviews and edits them. Most stations and systems use a form to display the information for the budget period, usually one year. Figure 2.1 is a 12-month calendar summary form employed by a radio multiple-station operator in an annual budget preparation.

Budgeting deals with the future. However, past experience suggests realistic revenue and expense amounts. Generally, a reserve account is maintained to cover emergencies. During the year, regular budget reports permit the general manager to compare planned and actual results and to make necessary adjustments.

Budgeting and cost controls, together with financial forecasting and planning, are among the major responsibilities of the business department. Other responsibilities include banking, billings to and collections from advertisers and advertising agencies, payroll administration, processing of insurance claims, tax payments, purchasing, and payments for services used.

Fundamental to the efficient discharge of the accounting function are the establishment and maintenance of an effective and informative accounting system that will protect assets and provide financial information for decision-making and the preparation of financial statements and tax returns. Such a system is based on financial records. As noted above, most such records are produced for electronic media concerns via specialized computer software.

PLANNING FINANCIAL RECORDS

No matter what the electronic media business is—radio, television, cable, or other—management requires certain basic information to function. It

33

34

Station _____

Delta Starr Broadcasting

2005 Proposed Budget

2005	Jan	Feb	Mar	Apr	May	Jun	Jul	Aug	Sep	Oct	Nov	Dec	Total
Income													
Local Spot Sales													
Other Local Sales													
Total Local Sales													
National Sales													
Regional Spot Sales													
Total Time Sales													
Non-Broadcast Rev. (Rental etc.)													
Total Gross Income													
Cost of Goods Sold													
Local Agency Comm. (15%)													
National Agency Comm (15%)													
Regional Agency Comm (15%)													
Regional Rep. Comm (15%)													
National Rep. Comm (15%)													
Total COGs													
Gross Profit													
Engineering Expense													
Payroll													
Outside Labor-Contract													
Repair & Maintenance													
Parts & Supplies													
Equipment Rental													
Freight on Equipment													
Auto Expenses													
Total Engineering Expense													

FIGURE 2.1 Budget worksheet used by a multiple radio station operator.

Station _____

Delta Starr Broadcasting

2005 Proposed Budget

2005	Jan	Feb	Mar	Apr	May	Jun	Jul	Aug	Sep	Oct	Nov	Dec	Total
Program Expense													
Payroll													
Payroll Taxes (12%)													
Talent Fees—Pd by Client													
Production Supplies													
Promotion/Prizes													
Advert & Promo													
Special Programs													
Supplies													
Program Expense Other													
Total Program Expense													
Sales Expenses													
Payroll													
Commissions													
Payroll Taxes (12%)													
Sales Promotion													
Telephone—Promotions													
Sales Promotion—Other													
Total Sales Expense													

FIGURE 2.1 *Continued.*

36

Station _____

Delta Starr Broadcasting

2005 Proposed Budget

2005	Jan	Feb	Mar	Apr	May	Jun	Jul	Aug	Sep	Oct	Nov	Dec	Total
General Administrative Expenses													
Payroll													
Payroll Taxes (12%)													
Contract Labor													
Commissions													
Employee Benefits (Health, etc.)													
Bonuses													
Employee Benefits—Other													
Tower Rent													
Rent													
Transmitter Monitoring													
Telephone													
Electricity													
Gas													
Water/Sewer													
Cablevision													
Trash Service													
Bldg Maintenance & Repair													
General Taxes													
Insurance													
Office Supplies													
Office Equipment Leases													
Office Equipment Repair/Maint													
Office Equipment Purchase													
Computer Maintenance													

FIGURE 2.1 *Continued.*

Station _____

Delta Starr Broadcasting

2005 Proposed Budget

2005	Jan	Feb	Mar	Apr	May	Jun	Jul	Aug	Sep	Oct	Nov	Dec	Total
Computer Internet Service													
Postage													
Postage Meter Rental													
Postage-Other (FedEX etc.)													
FCC Fees													
BMI/ASCAP/SESAC Fees (3.9%)													
Memberships/Dues													
Subscriptions/Publications													
Printing													
Client Entertainment/Meals													
Personal Property Taxes													
Miscellaneous													
Legal													
Legal FCC													
Bank Service Charge													
Bad Debt W/O's													
Total General Admin Expense													
Corporate/Expenses													
Administrative Allocation													
Total Corporate Expenses													
Total Expenses													
Net Income													
Total Multistation Sales													

FIGURE 2.1 _Continued._

37

includes amounts and sources of revenues and expenditures, and levels of operational profitability on a monthly and annual basis.

Cable system operators are concerned about their main revenue source, subscribers, while broadcasters want details of advertising sales. On the expenditure side, both cable and broadcast managers require information on programming costs. Cable operators need figures on pole rent and contract labor. Broadcasters care about the cost of maintaining the transmission plant.

Whatever the particular need, the quest for management financial information must begin with the design of a recordkeeping system that will produce the desired results. Every manager embarking on the task of setting up financial records is looking for guidance (i.e., What is a good model? or What has worked well for others?). Fortunately, excellent materials are available on records planning.

The principal sources utilized to set up accounting records are software companies that design and customize traffic and accounting systems for single and multiple station operators. Figure 2.2 presents a proposal submitted to a multiple station radio operator for such a system. You will note that the proposal provides for the design and implementation of financial reports. Figure 2.3 depicts how a centralized traffic and accounting system might be configured.

Another source is the National Association of Broadcasters (NAB), which has published an accounting manual for radio stations.[5] Included are chapters on financial statements, accounting records, charts of accounts with explanations, and accounting system automation.

Still another source of information is the Broadcast Cable Financial Management Association (BCFM). This organization, composed of industry members, concentrates on financial questions of import to its membership. It, too, publishes an accounting manual.[6] The contents are principally detailed charts of accounts with explanations, and model financial statement forms.

Whether the system chosen is manual or computerized, it must be designed to deliver to management certain basic information and to render financial reports. It will consist of a number of journals and ledgers that record and summarize all financial transactions and events.

The records most commonly generated are the following:

Cash receipts journal shows all monies received, listed by revenue account number. It identifies the payer and—in the case of receipts for advertising—gross amounts, discounts, and agency commissions, and resulting net amounts. Journal entries cover a given period of time, at the end of which all amounts are totaled and posted to the general ledger. Individual client payments are credited to the appropriate account in the accounts receivable ledger (Figure 2.4).

Cash disbursements journal records all monies paid out. Often, it is organized by major expense category and account number and lists the check number, date, amount, and the company or person to whom payment was made. Totals are posted to the general ledger (Figure 2.4).

Sales journal lists all transactions after the commercial schedule has run and has been billed to the client. No entries are recorded until this happens.

**CBSI CustomClassic System
12-Stations Centralized
Lease Terms**

CBSI CUSTOMCLASSIC SYSTEM, Multi-Terminal, w/Windows

Includes: License of CBSI Radio Program Log
             License of CBSI Radio Accounts Receivable
             License of CBSI Radio Sales Analyzer
             License of CBSI Radio Co-op/Copywriter
             License of CBSI Radio Auto Weekly Scheduler
             License of CBSI Radio Daily Report
             License of CBSI Radio Operator Rights
             License of CBSI Radio Programmable Avails
             License of CBSI Radio Customer/Collection Letters
             License of CBSI Radio Satellite/Event
             License of CBSI Radio CustomReports
             License of CBSI Radio Agency Management
             License of CBSI Radio Power+PLUS
             CBSI Multi-Terminal Software — up to 8 Terminals
             Niakwa RT (8 Terminal/Windows/Novell)
             Pre-Loading of Station Data at CBSI
             20 Days On-Site Operator Training**

CBSI INTERACCT ACCOUNTING SYSTEM, Level One

Includes:		
General Ledger Accounts	Operator Rights
Vendors Accounts	Import/Export
Bank Reconciliation	Project Accounting
15-84 Accounting Periods w/Detail	Vendor Tables
Full Security/Operator Audit Trail	1–12 Secondary Tables
Notations	Report Sequence
Password Security	Payroll
Design Financial Reports	
2 Days On-Site Operator Training**	

TOTAL SYSTEM TRAINING & INSTALLATION $16,402.00
MONTHLY SOFTWARE FEE $2,004.00/mo

39

FIGURE 2.2 Vendor proposal to design and install a traffic and accounting system for a group radio operation.

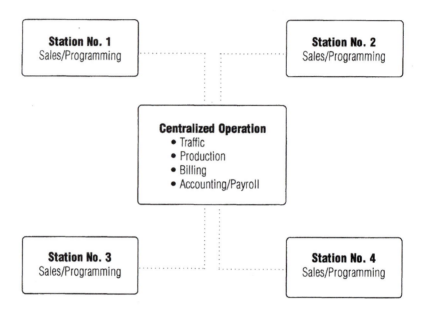

Centralization

Realizing your goals:
- Greater dominance in your market
- Better use of your talent
- Improved control
- Greater operational efficiency
- Increase your bottom line

| Station No. 1 | | Station No. 2 |
| Sales/Programming | | Sales/Programming |

Centralized Operation
- Traffic
- Production
- Billing
- Accounting/Payroll

| Station No. 3 | | Station No. 4 |
| Sales/Programming | | Sales/Programming |

Note: *All sales, programming and/or administration at individual station may be local or centralized*

FIGURE 2.3 Proposal for a multistation centralized traffic and accounting system.

Entries are triggered by performance against the contract and not when the contract is signed. When made, sales journal entries include the client's name, invoice number, date, amount, and the name of the staff member who made the sale. If part of the cost results from the sale of talent or program materials and facilities, that information is entered. So, too, are details of tradeouts—the exchange of advertising time for goods or services. Entries for a given period are totaled and posted to the general ledger. Each gross billing figure is entered on the client's page in the accounts receivable ledger (Figure 2.4).

General journal includes noncash transactions and adjustments, such as depreciation and amortization, and accrued bills not yet paid.

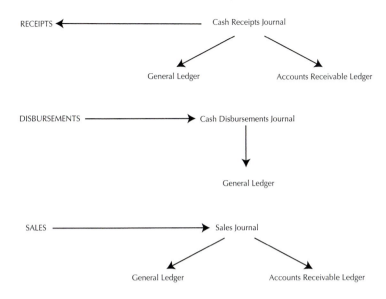

FIGURE 2.4 Financial recordkeeping process.

Accounts receivable ledger records money owed to the business by account. Using the ledger, the station or system prepares an aging sheet showing accounts that are current and those that are delinquent.

Accounts payable ledger lists monies owed by the business and includes the name of the creditor, invoice date and amount, and the account to be charged.

General ledger is the basic accounts book. It contains all transactions, posted from various journals of original entry to the appropriate account. The general ledger consists of two sections. One records figures for assets, liabilities, and capital, and the other the income and expense account figures.

Information from the general ledger is used to prepare two major financial records, the *balance sheet* and the *income statement*.

Balance Sheet   The balance sheet is a statement of the financial position of the station or system at a given time. It comprises three parts:

- *assets*, or the value of what is owned
- *liabilities*, or what is owed
- *net worth* or *equity*, or the financial interest of the enterprise's ownership

The term *balance sheet* is derived from the fact that total assets should equal total liabilities plus net worth or equity. The two sides of the sheet are, therefore, in balance.

ASSETS   Assets are classified as follows:

Current assets are those assets expected to be sold, used, or converted into cash within one year. They typically include cash, marketable securities, notes, accounts receivable, inventories (including programming), and prepaid expenses.

Fixed assets are those assets that will be held or used for a long term, meaning more than one year. Land and improvements (e.g., a parking lot), buildings, the transmitter, tower, satellite uplinks and downlinks, antenna system, studio and mobile equipment, vehicles, office and studio furniture, and fixtures are among items considered fixed assets.

Fixed assets are tangible assets—things. They depreciate, which means that use over time reduces their value. Depreciation is a business expense. The amount of time over which a tangible asset may be reduced systematically in value is determined by Internal Revenue Service (IRS) guidelines. A more detailed discussion of depreciation occurs later in this chapter.

Other assets is a category that includes mainly intangible assets—those having no physical substance. Examples are the Federal Communications Commission (FCC) license, organization costs, and goodwill. These assets are amortized, or written off, for financial statement reporting purposes.

Amortization, or write-off, of the goodwill amount means that the total amount is systematically reduced over a period of time by charging equal annual amounts to the profit and loss statement. Goodwill primarily represents the value of the broadcast license or cable franchise. For example, if a station were purchased for $6 million, and the value of its tangible assets were $3 million, then the goodwill amount would be $3 million. That amount would be charged to the station profit and loss account in equal annual amounts. For reasons discussed later in Chapter 10, "Entry into the Electronic Media Business," some intangible amounts, while deducted for financial statement reporting purposes, cannot be deducted for tax purposes.

An additional example of other assets is the network affiliation agreement of most television stations. In the mid-1980s, some stations began for tax purposes to write-off these agreements. However, such attempts occasioned significant IRS controversy and litigation. Most of these disputes were resolved by the Omnibus Budget Reconciliation Act of 1993. The act provided that certain intangible or other assets could be amortized over a 15-year period. Under the law, examples of permitted deductions are government licenses and permits, noncompete agreements, network affiliation agreements, franchises, trademarks, trade names, and goodwill. In the situation cited above, the acquired station's goodwill of $3 million would be amortized for tax purposes over 15 years, at the rate of $200,000 per year.

Prepaid and deferred charges include all prepayments made. Insurance, taxes, and rents are examples.

LIABILITIES   Liabilities reflect short- and long-term debts. They are listed as follows:

Current liabilities include accounts, taxes, and commissions payable. Monies owed for supplies, real estate, personal property, social security and withholding taxes, music license fees, and sales commissions fall into this category. Current liabilities also include amounts due on program contracts payable within one year.

Long-term liabilities include those liabilities not expected to be paid within one year. Examples of such liabilities are bank debt, mortgages, and amounts due on program contracts beyond one year.

NET WORTH   Net worth, or equity, records ownership's initial investment in the broadcast station or cable system, as increased by profits generated or reduced by losses suffered.

Preparing Financial Statements

Financial statement preparation begins with a chart of accounts, a list of account classifications. Each account is assigned a number.

The following balance sheet chart of accounts is used by LaTerr Broadcasting Corporation, licensee of KTIB-AM, Thibodaux, Louisiana (Figure 2.5). Asset accounts are numbered 1000 to 2800, 5010 to 5040, and 9520 to 9540. Liability accounts are 3100 to 3400, 6010 to 6500, and 9990. Equity accounts are 4000 to 4150.

It is from records of the kind detailed here that the balance sheet is prepared (Figure 2.6).

The financial health of a company is often judged by examining two ratios computed from the balance sheet numbers. The first of these is *current ratio*, which is obtained by dividing total current liabilities into total current assets. A good current ratio is 1.5 to 1. The second is the *debt-to-equity ratio*. It is computed by dividing stockholders' equity by long-term debt. A satisfactory debt-to-equity ratio is considered to be 1 to 1.

Income Statement   The income statement also is known as the *operating* or *profit and loss (P and L)* statement. It summarizes financial transactions and events over a given period of time. The difference between revenues and expenses is the profit or loss for that period.

REVENUES   A major source of revenue for all broadcast stations is the sale of time to local, regional, and national advertisers. Network compensation may be an additional source for network-affiliated television stations and some radio stations. Another source is Non-Traditional Revenue (NTR) (see Chapter 5, "Broadcast Sales). Other broadcast revenues include the sale of programs and talent and the rental of station facilities. Rents received for the use of station-owned towers or land, and interest and dividends are examples of nonbroadcast revenues.

Revenue sources for cable systems are somewhat different. Most revenue is derived from subscribers. However, systems are developing their advertising revenue through the sale of local and national spots, principally in local availabilities in advertiser-supported networks. Pay-per-view (PPV), video-on-demand

43

Account No.	Account Name	F/S Line Description	F/S #	Last JE	Print Status	Balance
1000	Cash - Hibernia	Cash	10	12/31/2002	Summarized	$861.75
1050	Cash - Payroll	Cash	10	12/31/2002	Summarized	$687.61
1060	Petty cash account	Cash	10	12/31/2002	Summarized	$154.69
1070	Petty cash	Cash	10		Summarized	$110.00
1080	Cash transfer	Cash	10	12/31/2002	Summarized	$0.00
1100	Accounts receivable	Accounts Receivable-Net Allo	13	12/31/2002	Summarized	$23,358.45
1150	Allowance for bad debts	Accounts Receivable-Net Allo	13	12/31/2002	Summarized	$700.75-
1200	Due from Delta Starr Broadcasting	Accounts Receivable-Net Allo	13	12/31/2002	Detailed	$29,350.00
1210	Due from Mike Starr, Jr.	Prepaid Expenses	15		Detailed	$0.00
1240	State estimated taxes	Prepaid Expenses	15		Summarized	$0.00
1245	Federal estimated taxes	Prepaid Expenses	15		Summarized	$0.00
1250	Other receivables	Prepaid Expenses	15		Detailed	$0.00
1300	Prepaid insurance	Prepaid Expenses	15	12/31/2002	Summarized	$417.32
1350	Due from employees	Prepaid Expenses	15	10/31/2002	Detailed	$0.00
2000	Equipment-group acquisition	Equipment-Group Acquisition	23		Summarized	$75,494.45
2010	Leasehold improvements	Leasehold Improvements	25	4/30/2001	Detailed	$3,980.00
2030	Office Equipment & Fixtures	Furniture & Fixtures	24	11/30/2002	Summarized	$56,685.93
2040	Radio Tower	Radio Tower	26		Summarized	$281,175.60
2050	Studio & Technical Equipment	Studio and Technical Equipme	22	10/31/2001	Summarized	$61,938.77
2060	Transmitting Equipment	Transmitting Equipment	27		Summarized	$35,840.63
2200	Accumulated Depreciation	Accumulated Depreciation	28	12/31/2002	Summarized	$486,473.03-
2501	Goodwill	Other Assets	29		Detailed	$43,654.44
2800	Meter Deposits	Other Assets	29		Detailed	$755.10
3100	Accounts payable	Accounts Payable	32	12/31/2002	Summarized	$36,566.71-
3200	State withholding	Payroll Taxes Payable	33	12/31/2002	Summarized	$554.28-
3210	Federal withholding	Payroll Taxes Payable	33	12/31/2002	Summarized	$11,387.50-
3220	F I C A Withholding	Payroll Taxes Payable	33	12/31/2002	Summarized	$8,137.28-
3230	Accrued payroll Taxes	Payroll Taxes Payable	33	12/31/2002	Summarized	$8,414.35-
3250	Income taxes payable	Payroll Taxes Payable	33		Detailed	$0.00
3260	Due to Mike Starr	Accrued Expenses	34	12/31/2002	Detailed	$62,859.32-
3270	Due to KTIB Broadcasting, Inc.	Accrued Expenses	34		Detailed	$0.00
3280	Due to Vincent Bruno	Accrued Expenses	34		Detailed	$0.00
3300	Accrued property taxes	Accrued Expenses	34	12/31/2002	Summarized	$0.00
3350	Note payable - Michael Starr	Note Payable - John Treen	41		Detailed	$0.00
3400	Deferred income taxes	Deferred Taxes	43	12/31/2002	Summarized	$850.00-
4000	Common stock	Capital Stock	45		Summarized	$29,400.00-
4148	Retained earnings	Retained Earnings	48		Summarized	$20,929.81
4149	Dividends paid	Retained Earnings	48	12/31/2002	Detailed	$0.00
4150	Current earnings	Current Year Income (loss)	49		Summarized	$0.00
5010	Sales	Sales	51	12/31/2002	Detailed	$316,356.57-
5030	Agency commissions	Sales	51	12/31/2002	Detailed	$7,103.42
5040	Other income	Other Income	62		Summarized	$0.00
6010	Advertising	Salaries & Wages	71	12/31/2002	Detailed	$20,637.57
6020	Dues and subscriptions	Salaries & Wages	71	12/31/2002	Detailed	$3,246.36
6030	Entertainment	Salaries & Wages	71	12/31/2002	Detailed	$4,284.63
6040	Freight	Salaries & Wages	71	7/31/2002	Detailed	$459.84
6050	Insurance	Salaries & Wages	71	12/31/2002	Detailed	$14,044.89
6070	Miscellaneous	Salaries & Wages	71	12/31/2002	Detailed	$5,485.01
6080	News service	Salaries & Wages	71	12/31/2002	Detailed	$3,625.54
6090	Office supplies	Salaries & Wages	71	12/31/2002	Detailed	$8,631.05
6100	Records and programs	Salaries & Wages	71	12/31/2002	Detailed	$6,455.00
6110	Rent	Salaries & Wages	71		Detailed	$0.00
6120	Technical repairs	Salaries & Wages	71	12/31/2002	Detailed	$9,836.62
6130	Other repairs	Salaries & Wages	71	12/31/2002	Detailed	$2,178.57
6140	General and adm. salaries	Salaries & Wages	71	9/30/2002	Detailed	$36,705.86
6150	Technical salaries	Salaries & Wages	71		Detailed	$0.00
6160	Broadcasters' salaries	Salaries & Wages	71	12/31/2002	Detailed	$55,355.37
6171	Social security taxes	Salaries & Wages	71	12/31/2002	Detailed	$11,915.09
6172	State unemployment taxes	Salaries & Wages	71	12/31/2002	Detailed	$165.22
6173	Federal unemployment taxes	Salaries & Wages	71	12/31/2002	Detailed	$600.82
6174	Property taxes	Salaries & Wages	71	12/31/2002	Detailed	$4,007.83
6175	Other taxes and licenses	Salaries & Wages	71	10/31/2002	Detailed	$107.75
6180	Telephone	Salaries & Wages	71	12/31/2002	Detailed	$13,692.90
6190	Utilities	Salaries & Wages	71	12/31/2002	Detailed	$6,738.94
6200	Interest	Salaries & Wages	71		Detailed	$0.00
6210	Transmitter power	Salaries & Wages	71	12/31/2002	Detailed	$7,270.01
6220	Talent fees	Salaries & Wages	71	12/31/2002	Detailed	$4,300.00
6230	Music royalties	Salaries & Wages	71	12/31/2002	Detailed	$10,623.76
6241	Legal fees	Salaries & Wages	71	12/31/2002	Detailed	$5,014.82
6242	Accounting	Salaries & Wages	71	12/31/2002	Detailed	$5,000.00
6250	Commissions	Salaries & Wages	71	12/31/2002	Detailed	$66,015.79
6260	Donations	Salaries & Wages	71	10/31/2002	Detailed	$500.00
6280	Depreciation	Salaries & Wages	71	12/31/2002	Detailed	$8,403.51
6290	Postage	Salaries & Wages	71	12/31/2002	Detailed	$146.25
6300	Coffee	Salaries & Wages	71	6/30/2002	Detailed	$0.00
6310	Equipment rental	Salaries & Wages	71	8/31/2001	Detailed	$0.00
6320	Travel	Salaries & Wages	71	12/31/2002	Detailed	$12,084.22
6330	Bad debts	Salaries & Wages	71	12/31/2002	Detailed	$607.29
6340	Maintenance contracts	Salaries & Wages	71		Detailed	$0.00
6350	Outside engineering	Salaries & Wages	71	12/31/2002	Detailed	$12,332.58
6370	Sales expense	Salaries & Wages	71	2/28/2001	Detailed	$0.00
6380	Group insurance	Salaries & Wages	71	12/31/2002	Detailed	$7,980.50
6390	Conventions	Salaries & Wages	71	8/31/2001	Detailed	$0.00
6400	Directors fees	Salaries & Wages	71		Detailed	$0.00
6430	Automobile	Salaries & Wages	71	12/31/2002	Detailed	$1,920.90
6440	F C C user fees	Salaries & Wages	71	9/30/2002	Detailed	$2,605.00
6450	Prizes and contests	Salaries & Wages	71	11/30/2002	Detailed	$10,550.33
6480	Sales support and training	Salaries & Wages	71	12/31/2001	Detailed	$0.00
6500	Management fees	Salaries & Wages	71		Detailed	$0.00
9520	Interest income	Gain/Loss on Disposal Assets	90		Detailed	$0.00
9530	Miscellaneous income	Gain/Loss on Disposal Assets	90	9/30/2002	Detailed	$44,500.00-
9540	LMA rental fee	Gain/Loss on Disposal Assets	90		Detailed	$0.00
9990	Income taxes	Income Taxes	95	12/31/2002	Summarized	$172.00

| | | Total: | | | | $0.00 |

44

FIGURE 2.5 Balance sheet chart of accounts. (Source: LaTerr Broadcasting Corporation. Used with permission.)

```
                        BALANCE SHEET

                      December 31, Year 1


      Current Assets:
         Cash                                 $    350,000
         Accounts Receivable                     1,000,000
         Reserve for Bad Debt                      (50,000)
         Net Accounts Receivable                   950,000
         Prepaid Expenses                          100,000
      Total Current Assets                     $2,400,000

      Fixed Assets:
         Land                                  $    400,000
         Buildings                                  300,000
         Equipment                                  200,000
         Automobiles and Trucks                      25,000
         Office Furniture/Equipment                  50,000
         Leasehold Improvements                      25,000
      Total Fixed Assets                       $1,000,000
         Accumulated Depreciation              $ (100,000)
      Net Fixed Assets                         $   900,000
      Net Intangible Assets                      3,700,000

      Total Assets                             $7,000,000


      Current Liabilities:
         Accounts Payable                      $   300,000
         Accrued Expenses                          100,000
         Current Notes Payable                     600,000
      Total Current Liabilities                $1,000,000


      Long-Term Notes Payable                     3,000,000

      Shareholders' Equity:
         Common Stock                            1,000,000
         Retained Earnings Beginning             1,000,000
         Retained Earnings Current Year          1,000,000
         Retained Earnings Total                $2,000,000
      Total Shareholders' Equity               $3,000,000

      Total Liability and Equity               $7,000,000
```

FIGURE 2.6 Example of a broadcast station's balance sheet.

(VOD), high-speed Internet, telephone, and music channels are among significant growth areas. Cable operators are required by law to set aside channel capacity for lease to third parties, and some receive revenue from such leases.

EXPENSES   Expenses are classified either as *direct* or as *operating and other.* Direct expenses are commissions paid to agencies for the sale of time. Operating and other expenses are listed according to the organizational structure. Usually, they reflect the costs of operating the major departments or areas of activity. In broadcast stations, they are technical (engineering), program, sales, promotion, news, and general and administrative.

Other expenses are cash and noncash expenses incurred in the operation of the business. Depreciation is an example of a noncash expense and results from the write-off of tangible assets, such as plant and equipment. Typically, the asset is reduced by equal annual amounts over its life. The systematic annual reduction in the asset's value is an expense and is charged to the income statement.

U.S. tax laws divide tangible assets into useful life categories for purposes of calculating depreciation. For example, buildings have a useful life of 41 years and towers a useful life of 15 years. Other noncash expenses may be amortized, the systematic reduction of an account over a period of time. As noted earlier, an example of an expense that is amortized is goodwill.

The term *amortization* also is frequently applied to program contracts, which are a cash expense item. Various methods for amortizing program contracts exist. One method is *straight line,* which permits a deduction of the total contract in equal annual amounts over the term of the contract. The alternate approach is called *accelerated amortization.* Under this method, larger amounts are written off in the early years of a contract, the theory being that the initial runs of a program have the most value. More detail on the specifics of these two approaches can be found in industry publications such as BCFM's *Broadcast Accounting Guidelines.* It should be noted that amortized program contracts are tax deductible and are usually charged to the program expense account, not to the "other" category.

Another common "other" expense is *interest.* Interest is the premium paid on amounts borrowed to finance acquisitions, purchases of equipment, or construction of a new facility.

Expenses are charged to the department incurring them. Those that are necessary for the overall functioning of the operation, such as utilities, generally are counted against general and administrative costs. Salaries and wages represent an expense in all departments. The following are examples of other broadcast department expenses:

Technical

- parts and supplies for equipment maintenance and repair
- rental of transmitter lines
- tubes for transmitter and studio equipment

Program

- program purchases

- rights to broadcast events (e.g., sports)
- recordings
- music licensing fees
- supplies (e.g., tapes)
- line charges for remote broadcasts

Sales

- commissions paid to staff
- commissions paid to station rep company
- trade advertising
- audience measurement
- travel and entertainment

Promotion

- sales promotion
- advertising and promotion of programs
- research
- merchandising

News

- videotape
- recordings, tapes, and transcripts
- raw film
- wire service
- photo supplies
- art supplies

General and Administrative

- maintenance and repair of buildings and office equipment
- utilities
- rents
- taxes and insurance
- professional services (e.g., legal, accounting)
- office supplies, postage, telephone, and telegraph
- operation of station-owned vehicles
- subscriptions and dues
- contributions and donations
- travel and entertainment

47

Operating expenses are deducted from revenue to determine *profit* or *loss*. Profit is the amount by which revenue exceeds expenses. The profit resulting from the deduction of operating expenses from revenue is called *operating profit*. Such deductions do not include noncash expenses, such as the depreciation and amortization previously discussed. Once the operating profit has been determined, it is then further reduced by depreciation, amortization, and federal, state, and local taxes. Operating profit adjusted for other expenses and taxes is called *net profit*.

To operate effectively, electronic media managers must know how much cash their enterprise produces annually, not just how much profit. *Cash flow* is the term used to describe the cash generated. It is calculated by adding back to net profit the amounts charged to expenses for depreciation, amortization, interest, and taxes. It is the term *cash flow* that is used to determine the value of an electronic media property by applying multiples to it. For a more detailed treatment of these concepts, refer to the discussion of multiples and prices in Chapter 10, "Entry into the Electronic Media Business."

No income statement treatment can be complete without a discussion of trade-outs. A *trade-out* or *barter* transaction occurs when goods or services are provided in exchange for time. As direct transactions, they do not produce commissionable billings for advertising agencies and, depending upon individual station or system policy, may not result in commissions for account executives either. The transactions must be included on financial statements, with the major questions being the value to assign to them and when to record them.

The Broadcast Cable Financial Management Association recommends that the value of the transaction be equal to the cash saved as a result of the barter. On timing, the BCFM outlines three ways: (1) record income and expense in the same amount in the same period; (2) record income and expense in equal amounts over the term of the barter contract; or (3) record revenue as trade spots are run and expense as goods and services are used. One of these three methods must be selected and consistently applied. Figure 2.7 is an example of an income statement.

Different proportions of revenue are provided by each source to radio and television stations, and radio and television stations incur expenses differently. Regrettably, it is no longer possible to compare the specific revenue and expense differences between the two media. That is because the National Association of Broadcasters discontinued its Radio Financial Report in 1992. And, in the post-1996 environment, it is unlikely that the major consolidators will be willing to divulge financial information that could lead to a resurrected report.

The NAB continues to collect and report TV industry financial data. The 2004 report showed that local advertising accounted for more than 60 percent of gross advertising revenues for a typical affiliate of ABC, CBS, and NBC.[7] The biggest expense items for those stations were news (29.1 percent) and programming (20 percent).[8]

	YEAR ENDED DECEMBER 31,	
	2002	2001
INCOME		
Sales	$ 316,357	$ 404,325
Agency commissions	(7,103)	(6,187)
	309,254	398,138
OPERATING EXPENSES		
Advertising	20,638	69,876
Dues and subscriptions	3,247	5,389
Entertainment	4,285	7,667
Freight	460	277
Insurance	14,045	12,978
Miscellaneous	5,482	5,383
News service	3,626	3,520
Office supplies	8,777	6,420
Records and programs	6,455	1,626
Technical repairs	9,837	3,599
Other repairs	2,179	5,713
General and administrative salaries	36,706	69,621
Broadcasters' salaries	55,355	58,764
Taxes and licenses	16,797	20,665
Telephone	13,693	15,383
Utilities	6,739	7,346
Transmitter power	7,270	5,007
Talent fees	4,300	4,998
Music royalties	10,624	10,405
Legal fees	5,015	300
Accounting	5,000	4,950
Commissions	66,016	83,254
Donations	500	175
Depreciation	8,404	15,350
Coffee	-0-	452
Equipment rental	-0-	124
Travel	12,084	16,348
Bad debts	$ 607	$ 4,848
Outside engineering	12,333	5,020
Sales expense	-0-	225
Group insurance	7,981	12,419
Conventions	-0-	1,130
Automobile	1,921	988
FCC user fees	2,605	2,300
Prizes and contests	10,550	13,902
Sales support and training	-0-	2,415
TOTAL OPERATING EXPENSES	363,531	478,837
OPERATING (LOSS)	(54,277)	(80,699)
OTHER INCOME		
Insurance proceeds	44,500	-0-
	(9,777)	(80,699)
INCOME TAXES (BENEFIT)	172	(1,436)
NET (LOSS)	(9,949)	(79,263)
RETAINED EARNINGS, beginning of year	(20,929)	58,334
RETAINED EARNINGS, end of year	$ (30,878)	$ (20,929)

FIGURE 2.7 Broadcast station income statement. (Source: LaTerr Broadcasting Corporation. Used with permission.)

COST CONTROLS

Radio, television, and cable have discovered the importance of cost controls comparatively recently. For most of their history, all three enjoyed almost automatic and sizable annual revenue increases. In that climate, management increased profits primarily through such increases, not through reducing costs.

In the late 1980s, the equation changed for broadcast radio and television. The combination of general economic conditions, the rise of niche marketing due to cable, and the fragmentation of audience shares related to the FCC's liberal licensing policies all but eliminated the customary annual sales increases.

That tide was reversed with a booming economy in 1993 and has continued. Radio has increased its overall share of mass media advertising. Television is still growing in sales volume, but at a lower annual percentage than radio. Cable progress has been impacted by the emergence of DBS as a competitor. Cable rate regulation expired in 1999 under the terms of the 1996 Telecommunications Act. However, continued subscriber rate increases have caused Congress to contemplate possible reconsideration of that provision. Now that it passes 97 percent of the nation's 109 million TV households, cable must look to rate increases, new services, and advertising for revenue growth.

In the new environment, albeit at different times, radio, television, and cable turned to cost controls. The most effective control technique capable of producing significant immediate results is personnel reduction. The 1996 act permitted expanded ownership consolidation, especially in local radio. That development has occasioned extensive reduction. Radio and television eagerly seized on this method, occasionally producing headlines with it. Increasing reliance on sophisticated automation for television, and automation plus utilization of satellite formats for radio, accelerated staff cutbacks.

When cable's moment of truth came, it focused initially on personnel adjustments, too. Cable also relied on automation technology to achieve some of its personnel goals. In addition, it turned to outside contractors to perform some of the functions formerly undertaken by staff. Cable uses independent contractors for installation, rebuilds, and other technical duties and, in some instances, for the sale of local and spot advertising.

Once the immediate cost benefits of personnel reduction are realized, additional expense reduction is a lot more tedious and requires persistent management attention. Continuing vigilance and monitoring of certain expenditure categories historically have led to savings. Many of these items involve commonsense administration and are common to radio, television, and cable. They include the following:

1. Employee Performance

   A. Employees should be hired on the basis of their qualifications to carry out required tasks. If a staff member lacks the necessary skills, or has to be trained or assisted, performance will suffer and the station or system will not be receiving value for its salary or wage dollar.

B. Each employee's workload should be great enough to justify the position. Underemployment represents a waste of dollars and a drain on profits.

C. Employee efficiency is influenced by available resources. The company must provide the equipment and the space necessary to enable staff to produce quality work efficiently and economically.

D. The work environment must be conducive to productivity. Uncomfortable temperatures, noise, and interruptions detract from work, and may reduce accomplishments and profits.

E. Supervisory personnel should be conversant with the job description of each employee in their charge and, through example and direction, strive to ensure that each performs at maximum efficiency.

F. Clear policies should be established and enforced on employee working hours and privileges, such as the frequency and length of coffee or meal breaks. Abuse can result in lowered productivity. Similarly, policies should be set forth on personal use of the telephone and other facilities. An employee engaged in a personal telephone call or in personal use of a copying machine or computer may delay the completion of business. Further, the cost of long-distance telephone calls for personal reasons can be substantial.

51

G. Morale is an important element in the willingness of employees to assist in controlling costs. For that reason, management should not underestimate the significance of employer–employee relations and of other factors that contribute to morale.

2. Employee Compensation

Salaries and wages should be fair and competitive in the market. However, care must be taken with increases and overtime.

It is financially dangerous to lead employees to believe that they will receive automatic, periodic increases, unless that is company policy. Staff accustomed to receiving such increases will feel resentment if increases are not granted or are discontinued. Instead, some employers prefer to grant bonuses, which are not viewed as a right and need not be given automatically or regularly.

Employees who regularly receive overtime pay regard it as part of their salary. When overtime is reduced or eliminated, they consider it a cut. If work cannot be completed in the normal work day, consideration should be given to adding part-time personnel at the regular rate of pay, thus avoiding the premium rates that have to be paid for overtime.

3. Professional Services

Some professional services are necessary, but their use should be reviewed periodically and controlled. The services used most by broadcast stations and cable systems are:

A. Accounting and auditing

The staff bookkeeper should be able to carry out most of the accounting. If not, an accounting firm will have to be used, and at a substantially higher cost. However, such a firm usually is engaged to file tax papers and conduct audits.

B. Legal

Most stations find it advisable to retain a Washington, DC, attorney who is qualified to practice before the FCC. The attorney provides the station with timely information and advice, and is especially helpful in the preparation of license-renewal papers. The increasing burden and complexity of federal regulation also has led many cable systems to engage Washington counsel. Some systems are trying to minimize the expense by joining with others in a consortium. Engaging a local attorney in addition is not a wise expense for most stations or systems, since most of the help requested concerns the collection of overdue accounts. That is a service that can be rendered more economically by a collection agency.

C. Consulting

Stations often feel the need for outside advice on programming, news, sales, and promotion. Engaging consultants can be costly. A more economical approach is to try to include such assistance, if possible, among the services of the station rep company.

4. Facilities

A. Land and buildings

Even though the cost of purchasing land and buildings may be high, it is more advantageous for a station to own than to rent. This is true, particularly, of the land on which cable satellite downlinks or the broadcast transmitter tower and building are located. If the landowner demands an excessive amount of money to renew a lease, management faces a dilemma. It is especially acute for broadcasters, since the license to broadcast is granted on the present tower location. To move would involve costly engineering studies and attorney fees and would require FCC approval.

Rental of office and studio buildings poses fewer risks. However, it may be difficult or impossible to obtain the owner's approval to make structural changes aimed at increasing services or improving efficiency.

B. Equipment

All equipment should be purchased at the best price available and for its contribution to the quality, efficiency, or range of program or other services. If it will generate additional revenues or reduce costs, so much the better. The temptation to buy equipment for "prestige" should be avoided. The same is true of equipment that will not be used regularly. Renting rather than purchasing may make more sense. A similar approach should be taken with telephone equipment and services. They should be sufficient for the business's needs, but not extravagant.

5. Insurance

Insurance has become a major cost-increase item. Some insurance requirements are mandated by state law. An example is workers' compensation. Loan agreements with the station's or system's lenders may require certain coverage, such as fire, automobile, title, or errors and omissions. Cost efficiencies on some types of insurance may be achievable through state or national broadcast or cable associations.

The major problem in recent years has been medical insurance. Premiums have escalated dramatically and are a major expense item. Employers constantly monitor such costs and pursue methods designed to limit the significant annual increases. Today, many companies require up to one or two years of service before an employee qualifies for employer-paid (or partially paid) medical insurance. Generally, deductibles have been increased and benefits have been capped or limited to contain costs. Employees have come to expect that medical insurance will be included in their compensation package. How it is administered is a definite morale factor.

6. Bad Debts

Failure to collect payment for time sold to advertisers is a problem that confronts many stations and a growing number of cable systems. Elimination of the problem is impossible, but it can be reduced through the statement and enforcement of a policy on billing and payment procedures. It may be necessary to terminate delinquent accounts to prevent additional losses and send a message to other advertisers.

7. Budget Control

Close control should be exercised over all expenditures. For purchases, this can be accomplished through purchase orders that require the general manager's signature. A control system should exist for other expenditures, including the following:

A. Travel and entertainment

A policy should be established for employees who incur work-related travel and entertainment costs, not only to control them but also to satisfy the requirements of the Internal Revenue Service. Before reimbursing employees, many companies require submission of an approval voucher signed by a supervisor or the general manager. Usually, it gives the date and purpose of the travel, locations, and details of and receipts for travel, food, accommodation, and other items, such as parking fees, tips, and tolls.

B. Dues

Management must determine those associations or organizations in which the station or system should hold membership. The NAB or the National Cable Television Association (NCTA) usually are high on the priority list. Affiliation with the state broadcast or cable association and the local chamber of commerce also may be considered advantageous. However, all memberships should be chosen with an eye to the benefits they provide.

53

Many companies believe that department heads and others should join appropriate local, state, or national organizations to advance their careers or the employer's interests. If the company has a policy of paying employee membership fees, it is important that each proposal for membership be considered on the basis of the benefits that will accrue to the individual and the company. If membership contributes little or nothing, monies spent will be wasted.

C. Subscriptions

Most employers subscribe to selected newspapers, magazines, and journals, and make them available to staff. Publications should be chosen for their contributions to the interests of the employees and the company. Costs can be reduced by eliminating those that are not read or are of marginal interest.

D. Contributions

All stations and systems confront requests from nonprofit organizations for financial contributions or air time. To control such expenditures, a policy should be implemented that permits the discharge of the "good corporate citizen" role and prevents resentment by those whose requests cannot be granted. Many companies put a dollar value on each public service announcement aired and mail an invoice to the organization indicating that the amount represents a contribution. Such records also provide useful documentation for license- or franchise-renewal purposes.

E. Communications

Broadcasting and cable always have been the home of deadlines and time demands. With today's emphasis on productivity and lean staffs, time pressures are intensified. Such an atmosphere produces an employee reliance on expedited means of communication, which almost always add to costs. Dependence on telephone, fax, photocopies, and express delivery services have become the rule, not the exception. Experienced management knows that even little numbers can grow quickly into larger ones, to the point of becoming unpleasant surprises.

Accordingly, managers must be alert to these expenditures and must develop methods of monitoring and control. For example, most communication systems today have electronic entry codes. They ensure that only authorized staff incur expenses. If employees exceed their authority or abuse their access, remedial action can be taken. The use of such codes has an immediate and dramatic effect on telephone, fax, and photocopy excesses. Abuse of costly overnight delivery services as a defense against almost-missed deadlines is not as easy to control and requires real management diligence.

MONITORING FINANCIAL PROGRESS

Management can monitor financial performance in a number of ways. The most obvious is to compare actual results for a month, quarter, or year with the budget and the comparable period for the prior year. A good financial statement, balance sheet, or income statement will give a manager all that information on one piece of paper.

Another important monitoring technique is the comparison of the station's or system's financial progress with that of peers. As noted earlier, one of the principal sources that provided comparisons for radio stations has been discontinued. However, television stations still can benefit from an examination of the NAB/BCFM *Television Financial Report*.

There are other sources for comparative information. One consists of newsletters and annual reports issued by Paul Kagan Associates, Inc., of Carmel, California.[9] Annual reports include the *Radio Financial Databook*, *TV Station Deals & Finance Databook*, and the *Broadband Cable Financial Databook*. Additional sources are available from the Radio Advertising Bureau (RAB),[10] the Television Bureau of Advertising (TVB),[11] and the Cabletelevision Advertising Bureau (CAB).[12] Revenue reports for some markets are compiled by Miller, Kaplan, Arase & Company.[13]

Another useful tool is the NAB's Television Financial Monitoring System, whose customized reports allow for the comparison of financial results of a particular station with those of similar stations. To use the system, it is necessary to send the NAB a special order form with details of the stations for which comparative data are desired (Figure 2.8).

Additionally, in some markets, stations report their revenue results to an accounting firm retained by all stations. Where available, this procedure provides a method of determining a station's revenue performance as a percentage of the total for the market. Since stations are no longer required to report their financial results to the FCC, this can be a valuable method of monitoring station and market performance.

Financial results are now the most important measurement of a manager's effectiveness. The electronic media manager must be knowledgeable about these important matters.

55

(Photocopy this page if additional order forms are needed)

SPECIAL TELEVISION FINANCIAL REPORTS

COMPARE YOUR STATION'S FINANCIAL PERFORMANCE WITH YOUR STATION PEERS!

Just pick the criteria to select the stations that are closest to your station. As long as there are 10 stations that meet your criteria, NAB will provide you with a report, that you can use to compare your station's performance with those in similar situations. The report sent to you will be identical to the pages included in the *2003 NAB/BCFM Television Financial Report,* using the stations with which you want to compare.

You can select stations using the following criteria:
1. Affiliation (ABC, CBS, Fox, NBC, UPN, WB, Independent, or any combination)
2. Market Size (2001-02 DMA rankings)
3. Station Revenue Size (Net Revenues)
4. Region of the Country (Nine Census Regions, see below)
5. Station Type (VHF or UHF)

Select the criteria most suited to your needs. We will send you a two-page report with over 50 different revenue and expense categories to compare your station's performance.

Affiliation: Choose one or more category

☐ ABC   ☐ Fox   ☐ WB   ☐ All Stations
☐ CBS   ☐ NBC   ☐ UPN   ☐ Independent

Market Size: (Choose a Lower Limit, Upper Limit or All Markets)

Lower Limit _____   Upper Limit _____   ☐ All Markets

Station Revenues: Choose an Upper and Lower dollar limit

Lowest Net Revenue Limit $_____   Highest Net Revenue Limit $_____
☐ No Revenue Limits

Regions of the Country: Choose one region, any combination of regions, or all regions

☐ New England (CT, ME, MA, NH,RI,VT)   ☐ West North Central (IA,KS,MN,MO,NE,ND,SD)
☐ Mid Atlantic (NJ,NY,PA)   ☐ West South Central (AR,LA,OK,TX)
☐ South Atlantic (DE,DC,FL,GA,MD,NC,SC,VA,WV)   ☐ Mountain (AZ,CO, ID, MT, NV, NM, UT,WY)
☐ East North Central (IL,IN, MI, OH, WI)   ☐ Pacific (AK, CA,HI, OR, WA)
☐ East South Central (AL, KY, MS, TN)   ☐ All Regions

Station Type: ☐VHF   ☐UHF

Note: Every effort will be made to accommodate the criteria you have selected to define your Special Television Financial Report. However, certain restrictions are placed on the comparative station selection process to ensure confidentiality. A minimum of 10 stations must fit the specified criteria you have selected.

(Over please for Order Information)

FIGURE 2.8 NAB Special Television Financial Reports order form. (Reprinted with permission of the National Association of Broadcasters.)

WHAT'S AHEAD?

No one can predict the future in a consolidating, technology-driven industry like electronic media with any accuracy. All we can do is spot trends.

One emerging trend is publicly traded megacompanies that are vertically and horizontally integrated. Public companies are earnings-driven, and the market is unforgiving when profit forecasts are not fulfilled. As consolidation progresses, more and more publicly-traded entities will be operating radio and television stations, even in small, unrated markets.

The stock market has begun to question the underperformance and economics of these megacompanies.[14] As shareholders watch the declining value of their equities, it does not take too much imagination to understand how important financial performance skills will be.

More than ever, financial management will be the measure of management success. Accordingly, it is vital that any aspiring broadcaster, cablecaster, or future electronic mediacaster of whatever technical innovation comes along be well acquainted with financial terminology and concepts.

Electronic media students should include computer, business, accounting, and financial courses in their curriculum planning. The industry will become more centralized as to product and management. It will be more computer-driven, and the number of program staff will decline. What will be left largely will be financial, sales, and promotion personnel.

SUMMARY

Financial management demands an understanding of the accounting function, basic financial statements utilized by managers, methods of preparation, and the terminology employed.

The accounting function begins with the budget process, continues with the recording and reporting of transactions, and concludes with an analysis of financial results.

The budget is a planning and control document that plots the course of projected financial transactions (i.e., revenue, expense, profit, or loss). Actual daily results are recorded in journals and ledgers, and are transferred to financial statements by using charts of accounts. The two main financial reporting forms are the balance sheet and the income statement. The balance sheet reveals the condition of the business at a fixed point in time. It discloses total assets, liabilities, and capital of the operation. Ratios are then applied to balance sheet results to determine the relative strength or weakness of the company.

The income statement is another measure of financial health. It measures revenue and expenses, resulting in profit or loss for a given period of time.

After the results are reviewed and compared with the budget, cost control methods may be required. Even if financial results meet or exceed the budget, the electronic media manager might still be underperforming. Financial progress also is judged by a comparison of the results achieved with similar facilities inside or outside the market. Once made, those additional comparisons may require management to effect further changes in station or system operations.

CASE STUDY

Dustin Hoffman is busy burning his graduation shoe leather making the rounds of well-situated communications graduates from his alma mater, "I Can't Believe U."

57

Dustin's interviews have focused his attention on what he should have learned but did not. Collegiate Bowling 101 was a sure GPA builder but it was not accounting concepts. Mating habits of the North American Bison was no substitute for Software Concepts for Managing Information in a business that sells intangible products.

It seems that his best opportunity is with an ailing radio station blessed with a new owner, an alumnus, who pawns the station through intensive sales, electronic efficiency, and multiple-hat staff members.

Dustin's offer from WFIX-FM is an entry-level sales position. He must oversee the installation of a computerized accounting and monitoring system to track sales performance and profits.

It's either this or go to work in his father's waste management business. He takes the job, and has to solve the following problems.

EXERCISES

1. Where can he get some basic information on accounting terminology and methods for a stand-alone radio station?

2. Where can he find a specialized software company that can provide an "off-the-rack" user-friendly accounting system?

3. What basic accounting statements will Dustin want the software to produce? Why?

4. What tools are available to monitor his station's performance against its peers?

NOTES

[1] *Radio Business Report, Morning E-Paper,* July 16, 2004. http://www.rbr.com/epaper.

[2] "1994 Career Guide," *U.S. News and World Report,* November 1, 1993, pp. 78–112.

[3] Ken Kerschbaumer, "Data Is Power," *Broadcasting & Cable,* June 7, 2004, pp. 48–49.

[4] *Ibid.*

[5] *Accounting Manual for Radio Stations.* Washington, DC: National Association of Broadcasters, 1981.

[6] *Broadcast Accounting Guidelines.* Northfield, IL: Broadcast Cable Financial Management Association, 1996.

[7] NAB/BCFM 2004 *Television Financial Report,* p. 36.

[8] NAB/BCFM 2004 *Television Financial Report,* p. 37.

[9] http://www.kagan.com.

[10] http://www.rab.com.

[11] http://www.tvb.org.

[12] http://www.onetvworld.org.

[13] http://www.millerkaplan.com.

[14] *Radio Business Report, Morning E-Paper*, July 16, 2004. http://www.rbr.com/epaper.

ADDITIONAL READINGS

Jablonsky, Stephen F., and Noah P. Barsky. *The Manager's Guide to Financial Statement Analysis*, 2nd ed. Hoboken, NJ: John Wiley & Sons, 2001.

Radio & Television Business Report. Lake Ridge, VA: Radio & Television Business Report (published monthly).

TFM: The Financial Manager. Northfield, IL: Broadcast Cable Financial Management Association (published bimonthly).

Tracy, John A. *How to Read a Financial Report: Wringing Vital Signs Out of the Numbers*, 6th ed. Hoboken, NJ: John Wiley & Sons, 2004.

Understanding Broadcast & Cable Finance: A Handbook for the Non-Financial Manager. Northfield, IL: BCFM Press, 1994.

59

Human Resource Management

This chapter looks at the management of human resources and examines

- the chief functions of human resource management

- the management of unionized workers

- selected laws and regulations governing the recruitment, hiring, and treatment of employees

Broadcast stations in the same market, with comparable facilities and staffs of similar size, often achieve different levels of success. Some attain their objectives regularly, while others fare poorly. Why?

The reasons may be complex. Often, however, the difference may be traced to the way in which each station manages its personnel. The station that attracts qualified employees, compensates them fairly, recognizes and responds to their individual needs, and provides them with a pleasant working environment is rewarded with the amount and quality of work that lead to success. The station that pays more attention to the return on its financial investment than to its staff is plagued by low morale, constant turnover, and a continuing struggle in the competitive broadcast marketplace.

It has been observed that, "No other element of the broadcasting enterprise can deliver as great a return on investment as its human resources."[1] Recognizing this, many large stations have established a human resources department, headed by a manager or director. Working with the general manager and other department heads, the department is involved in the following functions: (1) staffing, including staff planning and the recruitment, selection, and dismissal of employees; (2) employee orientation, training, and development; (3) employee compensation; (4) employee safety and health; (5) employee relations; (6) trade union relations, if staff members belong to a trade union; and (7) compliance with employment laws and regulations.

In most stations, however, these functions are handled by a number of different people. Typically, department heads are largely responsible for the management of employees in their respective departments. They recommend to the general manager departmental staffing levels, the hiring and dismissal of staff, and salaries and raises. They approve vacation and leave requests, supervise staff training and development, and ensure departmental compliance with legal and regulatory requirements. Similarly, if their staff is unionized, they carry out the terms of the union contract.

The general manager approves staffing priorities, hirings and dismissals, and salaries and raises for employees in all departments. The general manager monitors, also, the station's compliance with all applicable laws and regulations and with trade union agreements. The business manager is charged with maintaining employee records and processing the payroll.

THE FUNCTIONS OF HUMAN RESOURCE MANAGEMENT

STAFFING

Planning To meet its objectives, a broadcast station must have an adequate number of employees with appropriate skills, both in the station as a whole and in each department. Ensuring that enough qualified staff are available requires the projection of future needs and the development of plans to meet those needs. Together, these activities are known as *personnel planning*, which consists of five components:

Job analysis identifies the responsibilities of the job, usually through consideration of the job's purpose and the duties that must be carried out in order to fulfill that purpose.

Job description results from the job analysis and includes purpose and responsibilities.

Job specifications grow out of the job description and set forth the minimum qualifications necessary to function effectively. Typically, they include a certain level of education and experience in similar work. Other specifications vary with the job.

Workload analysis is an estimate of the type and amount of work that must be performed if the station's objectives are to be met.

Workforce analysis involves consideration of the skills of current employees to determine if any of them have the qualifications to handle the job. If the analysis shows that some do, a selection may be made among them. If not, the station probably will seek a qualified candidate outside.[2]

To illustrate the personnel planning procedure, assume that a television station intends to expand its early-evening newscast from 30 minutes to 1 hour. The workload analysis indicates, among other things, that a co-anchor must be added. The workforce analysis finds that none of the existing news staff is qualified. The job analysis concludes that the chief responsibility is to co-anchor the newscast and that additional responsibilities include writing and reporting for both the early and late newscasts. The job description lists the position title and the responsibilities it carries. The job specifications call for a degree in broadcasting or journalism and experience in TV news anchoring, writing, and reporting.

63

Recruitment   Recruitment is the process of seeking out candidates for positions in the station and, if necessary, encouraging them to apply. Many stations have a policy of filling vacant jobs with current employees, whenever possible. Such a policy can help build morale among all employees, since it shows management's concern for the individual and suggests that everyone will have an opportunity for advancement. From the station's standpoint, the practice is advantageous because management knows its employees and their abilities. In addition, the employee is accustomed to working with other station staff and is familiar with the station's operation. Stations that are part of a group usually post the opening with other stations in the group. Similar advantages apply.

When recruitment takes place externally, the particular vacancy will suggest the most likely sources of applicants. Stations and groups usually post all vacancies on their Web site. Some stations supplement their online postings with advertisements in the local newspaper, especially for clerical positions. Advertisements in national trade magazines—*B&C Broadcasting & Cable* and *Television Week*, for example—may attract the attention of potential employees in a range of professional areas. Publications and Web sites of trade and professional organizations, such as the National Association of Broadcasters and state broadcasting associations, are another means of publicizing job openings.

Web-only sites are an additional option. They include Radio Online (http://www.radio-online.com) for radio and Broadcast Employment Services (http://www.tvjobs.com) for television. Both sites offer postings at no charge to stations. Vacancies in radio and television may be advertised at http://www.TvandRadiojobs.com, which charges a listing fee.

Station consultants may be helpful in suggesting candidates for positions, since they are familiar with employees in other markets.

As noted later in the chapter, the Federal Communications Commission (FCC) requires most stations to use recruitment sources and notify requesting organizations of every full-time vacancy.

A good source of applicants, particularly for entry-level positions, is the two-year college or university, especially if it has a broadcasting or communication department. Many stations in college and university towns conduct internship programs with such institutions and are able to identify potential employees during the internship. In the absence of an internship program, a call to the institution's placement office will bring the vacancy to the attention of students. Most placement offices keep files on recent graduates and will alert those with appropriate qualifications. If the office distributes a regular listing of positions to interested alumni, an even larger number of potential applicants will be reached.

Word of actual or anticipated vacancies spreads quickly through most stations. It is common, therefore, for employees to carry out informal recruiting by notifying friends and acquaintances. Additionally, many stations ask employees to suggest people who may be interested.

Most radio and television stations keep a file of inquiries about possible jobs. Persons visiting the station to ask about openings often are invited to complete an application for employment, even if no vacancy exists. The application may be filed for possible use later. A similar practice is followed with letters of inquiry. Obviously, the value of the file diminishes with the passage of time as those making the inquiry find other employment, and many stations remove from the file applications that are more than six months old. However, it may be a useful starting point.

Selection   When recruitment has been completed, the station moves to the selection process. This involves the identification of qualified applicants and the elimination of those who are not. Ultimately, it leads to a job offer to the person deemed most likely to perform in a way that will assist the station in meeting its objectives.

Stations typically require applicants to complete an employment application form. Stations and groups often include the form on their Web site. Generally, it asks for personal information, such as name, address, and telephone number, as well as details of the position sought, education and work experience, and the names and addresses of references. An example of an application for employment form is shown in Figure 3.1. It calls for other information that the station may use in the selection, such as legal authorization to work in the United States and criminal record. In addition, it states the station's policy on nondiscrimination in employment, which will be discussed later in the chapter.

Application For Employment

Hometown Broadcasting Company is an equal opportunity employer. All qualified applicants will be considered without regard to race, creed, color, sex, pregnancy, marital status, age, ancestry, national origin, or disabilities or any other classification protected by applicable state or local laws. Reasonable accommodations for the needs of otherwise qualified applicants with disabilities will be made upon request. NOTICE TO APPLICANTS WITH DISABILITIES: Please advise if you need assistance in completing this form or need an alternate form. If you believe that you have been discriminated against on any bases listed above, you may notify the Federal Communications Commission or any local, state, or federal agency charged with the responsibility of investigating such claims (e.g., the Equal Employment Opportunity Commission).

PERSONAL INFORMATION:

1. Name: _____

2. Social Security Number: _____

3. Phone Number: _____

4. Date of Application: _____

5. Present Address: _____
City: _____ State: _____ Zip: _____

6. Specific position for which you are applying: _____

7. Salary desired: _____

8. Date you can start: _____ Are you 18 years or older? _____

9. What is your availability to work? _____ Full-Time _____ Part-Time
_____ Days _____ Nights _____ Weekends

10. Do you hold a current FCC license? _____ Yes _____ No
If yes, issue date: _____

11. Have you ever been employed by or applied for employment with Hometown Broadcasting Company or this station? _____ Yes _____ No
If so, please state when, where, and what position held: _____
_____

12. At time of hire, will you be able to demonstrate that you are legally authorized to work in the United States? _____ Yes _____ No

13. Can you perform the essential functions for which you are applying, with or without reasonable accommodation? _____ Yes _____ No

14. Have you ever been convicted of or pleaded guilty to a felony or a misdemeanor (do not include traffic violations)? A conviction is not necessarily grounds for disqualification from employment. _____ Yes _____ No
If so, explain, giving date, court, and place where offense occurred: _____
_____ _____

EMPLOYMENT EXPERIENCE: Please list your last three employers, starting with your current or most recent position.

1. Company Name: _____

2. Address: _____

FIGURE 3.1 Sample of application for employment in a broadcast station.

City: _____ State: _____ Zip: _____

3. Position Title: _____

4. Starting Salary: _____ Ending Salary: _____

5. Starting Date: _____ Leaving Date: _____

7. Reason for leaving: _____

8. Supervisor's Name: _____

If currently employed, may we contact your employer? _____ Yes _____ No

1. Company Name: _____

2. Address: _____

City: _____ State: _____ Zip: _____

3. Position Title: _____

4. Starting Salary: _____ Ending Salary: _____

5. Starting Date: _____ Leaving Date: _____

7. Reason for leaving: _____

8. Supervisor's Name: _____

1. Company Name: _____

2. Address: _____

City: _____ State: _____ Zip: _____

3. Position Title: _____

4. Starting Salary: _____ Ending Salary: _____

5. Starting Date: _____ Leaving Date: _____

7. Reason for leaving: _____

8. Supervisor's Name: _____

REFERENCES: Please list three people, other than relatives or previous employers, whom you have known for at least one year.

1. Name & Business Relationship: _____

2. Address: _____

3. Phone Number: _____

1. Name & Business Relationship: _____

2. Address: _____

3. Phone Number: _____

1. Name & Business Relationship: _____

2. Address: _____

3. Phone Number: _____

FIGURE 3.1 *Continued*

EDUCATION:

Name & Location	Course Study/Degree	Did you graduate?
High School	_____	_____
College	_____	_____
Graduate	_____	_____
Apprentice, Business or	_____	_____
Vocational School	_____	_____

Please list any other licenses, certificates, or skills which are job-related: _____

_____

_____

CERTIFICATION OF APPLICANT

I hereby certify that the information I have supplied on this application is true and complete and does not contain any falsifications, omissions, or concealments of material fact. I understand that any false statements or material omissions will be sufficient cause for rejection of my application or, if I have been hired, will be cause for discharge.

I certify that I am not a party to any contract and do not have any other obligations that would limit, interfere with or restrict my ability to work for Hometown Broadcasting Company.

1. Applicant's Signature: _____

2. Date of Application: _____

67

FIGURE 3.1 *Continued*

The station may ask applicants to take a test to prove that they have the skills claimed on the form. Candidates for a clerical position, for example, may have to demonstrate speed and accuracy on a word-processing test. Some stations use writing tests for entry-level positions in the newsroom.

Applicants for many positions prefer to provide the station with a résumé, in addition to or instead of a completed application form. The résumé permits the person seeking employment to emphasize qualifications and to provide more details than most application forms can accommodate.

For on-air positions, the station usually asks applicants for an air check or tape containing examples of their work. In radio, the aim is to identify persons whose voice and style match station format, or whose news delivery commands credibility. In addition to considering voice, the television station is interested in physical appearance and manner of presentation.

Using the employment application form or résumé and, if appropriate, test results and the on-air samples, the station can reduce the list of applicants to those who match most closely the job qualifications. The process of elimination usually continues until only a few names remain.

At this point, interviews may be arranged with those whose applications will be pursued. However, many stations prefer to carry out background and reference checks before proceeding, and with good reason.

Applicants seek to present their education, experience, and skills in the most favorable light. Most list accomplishments of which they are proud and ignore their shortcomings. Some even stretch the truth and give themselves job titles they never held or claim to be proficient in tasks for which they have only rudimentary ability. Furthermore, listed references are likely to be persons who are disposed favorably to the applicant.

Checking on the education of applicants usually is not difficult. A telephone call, fax, or letter to a school, college, or university can produce the required information.

The work experience check sometimes presents problems, especially if the applicant has held jobs with several stations over a number of years. However, the stations' personnel files should contain records of the candidate's job titles and responsibilities, employment dates, and salary.

Many stations try to obtain from previous employers details of the applicant's quality of work, ability to get along with colleagues and superiors, strengths and weaknesses, and the reason for leaving. It is not unusual to discover that managers under whom applicants have worked at other jobs have moved in the meantime. When this happens, perseverance is required to track down the manager and, in the event of failure, to find others who remember the applicant and are willing to respond to questions.

Obtaining responses is difficult for another reason: the increasing incidence of legal actions by persons receiving negative recommendations. For that reason, it is not unusual for employers to provide only confirmation of a former employee's dates of employment, job title, and responsibilities.

If the applicant has a job, questions may be posed to the current employer. But stations usually do so only with the approval of the applicant. Permission of the applicant is required, also, if the station plans to carry out a credit check. This practice is not widespread, but many stations conduct such a check on prospective employees whose job will entail the handling of money.

Checks with the references listed by the applicant usually concentrate on the circumstances through which the reference and the applicant are acquainted, and on personal and, whenever appropriate, professional strengths and weaknesses about which the reference can provide information.

If the background and reference checks support the station's preliminary conclusions about the applicant's qualifications, an interview will be scheduled. Of all the steps involved in the selection process, none is more important than the interview. The station will use the results to make a hiring decision. A good choice of candidate will add to the station's competitive strength. A poor choice may lead to a decision to dismiss the chosen candidate after only a short period of employment, leading to yet another search with its attendant expenditures of time, money, and effort.

Interviews are time-consuming for station employees who will be involved and may be costly for the station if the interviewees live in distant cities and the station meets the expenses of travel, meals, and accommodation. However, while application forms, tests, résumés, air checks or tapes, and background and reference checks yield a lot of information about applicants and their qualifications, only a face-to-face interview can provide insights into those personal characteristics that often make the difference between success and failure on the job.

The interview gives the station the opportunity to make a determination about the applicant's suitability based on observation of factors such as appearance, manners, personality, motivation, and communication abilities. The applicant's awareness of commercial broadcasting's philosophy, practices, and problems, and their attitudes toward them also may be gleaned from responses to questions. In addition, conclusions may be drawn about the applicant's ability to fit into the station.

Interviewing procedures vary. Some stations prefer an unstructured, free-wheeling approach, while others follow a structured and formal method. The general manager may take part or merely approve or disapprove the hiring recommendation. In some stations, only the head of the department in which the vacancy exists participates; in others, the heads of all departments may be involved. Some stations include staff in the interviewing.

Whatever procedure is followed, the principal objective of the interview should be the same: an assessment of the candidate's suitability for the position. Of course, the interview may be used to obtain from the applicant additional details about qualifications or clarification of information contained on the application form or résumé. The interviewer may wish to provide the applicant with specific information about the station and the job to be filled. But such exchanges of information should be used only as a means of satisfying the principal objective, and not merely to fill the allotted time.

Those involved in conducting the interview can take certain actions to try to ensure that the objective is achieved:

69

BEFORE THE INTERVIEW

1. Become fully familiar with the responsibilities of the position to be filled and the education, experience, and skills necessary to carry them out. This will permit an understanding of what will be required of the new employee, and of the relative importance of education, experience, and skills.

2. Review the candidate's application form or résumé and, if appropriate, test results and air check or tape. This will help to assess the candidate's qualifications and suggest possible questions for the interview.

3. Confirm the date and time of the interview and ensure that enough time has been allowed for it.

4. Give instructions that the interview must not be interrupted by other staff or by telephone calls.

DURING THE INTERVIEW

1. Establish a friendly climate to put the interviewee at ease. This can be accomplished by a warm handshake, a smile, and some small talk.

2. Ask only job-related questions. Questions that do not lead to an assessment of qualifications for the position are wasted. They also may be dangerous if they suggest discrimination based on age, sex, or religion, for example.

3. Give the interviewee an opportunity to speak at some length and to answer questions fully. One method of doing this is to pose open-ended questions. If necessary, press the candidate with follow-up questions to obtain additional information.

4. Listen to the responses to the questions. Some interviewers prefer to make written notes during the interview, though this can be disturbing for an interviewee who is required to look at the top of someone's head during what should be a face-to-face exchange.

5. Give additional information about the job and the station to ensure that the candidate has a full understanding of them. Details of the full range of responsibilities, working hours, salary, and fringe benefits, and of the station's organization, goals, and role in the community are among the items that could be covered.

6. Allow time for the candidate to ask questions. In giving details of the job and the station, many interviewers assume that they are providing all the information a candidate requires. However, the interviewee may also be interested in considerations that are not job-related, such as the cost of housing, the quality of the public schools, and employment opportunities in the community for a spouse.

7. Pace the interview so that all planned questions are covered. Omission of questions and the responses may make a hiring decision difficult.

8. Terminate the interview politely. One way to end is to advise the candidate when a decision on filling the position will be made.

9. Ensure that the candidate is shown to the next appointment on the schedule. If the interview is the final appointment, arrange for the candidate to be accompanied to the exit.

AFTER THE INTERVIEW   Record the results of the interview immediately. Some stations use an evaluation form that lists the qualifications for the job and permits the interviewer to grade each candidate on a scale from "poor" to "outstanding" on each. Other stations ask the interviewer to prepare a written memorandum assessing the candidate's strengths and weaknesses. When interviews with all candidates have been completed, the memoranda are used in making a recommendation.

Oral evaluations are not satisfactory, since they leave a gap in the station's employment records. This leads to problems if questions about hiring practices are raised by an unsuccessful candidate or the FCC.

As soon as the decision has been taken to hire one of the interviewed candidates, a job offer should be made promptly. A telephone call will establish if the candidate is still available and interested, and if the offer is acceptable.

To ensure that the station's records are complete, and to avoid misunderstandings, a written offer of employment should be mailed, with a copy. Among other information, it should include the title and responsibilities of the position, salary, fringe benefits, and the starting date and time. If it is acceptable, it should be signed and dated by the new employee and returned to the station, where it will become part of the employee's personnel file. The copy should be retained by the employee.

A letter should be mailed to the unsuccessful candidates, also, advising them of the outcome. They may not welcome the news, but they will appreciate the action, and the station's image may be enhanced as a result.

The station should keep records of all recruitment, interviewing, and hiring activities to satisfy FCC requirements, discussed later. The documentation may be useful in identifying effective procedures, and it may be necessary to satisfy inquires about, or challenges to, the station's employment practices.

Dismissals Staff turnover is a normal experience for all broadcast stations. It is a continuing problem for stations in small markets, where many employees believe that a move to a larger market is the only measure of career progress.

Stations in markets of all sizes are familiar with the situation in which a staff member moves on for personal advancement. In such circumstances, the parting usually takes place without hard feelings on the part of either management or employee.

Another kind of staff turnover is more difficult to handle. It results from a station's decision to dismiss an employee, an action that may send panic waves through the station. If it involves a member of the sales staff, it may also bring reactions from clients. If an on-air personality is involved, the station may hear from the audience.

Of course, some dismissals do not reflect ill on affected employees. Changes in station ownership, the format of a radio station, or locally produced programming at a television station may result in the termination of some employees. Economic considerations, such as those occasioned by in-market radio station consolidation, often lead to reductions in staff.

The majority of dismissals, however, stem from an employee's work or behavior. No station can tolerate very long a staff member who fails to carry out assigned responsibilities satisfactorily. Nor can a station continue to employ someone who is lazy, unreliable, uncooperative, unwilling to accept or follow instructions, or whose work is adversely affected by reliance on abuse of alcohol or drugs.

This is not to suggest that management should stand by idly while an employee moves inevitably toward dismissal. Several steps may be taken to avoid such an outcome. For example, a department head should point out unsatisfactory work immediately and suggest ways to improve. The employee should be warned in writing that failure to improve could lead to dismissal. A copy of the warning should be placed in the employee's file.

Similarly, the supervisor's awareness of the employee's inability or unwillingness to act in accordance with station policies should be brought to the attention of the noncomplying staff member. Action should be taken when the behavior is observed or reported, since tolerating it may suggest that it is acceptable. If the station has a written policy against the behavior, it should be sufficient to draw the employee's attention to it. Again, it would be wise to write an appropriate memorandum to the employee and to place a copy in the employee's file. The memorandum should indicate clearly that continuation of the behavior may result in dismissal.

Management actions of this kind may not lead to improvement or correction, but they will eliminate the element of surprise from a dismissal decision,

71

and they will show that the station has taken reasonable steps to deal fairly with the employee.

If an employee is to be dismissed, the way in which the decision is reached is important. So, too, is the way in which it is carried out, since it is certain to produce a reaction from other employees. The most important reason for caution, however, is federal and state legislation.

Attorney John B. Phillips, Jr., has prepared a set of guidelines for management to follow before discharging an employee.[3] First, he recommends a review of the employee handbook to make sure that the station management has complied with all procedures identified therein. That review should be followed by a review of the employee's personnel file to determine if the documentation contained in it is sufficient to warrant the termination. It should show, for example, that the employee has been advised of the possibility of dismissal and has had ample opportunity to correct any problems or failures to perform as required.

Next, managers should evaluate the possibility of a discrimination or wrongful discharge claim. (Major federal laws on discrimination are described later in the chapter.) The following are among the questions that should be considered:

- How old is the employee?
- Is the employee pregnant?
- How many minority employees remain with the station?
- Does the employee have a disability?
- Who will replace the employee?
- How long has the employee been with the station?
- Does the documentation in the file support termination?
- Was the employee hired away from a long-time employer?
- Has the employee recently filed a workers' compensation claim or any other type of claim with a federal or state agency?
- Has the reason for termination been used to terminate employees in the past?

Phillips lists other questions that may have legal implications but that are primarily practical in nature:

- If the termination is challenged, can the station afford adverse publicity?
- To what extent has the station failed the employee?
- Assuming that the employee is not terminated and the problem is not removed, can the station tolerate its continuation?
- Is the employee the kind of person who is likely to "fight back" or file suit?
- What impact would termination have on employee morale and employer credibility? What about failure to terminate?

- Has the immediate supervisor had problems with other employees in the department?

- Does the employee have potential for success in a different department?

- Are there nonwork-related problems that have created or added to the employee's problems at work?

- Has the employee tried to improve?

- Even if the termination is legally defensible, is it a wise decision?

Having reached a tentative decision to terminate, a manager may wish to let a noninterested party evaluate the decision before acting. However, this should not be viewed as a substitute for seeking legal advice if problems are anticipated.

If it is determined that dismissal is appropriate, Phillips suggests a termination conference with the employee. He offers the following guidelines:

1. Two station representatives should be present in most cases.

2. Within the first few minutes, tell the employee that he or she is being terminated.

3. Explain the decision briefly and clearly. Do not engage in argument or counseling, and do not fail to explain the termination.

4. Explain fully any benefits that the employee is entitled to receive and when they will be received. If the employee is not going to receive certain benefits, explain why.

5. Let the employee have an opportunity to speak, and pay close attention to what is said.

6. Be careful about what you say, since anything said during the termination conference can become part of the basis of a subsequent employee claim or lawsuit. In other words, do not make reference to the employee's sex, age, race, religion, or disability or to anything else that could be considered discriminatory.

7. Review the employment history briefly, commenting on specific problems that have occurred and the station's attempts to correct them.

8. Try to obtain the employee's agreement that he or she has had problems on the job or that job performance has not been satisfactory.

9. Take notes.

10. Be as courteous to the employee as possible.

11. Remember that you are not trying to win a lawsuit; you are trying to prevent one.[4]

73

What the employee was told and what the employee said should be included in the documentation of the conference, and it should be signed by all employer representatives in attendance.

ORIENTATION, TRAINING, AND DEVELOPMENT

All newly employed staff are new even if they have already worked in a radio or television station. They are with new people in a new operation. Accordingly, they should be introduced to other employees and to the station, a process known as *orientation*.

The introduction to other staff members may be accomplished through visits to the various departments, accompanied by a superior or department head. Such visits permit the new employee to meet and speak with colleagues and to develop an understanding of who does what. Some stations go further and require newcomers to spend several hours or days observing the work of personnel in each department.

An employee handbook designed for all staff often is used to introduce the new employee to the station. Typically, it includes information on the station's organization; its policies, procedures, and rules; and details of employee benefit programs and opportunities for advancement. Among the items usually covered in the section on policies, procedures, and rules are the following: working hours, absenteeism, personal appearance and conduct, salary increases, overtime, pay schedule, leaves of absence, outside employment, and discipline and grievance procedures. Information on employee benefits might include details of insurance and pension programs, holidays and vacations, profit-sharing plans, stock purchase options, and reimbursement for educational expenses.

One of the major purposes of an employee handbook is to ensure that all staff are familiar with the responsibilities and rewards of employment, thereby reducing the risk of misunderstandings that could lead to discipline or dismissal. It is important, therefore, that the employee read it and have an opportunity to seek clarification or additional details.

Training is necessary for a new employee who has limited or no experience. Often, it is necessary for an existing employee who moves to a different job in the station. Training is also required when new equipment or procedures are introduced.

Closely allied to training is employee *development*. Many stations believe that the existing staff is the best source of personnel to fill vacated positions. However, it will be a good source only if employees are given an opportunity to gain the knowledge and skills required to carry out the job.

A successful development program results in more proficient employees and, in turn, a more competitive station. Workshops and seminars are frequent vehicles for employee development. Many stations encourage attendance at professional meetings and conventions, as well as enrollment in college courses.

However, probably the most fundamental part of a development program is a regular appraisal session during which the department head reviews the employee's performance. The following are among the functions that may be evaluated:

- attendance and punctuality
- commitment to task

- initiative
- knowledge of company policies, and procedures
- professional appearance
- quality and quantity of work
- spoken and written communication
- teamwork and interaction with others
- versatility

Many stations use a performance review form with a grading scale. After grading all factors, the department head invites the employee to sign the form and indicate agreement or disagreement. In the event of disagreement, the employee may appeal the evaluation to the general manager. One copy of the form is retained by the employee and a second is placed in the employee's personnel file.

Performance reviews should enable employer and employee to exchange job-related information candidly and regularly. In addition to providing an opportunity to identify employee strengths, they also permit the department head to discuss weaknesses and ways in which they may be corrected, and to assess candidates for merit pay increases and promotion. At the same time, they may result in a demotion or dismissal.

A more comprehensive approach to employee development is afforded by the practice known as *management by objectives* (MBO), enunciated by Peter Drucker in *The Practice of Management*. Designed as a means of translating an organization's goals into individual objectives, it involves departmental managers and subordinates, jointly, in the establishment of specific objectives for the subordinate and in periodic review of the degree of success attained. At the end of each review session, objectives are set for the next period, which may run for several months or an entire year.

The MBO approach offers many advantages. It can lead to improved planning and coordination through the clarification of each individual's role and responsibilities, and the integration of employees' goals with those of the department and the station. Communication can be enhanced as a result of interaction between managers and subordinates. In addition, it can aid the motivation and commitment of employees by involving them in the formulation of their objectives.

However, if the practice is to be successful, objectives must be attainable, quantifiable, placed in priority order, and address results rather than activities. Furthermore, rewards must be tied to performance. If they are not, cynicism probably will result and the worth of the endeavor will be diminished.

COMPENSATION

The word *compensation* suggests financial rewards for work accomplished, but staff members seek other kinds of rewards, too. Approval, respect, and recognition are expectations of most employees. So, too, are working conditions that permit them to perform their job effectively and efficiently. The station that

75

recognizes and rewards individual employee contributions and achievements will make employees feel good about themselves and the station. Their positive feelings will be enhanced if the station provides a pleasant work environment that facilitates the fulfillment of assigned responsibilities.

Salary The Fair Labor Standards Act sets forth requirements for minimum wage and overtime compensation. It stipulates that employees must be paid at least the federal minimum wage. Stations in states with a rate higher than the federal minimum must pay at least the state minimum.

The act exempts from minimum wage and overtime regulations executive, administrative, and professional employees and outside salespeople, or those who sell away from the station. Small market stations also may exempt from overtime regulations announcers, news editors, and chief engineers.

As the major part of employees' compensation package, salaries must be fair and competitive. They must recognize each employee's worth and must not fall behind those paid by other employers for similar work in the same community. A perception of unfairness or lack of competitiveness may lead to staff morale problems and turnover.

Many stations pay bonuses to all employees. A Christmas bonus is common. Some stations provide employees with a cash incentive bonus, based on the station's financial results. Both kinds of bonus can generate goodwill and contribute to the employee's feelings of being rewarded.

Financial compensation for sales personnel differs from that of other staff and will be discussed in Chapter 5, "Broadcast Sales."

Benefits Fringe benefits provide an additional form of financial compensation. Benefit programs vary from station to station and market to market. Some benefits cover employees only, while others include dependents. The cost of benefits may be borne totally by the station or by both the station and the employee.

The National Association of Broadcasters (NAB) conducts an annual survey of television employee compensation and fringe benefits. It lists the following benefit programs:

Health benefits: Hospitalization, surgical, and major medical insurance coverage for both employees and their dependents. Most stations share the cost with the employee.

HMO: Employee and dependent participation in a health maintenance organization. Again, the cost typically is shared.

Dental: Available to employees and dependents on a cost-sharing basis.

Vision: Offered to employees and their dependents, with a sharing of cost.

Accidental death: A majority of stations provide it only for employees and meet the cost in full.

Group life insurance: Mostly provided for employees only and fully paid for by the employer.

Disability: Restricted to employees and covers both short- and long-term disability. Generally paid in full by the employer.

Pension plan: Provided by fewer than one-half of stations, most of which pay the full cost.

401-K plan: An employee may defer taxation on income by diverting a portion of income into a retirement plan. In most stations offering the plan, contributions are made by both the employer and the employee.

Education/career development: Some stations encourage employees to develop their knowledge and skills through courses of study, workshops, seminars, and so on. They offer tuition reimbursements for courses completed, and many cover the cost of participation in workshops and seminars.[5]

This list is not exhaustive. Among other benefit programs offered by stations are:

Paid vacation and sick leave: The amounts usually are determined by length of service.

Paid holidays: These include federal, state, and, occasionally, local holidays.

Profit sharing: Part of the station's profit is paid out to employees through a profit-sharing plan. The amount of the payment usually is determined by the employee's length of service and current salary.

Employee stock option plan: This benefit offers an opportunity for an employee to purchase an ownership interest in the station through payroll deductions or payroll deductions matched by the employer. Some employers give stock as a bonus.

Thrift plan: The station pays into an employee's thrift plan (savings) account in some proportion to payments made by the employee.

Legal services: The employer usually pays the full cost for services resulting from job-related legal actions.

Jury duty: To ensure that employees on jury duty do not suffer financially, stations make up the difference between the amount paid for jury service and regular salary.

Paid leave: Some stations grant paid leave to employees attending funerals of close family members or performing short-term military service commitments, for example.

Good working conditions and a fair, competitive salary and fringe benefits program contribute much to an employee's attitude toward work and the employer. However, a pleasant working environment will not substitute for a salary below the market rate. Likewise, a good salary may be perceived as a poor reward for having to tolerate unreliable or antiquated equipment or a superior who is quick to criticize and slow to praise. In addition, fringe benefits will not be enough to make up for a station's failure to provide satisfactory working conditions or salaries.

SAFETY AND HEALTH

The workplace *should* be pleasant, but it *must* be safe and healthy. If it is not, the result may be employee accidents and illnesses, both of which deprive the station of the services of personnel and cause inconvenience and possibly added costs for the employer.

There is another important reason for protecting the safety and health of staff. Under the terms of the Occupational Safety and Health Act of 1970, an employer is responsible for ensuring that the workplace is free from recognized hazards that are causing, or are likely to cause, death or serious physical harm to employees. Many states have similar requirements. The act established the Occupational Safety and Health Administration (OSHA), which has produced a large body of guidelines and regulations. Many deal with specific professions, but a significant number apply to business and industry in general, including broadcasting.

Among general OSHA requirements imposed on all employers are the following:

- to provide potable water and adequate toilet facilities
- to maintain in a dry condition, so far as practicable, every workroom
- to keep every floor, working place, and passageway free from protruding nails, splinters, loose boards, and unnecessary holes and openings
- to remove garbage in such a manner as to avoid creating a menace to health, and as often as necessary or appropriate to maintain the place of employment in a sanitary condition
- to provide sufficient exits to permit the prompt escape of occupants in case of fire or other emergency

Some requirements are designed to protect employees who work closely with electrical power, heavy equipment, and tall structures, such as transmitter towers.

Even conscientious adherence to OSHA regulations does not guarantee an accident-free workplace. If an employee dies as a result of a work-related incident, or if three or more employees have to be hospitalized, OSHA requires that the employer report the fatality or hospitalization within eight hours to its nearest area office.

Obviously, the station cannot accept total responsibility for the safety and health of staff. Employees have an obligation to take care of themselves, and the 1970 act requires them to comply with safety and health standards and regulations. However, the station should take the lead in satisfying appropriate guidelines and regulations, requiring staff to do likewise, and in setting an example of prudent safety and health practices for employees to follow.

EMPLOYEE RELATIONS

Employees differ in their aspirations. Some may be content in their current job, while others may be striving for new responsibilities through promotion in their departments or transfer to another area of station activity. Still others may be using their present position as a stepping-stone to a job with another station.

But most employees share the need to feel that they are important, that they are making a valuable contribution to the station, and that their efforts are appreciated. Accordingly, the relationship between management and staff is important.

Good employee relations are characterized by mutual understanding and respect between employer and employee. They grow out of management's manifest concern for the needs of individual staff members and the existence of channels through which that concern may be communicated.

Much of the daily communication among staff is carried out informally in casual conversations in hallways, the lounge, or the lunchroom. Its informality should not belie its potential, for either good or ill. More rumors probably have started over a cup of coffee than anywhere else.

Managers should use the informality offered by a chance encounter with an employee to display those human traits of interest and caring that help set the tone for employer–employee relations. A smile, a friendly greeting, and an inquiry about a matter unrelated to work can do much to convince staff of management's concern. In addition, they can help establish an atmosphere of cooperation and build the kind of morale necessary if the station is to obtain from all employees their best efforts.

Informal communication is important, but limited. To guarantee continuing communication with staff, managers rely heavily on the printed word. A letter or E-mail to an employee offering congratulations on an accomplishment, or a memorandum posted on the bulletin board thanking the entire staff for a successful ratings book, are examples.

Many stations communicate on a regular basis through a newsletter or magazine. Such publications often are a combination of what employees want to know and what management believes they need to know. They want to know about their colleagues. Anniversaries, marriages, births, hobbies, travels, and achievements find their way into most newsletters. Employees also are interested in station plans that may affect them.

Often, employee information needs are not recognized by management until they have become wants. Managers who are in close communication with employees recognize the desirability of keeping them advised on a wide range of station activities. The newsletter is a useful mechanism for telling staff members what they need to know by not only announcing but explaining policies and procedures, reporting on progress toward station objectives, and clarifying any changes in plans to meet them. Rumor and speculation may not be eliminated, but this kind of open communication should reduce both.

Bulletin boards are used in many stations to provide information on a variety of topics, from job openings to awards won by individuals and the station. Some stations permit staff to use the boards for personal reasons, to advertise a car for sale or to seek a babysitter, for example.

To a large extent, memoranda, newsletters, and bulletin boards reflect management's perceptions of employee information wants and needs. The ideas and concerns of nonmanagement staff are more likely to be expressed orally, to colleagues and superiors. Regular departmental meetings provide a means of airing employee attitudes.

79

When concerns are of a private nature, most employees are reluctant to raise them in front of their colleagues. Recognizing this, many department heads and general managers have an open-door policy so that staff may have immediate access to a sensitive and confidential ear.

The perceptions of employees often are valuable, not only in enabling management to be apprised of their feelings, but in bringing about desirable changes. Suggestions should be solicited from staff. Some stations go further and install suggestion boxes, awarding prizes for ideas that the station implements.

Because of the interdependence of employees and the need for teamwork, many stations encourage a cooperative atmosphere through recreational and social programs. Station sports teams staff and family outings to concerts, plays, sports events, picnics, and parties and are examples of activities that can help develop and maintain a united commitment to the station and its objectives.

HUMAN RESOURCE MANAGEMENT AND TRADE UNIONS

Relations between management and employees in many stations, particularly in large markets, are influenced by employee membership in a trade union. Among the major unions that represent broadcast personnel are the following:

Union	Examples of Employees Represented
American Federation of Musicians of the United States and Canada (AFM)	Musicians in live or recorded performance in radio and television
American Federation of Television and Radio Artists (AFTRA)	Performers in radio and television programs and in taped radio and television commercials
Directors Guild of America (DGA)	Associate directors in radio; television directors, associate directors, stage managers, and program assistants
International Alliance of Theatrical Stage Employees, Moving Picture Technicians, Artists and Allied Crafts of the United States, Its Territories and Canada (IATSE)	Radio engineers and audio operators; television technicians, stage hands, camera operators, grips, and electricians
International Brotherhood of Electrical Workers (IBEW)	Radio and television technicians; television floor directors, film editors, announcers, camera operators, news writers, clerical and maintenance personnel

(continues)

Union	Examples of Employees Represented
National Association of Broadcast Employees and Technicians (NABET)	Radio: continuity writers; traffic personnel; secretaries; board operators; disc jockeys; announcers and news anchors; producers; news and sports writers; and reporters
	Television: continuity writers; traffic personnel; secretaries; videotape and audio operators; projectionists; switchers; transmitter, camera, and character generator operators; floor directors; directors and lighting directors; news and sports anchors; writers and reporters; news photographers; assignment editors and producers; and weather anchors
Screen Actors Guild (SAG)	Actors in television series, filmed television commercials, and music videos
Writers Guild of America, East (WGAE)	Radio and television news writers, editors, researchers, and desk assistants; television promotion and continuity writers and graphic artists
Writers Guild of America, West (WGAW)	Writers of radio and television programs

The basic unit of a national or international union is the "local" union, which represents employees in a common job in a station or limited geographic area.

Like all employees, union members seek approval, respect, and recognition, and expect a safe and healthy workplace. They have similar concerns about salaries, fringe benefits, and job security.

However, management's treatment of unionized employees differs from that in nonunion stations. Take, for example, the matter of complaints. A nonunion employee generally presents the complaint directly to the supervisor or department head and, if necessary, to the general manager. If the employee is a member of a union, the complaint usually will be presented to management by a job steward. This procedure is one of many detailed in the document that governs management–union employee relations: the *union agreement* or *contract*.

THE UNION CONTRACT

The union contract covers a wide range of content and reflects the interests and needs of the employees covered by it. Creative personnel may be concerned about their creative control and the way in which they are recognized in program credits. Technical staff, on the other hand, may be much more interested in the possibility of layoffs resulting from new equipment or the use of nontechnical personnel in traditionally technical tasks.

Most contracts contain two major categories of clauses: *economic* and *work and relationship*.

In the economic category, provisions on wages and fringe benefits dominate. The contract will set forth hourly rates of pay, premium rates for overtime and holiday work, and, in some cases, cost-of-living adjustments. Among the fringe benefits generally covered are paid vacations and sick leave, insurance, pension, severance pay, and paid leave for activities such as jury duty.

The work and relationship section usually contains some or all of the following provisions:

Union recognition: The station recognizes the union as the bargaining unit for employees who are members of the union and agrees to deal exclusively with it on matters affecting employees in the unit.

Union security: The union may require, and the station may agree, that all existing employees in the bargaining unit become and remain members of the union and that new employees join the union within a specified period. Such a requirement is not permitted in so-called "right-to-work" states.

Union checkoff: The station agrees to deduct from the wages of union members all union dues, initiation fees, or other assessments, and to remit them promptly to the local union.

Grievance procedure and arbitration: This is a description of the procedure whereby employees may present or have grievances presented to their supervisors and, if necessary, the general manager. If the grievance is not withdrawn or settled, the contract may provide for its presentation to an arbitrator, whose decision will be final and binding on the station, union, and employee during the term of the contract.

No strike, no lockout: Contracts in which the grievance procedure requires the use of an arbitrator to settle grievances usually contain a clause forbidding strikes, work stoppages, or slowdowns by employees, and lockouts by management.

Seniority: Most unions insist on the use of seniority in management decisions on matters such as promotions, layoffs, and recalls. Preference in promotion is given to employees with the longest service to the station, provided that the employee has the qualifications or skills to perform the work. In the same way, senior employees will be the last to be affected by layoffs and the first to be recalled after a layoff.

Management rights: The contract recognizes the responsibility of station management to operate the station in an orderly, efficient, and economic way. Accordingly, the station retains the right to make and carry out decisions on personnel, equipment, and other matters consistent with its responsibility.

Many other provisions may be contained in the contract, including clauses on procedures for suspension or discharge of employees, the length and frequency of meal breaks, reimbursement to employees for expenses incurred in carrying out their work, and safety conditions in the station and in company vehicles. Many contracts also contain clauses permitting the station to engage nonstation employees to carry out work for which employees do not have the skill, and jurisdictional provisions stating which employees are permitted to carry out specific tasks.

UNION NEGOTIATIONS

The contract between a broadcast station and a labor union represents a mutually acceptable agreement and is the result of bargaining or negotiations between the two parties. To ensure that it serves the best interests of the station and its employees, management should take certain actions before and during the negotiations, and after the contract is signed.

Before the Negotiations

1. Assemble the negotiating team. The team should include someone familiar with the station's operation, usually the general manager. Familiarity with labor law or labor relations is desirable and, for that reason, an attorney often is part of the team. If an attorney is not included, the station should obtain legal advice on applicable federal, state, and local requirements pertaining to bargaining methods and content.

2. Designate a chief negotiator to speak for the station. The person selected should have good communication skills, tact, and patience.

3. Ensure that members of the negotiating team are familiar with the existing contract and with clauses that the station wishes to modify or delete, and the reasons. They should also be aware of the union's feelings about the current contract and any changes it is likely to seek.

4. Determine the issues to be raised by the station and those likely to be raised by the union.

5. Establish the station's objectives on economic as well as work and relationship matters.

6. Anticipate the union's objectives.

7. Determine the station's positions and prepare detailed documentation to support them. In most cases, the station will identify provisions it must have and others on which it is willing to compromise.

During the Negotiations

1. Take the initiative. One method is to put the union in the position of bargaining up from the station's proposals. For example, the station may prepare a draft of a written contract for the negotiations, thereby placing on the union the burden of showing the reasons to change it.

2. Listen carefully to union requests and ask for clarification or explanation so that they may be understood fully. This will permit the station's

team to prepare counterproposals or indicate parts of the proposed contract that meet the union's concerns or needs.

3. Keep an open mind. Refrain from rejecting union requests out of hand. Remember that, like the station, the union starts by asking for more than it expects to obtain and that the final contract will reflect compromises by both parties.

4. Be firm. An open mind and flexibility should not lead the union to believe that the station team is weak and can be pushed around. The station's chief negotiator should exhibit firmness when necessary, and support the station's arguments with a rationale and documentation.

5. Avoid lengthy bargaining sessions, since a tired and weary negotiating team may agree to provisions that prove to be unwise later.

6. Ensure that the language of the contract is clear and unambiguous. A document that is open to misunderstanding or misinterpretation will be troublesome to station management.

After the Contract Is Signed

1. Follow the contract diligently and expect the union to do the same.

2. Ensure that all department heads and other supervisory personnel are familiar with the contract. If they are not, and they fail to adhere to it, trouble could result.

REASONS FOR JOINING A UNION

Broadcast union members are found most often in large-market radio and television stations. However, that does not mean that stations in smaller markets are immune to attempts to organize employees. In addition, such organizing often results not from the strength of a union but from management's insensitivity to employee interests and needs.

Management that values its staff and treats them fairly may never experience a threat of unionization. Management that fails to do so may confront an attempt due to one or more of the following factors:

1. *Economic*

   A. Salaries that fall behind those of the competition in the market.
   B. Pay rates that are not based on differences in skills or the work required.
   C. Fringe benefits that do not match those of competing stations in the market.

2. *Working Conditions*

   A. Absence of guidelines or policies on matters such as promotions, merit pay increases, and job responsibilities.
   B. A workplace characterized by dirty offices; poor lighting, heating, and ventilation; unreliable equipment; and safety or health hazards.

84

3. *Management Attitudes and Behavior*

   A. Noncommunicative management, which leads, inevitably, to speculation, gossip, and rumor. This is particularly dangerous when changes are made without explanation in personnel, equipment, or operating practices.

   B. Unresponsiveness to employee concerns. Employee questions that go unanswered often become major problems, especially if employees believe that management is trying to conceal information on actions that may affect their status or job security.

   C. Favoritism. If management treats, or is perceived as treating, some employees differently from others, resentment may occur.

   D. Discrimination. Even though discrimination is illegal, management actions may be interpreted by some employees as being discriminatory and based on considerations of race, color, religion, national origin, sex, age, or disability.

   E. Ignoring seniority. Many employees believe that seniority and dedication to a station over a long period should be recognized by management in decisions on matters such as promotions. Union organizers will promise to obtain management recognition of seniority.

   F. Us versus them. Management that encourages its department heads and other supervisors to put a distance between themselves and their staff and to establish a combative rather than a cooperative environment will meet with resentment and distrust from most employees.

4. *The Troublemaker*

   Most stations are familiar with the complainer, the person who finds fault with most things or, failing to find a problem, invents one. In some cases, the complainer goes further and becomes an agitator, claiming that a union would meet every employee concern and solve every problem. Often, the arguments sound so persuasive that other employees go along and the likelihood of unionization becomes real.

5. *Competing Station*

   Union organization of staff at a competing station may result in an attempt at unionization, particularly if it succeeds in obtaining better salaries, fringe benefits, and terms and conditions of employment at that station.

85

WORKING WITH UNIONS

If, despite efforts to prevent it, a union is organized, management should view it not as a threat but as an opportunity to work cooperatively toward identified goals. That may be easier in theory than practice, but most union members recognize that their job satisfaction depends largely on the degree of success the station attains.

To help in any adjustment to the presence of a union, the following pointers are suggested:

1. Unionism is an accepted fact. Management must recognize that unions generally have reached a point of very high efficiency in bargaining and maintaining strength. Learn to live and work with them when necessary.

2. Management should take a realistic view of all mutual agreements and be very careful about altering, modifying, or making concessions in the established contractual arrangement.

3. Remember that rights or responsibilities that have been relinquished are hard to regain at the bargaining table. Similarly, granting concessions on grievances that have not been properly ironed out can cause future trouble, and rarely brings goodwill or satisfaction to the parties concerned.

4. Supervisors should be vigorously backed up. This does not imply that errors should be defended, but supervisors need support to maintain morale and company strength.

5. Dual loyalty is possible. In pursuing a positive approach, management must realize that in a well-run company the majority of clear-thinking union members know that a strong and progressive management is their best guarantee of security.

6. In employee communications, honesty is the best policy, even in the face of mistrust and disinterest. Candid communication of information about the company, its business outlook, and projected changes can help ensure the acceptance of its policies and principles.

7. Management should establish a working rapport with union officers and recognize the natural leadership they frequently display. Mutual respect should be reflected in efficient administration of all matters concerning management and the union.

8. A realistic effort should always be made to avoid either overantagonism or overcooperation. Either can be self-defeating and lead to an erosion of rights. Mature judgment is a must in preventing hasty or ill-considered decisions by union or management

9. Management must manage. It can and should be fair and just in all its labor relations, but it should live up to all obligations and expect the union to do the same. A contract should never be a club for either to wield, but rather an agreement to be respected and obeyed.[6]

HUMAN RESOURCE MANAGEMENT AND THE LAW

Like other employers, broadcasters are required to comply with a large number of laws dealing with the hiring and treatment of employees. Among the most important federal laws are the following:

Civil Rights Act of 1964, as amended, makes it unlawful for an employer to discriminate in hiring, firing, compensation, terms, conditions, or privileges of employment on the basis of race, color, religion, sex, or national origin.

Age Discrimination in Employment Act of 1967, as amended, forbids employers with 20 or more employees from discriminating against persons 40 years of age or older with respect to any term, condition, or privilege of employment, including, but not limited to, hiring, firing, promotion, lay-off, compensation, benefits, job assignments, and training.

Equal Pay Act of 1963, as amended, prohibits wage discrimination between male and female employees when the work requires substantially equal skill, effort, and responsibility, and is performed under similar working conditions.

Pregnancy Discrimination Act of 1978, an amendment to the 1964 Civil Rights Act, forbids discrimination based on pregnancy, childbirth, or related medical conditions. The act seeks to guarantee that women affected by pregnancy or related conditions are treated in the same manner as other job applicants or employees with similar abilities or limitations.

Americans with Disabilities Act of 1990 prohibits employers with 15 or more employees from discriminating against qualified individuals with disabilities in job application procedures, hiring, firing, advancement, compensation, job training, and other terms, conditions, and privileges of employment. Individuals are considered to have a "disability" if they have a physical or mental impairment that substantially limits one or more major life activities, have a record of such an impairment, or are regarded as having such an impairment.[7]

Family and Medical Leave Act of 1993 requires employers with 50 or more employees to make available to qualified employees (i.e., those who have been employed for at least 12 months) up to 12 weeks of unpaid leave during any 12-month period for one or more of the following reasons: for the birth and care of the newborn child of the employee; for placement with the employee of a son or daughter for adoption or foster care; to care for an immediate family member (spouse, child, or parent) with a serious health condition; or to take medical leave when the employee is unable to work because of a serious health condition. Upon return from leave, employees must be restored to their original job, or to an equivalent job with equivalent pay, benefits, and other employment terms and conditions.

EQUAL EMPLOYMENT OPPORTUNITY

The Equal Employment Opportunity Commission (EEOC) is primarily responsible for ensuring compliance with federal laws prohibiting discrimination in employment practices. However, the FCC has enacted equal employment opportunity rules (EEO) to which broadcasters must also adhere.[8]

The rules require that broadcast stations afford equal opportunity in employment to all qualified persons and refrain from discriminating on the basis of race, color, religion, national origin, and sex. Religious broadcasters may establish religious beliefs or affiliations as a job qualification for all station employees. However, they may not discriminate in any of the above areas among those who share their beliefs. Stations also must establish, maintain, and carry out a positive continuing program of specific practices designed to ensure equal opportunity and nondiscrimination in every aspect of station employment policy and practice. Under the terms of its program, a station must

- define the responsibility of each level of management to ensure vigorous enforcement of its policy of equal opportunity, and establish a procedure to review and control managerial and supervisory performance
- inform its employees and recognized employee organizations of the equal employment opportunity policy and program and enlist their cooperation
- communicate its equal employment opportunity policy and program and its employment needs to sources of qualified applicants without regard to race, color, religion, national origin, or sex, and solicit their recruitment assistance on a continuing basis
- conduct a continuing program to exclude all unlawful forms of prejudice or discrimination based upon race, color, religion, national origin, or sex from its personnel policies and practices and working conditions
- conduct a continuing review of job structure and employment practices and adopt positive recruitment, job design, and other measures needed to ensure genuine equality of opportunity to participate fully in all organizational units, occupations, and levels of responsibility[9]

In carrying out their equal employment opportunity program, licensees with five or more full-time employees (those who work at least 30 hours per week), must

- recruit for every full-time vacancy
- use recruitment sources to ensure wide dissemination of the vacancy
- notify organizations involved in assisting job seekers, if those organizations request notification
- engage in recruitment initiatives that go beyond efforts to fill specific vacancies. The goal is to reach persons who may not be aware of opportunities in the broadcasting industry or who may not yet have the experience to compete for current vacancies. Station employment units (i.e., a single station or multiple station cluster in a local market) with five to ten full-time employees and small market licensees must complete at least two such initiatives in each two-year period. Units with more than ten full-time employees should complete at least four initiatives in the period. Among the sixteen initiatives are hosting, co-sponsoring, or participating in job fairs, establishing an internship program, and participating in job banks and scholarship programs.
- analyze the recruitment program on an ongoing basis to ensure its effectiveness and address any problems identified as a result of the analysis

- analyze periodically measures taken to implement the equal employment opportunity program

- retain records to document satisfaction of the recruitment and initiative requirements[10]

Licensees with fewer than five full-time employees must comply only with the nondiscrimination requirements.

The FCC uses three documents to monitor compliance with its EEO rules:

1. An annual EEO public inspection file report, which describes the licensee's EEO efforts during the preceding year. The file report must include the following information:

   - a list of all full-time vacancies filled by the station's employment unit during the preceding year, identified by job title

   - for each such vacancy, the recruitment sources used to fill the vacancy identified by name, address, contact person, and telephone number. Organizations that have asked to be notified of job vacancies must be identified separately.

   - the recruitment source that referred the hiree for each full-time vacancy during the preceding year

   - data reflecting the total number of persons interviewed for full-time vacancies during the preceding year and the total number of interviewees referred by each recruitment source used in connection with such vacancies

   - a list and brief description of initiatives undertaken in the preceding year[11]

2. An EEO Program Report, FCC Form 396 (Figure 3.2), which is filed with the station's application for license renewal. The report asks for information on the licensee, contact person (if other than the licensee), and any pending or resolved discrimination complaints.

   Stations with fewer than five full-time employees complete only the first two pages of the form. Those with five or more also must complete page three, which requests

   - the name and title of the station official responsible for the EEO program

   - the submission of two attachments. One is a copy of the EEO public file reports from the previous two years. The second is a narrative statement demonstrating how the station achieved "broad and inclusive outreach" in the two-year period prior to the filing of the renewal application.

3. A Broadcast Mid-Term Report, FCC Form 397. The report is filed four years after a station's application for license renewal. The public inspection file reports for the preceding two years are submitted as attachments.

   The FCC may conduct inquiries of licensees at random or if it has evidence of a possible violation of its EEO rules. In addition, it completes random audits of about 5 percent of radio and television

89

Federal Communications Commission
Washington, D. C. 20554

Approved by OMB
3060-0113

BROADCAST EQUAL EMPLOYMENT
OPPORTUNITY PROGRAM REPORT

(To be filed with broadcast license renewal application)

(For FCC Use Only)

Code No.

Legal Name of the Licensee	
Mailing Address	

City	State or Country (if foreign address)	ZIP Code

Telephone Number (include area code)	E-Mail Address (if available)

	Facility ID Number	Call Sign

TYPE OF BROADCAST STATION :

Commercial Broadcast Station   Noncommercial Broadcast Station

☐ Radio   ☐ TV   ☐ Educational Radio

            ☐ Low Power TV   ☐ Educational TV

90

            ☐ International

List call sign and location of all stations included on this report. List commonly owned stations that share one or more employees. Also list stations operated by the licensee pursuant to a time brokerage agreement. Indicate on the table below which stations are operated pursuant to a time brokerage agreement. To the extent that licensees include stations operated pursuant to a time brokerage agreement on this report, responses or information provided in Sections I through IV should take into consideration the licensee's EEO compliance efforts at brokered stations, as well as any other stations, included on this form. For purposes of this form, a station employment unit is a station or a group of commonly owned stations in the same market that share at least one employee.

Call Sign	Facility ID Number	Type (check applicable box)	Location (city, state)	Time Brokerage Agreement (check applicable box)
		☐ AM ☐ FM ☐ TV		☐ Yes ☐ No
		☐ AM ☐ FM ☐ TV		☐ Yes ☐ No
		☐ AM ☐ FM ☐ TV		☐ Yes ☐ No
		☐ AM ☐ FM ☐ TV		☐ Yes ☐ No
		☐ AM ☐ FM ☐ TV		☐ Yes ☐ No
		☐ AM ☐ FM ☐ TV		☐ Yes ☐ No
		☐ AM ☐ FM ☐ TV		☐ Yes ☐ No
		☐ AM ☐ FM ☐ TV		☐ Yes ☐ No
		☐ AM ☐ FM ☐ TV		☐ Yes ☐ No

FCC 396
March 2003

FIGURE 3.2 Broadcast Equal Employment Opportunity Program Report (FCC 396).

CONTACT PERSON IF OTHER THAN LICENSEE

Name			Street Address
City	State	Zip Code	Telephone No. ( )

FILING INSTRUCTIONS

Broadcast station licensees are required to afford equal employment opportunity to all qualified persons and to refrain from discriminating in employment and related benefits on the basis of race, color, national origin, religion, and sex. See 47 C.F.R. Section 73.2080. Pursuant to these requirements, a license renewal applicant whose station employment unit employs five or more full-time station employees must file a report of its activities to ensure equal employment opportunity. If a station employment unit employs fewer than five full-time employees, no equal employment opportunity program information need be filed. If a station employment unit is filing a combined report, a copy of the report must be filed with each station's renewal application.

A copy of this report must be kept in the station's public file. These actions are required to obtain license renewal. Failure to meet these requirements may result in sanctions or license renewal being delayed or denied. These requirements are contained in 47 C.F.R. Section 73.2080 and are authorized by the Communications Act of 1934, as amended.

DISCRIMINATION COMPLAINTS. Have any pending or resolved complaints been filed during this license term before any body having competent jurisdiction under federal, state, territorial or local law, alleging unlawful discrimination in the employment practices of the station(s)? ☐ Yes ☐ No

If so, provide a brief description of the complaint(s), including the persons involved, the date of the filing, the court or agency, the file number (if any), and the disposition or current status of the matter.

Does your station employment unit employ fewer than five full-time employees? ☐ Yes ☐ No
Consider as "full-time" employees all those permanently working 30 or more hours a week.

If your station employment unit employs fewer than five full-time employees, complete the certification below, return the form to the FCC, and place a copy in your station(s) public file. You do not have to complete the rest of this form. If your station employment unit employs five or more full-time employees, you must complete all of this form and follow all instructions.

CERTIFICATION

This report must be certified, as follows:
A. By licensee, if an individual;
B. By a partner, if a partnership (general partner, if a limited partnership);
C. By an officer, if a corporation or an association; or
D. By an attorney of the licensee, in case of physical disability or absence from the United States of the licensee.

WILLFUL FALSE STATEMENTS ON THIS FORM ARE PUNISHABLE BY FINE AND/OR IMPRISONMENT
(U.S. CODE, TITLE 18, SECTION 1001), AND/OR REVOCATION OF ANY STATION LICENSE OR CONSTRUCTION PERMIT
(U.S. CODE, TITLE 47, SECTION 312(a)(1)), AND/OR FORFEITURE (U.S. CODE, TITLE 47, SECTION 503).

I certify to the best of my knowledge, information and belief, all statements contained in this report are true and correct.

Signed	Name of Respondent
Title	Telephone No. (include area code)
Date	

FCC 396 (Page 2)
March 2003

FIGURE 3.2 *Continued*

CONTACT PERSON IF OTHER THAN LICENSEE

Name			Street Address
City	State	Zip Code	Telephone No. ( )

FILING INSTRUCTIONS

Broadcast station licensees are required to afford equal employment opportunity to all qualified persons and to refrain from discriminating in employment and related benefits on the basis of race, color, national origin, religion, and sex. See 47 C.F.R. Section 73.2080. Pursuant to these requirements, a license renewal applicant whose station employment unit employs five or more full-time station employees must file a report of its activities to ensure equal employment opportunity. If a station employment unit employs fewer than five full-time employees, no equal employment opportunity program information need be filed. If a station employment unit is filing a combined report, a copy of the report must be filed with each station's renewal application.

A copy of this report must be kept in the station's public file. These actions are required to obtain license renewal. Failure to meet these requirements may result in sanctions or license renewal being delayed or denied. These requirements are contained in 47 C.F.R. Section 73.2080 and are authorized by the Communications Act of 1934, as amended.

DISCRIMINATION COMPLAINTS. Have any pending or resolved complaints been filed during this license term before any body having competent jurisdiction under federal, state, territorial or local law, alleging unlawful discrimination in the employment practices of the station(s)? ☐ Yes ☐ No

If so, provide a brief description of the complaint(s), including the persons involved, the date of the filing, the court or agency, the file number (if any), and the disposition or current status of the matter.

Does your station employment unit employ fewer than five full-time employees? ☐ Yes ☐ No
Consider as "full-time" employees all those permanently working 30 or more hours a week.

If your station employment unit employs fewer than five full-time employees, complete the certification below, return the form to the FCC, and place a copy in your station(s) public file. You do not have to complete the rest of this form. If your station employment unit employs five or more full-time employees, you must complete all of this form and follow all instructions.

CERTIFICATION

This report must be certified, as follows:
A. By licensee, if an individual;
B. By a partner, if a partnership (general partner, if a limited partnership);
C. By an officer, if a corporation or an association; or
D. By an attorney of the licensee, in case of physical disability or absence from the United States of the licensee.

WILLFUL FALSE STATEMENTS ON THIS FORM ARE PUNISHABLE BY FINE AND/OR IMPRISONMENT
(U.S. CODE, TITLE 18, SECTION 1001), AND/OR REVOCATION OF ANY STATION LICENSE OR CONSTRUCTION PERMIT
(U.S. CODE, TITLE 47, SECTION 312(a)(1)), AND/OR FORFEITURE (U.S. CODE, TITLE 47, SECTION 503).

I certify to the best of my knowledge, information and belief, all statements contained in this report are true and correct.

Signed	Name of Respondent
Title	Telephone No. (include area code)
Date	

FCC 396 (Page 2)
March 2003

FIGURE 3.2 *Continued*

licensees each year.

Managers can take steps to avoid problems that might result from an inquiry or audit. At the least, they should

- demonstrate serious attempts to comply with the rules
- ensure that all station employees involved in the recruitment and hiring processes are familiar with the rules and adhere to them
- keep current all information relating to the recruitment and initiative requirements
- maintain records sufficient to verify the accuracy of information provided in the EEO public file reports, Form 396, and Form 397

SEXUAL HARASSMENT

One form of discrimination to which managers are paying more attention today is sex discrimination resulting from sexual harassment in the workplace.

Pressure to treat the issue seriously was reinforced by four Supreme Court decisions during the 1990s. In 1993, the court agreed unanimously that employers can be forced to pay monetary damages even when employees suffer no psychological harm. In 1998, in another unanimous ruling, it determined for the first time that unlawful sexual harassment in the workplace extends to incidents involving employees of the same sex.

Later in the year, in two 7-2 decisions, justices held that an employee who resists a superior's advances need not have suffered a tangible job detriment in order to pursue a lawsuit against an employer. But the court said such a suit cannot succeed if the employer has an antiharassment policy with an effective complaint procedure in place and the employee unreasonably fails to use it.

In the two latter decisions, the court established that

- employers are responsible for harassment engaged in by their supervisory employees
- when the harassment results in "a tangible employment action, such as discharge, demotion, or undesirable reassignment," the employer's liability is absolute
- when there has been no tangible action, an employer can defend itself if it can prove (1) that it has taken "reasonable care to prevent and correct promptly any sexually harassing behavior," such as by adopting an effective policy with a complaint procedure; (2) that the employee "unreasonably failed to take advantage of any preventive or corrective opportunities" provided

Harassment may take many forms. Under guidelines issued by the EEOC, unwelcome sexual advances, requests for sexual favors, and other verbal or physical conduct of a sexual nature constitute sexual harassment when (1) submission to such conduct is made either explicitly or implicitly a term or condition of an individual's employment, (2) submission to or rejection of such conduct by an individual is used as the basis for employment decisions

93

affecting such individual, or (3) such conduct has the purpose or effect of unreasonably interfering with an individual's work performance or creating an intimidating, hostile, or offensive working environment.[12]

The licensee is held responsible for acts of sexual harassment committed by its "agents" and supervisory employees, even if it has forbidden them. If the conduct takes place between fellow employees, again, the licensee is responsible when it knew, or should have known, of the conduct, unless it can show that it took immediate and appropriate corrective action.[13]

To guard against the employee absenteeism and turnover that often accompany sexual harassment, the adverse impact on productivity and morale, and the filing of charges and lawsuits, managers should take the following actions:

1. Develop a written policy that defines sexual harassment and states explicitly that it is a violation of law.

2. Make sure that all employees are aware of the policy and understand it.

3. Train employees, especially supervisory personnel, to recognize harassment so that they may take action if they suspect it and, thus, prevent potentially more serious consequences if the behavior goes unchecked.

4. Establish a procedure that encourages victims to come forward and assures them that their complaints will be handled promptly and professionally.

5. Investigate all complaints immediately and thoroughly and advise the parties of the outcome, even if the allegations are not substantiated.

6. Document all complaints and their disposition. Complete records will be useful if legal action is initiated.

COMPUTER USE

Productivity loss and the potential for sexual harassment and other lawsuits also may result from unrestricted employee use of station computers. To guard against such eventualities, some companies have installed software tools to monitor individual computer activity. The expectation is that staff members will be wary of spending large amounts of time on personal E-mail or Web surfing if they know that checks may be made on how they spend their "working" hours.

Of no less concern to managers is the fear that employee-originated E-mail or online chat room messages or the downloading of some Internet content may expose the station to an array of lawsuits. In addition to sexual harassment, the risks include defamation, discrimination, the dissemination of trade secrets, and copyright and trademark infringement.

Stations that reject monitoring because of its "big brother" aura may opt for filtering software to limit access to the Internet. However, that will not necessarily remove the possibility of inappropriate E-mail or chat room activity and legal liability.

Managers are advised to develop and enforce an "acceptable use policy" (AUP) for computers. The following are among the provisions that should be considered for inclusion:

- computers, software, and Internet and E-mail accounts are the property of the company and should be used for business purposes only
- Internet and E-mail accounts cannot be used for an employee's personal interests
- downloading copyrighted software is prohibited
- accessing or sending sexually explicit material is forbidden
- participation in any online chat room or discussion group must be approved in advance and must not include statements about the company or its competitors
- email cannot be used to communicate trade secrets or other confidential information without prior written permission
- encryption is required for sensitive E-mail messages and accompanying files
- sending offensive or improper messages, such as those involving racial or sexual slurs or jokes, is prohibited
- employee access to a coworker's E-mail files must be authorized in advance
- email messages and Internet activity will be monitored from time to time by the employer
- violation of the policy will result in disciplinary action, up to and including dismissal

In time, other problems may arise and require modifications or additions to the AUP.

To ensure that all staff members are familiar with the policy, a copy should be placed in the employee handbook. However, given the potential gravity of abuse of the company's computers, it may be advisable to conduct a training session on appropriate use and to require employees to sign an acknowledgment that they have received and understand the policy.

WHAT'S AHEAD?

Many challenges confront staff members who are responsible for human resource management. Among the most important are those posed by an increasingly diverse workforce and changing employee values.

Today's workforce is the most diverse in American history. The first wave of baby boomers, most of them white and male, is retiring but is not being replaced by employees of like color and gender. In fact, white males comprise a much smaller percentage of new hires than in earlier years.

Women now constitute the majority of new job entrants. Some are recent school or college graduates. Other are older and are re-entering the job market after an absence of some years to raise children.

Many new employees are members of minority groups, chiefly African American and Hispanic and, in some parts of the country, Asian. According to some estimates, by 2010 almost half of the nation's new workers will be people traditionally classified as minorities. Many will be first-generation immigrants, and almost two-thirds of them will be women.[14]

Managing diversity will not be easy for those who are unprepared for it. Nonetheless, managers must recognize and respond to this new reality in their recruiting, selection, orientation, and training activities.

If they are to succeed, they must demonstrate an understanding of, and sensitivity to, the varied backgrounds, experiences, and ambitions of new staff and strive to ensure that other employees demonstrate similar traits.

Certainly, there is much work to be done. Even though the minority workforce in television increased from 18.1 percent to 21.8 percent between 2003 and 2004, the latest figure is only 3.8 percent higher than it was ten years earlier. And much of that growth results from employment in Hispanic stations.[15] Minorities accounted for 11.8 percent of the radio workforce, a dramatic increase over the 6.5 percent recorded in 2003. However, it is only one-half percent higher than it was in 1994.[16]

Managers will have to realize, also, that women have special responsibilities to family as well as job. That may require a greater degree of flexibility than has been customary in areas such as working hours and job sharing. But it will be necessary if employees are to find an acceptable balance between the demands of work and home.

Accompanying the changes in the composition of the workforce are differences between the values of many new employees and of those they are replacing.

Dedication to work, striving for career advancement and economic security, and loyalty to employer are characteristics associated with retiring and soon-to-retire baby boomers. They are being succeeded by members of "Generation X," who bring to their jobs a new set of perceptions about society, life, and work, fashioned by their experiences as children of often-absent working or divorced parents. Some saw their parents and relatives laid off during the downsizing that characterized corporate America in the 1990s. All witnessed the corporate scandals that were a product of the same era.

Perhaps it is not surprising that these "boomer babies" harbor economic uncertainty and are much more likely than their predecessors to place their own interests above those of their employer.

Motivating and encouraging them to view themselves as part of a team striving for mutually beneficial goals will be difficult for managers. But an effort must be made to reconcile the values of these employees with the more traditional values of employers if both are to find satisfaction and success in their endeavors.

Of course, many members of Generation X already have moved into managerial and supervisory positions and confront similar generational challenges. One is the loss of self-esteem and resentment often felt by older employees who have been passed over for promotion in favor of someone younger. They may conclude that their wisdom and loyalty have been ignored. They may feel uncomfortable having to answer to superiors who remind them more of their children than of their bosses. Overcoming these kinds of tensions will be a continuing challenge and will be accomplished only if members of the different generations attempt to understand each other's values and recognize each other's contributions.

SUMMARY

No asset is more important to a broadcast station than its human resources. In many large stations, human resource management is the responsibility of a human resources department, whose head reports directly to the general manager. However, in the majority of stations, personnel matters are the responsibility of several people, including the general manager and the heads of the various departments, including the business manager.

The basic functions of human resource management are staffing; orientation, training, and development; compensation; safety and health; and employee relations.

Staffing involves staff planning and the recruitment, selection, and dismissal of employees. Orientation seeks to introduce employees to their colleagues and the station, while training and development are attempts to develop employee talents and skills. Compensation includes financial rewards as well as approval, respect, and recognition. Safety and health involve the provision of a safe and healthy workplace. Employee relations are characterized by mutual understanding and respect between management and staff.

In many stations, the responsibilities and rewards of employment are described in an employee handbook. A union contract sets forth the relationship between management and trade union employees.

Broadcasters must adhere to laws dealing with the hiring and treatment of personnel. Among the most important federal laws are the Civil Rights Act of 1964, the Age Discrimination in Employment Act of 1967, the Equal Pay Act of 1963, The Pregnancy Discrimination Act of 1978, the Americans with Disabilities Act of 1990, and the Family and Medical Leave Act of 1993. In addition, they must comply with the FCC's equal employment opportunity rules and with rules governing sexual harassment in the workplace. Managers must also be attentive to the possibility that a variety of laws could be broken by unrestricted employee access to company computers.

Among the challenges confronting human resource managers are the growing diversity of the workforce and the contrasting values of different generations of workers.

CASE STUDY: TELEVISION

A television station's news crew is covering the anniversary of the September 11, 2001, tragedy in New York City. The crew consists of a reporter, a photographer, and a driver. The reporter is female, Caucasian, Christian, and under 40 years of age. The photographer is male, Pakistani, Muslim, and under 40 years of age. The driver is male, African American, Christian, and over 40 years of age.

On the drive to New York City, the reporter tells the photographer and the driver that she believes the United States should close all its borders and not let anybody who is not American and not a Christian into the country ever again. When the photographer tells her she needs to keep her opinions to herself, she replies: "What do you know, old man? You are older than dirt. You're lucky you have a job."

When they next stop for gas, the photographer says he is quitting as a result of the reporter's comments. In the meantime, the driver calls the station manager on the telephone and complains about her comments.

An investigation is later conducted by the station manager. It is decided that the reporter was out of line with her comments, and she is given a written warning. It is also decided that the driver's work performance has been below satisfactory for the last couple of months, and so he is terminated.

EXERCISES

1. Can the station be held liable for the "constructive discharge" of the photographer? Can the reporter be held personally liable?

2. What claims might the driver assert against the station? Assuming that the driver did, in fact, exhibit poor performance over the last several months, how could the station manager have better handled the circumstances?

3. Assume that there was a fourth crew member on the trip and that the station manager interviews her during the investigation. Does she have any rights regarding the station's conduct (or misconduct) toward her following her participation as a witness in the investigation?[17]

CASE STUDY: TELEVISION

A television station's control room supervisor checks into a clinic for rehabilitation. His treatment last six weeks, during which time he is unable to go to work. In the first week of the treatment, the station manager demotes him to a position on the third-shift sanitation crew.

Upon returning to work, the former supervisor explains to a couple of employees who ask him that he was a cocaine addict. He adds that his treatment was successful and that he is 100 percent drug- and cocaine-free. Over the next several weeks, these employees stop calling him by his name and, instead, call him "druggie."

Several weeks later, the former supervisor destroys a $4,000 piece of equipment when he's trying to move it in order to clean under it. The station manager sends him for a drug test, which he fails. As a result, he is terminated.

EXERCISES

1. Was the station manager within his rights to demote the control room supervisor while he was in the rehabilitation clinic?

2. Can the station be held liable for its employees calling him a "druggie"? What if they never said it to his face, but said it to co-employees when he was not present? Can the employees be held personally liable?

3. What if, after being terminated, the former supervisor applies for another position at the station? Assuming he is the most qualified for the position, does the station have to hire him? What if the station does not have a no-rehire policy for employees that have previously been terminated?

NOTES

[1] James A. Brown and Ward L. Quaal, *Radio-Television-Cable Management*, p. 111.

[2] R. Wayne Mondy, Robert E. Holmes, and Edwin B. Flippo, *Management: Concepts and Practices*, pp. 276, 280.

[3] John B. Phillips, Jr., *Employment Law Desk Book*, pp. 239–240.

[4] *Ibid.*, pp. 241–242.

[5] 2003 *Television Employee Compensation and Fringe Benefits Report*.

[6] J. Leonard Reinsch and E. I. Ellis, *Radio Station Management*, p. 266. Reprinted by permission.

[7] The act defines a "qualified" individual as a person who has the skill, experience, education, or other requirements to perform the essential functions of the position, with or without reasonable accommodation. Such accommodation is any modification or adjustment to a job or the work environment. It includes making existing facilities readily accessible to and usable by a person with a disability, restructuring a job, modifying work schedules, acquiring or modifying equipment, and providing qualified readers or interpreters. However, it does not require the employer to make an accommodation if it would impose an "undue hardship," that is, an "action requiring significant difficulty or expense" in light of the employer's size, resources, nature, and structure.

[8] 47 *CFR* 73.2080.

[9] *Ibid.*, (b).

[10] *Ibid.*, (c).

[11] *Ibid.*

[12] 29 *CFR* 1604.11(a).

[13] *Ibid.*, (d).

[14] Richard L. Daft, *Management*, p. 443.

[15] Bob Papper, "Recovering Lost Ground," *Communicator*, July/August 2004, p. 24.

[16] *Ibid.*

[17] This case study and the one that follows were prepared by J. Y. Elliott, III, of Miller and Martin, which has offices in Chattanooga, Nashville, and Atlanta.

ADDITIONAL READINGS

Berkman, Robert I., and Christopher A. Shumway. *Digital Dilemmas: Ethical Issues for Online Media Professionals.* Ames: Blackwell, 2003.

Drucker, Peter F. *The Practice of Management.* New York: Harper & Row, 1954.

A Guide to Disability Rights Laws. Washington, DC: U.S. Department of Justice Civil Rights Division, 1996.

Nelton, Sharon. "Sexual Harassment: Reducing the Risks," *Nation's Business,* March, 1995, pp. 24–26.

Plummer, Deborah L. (ed.). *Handbook of Diversity Management: Beyond Awareness to Competency Based Learning.* Lanham, MD: University Press of America, 2003.

Ripley, David E. "How to Determine Future Workforce Needs," *Personnel Journal,* January, 1995, pp. 83–89.

Broadcast Programming 4

This chapter treats the programming of radio and television stations and examines the

- role of the program department and the responsibilities of the program manager and other departmental staff

- types and sources of broadcast programs, and the strategies employed to air them with maximum effect

- major differences between programming a television station affiliated with one of the three original networks and programming an affiliate of another network or an independent station

Commercial radio and television stations air thousands of hours of programs each year. Individual programs may be produced by the station itself or obtained from another source. They may be designed chiefly to entertain, inform, or educate. They may be sponsored or sustaining. They may attract audiences numbering a few hundred or many thousands.

Despite the differences, the programming of all stations is determined by four influences:

The audience, which seeks out a station for its programs. Listeners or viewers may be exposed to other content, such as commercials and public service and promotional announcements, but their principal goal is to hear or view program content that satisfies their need at a particular time. Programs that fail to attract listeners or viewers, or fail to satisfy their needs, are imperiled. So are the financial fortunes of the station.

The broadcaster, who is responsible for operating the station profitably for its owners. The greater the audience, the greater the likelihood that a profit can be realized. Accordingly, the broadcaster selects and schedules programs to attract as many people as possible among the targeted audience.

The advertiser, whose principal interest in using a radio or television station is to bring a product or service to the attention of those most likely to use it. Programs that attract potential customers stand the best chance of attracting advertising dollars, especially if the number of people is large and the cost of delivering the commercial to them is competitive.

The regulator, or government and several of its agencies, notably the Federal Communications Commission (FCC). Its goal is to ensure that the station is operated in a way that serves the public interest. Since passage of the Radio Act of 1927, the regulator has taken actions aimed at compelling or encouraging broadcasters to engage in certain programming practices to satisfy that goal.

Much is said and written about broadcast programming. However, it would be unwise to identify any one influence for praise or condemnation. The programming we hear and see results from the interaction of all four forces. In this chapter, we shall consider the audience and the broadcaster. The advertiser and the regulator will be treated later.

THE AUDIENCE

More than 98 percent of U.S. households have radio and television receivers. The programs they carry attract males and females of all ages and from all socioeconomic categories and ethnic groups.

The pervasiveness and appeal of radio are indicated by the following facts:

- radio reaches more than 94 percent of persons aged 12 and over each week[1]

- four out of five adults are reached by car radio each week[2]

- the average listener spends almost 20 hours per week listening to radio[3]

The reach of television and the extent of its use are no less significant:

- 79 percent of U.S. households own two or more receivers
- television is the main news source for more than 75 percent of the U.S. public
- the average household views about 8 hours daily[4]

The size and composition of the audience for the two media fluctuate. The weekday radio listenership peaks at 7:00 A.M. It holds fairly steady from 9:00 A.M. to 4:00 P.M., then begins to drop. On weekends, listenership is at its highest between 9:00 A.M. and 3:00 P.M.[5] Men listen more than women, with men aged 35 to 44 listening most. They are followed by men 45 to 49 and 50 to 54.[6]

The television audience grows throughout the day and reaches a peak between 9:00 and 9:30 P.M. (EST). People spend more time viewing during the winter than the summer. Sunday evening attracts the largest number of viewers, and Friday evening the smallest.[7] Women watch TV more than men, and older men and women more than younger adults. Teenagers and children aged 2 to 11 watch least.[8] Larger households and those with children view more than smaller households and those without children. There is more use of television in pay-cable households than in those with basic cable or no cable at all. Differences among income classifications are not great, but households with an annual income of less than $30,000 view more than those with income exceeding that amount.[9]

103

THE PROGRAM DEPARTMENT

Of all the factors that determine the financial success of a radio or television station, none is more important than programming. It is programming that brings listeners or viewers to the station. If the number of listeners or viewers is large, and if they possess the characteristics sought by advertisers, the station will attract advertising dollars. Accordingly, the station's revenues and potential profits are influenced largely by its programming. Responsibility for programming is entrusted to a program department.

FUNCTIONS

The major functions of the program department are

- the planning and selection of program content that will appeal to targeted audiences
- the acquisition or, for non-news content, the production of programs
- the scheduling of programs
- the monitoring of programs to ensure compliance with the station's standards and regulatory and legal requirements

ORGANIZATION

The program department is headed by a *program manager* or *program director*, who reports directly to the general manager. In some stations, programming and production are combined in one department under an *operations manager*.

The number of people who report to the program manager, their titles, and their responsibilities vary. In addition, the titles and responsibilities of the program personnel in a radio station differ from those in a television station. We shall examine the two media separately.

Radio　The program department staff in a radio station with a music format generally includes the following:

MUSIC DIRECTOR　The music director is responsible for

- additions to, and deletions from, the station's playlist of music
- preparation of the playlist and supervision of its execution
- auditioning of new recordings
- consultation with the program manager on music rotation
- liaison with representatives of recording companies to obtain new releases
- contact with music stores on sales of compact discs
- cataloguing and filing of compact discs (in large markets, this responsibility may be handled by a music librarian)
- in small markets, an air shift and some local production

ANNOUNCERS　Announcers frequently are called *disc jockeys* or *deejays*. Their major responsibility is an air shift, which includes

- introduction of recordings and programs
- reading of live commercials and promotional, public service, and station identification announcements
- delivery of time and weather checks and traffic reports
- operation of control room equipment

In addition, announcers may

- produce commercials and other announcements
- serve as talent for commercials and other announcements
- double as music director or production director

In many stations, *continuity* or *creative services* and *traffic* staff report to the sales manager. In others, their activities are supervised jointly by the program manager and the head of the sales department. Continuity writers often are responsible for a variety of copy, including commercials and public service and promotional announcements. They also check copy for compliance with the station's program and advertising standards. Traffic personnel place on the schedule details of all program and commercial content to be aired.

At news-format stations, the program manager is, in essence, a news director. The staff consists of editors, anchors, reporters, writers, and desk assistants.

The staff of news/talk stations comprises personnel responsible for news, such as anchors and reporters, and for talk, including producers, hosts, and telephone screeners.

Television In many television stations, the program "department" may consist of only a program director (PD), whose major responsibility is the development of program schedules. As noted later, the PD also works with the general manager and others on the acquisition of syndicated programs.

THE PROGRAM MANAGER

RESPONSIBILITIES

Program managers in small and medium markets are involved in a broader range of activities than their counterparts in large markets. Obviously, there are differences between programming a radio station and a television station. In addition, in television, the amount of time spent on programming responsibilities is influenced greatly by the station's status as a network affiliate or independent. However, all program managers engage in four basic tasks: the *planning, acquisition, execution,* and *control* of programs.

Program Planning Program planning involves the development of short-, medium-, and long-range plans to permit the station to attain its programming and financial objectives.

As we shall see later in the chapter, the principal focus in radio is on the selection of a format and other program content to attract and satisfy the needs of particular demographics. Planning also includes the hiring of announcers or hosts whose personality and style are compatible with the station's format.

In television, planning is directed toward the selection and scheduling of programs to appeal to the largest number of people among the available audience. Affiliated stations also must consider which network programs they will broadcast and which they will reject or delay.

Since programming is the essential ingredient in attracting audiences, and since some audiences are sought more than others by advertisers, planning usually is done by the program manager in consultation with the head of the sales department and the general manager.

Program Acquisition The program manager implements program plans by having programs produced by the station itself or by obtaining them from other sources. The major sources of radio and television programs are described later in the chapter. Again, the head of the sales department and the general manager are involved.

Program Execution   Execution involves the airing of programs in accordance with the plans. The strategies of both radio and television program execution are described later.

The program manager coordinates the scheduling of content with traffic personnel, and its promotion with the promotion and marketing director.

Program Control   The program manager often is called the "protector" of the station's license because of the responsibility for ensuring that the station's programming complies with the terms of its license.

As protector, the program manager

- develops the station's program standards
- supervises all program content for adherence to the station's standards, the FCC's Rules and Regulations, and other applicable regulations and laws
- maintains records of programs broadcasted

The program manager also controls

- the direction and supervision of departmental staff and their activities
- the station's compliance with certain contracts, such as those with a network, program suppliers, and music licensing organizations
- program costs, to ensure that they do not exceed budgeted amounts

QUALITIES

The program manager should be *knowledgeable* and should possess administrative and professional *skills* and certain *personal qualities*.

Knowledge   The program manager should have knowledge of

Station ownership and management: Their goals and the role of programming in achieving them.

The station and staff: Programming strengths and shortcomings, the relationship of the program department to other station departments, and the skills and limitations of departmental employees.

The market: Its size, demographic composition, economy, and the work and leisure patterns of the population as a whole and its various demographic groups; the community's problems and needs; for radio, the music and information tastes of the community, and for television, program preferences.

The competition: Current programming of competing stations, their successes and failures, and their program plans.

Program management: The duties of the program manager and how to discharge them. This includes knowledge of the sources and availability of program content; production process and costs; salability of programming and methods of projecting revenues and expenses; sources and uses of program and audience research; programming trends and developments in broadcast technology; laws and regulations pertaining to programming.

Content and audiences: Formats, programs, and other content; their demographic appeal; and the listening or viewing practices of the audience.

Skills   The program manager must possess administrative and professional skills, among them the ability to

- develop program plans through consideration of need, alternative strategies, and budget
- evaluate ideas for local programming and coordinate the activities of staff responsible for program production
- analyze and interpret ratings and other audience research, and assess the potential for the success of locally produced programs and those available from other sources
- select and schedule content to maximize availability and appeal to targeted demographics
- negotiate contracts with program suppliers, freelance talent, music licensing organizations, and others

107

Personal Qualities   Audiences and station staff have strong feelings about the programming of radio and television stations and are not hesitant to express them. Accordingly, the program manager must be

- *patient* in listening to various, often contradictory, viewpoints offered by telephone, letter, fax, or E-mail from listeners or viewers and community groups, and in meetings with colleagues
- *understanding* of the needs and interests of audience members and of the motivations of fellow employees
- *flexible* in adapting to changing public tastes and programming and technological trends
- *creative* in developing and executing program and promotion ideas
- *ethical* in dealings with others in and outside the station and in programming practices

INFLUENCES

The program manager's decisions and actions are influenced by many factors. A model developed by The Arbitron Company (Figure 4.1) identifies 21 factors that comprise the decision-making environment in a radio station

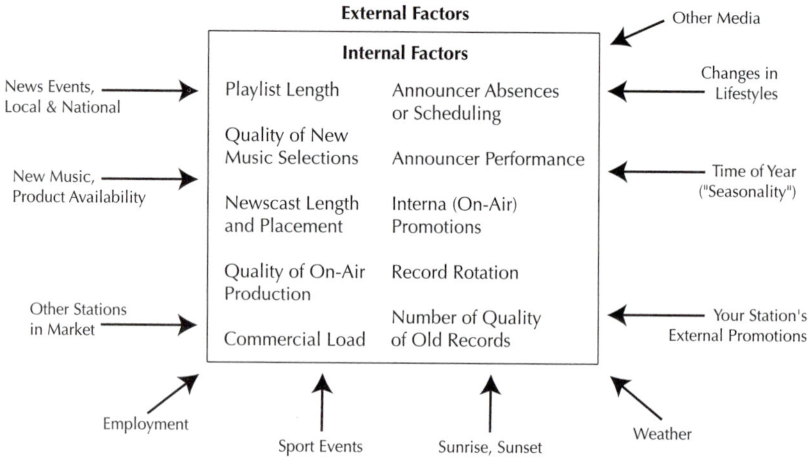

FIGURE 4.1 Music-format decision-making environment. (Source: The Arbitron Company. Reprinted with permission.)

108

with a music format. Obviously, the station can control all the internal factors listed, such as the performance of announcers, the quality of on-air production, and the music rotation. However, only one of the external factors—external station promotions—is within the station's control. The station has no control over such influences as the availability of new music in its format, the activities of competing stations or other media, and changing lifestyles that may affect audience habits and tastes.

J. David Lewis used responses from 301 stations in the United States to determine influences in television station programming. He developed eight categories, in no particular order of priority:

- *direct feedback* from the audience, including letters, telephone calls, and conversations
- *regulatory*, or rules and standards of practice, such as commitments to the FCC, its rules and regulations, and the station's own policy statement
- *inferential feedback*, or ratings
- *conditional*, a mix of factors including comments of critics and opinions of friends outside the station
- *production staff*, the opinions of station personnel with production responsibilities
- *personal* or *subjective judgment*, including instinct, common sense, and knowledge of the community
- *financial*, or factors related to the station's income and expenditures, such as sales potential, sales manager's opinion, and cost

- *tactical*, that is, methods of program planning, the arrangement of the schedule, and viewing trends[10]

RADIO STATION PROGRAMMING

The programming of most radio stations is dominated by one principal content element or sound, known as a *format*. It is designed to appeal to a particular subgroup of the population, usually identified by age, socioeconomic characteristics, or ethnicity.

In reality, few listeners probably know or care what name is used to describe the format of their favorite station. However, the selection of a name is important to management and the sales staff in projecting the station's image and in positioning the station for advertisers.

FORMATS

There are dozens of formats, but all can be placed in one of the following categories: *music*, *information*, and *specialty*.

109

Music   The music format is the most common among commercial radio stations. Describing the format of a particular station in one or two words has become increasingly difficult with the fragmentation of formats and the appeal of some artists in more than one format. In addition, stations use different names to characterize similar sounds. Arbitron identifies the following as America's favorite music formats:[11]

ADULT CONTEMPORARY (AC)   AC and its variants—*soft/light AC, hot AC, mainstream AC, full-service AC,* and *adult rock*—have a basic format that consists of well-known rock hits and pop standards. Women constitute about two-thirds of the formats' audience. More than half of all listeners are aged 25 to 49.

ADULT STANDARDS   Characterized by pre-rock era music, this classification includes *easy listening, middle-of-the-road, nostalgia,* and *variety.* Half the listeners are 65 and older. No other format has such a large share of its audience in a single age group.

ALTERNATIVE   The format includes stations identifying themselves as *album alternative* and *new rock.* Men account for almost two-thirds of the audience, nearly 85 percent of which is made up of persons aged 44 or younger.

CLASSICAL   This format consists chiefly of recorded classical music and live performances of symphonies, opera, and chamber music. Many stations program short music selections during the day and concerts in the evening. Its greatest appeal is to middle-aged (35–54) and older (55+) listeners, who constitute 90 percent of the audience. It attracts more college graduates (64 percent) than any other format. Listeners are relatively affluent, also, with 40 percent earning more than $75,000 a year.

CONTEMPORARY HIT RADIO (CHR)   This format includes stations specializing in *pop CHR* and *rhythmic CHR*. Basically, the format is characterized by a tightly controlled playlist of top-selling rock singles, selected new recordings that are on their way up, and occasional oldies. It attracts the largest share of teens (26 percent) of all formats. About three-quarters of the audience are 34 or younger.

COUNTRY   This format embraces both traditional and modern country music. The format has broad appeal to men and women in all age ranges. However, those aged 35 to 44 are the most frequent listeners.

NEW AC/SMOOTH JAZZ   This format includes *jazz, new age*, and *new adult contemporary* formats. The format consists of instrumentals, with some compatible vocals. Adults aged 35 and over make up the core audience.

OLDIES   The focus is on rock-era oldies and includes '70s *hits* and *rhythmic oldies*. The format appeals equally to men and women and draws more than half its audience from those aged 35 to 54.

ROCK   This format is rock-based music from the mid-1970s to the present, including *album rock* and *classic rock*. The music has huge appeal to men. They constitute more than 70 percent of the audience, the largest adult male share of any format. Adults aged 25 to 44-year-olds make up more than half the listenership.

URBAN   This format includes *urban AC* and *urban oldies*. The basic format specializes in contemporary rhythm and blues music. African Americans make up more than 80 percent of the audience. Listeners tend to be young—about one-third are aged 12 to 24.

While music is the dominant element in music-format stations, a variety of other program content is aired. The kind, amount, and frequency of such content are determined by a number of factors, such as format, the composition of the audience, and the size and location of the community. Examples of nonmusic content include

Community bulletin board: Information on community events.

Editorials: The opinions of the station's ownership on local or national issues and events.

Features: Stories on a wide range of topics of interest to the station's listeners.

Market reports: Both agricultural and business reports.

News: Local, regional, national, and international news.

Public affairs: Generally interview programs on local or national issues and events.

Public service announcements: Announcements for government and non-profit organizations.

Religion: Services of various religious denominations or discussions on religion.

Sports: Scores, reports, and play-by-play.

Traffic reports: Local traffic conditions, especially in large communities and most frequently in drive times.

Weather reports: Local and regional conditions and forecasts, but more extensive in times of weather emergencies.

Information   There are two basic information formats, *all news* and *all talk*—one-third consists of a combination of the two, and is called *news/talk*. Some stations restrict their news and talk content to sports and combine it with live coverage of sporting events in an *all-sports* format.

ALL NEWS   The all-news format consists of news (local, regional, national, and international), information and service features, analysis, commentary, and editorials. It appeals mostly to adults aged 35+, especially better-educated males.

Stations assume that the audience will tune in only for short periods of time to catch up on the latest developments. Accordingly, they program the format in cycles of 20 or 30 minutes, with frequent repetition of the top stories. This characteristic often is used in promotion, with slogans such as "Give us 20 minutes and we'll give you the world."

The format requires a large staff of anchors, writers, reporters, editors, desk assistants, and stringers, as well as mobile units and numerous news services. As a result, it is expensive and tends to be successful financially only in large markets.

ALL TALK   Interviews and audience call-ins form the basis of the all-talk format. The subject matter varies greatly. Interview guests may generate discussion of their personal or professional lives. A call-in may focus on a timely or controversial topic. Many stations have hosts with expertise as psychologists, marriage counselors, and sex therapists, and callers use the program to expound on their personal problems.

Adults aged 35 to 65+ are the most consistent listeners. Most often, they are persons in search of companionship or a forum for their views.[12]

Each hour or daypart is programmed to appeal to key available demographics. Success is tied closely to the skills of the host, who must be knowledgeable on a wide range of topics, easy in conversation, and perceptive. Good judgment and the ability to maintain control of the conversation are other desirable attributes.

The format also requires producers who have a keen awareness of local and national issues, and the ability to schedule guests who are informed, eloquent, and provocative. Screeners are used to rank incoming calls for relevance and to screen out crank calls.

NEWS/TALK   This combination of the all-news and all-talk formats takes different forms. Typically, it consists of news in morning and afternoon drive times, with talk during the remainder of the broadcast day. Some stations air play-by-play sports on evenings and weekends. The format's chief demographic appeal is to persons aged 35 to 65+.

111

Specialty There are many specialty formats. However, the following are the most common:

ETHNIC Ethnic formats are targeted toward ethnic groups or people united by a language other than English. African Americans constitute a major ethnic group in many large markets and in towns of various sizes in the South. Stations targeting this group often combine disco and hip-hop music with information of interest to the African-American community.

Spanish-language stations program music and information for Cuban Americans, Mexican Americans, Puerto Ricans, and others whose primary language is Spanish. In addition, many stations broadcast a variety of content in one or more foreign languages, including French, Polish, Japanese, and Greek.

RELIGION This format is characterized by hymns and other religious music, sermons, religious services, talks, interviews, and discussions. The particular program makeup is influenced heavily by the type of licensee. Some stations are licensed to churches and religious organizations that are more interested in spreading their message than in the size or composition of the audience. However, ratings and demographics are of major concern to a second type of licensee, the conventional entrepreneur, who sells blocks of time to churches and religious organizations and spots to advertisers.

112

VARIETY The variety format exists chiefly in one-station markets or where other formats do not meet the music or information needs of several desirable demographics. In a one-station market, for example, the format may include music for all age groups, news, weather, sports, and public affairs. Features would be selected for their appeal to the makeup of the community.

The format is programmed to satisfy the available audience. During the morning hours, music may be suited to adults at home. In the afternoon and evening, the sound may become more contemporary for teenagers and young adults.

PROGRAM SOURCES

Radio stations use three major sources of programs: *local*, *syndicated*, and *network*.

Local Local programming is the principal source for most stations. For stations with a music format, it includes both music and information content.

Recording companies are anxious to have their product played on radio stations, since air play is an important determinant of sales. Accordingly, they provide most stations with free, promotional copies. To ensure good service, the station must nurture close relationships with the companies. That can be done by maintaining regular contact, sending them copies of the playlist, and keeping them informed of success in reaching those demographics to which the recordings appeal.

Some stations obtain recordings from local stores under a trade-out arrangement. Stations in many small markets do not receive promotional copies and subscribe to a recording service for current releases.

Examples of locally produced information content on a music-format station include news, sports, and public affairs. Stations with an information format rely heavily on local production for news, talk, features, sports, and public affairs.

Radio stations also engage in remotes from retail stores, malls, and other business locations. Such broadcasts can be a useful promotional tool. Indeed, some stations have bought fiberglass or inflatable studios in the shape of giant radio receivers to increase their visibility on such occasions. However, remotes must be selected with care, since they may interrupt the regular flow of programming. They must also be planned in close cooperation with the sales department.

Syndicated Syndicators provide stations with *programs* and with complete music *formats*.

PROGRAMS Syndicated offerings range from 60- or 90-second features on health, finance, politics, and assorted other subjects, to programs of several hours' duration.

Long-form programming featuring nationally known talk personalities like Rush Limbaugh and Sean Hannity offers stations quality and cost-efficient content. Such is the appeal of syndicated product that it has even taken over the traditionally locally produced morning drive period on many stations and replaced station hosts with the likes of Don Imus and Howard Stern. Regional morning team programs are also available, especially in the South.

Barter is the primary method of syndicated program acquisition. Other programs are offered on a cash basis, the price determined by factors such as market size, the appeal of the program, and competition for it. Still other programs are available to the station without charge.

FORMATS The entire music programming of some stations is provided by format syndicators.

Stations receive from the syndicator, typically via satellite, music in the desired format and then insert commercials, promotional, public service, and ID announcements, and other nonmusic content.

Syndicated formats are found mostly in fully automated stations. However, many formats may be used in semi-automated and live-operated stations.

Some formats are sold to stations and others are leased. Cost is determined mostly by the type of format and size of the market.

In addition to providing music, many format syndicators offer their services to stations as consultants on programming, promotion, and research.

Network The programming of most national networks is designed for specific demographics or formats. The staples are music, news, and talk. Other programs vary according to the interests of the targeted audiences.

Many stations also receive news and other informational programming from regional or state networks. Ad-hoc networks are organized in many parts of the country for the coverage of special events and sports.

113

Strategies

Selection of a format is the first and most important step in the development of a station's programming strategy. It is also the most difficult. In most markets, music formats with the greatest appeal to the most-sought demographics (persons aged 25 to 54) already have been taken. AM stations experience particular problems, as evidenced by their movement away from music formats and toward news, talk, or a combination. With the increasing fragmentation of formats, FM stations also face difficulties in trying to position themselves in a way that sets them apart from stations with similar formats. "Niche programming" has become the key.

Among the factors that influence the format selection are

Market Size

Generally, the larger the market, the more specialized the format must be to attract an audience.

Community Composition and Location

Demographic characteristics and trends are important in predicting the appeal of particular formats since, as we have seen, music and other program preferences are linked closely to age, gender, income level, and ethnicity. The makeup of the workforce and the proportion of professional, industrial, and agricultural employees also provide useful pointers. The region of the country in which the station is located and the extent to which it serves chiefly urban, suburban, or rural residents, or some combination, give additional clues to content appeal.

Competition

Consideration of the degree to which competing stations have targeted all desirable demographics will indicate if there is a void in the marketplace. Persons deemed most desirable by advertisers are, in order, adults aged 25 to 54, 18 to 49, and 18 to 34. If there is a void, the station may select a format that meets the needs of the unserved or underserved audience. On the other hand, it may be determined that one or more stations are vulnerable to direct format competition, and that audience may be taken from them by better format execution and promotion.

Potential Audience and Revenues

The size and demographic composition of the audience are key factors in generating advertising dollars. For that reason, projections of the potential audience and of advertising revenues are major criteria in the format-decision process.

Technical Considerations

The size of the potential audience is determined by the number of people who can receive the station's programs. Accordingly, the power at which a station is authorized to broadcast is important. The greater the power, the greater the coverage. Coverage also is influenced by the frequency of an AM station and the antenna height of an FM station. The lower the frequency and the higher the antenna, the greater the range of the station's signal.

Format selection may take into account another technical consideration. The superiority of FM over AM sound fidelity has attracted a majority of music listeners to FM stations and posed programming dilemmas for AM stations in many markets.

Finances

The financial cost of the format and of promoting the station to capture enough listeners to appeal to advertisers must be considered.

Stations that opt for a music format also must decide on other content elements to include in their programming.

Next, the station decides how to execute the programming to attract and retain the target audience. The decision must take into account the needs and expectations of the listeners.

People turn to a music-format station chiefly for entertainment or relaxation, to an all-news station for information, and to an all-talk station for a variety of reasons, including information, opinion, and companionship. They expect to hear a familiar sound, one with which they feel comfortable. The format, therefore, must be executed with consistency.

The most common tool to obtain consistency is the *format wheel* or *format clock*, which identifies the mix and sequence of program elements in a one-hour period. Figure 4.2 shows a format wheel for a contemporary hit station in morning drive time.

The particular composition of an audience, its needs, moods, and the activities in which it engages change during the day. Stations attempt to respond to those changes through *dayparting*. On weekdays, the dayparts are

Morning drive time (6:00 A.M. to 10:00 A.M.): Most listeners want to be brought up-to-date with news and with weather and traffic conditions.

Midday (10:00 A.M. to 3:00 P.M.): The majority of listeners are homemakers and office workers, and both music and information programming are tailored to their needs.

Afternoon drive time (3:00 P.M. to 7:00 P.M.): Teenagers return from school and adults drive home from work. For the most part, the former seek entertainment and the latter a mix of entertainment and information.

Evening (7:00 P.M. to midnight): The audience of most stations is composed chiefly of people desiring entertainment or relaxation.

Overnight (midnight to 6:00 A.M.): Shift workers, college students seeking entertainment, and persons seeking companionship constitute the bulk of the audience.

All-news stations broadcast their content in cycles, with a certain time elapsing before each element is repeated. Figure 4.3 shows a format wheel for such a station.

Audience size is computed by quarter hour, and so stations strive to attract the maximum possible audience in each quarter-hour period. However, audi-

115

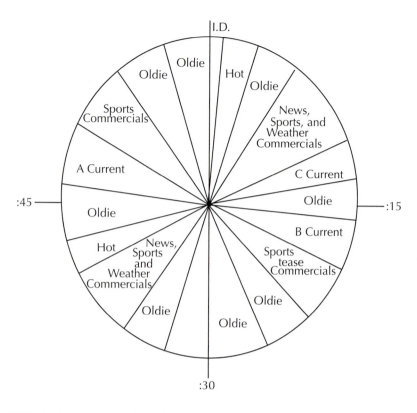

FIGURE 4.2 Morning drive format wheel: contemporary hit radio station. Hot: chart position 1–10; A Current: 11–20; B Current: 21-30; C Current: 31–40.

ence members do not have to listen continuously for fifteen minutes to be counted. Audience measurement companies credit a station with a listener if a person is tuned in for five or more minutes in any quarter hour. One technique to retain listeners from one quarter hour to the next is to schedule a *music sweep* (i.e., uninterrupted music) over each quarter-hour mark. Nonmusic content, which often prompts dial-switching, is placed within the quarter hour. Another is a *tease* or *bumper*. Here, the disc jockey or talk host previews what is coming up in the next segment.

A station's success in maintaining audience may be judged by the amount of time a person listens during a specific daypart. This is known as *time spent listening*, or *TSL*. It is calculated by multiplying the number of quarter hours in a daypart by the average quarter-hour audience and dividing the result by the cumulative audience. For example, a station has an average audience of 5,700 and a cumulative audience of 25,500 among persons aged 25 to 49 during morning drive Monday through Friday. The TSL is 80 (number of quarter hours) times 5,700 (average audience) divided by 25,500 (cumulative audience), or 17.9 quarter hours. To determine audience turnover, or the number of times an audience changes during a time period, the cumulative audience is divided by the average audience. In this example, it is 4.5.

116

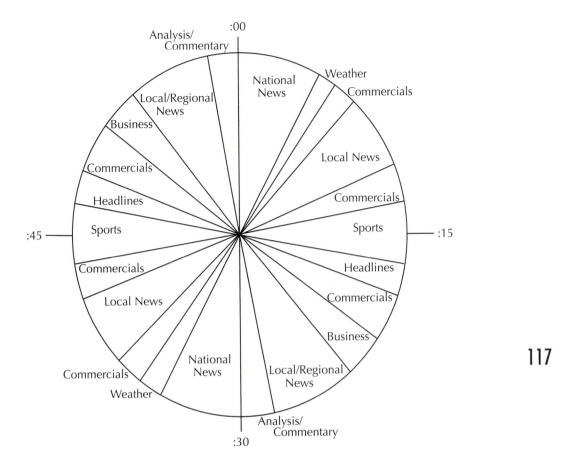

FIGURE 4.3 Format wheel: all-news station.

117

Essentially the same music is available to all stations in a market with a particular format. An important strategic consideration, therefore, is the selection of recordings for the *playlist* and their *rotation*. The playlist is the listing of recordings played over the course of a period of time, usually a week. Rotation refers to the frequency with which each is played.

Stations rely on several sources in deciding what to keep on the playlist and what to add and delete. Among those used most often are trade magazines, such as *Billboard* and *R&R* (*Radio & Records*), tip sheets, and newsletters. They reflect the popularity of recordings in different formats across the nation. To determine local appeal, stations check on sales with area music stores.

To increase their information base, many stations engage in continuing efforts to obtain listener feedback to the music being played or contemplated for addition to the playlist. The most common method is *call-out research*. The station plays over the telephone short excerpts (called "hooks") of music selections and asks respondents for their reactions. The results are tabulated and assist in tracking the popularity of recordings and making decisions on playlist content. Such research is relatively inexpensive, but only a limited number of hooks can be played before participants grow tired.

Another method is *auditorium testing*. Several dozen people are invited to a large room or auditorium and asked to rate as many as 400 hooks. They are paid and, generally, are chosen from the age group targeted by the station. They may be regular listeners, those who favor a competing station, or a combination. Auditorium testing is more expensive than call-out research and usually is attempted only periodically. That prevents close monitoring of changing music preferences and regular refinement of the playlist.

In an attempt to ensure that programming is tuned to the needs of the target audience, stations are paying increased attention to nonmusic research. Many are building *databases* to develop listener profiles. Income, lifestyle, product usage, and leisure activity are examples of information that is collected and stored. Images of the station, its programming, personalities, and other elements are obtained through *focus groups*, which bring together 10 to 12 people for a controlled discussion led by a moderator. Often, the results provide ideas for more extensive research. *Market perceptual studies* are conducted by telephone interview or mail survey among targeted listeners to identify perceptions of a station's position in the market and its various characteristics. Telephone interviews also are used in *format searches*, attempts to ascertain if there is a need or place for various formats or elements within a format.

In some formats and on some stations, primary emphasis is given to the music or information content. The personality of the announcer is secondary. However, since the announcer is the link between the station and the audience, many stations encourage announcers to project their personality with the expectation that it will provide another competitive weapon. In either situation, announcers are important in the creation of a station's image and are chosen to reflect that image. If personality is emphasized, announcers are scheduled during those dayparts when their personality suits the mood of the audience.

Strategy considerations also may involve the possible use of automation. The station must decide whether its benefits outweigh its shortcomings and whether it may be used advantageously over the entire broadcast day or in certain dayparts. Automation offers the advantages of a consistent, professional sound, eliminates personnel problems, and may result in cost savings. However, it removes the element of personality and deprives the station of spontaneity and flexibility.

Programming must be promoted constantly to retain the existing audience and to attract new listeners. The role of promotion is discussed in Chapter 6, "Broadcast Promotion and Marketing." It should be noted here that stations seek to gain competitive advantage through on-air and off-air promotion of image, programming, and personalities. They hope that the result will be a clear public perception of what the station does and how it can satisfy audience needs.

A final and most important strategic consideration is the station's commercial policy. Most listeners to music-format stations have little tolerance for interruptions in music and may seek out another station when commercials air. Commercial policy usually sets forth the commercial load (i.e., the number of commercials allowed per hour) and the frequency of breaks for commercials and other nonmusic content. Commercial policy is discussed further in Chapter 5, "Broadcast Sales."

TELEVISION STATION PROGRAMMING

Programming a commercial television station differs markedly from programming a radio station. While the radio programmer identifies a specific audience and broadcasts to it throughout the day, the television programmer targets a general audience and attempts to respond to the preferences of those persons who are available to view.

A radio station competes for audience primarily against the other radio stations in the market that seek to attract similar demographics. A television station is in competition against all other television stations in the market and against cable and direct broadcast satellite. Additional competition for the viewers' time comes from videocassette recorders, DVD players, and the Internet.

Network programming occupies only a minor place in the schedule of most radio stations. It is a dominant force in television, providing a major part of the schedule for stations affiliated with the three original networks—ABC, CBS, and NBC. It plays a lesser, though still very important, role in the offerings of affiliates of Fox, The WB, and UPN. (At the time of writing, the future of PAX TV was uncertain. Accordingly, it will not be considered here.)

Programming success in television rests heavily on the ability to produce or buy programs with audience appeal, air them at times when they can be seen by the audience to which they appeal, and build individual programs into a schedule that encourages viewers to tune to the station and remain with it from one program to another.

PROGRAM SOURCES

Television stations affiliated with a network rely on three principal sources of programs: the *network, program syndicators*, and *local production*. Independent stations (i.e., those not affiliated with a permanent network) use syndicated and local production and receive sports and specials from ad-hoc networks.

Network   ABC, CBS, and NBC provide affiliates with the bulk of their programming. Weekday daytime hours consist of news magazines, soap operas, a game show, and network news. In prime time, entertainment, news magazines, and some sports are broadcast. Talk-variety, news interviews, and news characterize the late night and overnight periods.

On weekends, they schedule news magazines and programs for children and teenagers on Saturday mornings, sports in the afternoon, and entertainment in prime time. Daytime on Sundays includes news-magazine and news-interview programs and sports, followed by prime-time entertainment.

The networks produce their news and sports broadcasts and a growing number of their prime-time entertainment programs. However, they continue to purchase a significant amount of entertainment from independent production companies.

Fox, The WB, and UPN supply fewer hours for their affiliates than the original networks. Weekdays, Fox programs two hours of entertainment in prime time. On Saturday, children's programs are aired in the morning, sports in the afternoon, and entertainment in prime time, followed by more entertainment. A morning news-interview program, afternoon sports, and three hours of prime-time entertainment make up the Sunday schedule.

The WB airs a two-hour, young-adult entertainment block weekday afternoons and two hours of entertainment in prime time. Five hours of morning children's programming are the network's only offerings on Saturday. The network's Sunday schedule consists of two hours of prime-time entertainment.

UPN programs two hours of entertainment in prime time Monday through Friday and a movie on Saturday afternoons.

Program Syndicators   Syndicated programs are used by network-affiliated stations to fill many of the periods during which the network does not provide programming. Independent stations rely heavily on such programs during all dayparts.

There are two major categories of syndicated programs:[13]

> *Off-network*, which denotes that the programs have been broadcast on a network and now are available for purchase by stations and other outlets. They include a large number of situation comedy and dramatic programs that attract large and loyal audiences during their network runs.

> *First-run*, which describes programs produced for sale directly to stations. The kind of content available varies from year to year. In the early years of the twenty-first century, among the most plentiful and popular offerings, were talk, game, and court shows.

Feature films and cartoons also are distributed by syndicators. Decisions on syndicated program acquisitions are based on program availability, cost, and audience appeal.

As noted later in the chapter, the station rep company is an important source of information on available programs. Many stations use additional sources, such as the annual *Television Programming Source Books*, published by BiB Channels. This three-volume series contains information on films and film packages, and lists short- and long-form TV film and tape series, with details of program length, number of episodes, story line, distributor, and distribution terms. Product is available to a station only if it has not already been obtained by another station in the market.

Even though stations often announce that they have bought a syndicated program, what they have bought, in fact, are the exclusive rights to broadcast a program over a specific period of time. The rights are contained in a license agreement between the syndicator and the station. It details, among other items, the series title, license term, number of programs, license fee, method of delivery, and payment terms. The fee is based on a number of factors, including the size of the market, competition for the program from stations in the market, the age of the program, and the time period during which it will be broadcast. The negotiating skills of the person representing the station also may be influential. In the case of feature films, market size, competition, and the age of the films are taken into account, as well as the success they achieved during their showing in movie theaters or on a network.

The dramatic increase in the cost of syndicated product, combined with the emergence and growth of barter programming (discussed below), have led to an important change in the program manager's traditional role in syndicated program purchasing. Today, because of the increased emphasis on the bottom line, the programmer is likely to be only one of several key station personnel involved in purchasing decisions. Others include the general manager, sales manager, and business manager. In many stations, the general manager has primary responsibility, while the program manager merely administers decisions.

In determining what to buy and how much to pay, the station should give particular attention to the ratings potential and projected revenues of syndicated programs. Their appeal may be ascertained by studying their performance in other markets, particularly those with a similar population makeup. Nielsen's *Report on Syndicated Programs* provides detailed information on the size and demographic composition of the audiences for syndicated programs in all markets, in different dayparts, and against different program competition. Clues to the appeal of off-network programs may be gleaned from their performance in the market when they aired on a network.

Calculating revenue potential requires consideration of (1) spot inventory, or the number of 30-second spots available in each program; (2) the average selling price in the daypart in which the program will be broadcast; and (3) the selling level, that is, the percentage of spots likely to be sold. Multiplying the selling price by the number of spots available produces the *gross revenue*. The gross is reduced by 15 percent to allow for commissions paid by the station to account executives, reps, and advertising agencies, producing the *net*. That figure is reduced further by the projected selling level (most stations use 80 percent) to give what is known as the *net net*.

Assume that a network-affiliated station is contemplating the purchase of a half-hour, off-network series. Six commercial minutes are available and the average selling price in the daypart for a 30-second spot is $400. The calculation would be as follows:

Selling price	$400
30-second commercials	× 12
Gross	$4,800
Net revenue level (after commission)	× .85
Net	$4,080
Selling level	×.80
Net net	$3,264

121

The projected revenue of $3,264 for each episode applies only to the first year. Projections for subsequent years will take into account possible changes in the spot rate. For example, rates in the daypart may increase to keep pace with inflation. A decrease might result if the program were moved to a less costly daypart.

Having calculated the net net revenue potential of each episode over the life of the contract, the station must then consider how much it can afford to pay per episode. The actual price will be determined through negotiations between the syndicator and the station.[14]

When the contract is signed, the station usually makes a down payment and pays the balance in installments. As noted in Chapter 2, "Financial Management," costs are assigned according to an amortization schedule for accounting purposes. The station may select the *straight line* method, which means that an equal value is placed on each broadcast of each episode. Alternatively, it may opt for *accelerated amortization* or the *declining value* method, which assumes that the value of each episode decreases with each broadcast. Accordingly, the station assigns to each broadcast a declining percentage of total cost. A program with six runs may be expensed as follows: run 1—40 percent; 2—30 percent; 3—15 percent; 4—10 percent; 5—5 percent; 6—0 percent.

122

It is becoming increasingly difficult for stations to buy attractive syndicated programs for cash. Some are available only through *barter*.

In a barter transaction, the syndicator provides the program at no cost but, in return, retains for sale some of the commercial inventory. In a 30-minute program, for example, two minutes may be retained, leaving four minutes for sale by the station. More common is the *cash + barter* arrangement, whereby the station pays a fee for the program and also surrenders time to the syndicator.

At its inception, barter was viewed as a means whereby stations could control soaring program costs. Syndicators emphasized that the value of the commercial time surrendered would represent a much lower cost to the station than if the program were bought on a straight cash basis. Furthermore, the small amount of inventory retained by the syndicator probably would not hurt profits, since 10 to 15 percent of commercial time generally remains unsold.

Barter does permit stations to obtain competitive product without putting out large amounts of cash, and to exchange time that might not be used for lower overall program costs. However, it has become such a dominant force that stations that would be willing to pay cash do not have that option. In addition, program costs have continued to escalate and stations have been left with less inventory to recoup their programming investment. Furthermore, barter now places stations in direct competition with syndicators for the sale of time to national advertisers in the same program.

Local Production   The focus of local production is on local newscasts and public affairs programs, chiefly face-to-face interviews. Other local productions may include magazine, music video, exercise, sports, and children's programs, and occasional documentaries.

PROGRAMMING FACTORS

The TV program manager weighs many factors in making program acquisition and scheduling decisions. Among the more important are these:

Strength or Weakness of Competing Stations

Since the size of the television audience is predictable in each daypart, a
station attracts viewers at the expense of its competitors. Noting the
strength or weakness of the competition, both among total viewers and particular demographics, the station can schedule appropriate programs. In a
single time period, there are two basic options. One is to try to draw viewers from competing stations with a program of similar audience appeal.
The second is to schedule a program with a different appeal to attract those
whose interests are not being addressed.

Building Audience Flow

It is advantageous to a station to air programs that attract large audiences.
It is much more advantageous if audiences can be inherited from preceding programs and retained for those that follow. In scheduling, consideration is given to both possibilities.

A challenge in scheduling programs to capitalize on this so-called *audience flow* has grown out of the spread in ownership of remote-control pads.
Viewers use them to switch from channel to channel within and between
programs to explore their options. This practice is known as *flipping*.[15]

Building Audience Habit

Series programs scheduled in the same time period each weekday can
become part of the audience's daily television viewing routine.
Encouraging such habit formation usually is an important goal.

Available Audience

The audience of a market, and the availability of different parts of the audience in various dayparts, are major determinants of program selection and
scheduling. Figure 4.4 shows the dayparts on weekdays and the audience
available in each.

Weekends present a different picture. In theory, all children and many
adults are potential viewers. However, shopping, social, and sporting activities influence the number and kind of people who are free to watch television on Saturdays. The nature of the local economy is important, too.
More adults usually are available in white-collar than in blue-collar communities, where Saturday work is not uncommon. On Sundays, religious
pursuits may be added to shopping, social, and sporting activities as alternatives to television viewing.

Audience Interest

Audiences are attracted in large numbers to many entertainment programs. If audience interest in other kinds of content is high in a particular

market, or if the station believes that interest can be stimulated, it may wish to produce or buy programs that respond to such interest.

Advertiser Interest

To be successful, programs must attract advertisers as well as audiences. The principal target of most local TV advertisers is adults aged 25 to 54. Selecting programs with low audience appeal, or with appeal chiefly to demographics in which advertisers are not interested, leads to financial problems.

Budget

The amount of money available for program production and purchases is an important determinant of what can be programmed. Costs of many popular off-network programs have been driven up significantly in recent

Daypart	Available Audience
Early Morning [6:00 A.M. to 9:00 A.M.]	Children, homemakers, adult men and women who work outside the home, retired persons. Schoolchildren and working adults are preparing to leave, and most have left by the end of the daypart.
Morning [9:00 A.M. to Noon]	Mostly preschoolers, homemakers, the retired, and shift workers.
Afternoon [Noon to 4:00 P.M.]	Early in the daypart, working adults who eat lunch at home are added to the morning audience. They leave, and are replaced from about 2:00 P.M. by children returning from school.
Early Fringe [4:00 P.M. to 6:00 P.M.]	The return of most working adults begins and, in many small and medium markets, is completed.
Early Evening [6:00 P.M. to 7:00 P.M.]	In all but the largest markets, all segments of the audience are home.
Prime Access [7:00 P.M. to 8:00 P.M.]	All audience segments are available to view.
Network Prime Time [8:00 P.M. to 11:00 P.M.]	During the first hour or so, the same as that for prime access. A decrease begins at about 9:30 P.M., chiefly among children, those who have to get up early, and the retired.
Late Fringe [11:00 P.M. to 11:35 P.M.]	Mostly adults.
Late Night [11:35 p.m. to 2:05 A.M.]	Again, mostly adults, including shift workers.
Overnight [2:05 a.m. to 6:00 A.M.]	Shift workers comprise the largest part of the comparatively small available audience.

FIGURE 4.4 Television dayparts and available audience (all times are EST).

years, making it difficult for a station to use large numbers of such programs as a stepping-stone to success.

Program Inventory

Many syndicated program and feature film contracts permit multiple broadcasts over a period of years. In addition to recently purchased product, such content still may be available for airing.

Local Production Capabilities

It has been noted that most stations produce few programs, except news and public affairs. However, a station with an adequate budget, equipment, and technical facilities, competent production personnel, and sources of appropriate talent may contemplate producing other kinds of programs, especially if audience and advertiser interest are strong.

SCHEDULING STRATEGIES

Consideration of the above factors will suggest program scheduling strategies suited to the competitive situation in which the station finds itself. The following strategies are among those used most commonly:

Head-to-head: A program that appeals to an audience similar to that being sought by a competing station or stations. Early- and late-night newscasts usually are scheduled against each other on stations affiliated with the original networks and provide an example of this strategy.

Counter: A program that appeals to a different audience from that targeted by the competition. A program with principal appeal to adults at the same time as a children's program on another station is an example of counter-programming.

Strip: Scheduling a program series at the same time each day, usually Monday through Friday. This practice, also known as *horizontal programming*, encourages habit formation by the audience. However, if the program does not attract a sizable audience, the strategy may backfire, since failure will be experienced every day. With syndicated series, the strategy is desirable only if there are enough episodes to schedule over several months, at least.

Checkerboard: Airing a different program series in the same time period daily. This strategy has several drawbacks. It is expensive, since the station may have to buy as many as five different series. It is difficult to promote. Finally, it does not permit the station to capitalize on the element of audience habit.

Block: Scheduling several programs with similar audience appeal back-to-back, usually for two hours or more. This strategy also is called *vertical programming* and seeks to encourage audience flow.

Feature films pose a special scheduling challenge. Film packages contain both good and not-so-good movies, and not all have similar audience appeal.

Many stations try to surmount the problem by airing films under an umbrella series title and identifying an element for promotional emphasis. If the movie has won awards, for example, the award-winning elements lend themselves to such an approach.

Three decades ago, Philip F. von Ladau, vice president and general manager of Marketron, Inc., set forth ten basic programming principles. Despite changes in audience habits resulting from the massive growth in the number of viewing options and the impact of the remote-control pad, judicious application of the principles can still lead to successful scheduling. They are

1. *Attack where shares of audience are equally divided.* It's a lot easier to take a little audience from each of several stations than a lot of audience from a dominant program.

2. *Build both ways from a strong program.* Take advantage of early tune-in to a strong program creating "free" sampling of a good preceding show; late tune-outs to accomplish the same for the following. This falls under the principle that it's easier to sustain an audience than to build one.

3. *Sequence programs demographically.* Don't force unnecessary audience turnover.

4. *When a change in appeal is called for, accomplish it in easy stages.* When the available audience dictates a change, do so with a program type that will hold as large a share of the preceding audience as possible, rather than attempting to completely change the demographic appeal.

5. *Place "new" programs at time periods of greatest tune-in.* This amounts to free advertising through happenstance sampling. People turning on their sets generally leave them at the station last used; thus, at times of building (increasing) set usage, a significant number of people may inadvertently be exposed to your new show.

6. *Keep a "winning" program in its current position.* Changing competition must, of course, be taken into consideration. But when people are in the habit of finding a popular program in a particular time period, moving it risks an audience loss.

7. *Counter-program to present viewers with a reasonable alternative to the other fare.* It's generally better to offer something different than just another version of the types of programs already being aired by the competition.

8. *Program to those people who are available.* A lot of errors are made here by considering the age/sex makeup of all the audiences using TV. What is really available to most programs, particularly independent and/or individual-station-placed programs, is just the audience that remains after the dominant show has commanded its share.

9. *In buying, always consider how it would be to have the offered program opposite you.* It may be worth a small going-in monetary loss as opposed to the big one that might be created with the subject program opposite your existing properties.

126

10. *Don't place an expensive program in a time period where there is insufficient audience or revenue potential,* enough at least to break even in combination with its preceding and following properties.[16]

PROGRAMMING THE NETWORK AFFILIATE

Even though stations affiliated with the Fox, The WB, and UPN networks are "network affiliates," their networks' schedules are much more limited than those of ABC, CBS, and NBC. As a result, they operate like independent stations much of the time. For that reason, they will be considered with the independents later in the chapter.

Affiliation with one of the three original networks offers many advantages. It has been noted that the network fills a significant part of an affiliate's program schedule, mostly at no direct cost.

Many network programs attract large audiences, thus increasing the value of the time the station sells in and around them. Skillful scheduling and promotion also permit the station to attract audiences to locally scheduled programs before, between, and after network offerings. Similar assistance in boosting audiences is afforded through the network's publicity and promotion.

However, the affiliate programmer's job is not without challenge. Cable and DBS allow viewers to select from dozens of channels, which offer stiff competition and which have cut deeply into the affiliates' audiences.

127

NETWORK-AFFILIATE RELATIONS

The relationship between a network and an affiliated station is governed by an affiliation contract. Specific contracts differ from network to network and are undergoing some changes, particularly on the terms of compensation that networks traditionally have paid to their affiliates. Generally, however, they contain the following clauses:

1. The network agrees to provide, and deliver to the station, a variety of programs.

2. The station has the right of first refusal. In other words, the network must offer programs first to its affiliated station in the market.

3. The station may reject any network program it believes to be unsatisfactory, unsuitable, or contrary to the public interest. In such cases, the network may offer the program to another station or program transmission service in the market. In practice, affiliated stations clear (i.e., carry) most of their network's programs. When they refuse, it is generally because they consider the program too controversial or because they wish to broadcast a program of special local interest.

4. The station may broadcast a network program on a delayed basis, but only with network approval. When the delayed broadcast occurs, the station must announce that the program was presented earlier on the network.

5. The station may not add or delete material from a network program without prior written authorization from the network.

6. Within a network program period, the station may not delete any network identification, program promotion, or production credit announcement, except promotional announcements for a program the station will not carry. In such cases, only a network or station promotional announcement or public service announcement may be substituted.

7. The network may cancel a previously announced program and substitute another program.

8. The station may broadcast locally originated announcements in station break periods between and during network programs. However, the placement and duration of such periods are determined by the network.

9. When an affiliated station is sold, the network has the right to determine whether to accept the change.

NETWORK PROGRAMMING

128

The original networks provide their affiliates with programs in most dayparts.

Weekday early-morning network programming consists of news magazines. A woman's magazine program (ABC) and game show (CBS) fill part of the morning, followed by an afternoon block of soap operas and news in early evening on all three networks. Network prime time comprises a variety of programs: reality, situation comedies, dramas, feature films and made-for-TV movies, news magazines, specials, and sports. Late night is made up of news-interview and talk-variety programs. ABC and CBS air news during all or part of the overnight daypart.

The networks' weekend lineup varies, chiefly as a result of sports coverage on Saturday and Sunday afternoons. News magazines, cartoons, and other child- and teen-appeal programs are aired on Saturday mornings. Sports characterize Saturday afternoons, usually followed by the network news. Network prime time consists of entertainment. NBC is the only network that programs the late-night slot, with "Saturday Night Live."

News magazines and news interviews are aired on Sunday mornings, and sports during the afternoons. Network news precedes prime-time programming, which starts at 7:00 P.M.

SCHEDULING

Since a network fills the major part of an affiliated station's broadcast day, the program manager's chief scheduling responsibility is for those periods during which the network is not feeding programs. Of course, if the station determines that it will not clear or will delay broadcast of a network program, additional scheduling decisions must be made. Programming possibilities on weekdays include the following.

Early Morning (6:00 A.M. to 9:00 A.M.) Many affiliates start the daypart with local news and/or news-magazine programs, and most join the networks at 7:00 A.M. for their respective news magazines. Children and teenagers are not being served. Locally produced children's programs, syndicated cartoons, and off-network sitcoms or drama-adventure series offer alternatives for part or all of the period.

Morning (9:00 A.M. to Noon) Homemakers are a principal target in this daypart. During the first two hours, the networks are not providing programs. Options include local or syndicated talk, discussion, or magazine programs oriented toward women, and game shows. Off-network situation comedies starring children or with slapstick elements may bring children as well as adults to the set. ABC and CBS return at 11:00 A.M. and most affiliates clear network programming through the end of the period. Syndicated talk is the choice of many NBC affiliates.

Afternoon (Noon to 4:00 P.M.) Between noon and 12:30, many affiliates opt for local news or a news magazine, both of which provide an opportunity to promote later newscasts. Syndicated entertainment, such as quiz or game shows and situation comedies, is an alternative. From 12:30 (CBS) or 1:00 (ABC and NBC), affiliates generally carry the network soap opera block. It runs until 4:00 P.M. on ABC and CBS. NBC affiliates have an opportunity to counter-program starting at 3:00 P.M. The alternatives include syndicated talk with strong appeal to women, or cartoons and situation comedies with teenage and child appeal to target returning schoolchildren and teenagers.

129

Early Fringe (4:00 P.M. to 6:00 P.M.) This is the start of the longest period for which an affiliate has programming responsibility. At the same time, it offers a station the opportunity to generate significant advertising revenues and build the adult audience for its local news.

The growth in audience size and diversity allows stations to engage successfully in counter-programming. Thirty-minute and one-hour off-network and first-run syndicated content fit easily into the period, and many stations have discovered that audiences respond well to blocks of programs of the same genre.

Placement of local news is a major strategic factor. Airing it at 5:00 P.M. or 5:30 P.M. rules out the possibility of back-to-back hour-long programs. However, a succession of two or three off-network situation comedies with increasingly older appeal can bring youngsters to the set first, followed by teenagers and adults. An hour-long syndicated talk program attracts the adult demographics desired for news at 5:00 P.M. Movies may be considered by stations that do not air local news until 6:00 P.M., but their appeal varies. They also pose some scheduling problems because of their varying lengths. Made-for-television movies are consistent in length, but have proven less appealing than feature films.

Early Evening (6:00 P.M. to 7:00 P.M.)   The length of the local newscast and the periods selected both for local and network news influence the schedule in this daypart. The 30-minute network newscast may be preceded or followed by a 30-minute local newscast. An hour-long local news program may be followed by network news in the first half hour of prime access, or a 90-minute news block may start with 30 minutes of local news, followed by network news, and a final 30 minutes of local news. In most major markets, longer news blocks are common.

Prime Access (7:00 P.M. to 8:00 P.M.)   The Prime-Time Access Rule restricting what could be shown by some network affiliates formerly influenced program choices in this daypart. With the rule's termination in 1996, stations in all markets are free to air whatever they please. Most stations have filled the time slot with syndicated programs. Quiz and game shows, as well as off-network situation comedies, have proved very strong in this period. News magazine programs enable stations to inherit adults from the preceding newscasts.

Network Prime Time (8:00 P.M. to 11:00 P.M.)   Most affiliates carry network programming during this entire daypart. If a network program is not competitive, or if most of the network's schedule on a given night is faring poorly, the station may consider preempting and substituting its own programming. Syndicated entertainment programs can fill a 30- or 60-minute period, while movies may produce the desired audience for periods of 90 minutes or two hours.

Late Fringe (11:00 P.M. to 11:35 P.M.)   Affiliated stations usually air their late local news in this time slot.

Late Night (11:35 P.M. to 2:05 A.M.)   NBC provides affiliates with programming for the entire period, and CBS programs all but 30 minutes. ABC fills only the 11:35 P.M. to 1:05 A.M. slot. Options for CBS and ABC affiliates include off-network situation comedies and, for ABC affiliates, syndicated talk or entertainment-based programs and off-network dramatic series.

Overnight (2:05 A.M. to 6:00 A.M.)   Affiliates that remain on the air usually carry news fed by the network during part or all of the period.

Weekend scheduling is influenced by network sports programming, which varies from season to season. On Saturday afternoons, the station may have to program a period of two or more hours. Syndicated entertainment and feature films are among the most popular options. Many stations air a 30-minute local newscast at 6:00 P.M. and follow network news with a one-hour or two 30-minute syndicated entertainment programs from 7:00 to 8:00 P.M. Local late news follows network prime time on many affiliated stations. ABC and CBS affiliates do not receive network programming during late night and often run movies, syndicated talk, off-network drama series, or situation come-dies in the time periods.

Many affiliates carry religion, public affairs, or children's programs on Sunday mornings before joining the network for news-magazine and news-interview broadcasts. Depending on the season, the station may have to schedule afternoon programs before or after network sports. Again, syndicat-ed entertainment and feature films are common choices, with local and net-work news between 6:00 and 7:00 P.M. After network prime time, most affil-iates air a 30-minute local newscast. Movies, syndicated entertainment, and religion are among the alternatives for the late-night period.

PROGRAMMING THE INDEPENDENT STATION

Programming an independent television station is a most challenging job. The challenge is less difficult for stations affiliated with Fox, The WB, and UPN, which receive varying amounts of programming from their networks. However, programmers still are left with many hours to fill each day, and independents cannot rely to the same degree as competing affiliates on net-work programs to encourage the flow of viewers into locally scheduled time periods, thus enhancing not only audience size but also the value of time the station sells to advertisers.

131

By definition, the true independent does not have access to programs on any permanent network, many of which attract large audiences to the affili-ates with which it competes. It does not benefit from network promotion and publicity, which draw viewers to the affiliates. Unlike the affiliate, the true independent must provide all the programs it airs, a task that has been aggra-vated by the increased competition for attractive off-network syndicated pro-grams and by their growing cost.

The independent does not enjoy the comparatively high rates that affiliates can charge advertisers for time in and around network programs. Further, the independent often has to contend with a negative attitude on the part of time buyers.

The challenge is difficult but not impossible. In large measure, independ-ents' achievements have been based on the wisdom of their program selection, the imagination of their promotion efforts and, above all, on the effectiveness of their program scheduling.

For the most part, the programming weapons of independents have been movies, syndicated talk, off-network entertainment programs—especially sit-uation comedies and action-drama series—syndicated or local children's pro-grams, and live sports. Many independents also carry specials and, occasion-ally, programs rejected by affiliates.

Network promotion has aided Fox affiliates in positioning themselves, while station promotion has enabled true independents to benefit from their image as a source of alternative programming or as the station to watch for movies or sports. However, positioning the independent is becoming more difficult with the increase in both alternative and specialized program offer-ings on cable and DBS.

At the heart of the strategy of many independents is the realization that it is unrealistic to try to beat affiliates in all time periods. Rather, they have identified dayparts in which they can compete and have programmed accordingly. Generally, the dayparts have been those in which all affiliates seek similar audiences or in which parts of the available audience have been unserved or underserved. Their strategy has been based chiefly on counter-programming.

The success of their counter-programming points to one of the few programming advantages enjoyed by true independent stations: flexibility in scheduling. Affiliates are expected to carry most of the programming of their networks. The network schedule also determines the amount and times of locally programmed periods. The independent, on the other hand, is free to develop its own schedule and to take advantage of the opportunities to attract audiences whose interests are not being satisfied. Among the best opportunities for counter-programming on weekdays are the following:

Early Morning

While most affiliates are carrying adult-appeal network or local news-magazine shows or local news programs, the independent can capture children with syndicated cartoons or locally produced children's programs.

Afternoon

With affiliates of ABC, CBS, and NBC airing network soap operas, the independent has taken advantage of the abundance of syndicated talk programs to offer an alternative. Off-network situation comedies and male-oriented action dramas also have proved effective options. As the daypart progresses, cartoons and other child- and teenage-appeal content is favored by many stations. WB affiliates receive young-adult programming from the network during the last hour of the period.

Early Fringe

The WB fills the first hour of the daypart for their affiliates with more young-adult programs. Many stations move to a block of off-network situation comedies with appeal to both adults and children. The strategy also serves as a counter to local news, which usually starts before the end of the period, and as a bridge to the adult-appeal programming that follows. True independents also look to situation comedies or counter with off-network reality shows and hour-long dramas.

Early Evening

An excellent opportunity to counter-program with off-network entertainment is offered during this traditional news block on affiliated stations.

Prime Access

The independent can benefit from audience flow in the 7:00 to 8:00 P.M. period by airing additional entertainment. An alternative for true independents would be to start a two-hour movie at 7:00 P.M. in an attempt to attract adults and hold them during the first hour of network prime time.

Late Fringe

During this period, most affiliates of the three original networks broadcast local news. Independents are able to counter with adult-appeal entertainment programs, such as situation comedies, action dramas, or movies.

Overnight

Entertainment of any kind geared toward adults provides an alternative to news broadcasts on affiliates of the original networks.

Most other periods do not offer significant advantages to independent stations, though effective counter-programming still is possible.

During the morning hours when affiliates are not receiving network programs, the independent is on an equal footing. Homemakers constitute a significant part of the available audience and are the principal target of advertisers. With their appeal to women in the 25 to 54 age group, movies could offer strong competition to the affiliates' offerings. Alternatives include syndicated talk and off-network situation comedies and dramatic series with strong female appeal. Similar programs may be the most effective way of competing against the network soap operas before the return of children in midafternoon.

Prime time poses a difficult problem for the true independent. The networks' lineup of entertainment programs attracts large audiences during this period. Movies, off-network dramatic series, and specials offer the best opportunities to attract audiences. From 10:00 to 10:30 or 11:00 P.M., the independent can counter entertainment on the affiliates with local news.

In the late-night daypart, syndicated talk-variety, off-network situation comedies and adventure dramas, or movies are effective competition against network programming.

Weekends provide true independent stations with several opportunities to counter-program. While affiliates are carrying network cartoons or other child- or teen-appeal programs on Saturday mornings, the independent may target adults and older teenagers with movies or sports, such as wrestling. Syndicated popular music, adventure drama, and movies offer alternatives to network sports during the afternoons.

As noted earlier, affiliate programming on Sunday mornings consists primarily of religion, public affairs, and network news magazines and news interviews. The independent station can attract children with cartoons, and young viewers and adults with situation comedies and adventure dramas. Movies are another vehicle to bring adults to the set. Popular-music programs and movies are among the most attractive alternatives to network sports on Sunday afternoons, though some independents go head-to-head against affiliates with regional or minor sports.

133

PROGRAMMING AND THE STATION REPRESENTATIVE

The traditional role of the station representative firm, or station rep, has been to sell time on client stations to national spot advertisers. However, in the increasingly competitive environment in which television stations operate, reps have assumed an important role in local station programming. Today, rep firms have departments that are experienced in advising stations on the purchasing, scheduling, and promotion of programs.

The move is not surprising. After all, the more attractive the station's programming, the easier it is to sell time. Competitive programming requires sound information and advice on which to base program purchase and scheduling decisions. The rep can provide such services.

The rep has access to a wealth of information that can be used to strengthen the station's position. Details of the current performance of network offerings and network program plans, including specials, can provide the station with useful insights for its own planning.

The rep knows which syndicated programs are available or are about to become available. Additionally, the rep is privy to a wide range of information on such programs, including the track records of those that have been broadcast, how they fared in other markets or geographic areas similar to that of the client station, their strength against different kinds of competing programs and among different demographics, and, with off-network programs, how they performed when they were broadcast originally in the market. Using this and other information, the rep can recommend desirable program purchases and realistic purchase prices.

With a proposed new program, the challenge is more difficult. An important consideration is whether it will actually make it to the air. The rep firm programming department can evaluate the program's prospects before the station commits to it. If a commitment is made, the rep can suggest likely demographic appeal and possible time periods.

The rep programmer also has information on the availability of feature film packages and the performance of individual films in movie theater and network showings.

It has been emphasized that a station's programming success derives not only from individual programs, but the way in which they are assembled in a schedule. Here, again, the rep's expertise can be valuable.

Through a close study of the market and competing stations, the rep can identify strengths and weaknesses in the station's current schedule and propose appropriate changes. It is unlikely that the rep will recommend program purchases in isolation. Generally, such purchases are proposed with an eye to strengthening a daypart, not just a time period.

The rep firm can help the station decide on expanding or contracting the amount of local news programming. For example, the station may be considering adding a half-hour to its early news, starting a Saturday morning newscast, or supplying a newscast to the local independent station. The rep can analyze what has happened in other markets under similar circumstances and can assist the station in making intelligent forecasts in its own market. To achieve the strongest possible lead-in for early news, the rep routinely aids the station in programming the early-fringe time period.

PROGRAMMING FOR CHILDREN

Television stations have wide discretion in selecting the programs they broadcast. Children's programming is a notable exception.

In accordance with the terms of the Children's Television Act (CTA) of 1990 and the FCC rules adopted under the act, commercial and noncommercial licensees are required to serve the educational and informational needs of children through their programming. Nonbroadcast efforts that enhance the value of such programming, and efforts to produce or support programming by another station in the market, also may contribute to meeting the requirements.

Children's programming constitutes an important part of the licensing process. To receive FCC staff-level approval of the CTA portion of its license renewal application, a licensee must demonstrate that it has aired at least three hours per week of *core programming*, averaged over a six-month period.[17] The FCC characterizes such programming as that which meets the following criteria:

1. It has serving the educational and informational needs of children ages 16 and under as a significant purpose;

2. It is aired between the hours of 7:00 A.M. and 10:00 P.M.;

3. It is a regularly scheduled weekly program;

4. It is at least 30 minutes in length;

5. The educational and informational objective and the target child audience are specified in writing in the licensee's *Children's Television Programming Report*; and

6. Instructions for listing the program as educational/informational, including an indication of the age group for which the program is intended, are provided by the licensee to publishers of program guides.[18]

A station that airs "somewhat less" than an average of three hours per week of such programming may still receive staff approval. However, it must show that it has broadcast a package of programming that demonstrates a commitment at least equivalent to airing three hours a week of core programming.

If a station fails to meet either the core or equivalent requirements, its license renewal application is reviewed by the FCC. At that time, the licensee has an opportunity to demonstrate attempts at compliance through nonbroadcast efforts and/or support for programming on another station.

FCC Form 398 (Figure 4.5) provides the means by which a commercial station may document its efforts to satisfy the children's programming requirements. It asks for details of both core and noncore educational and informational programming aired in the preceding calendar quarter, core programming planned for airing in the next quarter, and core programming

Federal Communications Commission
Washington, D. C. 20554

Approved by OMB
3060-0754

FCC 398
Children's Television Programming Report

Report reflects information for quarter ending (mm/dd/yy) _____

1. Call Sign	Channel Number	Community of License				
		City	State	County		ZIP Code
Licensee						

☐ Network Affiliation: _____	☐ Independent	Nielsen DMA	World Wide Web Home Page Address (if applicable)
Facility ID Number	Previous call sign (if applicable)	LicenseRenewal Expiration Date (mmddyy)	

Core Programming

2. State the average number of hours of Core Programming per week broadcast by the station. See 47 C.F.R. Section 73.671(c).

3. Does the licensee identify each Core Program at the beginning of the airing of each program as required by 47 C.F.R. Section 73.673? ☐ Yes ☐ No

4. a. Does the licensee provide information identifying each Core Program aired on its station, including an indication of the target child audience, to publishers of program guides as required by 47 C.F.R. Section 73.673? ☐ Yes ☐ No

   b. Identify publishers who were sent information in 4.a.

5. Complete the following for each program that you aired during the past three months that meets the definition of Core Programming. Complete chart below for each Core Program.

Title of Program:		Origination		
		Local	Network	Syndicated
Days/Times Program Regularly Scheduled:	Total times aired at regularly scheduled time	Number of Preemptions	If preempted, complete Preemption Report	
Length of Program: (minutes)				
Age of Target Child Audience: from _____ years to _____ years.				
Describe the educational and informational objective of the program and how it meets the definition of Core Programming.				

FCC 398 (Page 1)
April 2001

FIGURE 4.5 Children's Television Programming Report (FCC 398).

sponsored by the licensee and aired on any other station in the market. The form must be filed quarterly with the FCC and a copy placed in the station's public inspection file. Noncommercial stations are exempt from filing the form. However, they must meet the programming obligations.

Television broadcasters also are required to alert parents and others to the content of programs through use of a ratings system for all programs except news and sports. That obligation is in response to a mandate in the Telecommunications Act of 1996 and follows an FCC-approved agreement adopted jointly by the National Association of Broadcasters (NAB), the National Cable Television Association (NCTA), and the Motion Picture Association of America (MPAA), and titled *TV Parental Guidelines*.

Non-Core Educational and Informational Programming

6. Complete the following for each program that you aired during the past three months that is specifically designed to meet the educational and informational needs of children ages 16 and under, but does not meet one or more elements of the definition of Core Programming. See 47 C.F.R. Section 73.671. Complete chart below for each additional such educational and informational program.

| Title of Program: | | Origination | | |
		Local	Network	Syndicated

Dates/Times Program Aired:	Total times aired	Number of Preemptions	If preempted and rescheduled, list date and time aired.	
			Dates	Times
Length of Program: (minutes)				
Age of Target Child Audience (if applicable): from __ years to __ years.				
Describe the program.				

Does the program have educating and informing children ages 16 and under as a significant purpose?	☐ Yes ☐ No
If Yes, does the licensee identify each program at the beginning of its airing consistent with 47 C.F.R. Section 73.673?	☐ Yes ☐ No
If Yes, does the licensee provide information regarding the program, including an indication of the target child audience, to publishers of program guides consistent with 47 C.F.R. Section 73.673?	☐ Yes ☐ No

Other Matters

7. Complete the following for each program that you plan to air for the next quarter that meets the definition of Core Programming. Complete chart below for each Core Program.

| Title of Program: | | Origination | | |
		Local	Network	Syndicated

Days/Times Program Regularly Scheduled:	Total times to be aired	Length of Program: (minutes)	Age of Target Child Audience: from ___ years to___ years.
Describe the educational and informational objective of the program and how it meets the definition of Core Programming.			

8. Does the licensee publicize the existence and location of the station's Children's Television Programming Reports (FCC 398) as required by 47 C.F.R. Section 73.3526(e)(11)(iii)?   ☐ Yes ☐ No

FCC 398 (Page 2)
April 2001

137

FIGURE 4.5 *Continued.*

The guidelines apply to programs designed solely for children and to those designed for the entire audience, including children. They consist of seven categories of programs, with additional content indicators for sexual situations, violence, language, and dialogue (see Appendix A, "TV Parental Guidelines").

PROGRAMMING AND THE COMMUNITY

The Communications Act imposes on broadcasters the obligation to serve the public interest, convenience, and necessity. Programming is the principal tool used to satisfy that requirement.

9. List Core Programs, if any, aired by other stations that are sponsored by the licensee and that meet the criteria set forth in 47 C.F.R. Section 73.671. Also indicate whether the amount of total Core Programming broadcast by another station increased.

Name of Program	Call Letters of Station Airing Sponsored Program	Channel Number of Station Airing Sponsored Program	Did total programming increase?
			☐ Yes ☐ No
			☐ Yes ☐ No
			☐ Yes ☐ No

For each Core Program sponsored by the licensee, complete the chart below.

Title of Program:		Origination		
		Local	Network	Syndicated

Days/Times Program Regularly Scheduled:	Total times aired	Number of Preemptions	If preempted and rescheduled, list date and time aired.	
			Dates	Times

Length of Program: _____ (minutes)

Target Child Audience: from _____ years to _____ years.

Describe the educational and informational objective of the program and how it meets the definition of Core Programming.

10. Name of children's programming liaison:

Name	Telephone Number (include area code)
Address	Internet Mail Address (if applicable)
City	State

11. Include any other comments or information you want the Commission to consider in evaluating your compliance with the Children's Television Act (or use this space for supplemental explanations). This may include information on any other non-core educational and informational programming that you aired this quarter or plan to air during the next quarter, or any existing or proposed non-broadcast efforts that will enhance the educational and informational value of such programming to children. See 47 C.F.R. Section 73.671, NOTE 2.

WILLFUL FALSE STATEMENTS MADE ON THIS FORM ARE PUNISHABLE BY FINE AND/OR IMPRISONMENT (U.S. CODE, TITLE 18, SECTION 1001), AND/OR REVOCATION OF ANY STATION LICENSE OR CONSTRUCTION PERMIT (U.S. CODE, TITLE 47, SECTION 312(a)(1)), AND/OR FORFEITURE (U.S. CODE, TITLE 47, SECTION 503).

I certify that the statements in this application are true, complete, and correct to the best of my knowledge and belief, and are made in good faith.

Name of Licensee	Signature
Date	

FCC 398 (Page 3)
April 2001

FIGURE 4.5 *Continued.*

Entertainment dominates the programming of most commercial television stations and music-format radio stations. Information is included in the schedule of most stations and is the sole element for many radio stations.

Problems confronting the community of license must not be overlooked in programming. Every three months, licensees must place in their public file a quarterly list reflecting the station's "most significant programming treatment of community issues."

To help determine the issues of concern, the program manager and others in managerial capacities must develop a personal involvement with the community. Riding the bus to work and speaking with other passengers, and talking with garage attendants, laborers on construction projects, and others out-

PREEMPTION REPORT

Complete the chart below for each core program listed in Question 5 of FCC 398 that was preempted during the past three months.

Title of Program:		
Total Times to be Aired	Number of Preemptions	Number of Preemptions Rescheduled
Date Preempted/Episode #	If rescheduled, date and time rescheduled	Is the rescheduled date the second home? ☐ Yes ☐ No
If rescheduled, were promotional efforts made to notify public of rescheduled date and time? ☐ Yes ☐ No		
Reason for Preemption: ☐ Breaking News ☐ Other News	☐ Sports ☐ Public Interest	☐ Other

FCC 398 (Page 4)
April 2001

FIGURE 4.5 *Continued.*

side the broadcast workplace may result in some valuable insights. Membership in service clubs and nonprofit organizations can be useful too.

The public interest is served best, however, when the station demonstrates a sincere commitment to community service. Many stations render off-air service through participation in, and sponsorship of, selected events. Opportunities through use of the station's air time are numerous. They include the following:

Local Newscasts

Radio and television newscasts are important sources of information on day-to-day events and activities in the community. Investigative reports and series enable the station to bring to public attention questionable or illegal practices by individuals or institutions, often with results that are beneficial to the community.

Public Affairs Programs

Interview programs are the most common method of exploring community issues in depth. On television, such programs often are criticized for their reliance on "talking heads." Radio stations find it difficult to engage the sustained interest of listeners accustomed to almost continuous music. Nevertheless, public affairs programs of this kind can be instructive and allow the station to compensate for the brevity with which complex issues usually are covered in newscasts.

Station Editorials

Editorials offer the station the opportunity to focus listener or viewer attention on community issues and problems and to play a leadership role in effecting change.

Public Service Announcements (PSAs)

Most PSAs contain information about the activities of nonprofit groups. The NAB reported that they accounted for more than $7 billion of the estimated $9 billion plus in public service provided by broadcast stations in 2003.[19]

Radiothons and Telethons

Raising funds to support their activities is a constant challenge for most nonprofit organizations. Many broadcast stations have become partners in that endeavor by donating air time for radiothons or telethons or by making time available at a modest cost.

Such methods of serving the public interest can go far toward stilling criticisms that broadcast stations are merely vendors of entertainment. In addition, they can lead to improved ratings and increased business by enhancing the station's image in the community.

Active participation in the community, and service to it, are valuable tools for forestalling threats from citizen groups and fending off challenges to license renewal. They also permit the station to show that it is living up to its responsibility as a public trustee.

The discharge of that responsibility has become even more important in this era of deregulation. Instead of dictating standards, the FCC has entrusted to listeners and viewers the task of deciding the public's interest. However, the FCC retains its responsibility to ensure that broadcasters remain responsive to the needs, interests, and tastes of their audiences.

WHAT'S AHEAD?

Broadcast programmers will have to respond to the realization that the nation is growing older. The Census Bureau reported that, in 2004, the median age was 36, up from 33 in 1990 and 30 in 1980.[20] And it will continue to increase through 2035.

A dominant factor in this phenomenon is the almost 78 million babies born between 1946 and 1964, the so-called "baby boom" generation. Today, boomers account for about 28 percent of the population and about 48 percent of families.[21]

The aging of the United States offers opportunities for radio and television stations. To capitalize on the trend, they will have to be responsive to the needs of older audiences and their unprecedented buying power with relevant entertainment, news, and information content. However, the challenge may be more difficult than it appears. Account executives will be faced with the task of selling a greater number of persons aged 54+ to advertising agencies enamored with the 18- to 49-year-old demographic.

Programming for another element of the population will find greater favor with the advertising community: ethnics, especially Hispanics and Asians. Their numbers are going up more rapidly than those of any other audience segment. And their presence is not limited to certain markets. Indeed, in the 1990s, both groups registered increases in almost every state. Particularly appealing to advertisers is their significant economic clout. No less impressive is the fact that—with African Americans and other nonwhite ethnics—they constitute almost half of the under-24-year-old population.[22]

Nonetheless, attracting and retaining those and other audiences will not be easy for stations confronting fierce competition. The array of available entertainment and information choices is rendering consumers much more selective in their choice of medium and allocation of time. Finding the content that best suits their needs, and delivering it in a way that fits their lifestyle, will be difficult challenges.

More and more audiophiles are being attracted to the commercial-free music and other content of satellite radio. The number of subscribers to XM Satellite Radio more than doubled in 2004, to more than three million. Sirius Satellite Radio experienced a virtual quadrupling in its number, to over one million.[23] Even though satellite broadcasters' penetration of the radio market is relatively modest so far, it will continue to increase and to drain audience from terrestrial stations. A logical weapon for local broadcasters—one that their satellite competitors cannot match—is their localness, a characteristic that they must employ to their advantage in the struggle for audience.

Television stations have been grappling with the problem of declining audience shares for years. They, too, can benefit from identifying themselves closely with their market. However, one of their best hopes of reversing the flow of viewers to cable and DBS may lie in their utilization of their digital channel allocation.

Initially, most stations were simply using their expanded bandwidth to simulcast their analog feed. However, that was likely to change as the major networks developed their news and weather broadband services for affiliates. Additional impetus for multicasting was expected to result from station contemplation of the appeal of other kinds of content, especially that with pay or subscription potential.

Assistance may come from an unlikely quarter—telephone companies. Such an alliance could lead to a dramatic transformation in stations' traditional

141

business model. A significant boost to a station-telephone company partnership already has come from the chairman of Verizon, a telco striving to compete with cable and DBS in the delivery of television programs. He told broadcasters that his company would be willing to distribute stations' multicast channels over cellphones and its planned Fios TV service.[24] The move could permit broadcasters to profit from an income stream of which they could only dream thus far—subscriber revenues.

Others with video distribution ambitions may also come knocking on TV station doors. One, Crown Castle International, has announced plans for a Digital Video Broadcasting-Handheld (DVB-H) service, capable of delivering to cellphones at least eight television channels in a market. It offers an additional inducement to broadcasters: it would pay retransmission fees to stations providing content.

Another emerging technology that could enhance broadcasters' efforts to reach on-the-go consumers—and generate new revenues—is the iPod. Product sales have been brisk and have attracted the attention of both stations and advertisers. The audio-only digital device is well suited to the delivery of a range of radio station content. However, it may be attractive to TV stations, too. Some already have been willing to surrender their distinguishing video feature to offer "podcasts," sound-only versions of their newscasts.

Other TV stations are launching customized online newscasts or re-running edited versions of newscasts online. That practice is expected to grow.

These trends underline what is becoming a crucial programming goal: to attain the widest possible distribution and to mine as many advertiser and consumer dollars as possible.

SUMMARY

Radio and television station programming reaches virtually every household in the United States. It is influenced by the interests of the audience, the broadcaster, the advertiser, and the regulator.

Entertainment is the dominant program element both in radio and television, with the exception of information-format radio stations. However, most stations broadcast a variety of other programs.

Responsibility for a station's programming rests with the program department, headed by a program manager or program director. In a music-format radio station, department staff generally includes a music director and announcers. In a station with an information format, editors, producers, hosts, anchors, reporters, writers, and desk assistants constitute the majority of the staff. In many television stations, the program department comprises only of a program director. The principal duties of the head of the program department are to plan, acquire, execute, and control the station's programming. To carry out those duties effectively requires knowledge, administrative and professional skills, and certain personal qualities.

The programming of most radio stations revolves around one principal content element, called a format. Usually it is designed to appeal to a particular subgroup of the population, identified by age, ethnicity, or socioeconomic status. Music is the most common format. Other format categories are information and specialty.

The major sources of radio station programs are the station itself, syndicators who distribute both programs and entire music formats, and networks.

In developing a programming strategy, a radio station selects a format and decides how to execute it. Consistency of sound is a major consideration, and stations seek to attain it through use of a format wheel or clock. The wheel identifies the combination of content elements in a one-hour period and the sequence in which each element is aired. All-news stations broadcast their content in cycles, with a period of time elapsing before each element is repeated. Other important strategic considerations include dayparting, playlist selection, music rotation, and the frequency and length of commercial interruptions.

Television station programming is quite different from radio station programming. In radio, a major goal is to identify a segment of the population and broadcast to it throughout the day. In television, the programmer seeks to attract and retain those persons who are available to view.

Network affiliates use three major program sources: the network, program and feature film syndicators, and the station itself. Independent stations rely on syndicators, station productions, and ad-hoc networks.

In acquiring and scheduling programs, the television station program manager considers many factors. Chief among them are the programming of competing stations, the potential audience, and the station's program budget. Attention is also paid to the possibility of building audience flow and habit. The basic scheduling strategies are head-to-head, counter, strip, checkerboard, and block.

The three original networks—ABC, CBS, and NBC—fill a large part of their affiliates' schedules. Fox, The WB, and UPN provide considerably less programming to their affiliates. Independent stations, must program all time periods themselves.

Despite the challenge, many independents have achieved profitability by concentrating on dayparts in which they can compete effectively. Counterprogramming has played an important part in their success.

Many television stations seek program information from their rep company, which is aware of the availability and performance of all syndicated programming. Additionally, the rep can offer advice on scheduling and promoting programs.

Television stations are required to air programming that meets the educational and informational needs of children and to use a ratings system for all content, except news and sports.

Programming is the chief method whereby stations carry out their obligation to serve the public interest. They are required to treat community issues and can use their airtime in a variety of ways to demonstrate a commitment to public service. Service also can be rendered by station involvement in community activities.

Increasingly, broadcast station programmers will have to respond to the needs of audiences that are older and ethnically more diverse. One tool for staving off the intense competition they face is their localness. Partnerships with telephone companies offer the promise of wider program distribution and additional revenue streams for Radio Stations.

CASE STUDY: RADIO

You are program director of an FM station with an oldies format in a medium market in the Southwest.

The station adopted the format 15 years ago and has faced no format competition.

The total audience numbers have remained fairly consistent. Regularly, you place among the top ten stations in the 20-station market among persons aged 12+.

However, your audience has been aging. And that is having a negative impact on your appeal to ad agencies, whose primary demo is persons aged 25 to 54.

That demo dropped from 71 percent of your audience in 1998 to 68 percent in 2001. Today, it is down to just 60 percent and will continue to fall. Simultaneously, your aged 55+ audience is increasing. It has gone from 21 percent in 1998 to 32 percent and will keep on growing.

General manager Dan Smith has called you to a meeting. General sales manager Mary Reece also will attend. Dan is reacting to an inquiry from your group's regional manager, who is concerned about the decline in agency buys on the station. Mary has a similar concern. The goal of the meeting is to develop a plan of action.

Dan has concluded that there are three options: (1) change the format to appeal to a younger demo already targeted by one or more stations in the market; (2) adjust the current format to try to retain current listeners and attract new listeners from a younger demo; (3) try to sell your older demos to agencies.

EXERCISES

1. What are the pros and cons of each of Dan's options?

2. Are there additional options? If so, what are they?

3. How realistic is Dan's third option? Explain.

CASE STUDY: TELEVISION

You are program director of a CBS affiliate in a top-100 market in the Southeast. The market is also served by affiliates of ABC, Fox, NBC, The WB, and PBS. There is no UPN affiliate. Comcast provides cable services.

Your general manager has just returned from a meeting of the company's board of directors. There, a decision was taken that all stations in the group—including yours—must explore options of using their digital allocation for multicast services.

144

The board will be meeting again in four weeks. At that time, your general manager will be required to submit a report and the station's recommendations. The GM has asked for your thoughts on the following questions.

EXERCISES

1. Are additional network programs a possibility? If so, which?

2. Could locally produced, advertiser-supported programs be part of the mix? If so, describe them.

3. Are there possibilities for subscription or paid programming blocks? If so, what are they?

4. Are there other services that could be offered? If so, which?

5. What are your recommendations? How do you support them?

NOTES

[1] *Radio Today: How America Listens to Radio*, 2005 Edition, p. 3. http://www.arbitron.com.

[2] *2004–2005 Radio Marketing Guide and Fact Book*, p. 14. http://www.rab.com.

[3] *Radio Today: How America Listens to Radio*, 2005 Edition, p. 3.

[4] *TV Basics*. http://www.tvb.org.

[5] *Radio Today: How America Listens to Radio*, 2005 Edition, p. 6.

[6] *Radio Today: How America Listens to Radio*, 2005 Edition, p. 5.

[7] *1998 Report on Television*, p. 17.

[8] *Ibid.*

[9] *1998 Report on Television*, p. 18.

[10] J. David Lewis, "Programmer's Choice: Eight Factors in Program Decision-Making," *Journal of Broadcasting*, 14:1 (Winter 1969–1970), pp. 74–75.

[11] *Radio Today: How America Listens to Radio*, 2005 Edition.

[12] Harriett Tramer and Leo W. Jeffres, "Talk Radio—Forum and Companion," *Journal of Broadcasting*, 27:3 (Summer 1983), p. 300.

[13] Other categories are *off-first run*, *off-Fox*, and *off-cable*. The first refers to series produced for syndication with only a limited number of episodes but now with enough to permit daily broadcast, or stripping. The second indicates that the series was carried originally on the Fox network, and the third on a cable network.

[14] Syndicators of some highly successful network programs have sold off-network syndicated rights by confidential bid rather than negotiation. "The Cosby Show" and "Who's the Boss?" are examples.

[15] Remote-control pads have given rise to another habit that causes headaches for the program manager. Many viewers employ them to scan the dial continuously, a practice known as *grazing*. The virtual saturation of the remote control also has implications for the sales department as viewers practice *zapping*, the term given to

145

changing channels to avoid commercials. The device also permits *zipping*, the fast-forwarding of videocassette recorders through commercials in recorded programs.

[16] *Broadcast Financial Journal*, March 1976, p. 23. Used with permission of Broadcast Cable Financial Management Association.

[17] Broadcasters that use their digital channels to multicast six programming streams must offer up to 18 hours of educational and informational programming. Both analog and digital broadcasters also must display an on-air "E/I" symbol throughout such programming.

[18] 47 CFR 73.671(c).

[19] Harry A. Jessell, "Stations' Good Deeds Worth $9.6 Billion," *Broadcasting & Cable*, June 14, 2004, p. 13.

[20] http://www.census.gov.

[21] http://www.metlife.com.

[22] Steve Smith, "The Next Ethnic Wave: TV for Asian Americans," *TelevisionWeek*, October 25, 2004, p. 8.

[23] "Satellite Radio Posts Subscriber gains," *Chattanooga Times Free Press*, December 28, 2004, p. C5.

[24] Daisy Whitney, "Moving Beyond the Old TV Model," *TelevisionWeek*, April 25, 2005, p. 42.

146

ADDITIONAL READINGS

Broadcasting & Cable Yearbook. New Providence, NJ: R.R. Bowker, published annually.

Eastman, Susan Tyler, and Douglas A. Ferguson. *Media Programming: Strategies and Practices*, 7th ed. Belmont, CA: Thomson Wadsworth, 2006.

Hausman, Carl, Philip Benoit, Frank Messere, and Lewis O'Donnell. *Modern Radio Production: Production, Programming, and Performance*, 6th ed. Belmont, CA: Thomson Wadsworth, 2004.

Lynch, Joanna R., and Greg Gillispie. *Process and Practice of Radio Programming*. Lanham, MD: University Press of America, 1998.

MacFarland, David T. *Future Radio Programming Strategies: Cultivating Listenership in the Digital Age*, 2nd ed. Mahwah, NJ: Lawrence Erlbaum, 1997.

Miles, Peggy. *Internet World Guide to Webcasting: The Complete Guide to Broadcasting on the Web*. New York: John Wiley, 1998.

Norberg, Eric G. *Radio Programming: Tactics and Strategy*. Boston: Focal Press, 1996.

Perebinossoff, Philippe, Brian Gross, and Lynne S. Gross. *Programming for TV, Radio and the Internet: Strategy, Development and Evaluation*, 2nd ed. Boston: Focal Press, 2005.

Warren, Steve. *Radio: The Book*, 4th ed. Boston: Focal Press, 2004.

Broadcast Sales 5

This chapter considers

- the functions of the sales department and the responsibilities and attributes of its personnel
- the sale of time to local, regional, and national advertisers
- research methods and the uses of research in sales

A broadcast station serves two kinds of customers:

Audiences, which tune to a station to hear or view its programs and which make no direct payment for the product (i.e., programs) they receive. As we have seen, obtaining audiences is the responsibility of the program department.

Advertisers, who gain access to those audiences with information on their products and services by purchasing advertising time. Obtaining advertisers is the responsibility of the sales department.

Broadcast advertisers fall into three categories:

Local: Those in the immediate geographical area of the station.

Regional: Those whose products or services are available in the area covered by the station.

National: Those whose products or services are available nationwide, including the area covered by the station.

Time is sold to local and regional advertisers by members of the station's sales staff called *account executives*. Sales to national advertisers are carried out by the station's national sales manager or by its national sales representative, known as the *station representative (station rep) company*.

The sales department is the principal generator of revenues for the station. However, its ability to sell time is determined to a large degree by the program department's success in drawing audiences, especially those that advertisers want to reach. Good programming attracts audiences, which in turn attract advertisers and dollars. The greater the sales revenues, the better the programming the station can provide. Together, therefore, the program department and the sales department are important parts of a cycle that has a major impact on the station's financial strength.

THE SALES DEPARTMENT

The number of sales department employees of a particular station is influenced largely by market size. Local competitive conditions also may be influential. However, departments in markets of all sizes have similar responsibilities.

FUNCTIONS

The major functions of the sales department are to

- sell time to advertisers
- provide vehicles whereby advertisers can reach targeted audiences with their commercial messages at a competitive cost
- develop promotions for advertisers
- generate sufficient revenues to permit the station to operate competitively

- produce a profit for the station's owners
- contribute to the worth of the station by developing and maintaining a strong base of advertiser support

ORGANIZATION

The staff and activities of the department are directed by a general sales manager (GSM), who answers to the general manager and whose specific responsibilities are described later. The following are the principal department staff:

NATIONAL SALES MANAGER

Coordinating the sale of time to national advertisers through the station rep company and maintaining contacts with local offices of national accounts are the chief responsibilities of the national sales manager, who reports to the general sales manager. In many stations, the duties are carried out by the general sales manager.

LOCAL SALES MANAGER

The local sales manager reports to the general sales manager and is responsible for

- planning and administering local and regional sales
- directing and supervising account executives
- assigning actual or prospective clients to account executives
- establishing account executive sales quotas
- in some stations, carrying a list of clients

ACCOUNT EXECUTIVES

Account executives report to the local sales manager and

- seek out and develop new accounts
- service existing accounts
- prepare and make sales presentations
- in radio, often write and produce commercials

CO-OP COORDINATOR

Many manufacturers reimburse retailers for part of the cost of advertising that promotes the manufacturer's product. This arrangement is known as *cooperative*, or *co-op*, *advertising*, and stations often employ a coordinator to provide co-op data to account executives. However, the responsibilities may be more extensive and may consist of

- identifying co-op opportunities
- working with retailers in the development of co-op campaigns using advertising allowance credits, called *accruals*

- handling the various elements of the campaign, such as copy and production, and overseeing the campaign's execution
- assisting retailers in filing for reimbursement of co-op expenditures

In many stations, the co-op coordinator's job has evolved to include vendor support programs. They will be discussed later in the chapter.

Once sales orders have been received and checked by the sales manager, they are confirmed and processed. Those are among the responsibilities of the traffic department, which often is a unit of the sales department. It is headed by a *traffic manager*, who reports to the general sales manager. The traffic department also

- prepares the daily program log detailing all content to be aired, including commercials
- maintains and keeps current a list of availabilities, called *avails* — in other words, time available for purchase by advertisers
- advises the sales department and the station rep company of avails
- schedules commercials and enters appropriate details on the program log
- checks that commercials are aired as ordered and scheduled
- advises the general sales manager if commercials are not broadcast or are not broadcast as scheduled, and coordinates the scheduling of *make-goods*

Clients who do not use the services of an advertising agency often require the station's assistance in writing and producing commercials. The writing usually is assigned to copywriters in the *continuity* or *creative services department*, which may be a unit of the sales or program department and which is headed by a director. Commercial production is carried out by the production staff.

THE GENERAL SALES MANAGER

RESPONSIBILITIES

Like all managers, the general sales manager plans, organizes, influences, and controls. The proportion of time spent on those and other functions varies. In a large station, for example, the position may be chiefly administrative. In a smaller station, the general sales manager may be a combination national and local/regional sales manager and account executive. However, included in the major responsibilities of most general sales managers are the following:

- Developing overall sales objectives and strategies. They are drawn up in agreement with the station rep and national sales manager for national sales, and with the local sales manager for local and regional sales.
- Selecting the station representative company, in consultation with the general manager and the national sales manager.

- Preparing and controlling the department's budget, and coordinating with the business department collections, the processing of delinquent accounts, and credit checks on prospective clients.

- Developing the rate card and controlling the advertising inventory.

- Selecting, or approving the selection of, all departmental personnel and arranging for their training, if necessary.

- Setting and enforcing sales policies, and reviewing all commercial copy, recorded commercials, and sales contracts.

General sales managers engage in a variety of other duties, including the conduct of sales meetings, approval of account executive client lists, and the handling of *house accounts*, or accounts that require no selling or servicing and on which no commissions are paid. However, one of their most significant activities is the establishment of sales quotas.

The importance of revenue and expense projections in the preparation of the station's annual budget was noted in Chapter 2, "Financial Management." As the major generator of revenues, the sales department plays a key role in the station's success. If its projections are unrealistic and fall short of expectations, cost-cutting measures will have to be introduced to keep the budget in balance. Those measures might include the termination of personnel and the modification or elimination of plans for equipment purchases, programming, promotion, and other areas of station operation.

To try to avoid such an upheaval, most sales departments establish attainable annual dollar targets. In many stations, account executives are asked to submit their sales goals for each month of the next fiscal or calendar year, reflecting adjustments for the number of weeks per month compared to the current year and the proposed percentage increase. The GSM and the local sales manager review them, determine their appropriateness, and make changes they deem necessary. Finally, the sales managers meet with each account executive and, together, the three agree on a final quota. In the meantime, the GSM consults with the station rep to settle on targets for national sales.

When these steps have been completed, the GSM sends to the general manager the department's budget proposal listing projected revenues from local, regional, and national sales and estimated expenses. It is analyzed with the submissions from other departments, and adjustments are made to develop a balanced budget. They may consist of a reduction in requested expenditures, an increase in revenues, or both. If more revenues are called for, the GSM considers the options with the local sales manager, account executives, and the station rep, and higher goals are established by mutual agreement.

Monthly goals provide continuing, short-term targets. They may not always be met. A delay in receipt of an order, a change in a client's advertising schedule, or a temporary lull in the economy can play havoc with an account executive's expectations in a single month. Accordingly, much more serious attention is paid to the attainment of quarterly goals.

If business remains sluggish over an extended period, the general sales manager will contemplate steps to revive it. Rates may be lowered temporarily, for example. Additional sales incentives may be introduced. One station offered a ski trip to account executives who made calls on ten potential new clients

151

in two weeks and completed at least one sale. All met the challenge and won a trip, and the station wrote $10,000 in brand new business. Of course, if these and other actions fail to produce the projected revenues, the only alternative will be a reduction in expenditures.

QUALITIES

To be effective, a GSM must possess many attributes. Chief among them are *knowledge*, administrative and professional *skills*, and certain *personal qualities*.

Knowledge   The general sales manager should have knowledge of

Station ownership and management: The objectives and plans of the station's owners and the general manager, and the role of the sales department in accomplishing them.

The station and staff: The station's strengths and weaknesses as an advertising medium, and the ways in which the sales function relates to the activities and functions of other departments; awareness of the motivations, potential, and limitations of sales department employees, and of their working relationship with staff in other departments.

The market and the competition: Population makeup, employment patterns, cultural and recreational activities, and business climate and trends; the sales activities and plans of competing stations and media, their successes and failures.

Sales management: The responsibilities of sales management and ways of discharging them. This includes familiarity with techniques, practices, and trends in broadcast sales and advertising; methods of estimating revenues and expenses, and of increasing revenues and controlling costs; methods, sources, and uses of marketing, sales, and audience research; marketing and sales techniques and practices, especially those used by retail stores and service companies; and the business, sales, and advertising objectives of clients and their past and present advertising practices.

Content and audiences: Types of formats, programs, and other content, their demographic appeal, and audience listening or viewing habits.

Skills   Knowledge will be translated into success only if the general sales manager is able to combine it with both managerial and professional competence in

- planning the department's objectives and strategies, explaining and justifying them to the general manager, and coordinating their accomplishment with staff and other departments

- organizing personnel and activities to attain stated objectives, and stimulating and directing employees toward their attainment

- managing the advertising inventory—that is, balancing the number of commercial units, availabilities, and cost-per-spot to maximize revenue

- controlling the department's activities by careful attention to budget, personnel strengths and shortcomings, the achievements of competing stations and media, and research findings, and by taking appropriate actions

Personal Qualities   Selling often is referred to as a "people" business. For that reason, the GSM must be able to get along with people, both inside and outside the station. An outgoing personality, combined with a cooperative attitude and high ethical standards, are absolute necessities. But a friendly exterior will not spell success in the absence of other qualities.

General sales managers are charged with generating the bulk of the station's revenues. Accordingly, they have to be

- *ambitious* in striving for the accomplishment of objectives
- *competitive* in approaching their responsibilities and meeting the challenges posed by other stations and media
- *persuasive* in their dealings with clients, advertising agencies, and the station rep

Finally, they must be *adaptable* to changing business conditions, and *creative* in developing sales techniques and promotions and in motivating their staff.

153

TIME SALES

Time is sold to advertisers by the second. The majority of sales in radio are 60-second spot announcements, called *spots*. In television, the 30-second spot is standard, and a limited number of 15- and 10-second spots are also available. Many broadcast stations also sell blocks of time for the airing of programs.

THE RATE CARD

Traditionally, radio stations listed the cost of time on a published rate card. The major factors in determining cost were the time of day at which the spots were to run and the number of spots purchased, hence the name *frequency card*.

In time, most stations moved to a *grid card* in which the principal determinants are the supply of, and demand for, time. Grid cards are still used by many radio stations. Increasingly, however, computerization has permitted stations to introduce an *electronic rate card*. Using revenue goals and a variety of other variables, such as supply and demand, daypart, traditional sellout periods, and the flow of demand during the week, the station may select from a number of software programs to develop its rate structure.

The electronic rate card in Figure 5.1 shows that the station sells time in four dayparts and that the cost of a 60-second spot varies by daypart and day of the week. Morning and afternoon drive times Monday through Friday are in greatest demand and command the highest prices. Costs increase as the

	M	Tu	W	Th	F	Sat	Sun
6:00 A.M.. – 10:00 A.M.	85	85	90	90	95	25	10
10:00 A.M. – 3:00 P.M.	55	55	60	60	65	50	30
3:00 P.M. – 7:00 P.M.	60	60	65	70	70	50	35
7:00 P.M. – 12:00 A.M.	15	15	20	20	25	20	10

FIGURE 5.1 Radio station electronic rate card.

week progresses. Although not included in the rate card, 30-second spots also may be purchased. In addition, the station offers a *Total Audience Plan (TAP)*, whereby advertisers may obtain equal distribution of spots in the first three dayparts or in all four. The station also offers a discount when an advertiser buys an annual or long-term schedule. Stations are willing to give a price break in return for a guarantee of future revenue.

The electronic rate card offers several advantages. It compels the sales manager to pay continuing attention to inventory. As a result, inventory should be easier to manage and the station should be able to generate maximum revenues by pricing available time to reflect current supply and demand. At the same time, however, it reduces the account executive's flexibility because special rates cannot be offered. Clients also may conclude that rates are negotiable because of their wide variation.

In addition to selling by daypart, most radio stations sell sponsorships in certain programs (e.g., news, sports) and in daily features (e.g., business report), with specific rates for each.

For the most part, television stations sell time in, and adjacent to, programs and not by daypart. They have used grid cards for many years to adjust rates in response to demand.

Figure 5.2 shows part of a grid rate card used by a television station that sells at five levels. As an example of how the selling level is determined, assume that demand for time in "Entertainment Tonight" is low. An advertiser may be able to buy 30-second spots at level 5, or $100 each. However, if demand is high, the advertiser may have to pay $450 at level 1.

Note the following:

- Local news is in high demand and is priced accordingly.

- Prices of other programs rise and fall as audience size increases and decreases.

- The same rates are set for the one-hour game show block, the two-hour afternoon soap opera block, and the one-hour evening magazine block, without regard to the program in which the spot appears.

154

- Only the cost of 30-second spots is included on the card. However, other lengths are sold: 60-second spots at double the 30-second rate, and 15- and 10-second spots at 75 percent and 50 percent of the 30-second rate, respectively.

The station offers a discount to advertisers in its unsold inventory program. If time is not sold, the station is authorized to air participating advertisers' spots up to a maximum monthly dollar amount.

The rate card in Figure 5.2 reflects costs in regularly scheduled, Monday through Friday programs on a network-affiliated station. Costs vary according to audience size for network prime-time programs. They vary, too, for

Monday to Friday						
		30 Seconds				
		1	2	3	4	5
A.M.						
4:30–5:00	Early Today	50	40	30	20	10
5:00–5:30	Action News at 5:00	70	60	50	40	30
5:30–6:00	Action News at 5:30	150	125	100	80	60
6:00–7:00	Action News Today	300	250	200	175	150
7:00–9:00	Today Show	250	200	175	150	100
9:00–10:00	Today Show	125	100	80	70	60
10:00–11:00	Ellen	80	70	60	50	40
11:00–12:00	Starting Over	50	40	30	20	10
P.M.						
12:00–12:30	Hollywood Squares	50	40	30	20	10
12:30–1:00	Family Feud	50	40	30	20	10
1:00–2:00	Days of Our Lives	125	100	80	70	60
2:00–3:00	Passions	125	100	80	70	60
3:00–4:00	Dr. Phil	175	150	100	80	60
4:00–5:00	Montel Williams	100	70	60	50	40
5:00–5:30	Action News at 5:00	300	250	200	175	125
5:30–6:00	Action News at 5:30	325	300	250	200	150
6:00–6:30	Action News at 6:00	700	600	450	400	250
7:00–7:30	Entertainment Tonight	450	400	350	200	100
7:30–8:00	Inside Edition	450	400	350	200	100
11:00–11:35	Action News Tonight	500	450	400	350	200

FIGURE 5.2 Excerpt from television station grid rate card.

weekend network sports programs, specials, and movies, and are influenced by the anticipated appeal of each to the station's audience. Special rates are used for news updates, which usually include a 10-second spot and an open billboard announcing sponsorship.

Even though a rate card lists the costs of time, cash does not always change hands every time an advertiser obtains time on a broadcast station. Many stations exchange time for merchandise or services in a transaction known variously as a *trade*, *tradeout*, or *barter*. For example, advertisers may provide the station with travel, food, or furniture for its own use or as contest prizes, in return for advertising time with an equivalent cost. Some stations use trades to persuade hesitant businesses to advertise, and hope that they will be able to convert to a cash sale later. Merchandise or services instead of cash are accepted by many stations to settle delinquent accounts.

Barter programming also is used to acquire time. As noted in Chapter 4, "Broadcast Programming," it permits a syndicator to obtain time, at no cost, for sale to national advertisers in return for supplying programs to the station without charge.

Cooperative, or *co-op*, *advertising* was mentioned earlier in this chapter. It allows a retailer to enjoy the benefits of advertising at less than rate card prices. In a co-op deal, the retailer receives from the manufacturer reimbursement for part or all of the cost of advertising that features the manufacturer's product. The percentage of reimbursement usually is tied to the value of the retailer's product purchase and carries a dollar limit. For instance, a hardware store may buy $20,000 worth of lawnmowers and qualify for 50 percent reimbursement to a maximum of $2,000.

Vendor support programs enable a retailer to obtain manufacturer (vendor) dollars to cover the advertising costs. In a *direct vendor program*, the retailer develops a proposal (often in cooperation with a station account executive) to promote the sale of a product, and presents it to the vendor or product distributor for financial support. For example, a grocery store may plan to highlight a product in an in-store promotion. It may propose a schedule of radio commercials that would advertise both the product and the store. In a *reverse vendor program*, the vendor approaches the retailer with funding to support a promotion. Monies provided under a vendor program are not subject to the kinds of product purchase requirements that apply to co-op, and represent another method whereby a retailer may acquire time without paying rate card prices.

Another method is through *per-inquiry advertising*, whereby an advertiser pays on the basis of the number of responses generated by the advertising. The practice is not widespread, but it is used by some stations, especially with mail-order companies that pay the station a percentage of money received on sales of the advertised product.

Per-inquiry advertising is frowned on by most stations. So, too, is rate cutting, often called "selling below the card" or "selling off the card." Most stations express verbal opposition to cutting rates but many engage in it, especially when business is bad or when an advertiser threatens to make the buy on a competing station unless the rate is reduced.

Some stations disguise rate cutting by awarding advertisers *bonus spots*, also called *spins*. No charge is made for them since they are given as a consideration for buying other spots. The effect is that the advertiser receives time for less than the price quoted on the rate card.

Even though rate cutting may lead to a short-term spurt in sales for the station, it can result in a price war and create instability in the market. It conditions advertisers to believe that prices are negotiable and brings into question the value of commercial time on all stations. Ultimately, of course, it may be self-defeating, since stations have a limited amount of time to sell, and an increase in sales at less than the rate card price may not produce an increase in revenues.

SALES POLICIES

Time is a perishable commodity. Once it has passed, it cannot be sold to an advertiser. This fact imposes on the sales department an obligation to manage its commercial inventory in such a way that it produces the maximum possible financial return.

As a first step, the department must ensure that the rate card is realistic, based on considerations such as the size or characteristics of the audience, market size, and competitive conditions. But inventory management also requires the development of sales policies that will make time available and attractive to advertisers, and that will not result in audience tune-out.

Most stations have policies on the following:

Amounts of Time that May Be Purchased

As noted earlier, radio stations sell mostly commercial units of 60 seconds. Thirty-second units are the norm in television. Longer periods of time usually may be bought in both media for the broadcast of entire programs.

Number of Commercial Breaks per Hour

Most stations limit the number of breaks (called *stop sets* in radio) for commercials and other nonprogram material to reduce the possibility of alienating the audience with frequent interruptions in programming.

Number of Commercials per Break

Stations that have only a few breaks per hour may have to air several minutes of commercials in each to meet revenue needs. Infrequent breaks may please the audience but upset the advertiser, whose commercial may become lost in a succession of announcements, a situation known as *clutter*.

Number of Commercial Minutes per Hour

Again, the goal is to schedule enough commercials to satisfy revenue demands, but not so many as to drive away audiences, especially to competing stations. Many stations continue to adhere to the standards of the now-discontinued radio and television codes of the National Association of Broadcasters (NAB). Under the Radio Code, stations agreed not to broadcast more than 18 minutes of commercials per hour. The Television Code limited network-affiliated stations to not more than 9 minutes and 30 seconds of commercials and other nonprogram material (e.g., promotional announcements) in prime time, and 16 minutes at other times. For independent stations, the limits were 14 and 16 minutes, respectively.

Rate Protection

Most stations guarantee advertisers that the price in effect at the time a sales contract is signed will not change for a specific length of time, even if rates are increased in the meantime.

Product Protection

Advertisers prefer that commercials for competing products or services not be aired adjacent to, or in the same breaks, as theirs. A product protection policy guarantees that a certain time will elapse before such spots are broadcast. In practice, this has become a difficult policy for successful stations to implement. The demand for categories such as automotive, furniture, and fast food often exceeds the TV station's available spot inventory, especially in news and prime-time programs. As a result, many stations no longer guarantee protection. Radio stations often establish protection priorities: (1) one-hour separation, if possible; (2) top and bottom of the hour separation; (3) stop set separation; (4) first and last spot in a stop set. Stations that do guarantee protection may allow advertisers a choice of a rebate, credit, or make-good if spots for competitors run back-to-back for some reason.

Product Acceptance

A policy that states the categories of products or services for which the station will not accept advertising.

Continuity Acceptance

The wording and/or visuals of commercials must meet standards determined by the station.

Make-Goods

When a spot does not run or is aired improperly, the station offers the advertiser a *make-good*, or another time for the commercial.

Additional Costs

A policy on costs the advertiser will incur beyond the purchase of time. Many radio stations include production and talent costs in the rate card price. However, such costs may be added to the purchase price if the commercials are sent for broadcast on other stations.

With two exceptions, a station creates sales policies that are consistent with its revenue objectives and its perception of responsible operation. The first exception grows out of the Children's Television Act of 1990, which directed the Federal Communications Commission (FCC) to adopt rules limiting the amount of commercial matter that television stations may air during children's programming. As a result, the commission approved a restriction on commercial time in programs directed toward viewers 12 and under to 10.5 minutes per hour on weekends and 12 minutes per hour on weekdays. At the same time, it reaffirmed its long-standing prohibition on "program-length commercials" (i.e., programs associated with a product and within which a commercial for the product is broadcast), and on "host selling," or the use of program talent to advertise products.

The second exception applies to both radio and television stations and deals with the sale of time to candidates for public office. The following policies apply.

Access Section 312 of the Communications Act of 1934 As
amended, Section 312 gives the FCC the right to revoke a broadcast station's license "for willful or repeated failure to allow reasonable access to or to permit purchase of reasonable amounts of time for the use of a broadcasting station by a legally qualified candidate for Federal elective office on behalf of his candidacy."

Federal candidates are the only ones to whom a station must grant access or sell time. However, if time is sold to a candidate for any elective office, Section 315(a) of the Communications Act applies:

> If any licensee shall permit any person who is a legally qualified candidate for any public office to use a broadcasting station, he shall afford equal opportunities to all other such candidates for that office in the use of such broadcasting station: *Provided*, that such licensee shall have no power of censorship over the material broadcast under the provision of this section.

159

Charges Section 73.1942(a) of the FCC's Rules and Regulations This section stipulates the prices that the station may charge political candidates:

> The charges, if any, made for the use of any broadcasting station by any person who is a legally qualified candidate for any public office in connection with his or her campaign for nomination for election, or election, to such office shall not exceed: (1) During the 45 days preceding the date of a primary or primary runoff election and during the 60 days preceding the date of a general or special election in which such person is a candidate, the lowest unit charge of the station for the same class and amount of time for the same period. (i) A candidate shall be charged no more per unit than the station charges its most favored commercial advertisers for the same classes and amounts of time for the same periods. Any station practices offered to commercial advertisers that enhance the value of advertising spots must be disclosed and made available to candidates on equal terms. Such practices include but are not limited to any discount privileges that affect the value of advertising, such as bonus spots, time-sensitive make goods, preemption priorities, or any other factors that enhance the value of the announcement. . . . (2) At any time other than the respective periods set forth in paragraph (a) (1) of this section, stations may charge legally qualified candidates for public office no more than the charges made for comparable use of the station by commercial advertisers. The rates, if any, charged all such candidates for the same office shall be uniform and shall not be rebated by any means, direct or indirect. A candidate shall be charged no more than the rate

the station would charge for comparable commercial advertising. All discount privileges otherwise offered by a station to commercial advertisers must be disclosed and made available upon equal terms to all candidates for public office.

Discrimination   Section 73.1941(e)   This section provides that

In making time available to candidates for public office, no licensee shall make any discrimination between candidates in practices, regulations, facilities, or services for or in connection with the service rendered pursuant to this part, or make or give any preference to any candidate for public office or subject any such candidate to any prejudice or disadvantage; nor shall any licensee make any contract or other agreement which shall have the effect of permitting any legally qualified candidate for any public office to broadcast to the exclusion of other legally qualified candidates for the same public office.

Records-Section 73.1943   This section requires stations to maintain and make available for public inspection certain political records:

(a) Every licensee shall keep and permit public inspection of a complete and orderly record (political file) of all requests for broadcast time made by or on behalf of a candidate for public office, together with an appropriate notation showing the disposition made by the licensee of such requests, and the charges made, if any, if the request is granted. The "disposition" includes the schedule of time purchased, when spots actually aired, the rates charged, and the classes of time purchased. (b) When free time is provided for use by or on behalf of candidates, a record of the free time provided shall be placed in the political file. All records required by this paragraph shall be placed in the political file as soon as possible and shall be retained for a period of two years. As soon as possible means immediately absent unusual circumstances.

Time Requests   The candidate is responsible for requesting equal opportunities:

A request for equal opportunities must be submitted to the licensee within 1 week of the day on which the first prior use giving rise to the right of equal opportunities occurred: Provided, however, That where the person was not a candidate at the time of such first prior use, he or she shall submit his or her request within 1 week of the first subsequent use after he or she has become a legally qualified candidate for the office in question.[1]

Proof   Additionally, proving that the equal opportunities provision applies rests with the candidate:

A candidate requesting equal opportunities of the licensee or complaining of noncompliance to the Commission shall have the burden of proving that he or she and his or her opponent are legally qualified candidates for the same public office.[2]

160

LOCAL AND REGIONAL SALES: THE ACCOUNT EXECUTIVE

As indicated earlier, local and regional sales are the responsibility of staff members known as account executives.

Hiring   Success in attaining sales objectives is tied closely to the station's ability to attract and select persons with the appropriate background and personal attributes. If they are selected wisely, the station will reap significant financial returns; if not, the station will face constant turnover, resulting in lost sales, disruptions in relationships with clients, and the time, effort, and expense of finding and training replacements.

SOURCES   Many people are attracted to careers in broadcasting because of the glamour that accompanies work as a disc jockey or television news anchor, or the opportunity for creative expression through writing or production. Relatively few show an initial interest in sales, despite the fact that it offers better financial prospects and an avenue for advancement to top management.

In their search for account executives, stations turn to various sources:

Other stations: Persons working as account executives in other stations in the market bring with them familiarity with broadcast sales, local clients, and the community. Those hired from outside the market are familiar with the first, but have to develop relationships with clients and an awareness of the community.

Other media: Newspapers, outdoor, transit, and other advertising media provide a source of employees with knowledge of sales and advertising and an understanding of the methods, strengths, and shortcomings of the medium in which they have been employed.

Advertising agencies: Awareness of agency practices, clients, and the relative advantages and disadvantages of different media are among the qualities offered by advertising agency account executives and media buyers.

College or university graduates: Broadcasting or communication graduates bring to the position some knowledge of media theory and practices. Business graduates may be equipped similarly in sales and marketing. The best prospects are those who have included in their academic program an internship, or who have gained practical experience through part-time work.

Other: Other sources include persons currently working in the station, especially in sales, traffic, continuity or creative services, or production. They are familiar with the station and its personnel, and should understand the role and responsibilities of the account executive. Persons with a successful background in selling, especially in the sale of intangibles, also may have the experience and potential to succeed.

QUALIFICATIONS   Probably the best predictor of success as an account executive is a record of accomplishment in broadcast sales. However, in selecting among all candidates, the station should consider *knowledge, skills,* and *personal qualities.*

KNOWLEDGE Applicants for account executive positions should have, or show the ability to develop, knowledge of

Broadcast and other media: their operations, personnel, and relative strengths and weaknesses as advertising vehicles.

The station and its competitors: programming, personalities, coverage, and the characteristics of audiences for different formats or programs.

The market: employment, work hours, households, retail sales, consumer spendable income, buying habits, and the listening or viewing population.

Sales and marketing: techniques and practices, and the categories, sales cycles, and special sales periods of retailers.

Research: terminology, and the uses of research in sales.

SKILLS The account executive should have the ability or potential to set and attain objectives, plan and manage time, communicate effectively, keep accurate records, and relate to people and their problems. On a daily basis, skills in preparing and delivering sales presentations, selling and servicing accounts, and interpreting and using research are required.

PERSONAL QUALITIES Ambition, initiative, and energy are prerequisites for anyone seeking success in sales. Persistence, persuasiveness, imagination, integrity, and professionalism in behavior and dress are equally necessary for the broadcast account executive.

162

Training Stations recognize that new employees with little or no experience will be productive only if they understand what is expected of them and are equipped with the knowledge and skills to function effectively. To accomplish those goals, the Television Bureau of Advertising (TVB) partners with The Center for Online Learning in a self-administered and self-paced sales training course over the Internet. The Radio Advertising Bureau (RAB) provides a variety of training opportunities for radio sales personnel. Many stations prefer to organize customized training programs to introduce new account executives to their responsibilities and to the information and techniques they will be required to master to achieve success in the market.

Typically, a program includes details of the station's expectations on the number of contacts and sales presentations, and the amount of business that should be accomplished within a certain period of time. It introduces the employee to the medium, and to the station and its personnel, particularly those departments and people whose work affects, or is affected by, the sales department.

For example, the new account executive should become familiar as soon as possible with the station's format or programming, and with traffic, continuity or creative services, and production personnel and practices. Methods of prospecting or finding new business, preparing and presenting sales proposals, processing orders, maintaining records, and compiling activity reports should also be covered.

Figure 5.3 contains an example of a two-week training program for radio station account executives. In addition to the activities listed, trainees are

Day	Activities
1.	Tour of station and introduction to staff
	Role of the salesperson
	The radio medium
	Advertising on radio
	Presentation by the news director, program director, and a disc jockey
	Rate cards
2.	Attend sales meeting
	Audience research: how to read, understand, and use as a sales tool
	Exercise in the use of research
	Conducting research on clients and prospects
3.	Interpersonal relations: dealing with clients and prospects
	Role-playing exercises on interpersonal relations
	Prospecting
	Making the appointment
4.	Selling techniques
	Written sales proposals
	Sales presentations
	Time management
	Co-op advertising: opportunities and pitfalls
	Processing orders
	Availabilities
	Make-goods
5.	Competitive media: strengths and weaknesses
	Radio positioning proposals
	Attempt to schedule three appointments for days 7–9
6.	Follow-up appointments
	Collections
	Presentations by traffic manager, continuity director, sales secretary
	Sales promotions
7.	Appointments or introductions to clients
	Review of appointments or introductions
8.	Appointments
	Introduction to clients
	Ride with another account executive
9.	Prospecting/appointments for following week
	Appointments
	Introductions to clients
	Ride with another account executive
10.	Deliver sample sales presentation to general and local sales managers
	Presentation review
	Review of training program
	Appointments for following week
	Introduction to clients

163

FIGURE 5.3 Training program for radio station account executives.

required to complete daily readings, listen to audio tapes, view videotapes and slide-tape presentations, and spend part of each day observing the work of the sales department.

New employees with previous broadcast sales experience may not be required to participate in all training activities. However, they should attend those that permit them to become familiar with the station and its personnel and with the department's sales policies and practices.

Training does not end with an initial program of the kind outlined in Figure 5.3. It should be a continuing requirement for new and existing account executives so that they may enhance their knowledge, stay abreast of new sales techniques and strategies, and seek additional means of revenue enhancement.

One method employed by many stations is the generation of revenue beyond the sale of airtime. It is termed *non-traditional revenue* (NTR). RAB reported in 2004 that more than 60 percent of station survey respondents said they include the topic in their training. Topping the list of NTR activities in which stations engaged were event marketing, cause-related marketing, and the Internet.[3] One station organizes a sports and leisure show in a mall and derives revenue from the sale of booth space to event exhibitors. A station might identify financial support of the public schools as its cause and promote the sale of books containing discount coupons for use at restaurants, stores, and entertainment and cultural venues. To generate revenue, the station might sell mentions of participating companies in its on-air promotions. The sale of classified advertising on the station's Web site is an example of a way in which an increasing number of stations are using the Internet as a source of non-raditional revenue.

Sales Tools   The most important tool of the account executive is knowledge that will permit the creation of a sales proposal geared to the interests and needs of each client or prospect. Knowledge of the *market*, the *station*, and the *client* are of particular importance.

MARKET DATA   The account executive should be familiar with the people and business activity of the market, including the size and composition of the population, median income and purchasing power, and retail sales and buying patterns. Knowledge of the workforce and working hours, and of cultural and recreational pursuits, also should be part of the account executive's database.

STATION DATA   To show how the station can assist the client or prospect in attaining objectives, the account executive should have knowledge of the station's

- audience, especially those characteristics that are important to the advertiser and how they compare to the characteristics of audiences for competing stations or programs

- format or programs, and their appeal to the advertiser's actual or potential customers

- commercial policies, particularly those that will afford the advertiser distinctive, uncluttered access to the audience

- availabilities, to show how the prospect can gain access to targeted customers

- rate card, to present a package that meets the advertiser's objectives at an acceptable cost

Other data that may be helpful in making a sale include the success achieved by advertisers currently using the station, awards won by the station and its employees, and the quality of staff and the facilities available to produce commercial messages.

CLIENT DATA   One of the most frequent objections by advertisers is that account executives do not know the advertiser's business. Some stations try to alleviate that problem by inviting current advertisers to station sales meetings to educate the sales staff. However, in compiling a tailor-made proposal, the account executive must understand the particular needs of each client or prospect.

To do that effectively calls for detailed knowledge of the company, its products or services, its customers, and its competitors. Familiarity with the company's objectives, current advertising practices, and advertising budget also is required.

The process whereby an account executive obtains such information is known as a *client needs analysis*. RAB has developed a series of questions to complete the analysis and they are reproduced in Figure 5.4. Answers to the questions should permit the account executive to develop a profile of the business and to prepare a sales proposal that will be responsive to the prospect's needs.

Knowledge of the market, station, and prospective client may not be sufficient for prospects who have not engaged in paid advertising in the past. They may have to be convinced of the value of advertising and, for that reason, the account executive should be familiar with the benefits that advertising brings. RAB's list of ten reasons to advertise (Figure 5.5) provides useful information to meet such a challenge.

Prospects who have not used radio or television previously may have to be persuaded of the medium's advantages as an advertising vehicle. The radio account executive may cite some of that medium's strengths:

- it reaches virtually every U.S. consumer

- it accompanies customers and prospective customers wherever they go and whatever they are doing

- it offers desired targetability through a wide range of format and programming options

- it reaches the big spenders

- it allows advertisers to achieve the message frequency necessary to stand out from the competition

- it is the only truly portable, mobile medium

- it reaches customers and prospective customers right up to the time of purchase

165

RAB Sample Client Needs Analysis Questions

Company:
1. How long have you been in this business?
2. How did you get started?
3. If relatively new, what did you do prior to this?
4. What's most enjoyable about being in this business?
5. What's least enjoyable about being in this business?

Products/Services:
1. Do you consider your products to be average quality? High-end? Low-end?
2. What are your best sellers? Worst sellers?
3. Anything you consider your specialty?
4. Anything you like to feature (maybe because of higher profit margin)?

Customers:
1. Who are your current customers?
   a. %Male? % Female?
   b. Average age?
   c. Average income?
   d. Typical profession
   e. Typical level of education
2. Who would you like them to be?
   a. %Male? % Female?
   b. Average age?
   c. Average income?
   d. Typical profession
   e. Typical level of education
3. Has your client based changed in the last year?
   a. If so, why?
   b. Was this a good change? Why or why not?
4. Do you anticipate any changes in your business that would affect your current customer profile?
5. From how far away do your customers typically come to shop? Are you satisfied with this?
6. What is the average amount a typical customer spends each time they shop your store?
7. How much is a customer worth? (Amount they spend + number of referrals).
8. How would a typical customer describe the experience of shopping at your store?
9. What is the single largest misconception non-customers have about shopping with you?

Competition:
1. Who are your biggest competitors?
   For each competitor:
2. Why do people shop there?
3. What are their primary competitive advantages?

FIGURE 5.4 RAB sample client needs analysis questions. (© Radio Advertising Bureau. Used with permission.)

- it mixes well with other media, and takes up where those media fall short

The television account executive may point to that medium's

- persuasiveness, growing out of its combination of sight, sound, motion, and color

- reputation as the most memorable, credible, exciting, and influential advertising medium

4. What do they offer customers that you can't or won't?
5. Why do customers come to you?
6. What do you offer that your competitors can't/won't?
7. What is your single greatest competitive advantage?
8. What is your single greatest competitive disadvantage?
9. Do you anticipate any changes competitively? (New competition/old going out of business/new product lines, etc.)

Objectives:
1. Is your business experiencing the kind of growth you need/want? If not, why?
2. Do you have a positioning statement?
3. What do you feel is your unique selling position?
4. What is your primary business image: low price, large inventory, service, etc.?
5. What would you want your overall image to be, if different from above?
6. Do you feel there are any misconceptions about you/your business that you would like to address?
7. Could you describe your single biggest sales and marketing challenge?
8. How are you actively addressing this challenge?
9. How would you like to see your business change over the next 12 months?

Advertising:
1. What media do you currently use?
2. Which do you use most often?
   For each medium:
3. How often do you typically use this medium? Details?
4. What do you like best about this medium?
5. What do you like least about this medium?
6. What would you change about this medium?
7. What is your typical average monthly investment in this medium? What percent of your monthly advertising budget does this represent?
8. Do you utilize co-op? Details?
9. Are you taking advantage of discretionary vendor support? Details?
10. Dates and names of all major sales events
11. Two strongest sales events? Why are they the most successful?

Wrap-up:
1. Are there any other areas we should discuss before I begin to prepare some detailed analysis and recommendations based on today's meeting?
2. As I am collecting research on your industry over the next few days, are there any areas of special interest to you that I should research as well?
3. Are there any other individuals involved in making marketing and advertising decisions?
4. Do you have an advertising agency?
5. I'll have research and recommendations ready for your review on (date). Can we meet at (time) to discuss my findings?

167

FIGURE 5.4 *Continued*

- capacity to involve viewers emotionally
- ability to demonstrate products and plant in viewers' minds images of product packaging, uses, and benefits
- broad demographic appeal and ability to reach *all* demographics
- large daily audiences
- wide geographic coverage

1. Advertising Creates Store Traffic

Continuous store traffic is the first step toward increasing sales and expanding your base of shoppers. The more people who come into the store, the more opportunities you have to make sales. A National Retail Federation survey found that for every 100 items shoppers plan to buy, they make 30 unanticipated purchases.

2. Advertising Attracts New Customers

Your market changes constantly. Newcomers to your area mean new customers to reach. People earn more money, which means changes in lifestyles and buying habits. The shopper who wouldn't consider your business a few years ago may be a prime customer now.

3. Advertising Encourages Repeat Business

Shoppers don't have the store loyalty they once did. Shoppers have mobility and freedom of choice. You must advertise to keep pace with your competition. The National Retail Federation states: "Mobility and non-loyalty are rampant. Stores must promote to get former customers to return, and to seek new ones."

4. Advertising Generates Continuous Business

Your doors are open. Employees are on the payroll. Even the slowest days produce sales. As long as you're in business, you've got overhead to meet and new people to reach. Advertising can generate traffic now . . . and in the future.

5. Advertising Is an Investment in Success

Advertising gives you a long-term advantage over competitors who cut back or cancel advertising. A survey of more than 3,000 companies found . . .
- Advertisers who maintained or expanded advertising over a five-year period saw their sales increase on average of 100%.
- Companies which cut advertising grew at less than half the rate of those that advertised steadily.

6. Advertising Keeps You in the Competitive Race

There are only so many consumers in the market ready to buy at any one time. You have to advertise to keep regular customers, and to counterbalance the advertising of your competition. You must advertise to keep or expand your market share or you will lose to more aggressive competitors.

7. Advertising Keeps Your Business Top-of-Mind with Shoppers

Many people postpone buying decisions. They often go from store to store comparing prices, quality and service. Advertising must reach them steadily throughout the entire decision-making process. Your name must be fresh in their minds when they decide to buy.

8. Advertising Gives Your Business a Successful Image

In a competitive market, rumors and bad news travel fast. Nothing sets the record straight faster than advertising; it tells your customers and competitors that your doors are open and you're ready for business. Advertising that is vigorous and positive can bring shoppers into the marketplace, regardless of the economy.

9. Advertising Maintains Morale

Positive advertising boosts morale. It gives your staff strong, additional support. When advertising or promotion is suddenly cut or canceled, salespeople and employees may become alarmed or demoralized. They may start false rumors in the honest belief that your business is in trouble.

10. Advertising Brings in Big Bucks for Your Business

Advertising works. Businesses that succeed are usually strong, steady advertisers. Look around. You'll find the most aggressive and consistent advertisers are almost invariably the most successful. Join their ranks by advertising, and watch your business grow!

FIGURE 5.5 RAB's ten reasons to advertise. (© Radio Advertising Bureau. Used with permission.)

- record of bestowing prestige on advertisers and products

Many stations include relevant market and station data in a sales kit, a variety of materials usually contained in an attractive folder and designed to demonstrate the station's ability to generate traffic for the prospect. The kit might consist of details of the market's population, the size and characteristics of the audience, personality profiles, a coverage map, cost and effectiveness comparisons with other media, and reprints of newspaper or magazine articles about the station and of the station's trade and consumer advertising.

The Sales Proposal   In the past, account executives relied heavily on the sales kit to obtain an order. They expected that an impressive array of information about the station would be sufficiently persuasive. What they failed to realize is that advertisers are interested in the station only when they understand how it can help further their business.

Today, sales managers demand written, custom sales proposals. Instead of an all-purpose collection of materials, account executives are required to develop a personalized proposal that addresses the special needs of each potential client. The proposal includes frequent references to the prospect, and the material is organized for easy understanding. It is brief and to the point.

For example, a radio station's proposal to an above-ground pool retailer that does not advertise on radio might begin with a list of campaign objectives: for example, position the store as the best in the market and pool ownership as simple, economical, and fun; and identify the targets as families with children, living in outlying areas. That might be followed by a description of campaign strategy: a heavy schedule of commercials to make the message inescapable; a repetition of the themes of speed and ease of installation, simplicity of maintenance, and low monthly payments. A statement about radio's ability to reach families throughout the day and to do so at a lower cost than competing media might be followed by details of the target audience (adults aged 25 to 54) that listen to the station in outlying and rural areas where above-ground pools are very popular. Finally, the campaign objectives are repeated and a specific advertising schedule is presented, showing the number of spots proposed, when they would air, and the weekly cost.

Note that the proposal includes a recommended advertising schedule. Merely to sell time would bring the account executive a commission, but might not produce increased business for the advertiser and could make it difficult or impossible to obtain a subsequent order.

The most widely accepted measures of a schedule's effectiveness are *reach* and *frequency*. Reach refers to the number of different homes or persons targeted by the advertiser who see or hear the commercial. Frequency is the number of times the targeted homes or persons are exposed to it.

Both goals may be accomplished through a *saturation schedule*, a heavy load of commercials aired in time periods when the targeted homes or persons are tuned in. In contrast, a *spectrum plan* exposes different people to the commercial, but only occasionally. It involves the purchase of a moderate number of spots distributed throughout the day.

A *spot schedule* is a series of commercials aired in only one or two periods of the day, and is aimed at reaching the target audience that is most available during those periods. It is used to reach a large number of people in a particular demographic category.

A *rotation plan* gives an advertiser exposure to a similar or different audience over a period of time. With *horizontal rotation*, the commercials are broadcast at or about the same time daily. *Vertical rotation* places the commercials throughout the day.

Advertisers who want to stretch their campaign may buy time on an "on-and-off" basis. In other words, they may run a succession of two-week schedules with a one-week interruption between them. Some account executives refer to this practice as a *blinking schedule*.

The Sales Call

Account executives handle two kinds of accounts:

Direct: The account executive deals directly with the advertiser, obtaining the order and receiving the copy and/or spot or arranging for the commercial to be written and/or produced by the station. The station bills the advertiser.

Agency: An advertising agency writes and/or produces (or arranges for the production of) the client's commercial and buys time from the account executive on the client's behalf. The station bills the agency, which receives a commission of 15 percent on the dollar amount of time purchased.

Many new account executives have to prove they can develop new business and have a clear understanding of the sales process and client service before they are assigned to an active account. Once they have provided proof, they join other account executives in working on an exclusive list of accounts.

The most equitable method of compiling the list is to assign a variety of product or service categories to each salesperson. Assigning on a geographical basis so that all areas of the market are covered can lead to imbalances in sales opportunities and create morale problems. Assigning by category (e.g., furniture stores, automobile dealerships) enables the account executive to develop a good knowledge of the product and of category sales and marketing practices, but many advertisers object to dealing with someone who does business with competing companies.

In addition to equity, a major consideration in assigning accounts is compatibility. Usually, attempts are made to match an account executive with a prospect or client on the basis of their respective personalities and temperaments.

The purpose of sales calls is to obtain an order. However, few sales are made the first time an account executive calls on a prospect. Often, the first meeting is used to learn as much as possible about the prospect's business and needs so that a proposal may be prepared for presentation during a second visit.

To successfully generate initial and repeat sales to a direct account, the account executive should take certain actions *before*, *during*, and *after* the call:

BEFORE   Identify the person who handles the prospect's advertising and is authorized to buy time and sign a sales contract.

Make an appointment to meet with individuals at their convenience. Develop knowledge of the prospect's

- business or service
- customer characteristics

- past and present advertising activity
- advertising budget (or an approximation) and how and when it is allocated
- objectives and problems
- previous dealings with the station, if any

Be aware of the interests and personalities of the persons to whom the proposal will be presented, and of their buying habits (e.g., whether they buy in small or large quantities).

Prepare a proposal that addresses the prospect's needs and includes an advertising schedule and its costs.

Ensure that printed or other materials for the presentation are ready and taken on the call. Increasingly, account executives are turning to PowerPoint to present the proposal. It offers the opportunity for greater effect than the printed page through the inclusion of colorful graphics, audio, and still and moving pictures. If it is to be used, make sure that it is complete and free of errors.

DURING   Describe and explain the proposal, with frequent reference to the prospect's needs and the ways in which the proposal will help meet them. Remember to

- keep the presentation brief
- invite questions, and design the answers so that they reinforce major points contained in the proposal
- ask for the order
- have the client sign and date the sales contract
- obtain a production order if the client wants the station to write and/or produce the commercial

AFTER   Process the order. The routing of the order varies, but generally it is checked by the local sales manager and then cleared against availabilities. If requested times are available, details are sent to traffic for entry on the program log. If copy and/or production are required, relevant information is provided to the persons responsible. In some stations, bookkeeping receives a copy of the order for billing purposes; in others, clients are billed from the log.

Prepare a report on the call, noting the name of the client and the person seen, the date, the content of the presentation, its results, and comments.

Service the account. Diligent servicing paves the way for subsequent sales. It begins with monitoring the progress of the order from its delivery at the station to the time the commercial begins to air.

Problems can occur, and it is the responsibility of the account executive to ensure that they are resolved. Additionally, the account executive should check with the client regularly during the advertising's schedule to assess its results. Adjustments may be necessary if the commercial appears to be having limited or no effect. Maintaining contact with the client is a continuing responsibility, and should be accompanied by acts of appreciation, such as invitations to lunch or dinner;, offers of tickets to cultural, sports, and other events; or similar gestures.

If a sale did not result from the call, the account executive should analyze the reasons why and develop another proposal that addresses the prospect's reservations or concerns. Sometimes, the failure may be explained by the account executive's inability to position the station in such a way that a buy makes sense. Often, it may result from the way in which objections raised by the prospect are handled. Most are predictable, and the account executive should anticipate them and be ready to respond.

The following are among the objections mentioned most frequently, and the actions that may be taken to counter them:

"You're too expensive."

Probe to discover what the prospect is using for comparison. Another station? Another medium? Point to the prospect's selection of a superior (and more expensive) location for doing business or to something about the business (e.g., a large and impressive sign) that is expensive but, presumably, successful. Stress that the prospect will be buying much more than a schedule of commercials, such as the number of people who will be reached, their characteristics (underlining the fact that they are potential customers), the station's expertise in commercial production, and so on. Rather than speaking of the cost of the schedule, emphasize the cost of reaching individuals and how it compares to other stations or media. Use the experience of other advertisers on your station to show that you can help the prospect increase business and profits.

"I don't have enough budget."

If you don't know the prospect's current advertising budget and its disposition, try to find out. Use that information, or your estimate, to demonstrate the affordability of your station and its ability to reach more potential customers. If appropriate, raise the possibility of co-op or vendor support programs to exemplify how the prospect can enjoy the benefits of additional advertising at little or no added cost, and detail the assistance the station will give in carrying out such programs.

"Radio (or television) doesn't work."

Ask for more information. You will probably learn that the prospect bought a short and inexpensive schedule on a radio station or in a TV daypart with the wrong demographics, or that the commercial was poorly written or produced. Point out those likely causes of disappointment and explain how you will do things differently. Again, use facts and examples to illustrate the effectiveness of radio or television advertising and the ability of your station to reach the prospect's customers.

"My customers don't listen to (or watch) your station."

Refer to data on who buys what and show how many of them are reached by your station. This response also can be used to meet a price objection if the prospect is advertising on a radio station that does not attract large numbers of the prospect's potential customers, or in TV dayparts or programs that skew to less-than-desirable demographics.

"I tried your station once and I had a bad experience with your rep, John Smith. He screwed up everything."

Tell the prospect what happened to John Smith. If he has been fired, so much the better. You can use that information to emphasize your station's commitment to giving clients the best service. If he is still employed by the station, make the point that the station considers the prospect important enough to assign another account executive. Give an assurance that similar bad experiences will not occur in the future.

"I've been advertising with WAAA for years and I don't want to change."

This objection reflects a fear of change. Find out when the prospect first advertised with WAAA. Speculate aloud about the concerns that accompanied that decision and reinforce the success that resulted from it. How will the prospect's business grow from this point? Your station provides that opportunity by offering the means of reaching new or larger audiences of potential customers or by adding to the mix of customers. Again, it may be advantageous to compare your station's cost and production quality with those of WAAA.

The account executive should listen closely to every objection and seek clarification or additional details. For example, a blanket statement like, "I tried radio and it doesn't work" is not specific enough to understand what gave rise to it or to frame a satisfactory response. Further questioning may reveal that the prospect spent $250 on a schedule with a station whose listeners were not potential customers. Now, the objection has moved from radio in general to a specific radio station, and that is easier to handle. The account executive can use the new information to speak about radio's ability to target particular demographics and to describe the represented station's proven record of attracting listeners in the demographic group that buys the prospect's products.

The account executive's principal contact in agency accounts is with *media buyers*. Generally, they are much more knowledgeable than retailers about broadcast advertising, and their concerns are different. While a retailer is interested in results (i.e., generating more customers), a media buyer focuses on rating points and costs.

Assume that a decision has been made to buy a schedule on a television station. A request is made for a list of avails for the quarter. The buyer will identify the required demographic (e.g., men and women aged 25 to 54), restrictions (e.g., no time before 4:00 P.M. or after midnight), the amount budgeted (e.g., $25,000), and the cost-per-point sought (e.g., $20). The account executive uses an appropriate computer program to arrive at the most efficient schedule based on the buyer's stipulations. Negotiations continue until agreement is reached on schedule and cost. If the schedule fails to deliver the promised ratings, the media buyer usually requests additional spots at no cost to make up for the difference.

Sales presentations to agencies are prepared in much the same way as those for retailers and must be scheduled to meet the buyer's quarterly purchasing cycles. They pay special attention to client needs, but they also recognize the buyer's interest in rating points and costs, and are designed to address it.

173

Compensation   As noted in Chapter 3, "Human Resource Management," financial compensation for sales personnel differs from that of other staff. The seven principal methods are

Salary only: Sales managers who do not service clients, co-op coordinators, and trainees are most likely to be compensated on a straight salary basis.

Salary and bonus: Salary combined with a bonus based on net sales revenues; used mostly for sales managers. Some managers also receive an *override*, a percentage of total billings.

Straight commission: The most common method for account executives. It permits the more successful to earn comparatively large salaries.

Draw against commission: Account executives establish their own minimum compensation, or *draw*, and receive that amount as long as their sales commissions meet the goal during the specified period, usually a week or month. Commission is paid on all sales that exceed it. Some stations provide a guaranteed draw. In other words, the compensation is paid even if the sales goal is not met. However, the guarantee generally remains in force for a limited period.

Salary and commission: Used for managers with a client list, account executives, and co-op coordinators.

Salary, bonus, and commission: Managers who continue to service clients are most likely to fall into this category.

Straight commission with bonus: Account executives and managers servicing clients may be compensated in this way.

The account executive must receive enough money to enjoy a reasonable standard of living and a sense of security during the initial period of employment. Some stations attempt to provide both by using straight salary for several months, moving to commission and a smaller salary, and, ultimately, to straight commission.

Commissions may be paid on billings or on billings collected. If billings are used, commissions are adjusted later if payment is not received from the advertiser. The billings collected method usually leads the account executive to check the credit rating of prospective clients before attempting a sale, and to take extra effort to ensure that bills are paid and delinquent accounts settled.

With the exception of salary only, all compensation methods use commissions and quotas to stimulate effort and productivity. Most stations employ additional incentives, with monetary or other prizes as inducements.

Individual or team sales contests are common in many stations, with points determined on the level of accomplishment. For example, new accounts may be worth 25 points, new business from clients who have used competing stations, 20, and increasing sales to current accounts, 15. Other accomplishments meriting points might include generation of the greatest dollar amount of new business or the greatest percentage increase in business.

Other incentives include extra commissions, such as paying a higher percentage commission on new than on repeat business or on production beyond quota. One radio station rewards account executives who reach their established revenue goal with a four-day weekend by giving them a day off on the Friday preceding a Monday national holiday.

Prizes should take into account the motivations of employees. A small monetary reward may not be very appealing to an account executive earning more than $100,000 a year. Similarly, a trip to a nearby resort may not be viewed as valuable by someone who does a lot of traveling.

Contests that are won regularly by the same few people may injure rather than assist the sales effort. For that reason, many stations prefer group incentives. A television station awards a collective bonus when quarterly budgeted sales revenues are exceeded. Everybody has a reason to lend their best efforts to the endeavor since all benefit if the goal is achieved.

One way of reaching for any sales goal is through additional sales to existing clients. Another is through the attraction of new clients, a responsibility of all account executives. It is particularly important for the new employee, who may have only a short client list, or no list at all.

Monitoring other media can provide useful leads in identifying new accounts. Thumbing through the local newspaper and tuning to other stations will reveal who is advertising, what they are advertising, and the targets and appeals being used. Analyzing the ads permits the account executive to develop a sales proposal for the advertiser, using the products, audiences, and appeals of the current campaign.

Many newspapers carry stories announcing the opening of new businesses. Government offices maintain records of business licenses granted and building permits issued. These and other sources provide valuable clues for the account executive in search of clients.

NATIONAL SALES: THE STATION REP

Most national advertising is bought by advertising agencies with offices in large cities such as New York, Chicago, Los Angeles, Atlanta, and Dallas. Since it would be impossible for the majority of broadcast stations to maintain a sales staff in those cities where major agencies buy time, they engage a station representative company, or rep, to sell time on their behalf.

The rep is, in effect, an extension of the local sales force. Rep sales are billed by the station to the agency, which deducts its 15 percent commission. From the balance, the station pays the rep a commission, as set forth in the contract between the two. It may run from about 5 to 15 percent of the gross business ordered (i.e., the amount billed to the agency). One reason for the range in rates is the ability of multiple-station owners to negotiate a reduction based on the number of stations to be represented.

Selecting the Rep   National sales may account for as much as 50 percent of a station's sales revenues. Selection of a rep, therefore, is an important decision. Among the considerations to be weighed before contracting for the services of a rep firm are these:

Ownership and management: Who owns and who manages? Who provides direction and leadership, and how are they provided?

Services: In addition to national sales, what services will the company provide? Will advice be available on programming, promotion, research, and local sales? What about assistance in collecting past-due accounts?

Offices: Does the firm have enough offices, and are they located in appropriate cities to give effective national sales coverage?

Staff: How many employees are assigned to sales and to other services in the company's offices? What kind of educational and professional background do they have? How are they trained and compensated? Is the staff stable?

Stations represented: Does the company specialize in representing particular kinds of stations or stations in particular kinds of markets? How many stations does the company represent, and how long has it represented them? Which stations? Do they include similar properties?

Sales teams: How many sales teams does the rep have? How many stations are on each team? Are TV affiliates and independents mixed?

Reputation: What is the company's reputation with national advertising agencies and with stations already represented? How is it perceived by other station rep companies?

Sales philosophy and practices: Are they compatible with those of the station?

Cost: Is the commission realistic? How does it compare to that paid by similar stations in similar markets for the same services?

Rep Services   The basic service offered by a rep company is the sale of national spot advertising on stations it represents. Sales are accomplished through rep account executives, who make regular calls on media buyers in advertising agencies.

Much of the information used by the account executives is developed by rep employees engaged in research on, among other items, programming, products, advertisers, and broadcast markets and audiences. Their work enables the rep company to offer a second service: consulting on a range of station activities, all of which have an impact on the sales effort.

Most rep firms offer advice to stations on the following:

Sales and sales strategy: Sales includes rate card development, sales training, and presentation materials; sales strategy includes the basic posture of the station as it enters a given quarter and changes in that posture as time passes.

Budget development: The rep's projections of market and station billings for a future year.

Programming: Local programming and the purchase of syndicated programs and features.

Research: Research methods, interpretation of research, application of findings; information and analysis on business considerations (e.g., switching network affiliation, expanding local news, financial impact of airing a syndicated program instead of clearing the network lineup).

Promotion: Audience and sales promotion methods, preparation of trade and consumer advertisements, public relations.

176

To represent the station effectively and to maximize the advertising dollars flowing to the station, the rep must be supplied with data on the *station, competition,* and *market.* Information on the station would include

- availabilities and rate card
- audience coverage, ratings, and other research reports (e.g., local marketing research)
- format or program schedule, features, specials, and sporting events
- news releases on the station, its personnel, and achievements and awards
- promotions, and examples of trade and consumer advertising
- local, regional, and national clients, and advertising effectiveness as documented in communications from advertisers and agencies

The rep also would find it helpful to receive details of station facilities, especially those that distinguish it from the competition, the station's role and image in the community, and, for radio, an air check and personality profiles.

To the degree possible, the station should provide the rep with similar information on competing stations in the market, drawing particular attention to those characteristics that suggest, or demonstrate, the represented station's superiority.

The rep may have to sell agencies on the worth of the market as well as the station. Accordingly, the station should supply details of the community's media and their circulation, population makeup and trends, employment categories, major employers, and pay days. Details of the market's educational institutions and cultural and recreational activities also would give the rep a profile of the market.

Station-Rep Relations   The principal contact between the station and the rep company is the person responsible for national sales, usually the general sales manager or the national sales manager. If the relationship is to be productive, it must be characterized by trust and confidence.

To establish and maintain such an atmosphere requires open and constant communication. The station must satisfy the rep's information needs promptly and accurately. In particular, the rep must be aware of all availabilities and of modifications in the rate card, and must be provided with details and explanations if spots are not aired as ordered. The rep must also be advised of changes in the programming of the station and of competing stations. The station should be informed of the status of ongoing negotiations with agency buyers, and has a right to an explanation if potential sales are not closed by the rep.

Communication can be enhanced through regular visits to the rep's offices by the station's general manager as well as the general and national sales managers. Such visits provide opportunities to sell the market and the station and to exchange ideas and information. Similarly, appropriate members of the rep's management team should visit the station periodically.

The station should reply promptly to rep requests for availabilities, and clear and confirm sales orders as quickly as possible. Timely payment of commissions also contributes to good relations.

Since the rep company is a partner in the sales effort, it should be involved in the development of sales objectives and plans, and in the review of their progress. And the rep should be recognized for significant accomplishments through congratulatory letters and awards.

RESEARCH AND SALES

The sales department relies heavily on market and audience measurement research. For the most part, market research is qualitative. It includes, for example, information on new businesses and on demographic and employment changes, much of which the department may obtain from the chamber of commerce, business news announcements and stories in local newspapers, and census reports. More comprehensive data on factors such as the occupation, education, income, and buying habits of station audiences and the population in general may be purchased from market research companies.

Typically, audience research is quantitative and consists of a count of listeners or viewers categorized by age and gender. It is usually bought from independent companies. Account executives use it to provide clients with details of audiences that will be reached through a commercial schedule and to demonstrate the schedule's efficiency. It is also a useful tool for reviewing the rate card.

Three principal methods are used to estimate audiences for radio and television stations. A fourth is used only for television. Each employs a process known as random sampling, which means that each household or person in the population being surveyed has an equal chance of being selected. Accordingly, the viewing or listening behavior of persons or households in the sample group can be projected to that population. The measurements are estimates, and are subject to a sampling error. In other words, the actual audience may be a little larger or smaller than reported. The survey methods are as follows:

Diary: Daily viewing or listening activity is recorded in a small booklet or log for one week.

Telephone: Interviewers ask what station or program is being listened to or watched at the time of the call. This is known as the *telephone-coincidental* method. In the *telephone-recall* method, participants are asked which stations or programs were listened to or viewed during an earlier period of time (e.g., the previous day or evening).

Personal interview: Interviewers visit people in their homes and question them about their listening or viewing.

Meter: A monitoring device records the channel to which the television set is tuned and is connected by telephone to a central computer.

Each method has advantages and disadvantages, and some of them are listed in Figure 5.6.

The sales department, station rep, and advertising agencies use audience estimates compiled chiefly by Nielsen Media Research (television) and The Arbitron Company (radio).

Nielsen surveys all 210 television markets for four-week periods in

Advantages	Disadvantages
Diary	
Provides detailed information	Diary-keeper may
Reports individual viewing or listening behavior	—lie
	—fail to complete it
Relatively Inexpensive	—fail to return it
	—enter inaccurate information (e.g., call letters, dial position)
	—write illegibly
	—forget what was listened to or viewed before completing
	Diary has to be carried for away-from-home listening
	Slow results
	Infrequent surveys in many markets
Telephone-coincidental	
Eliminates possiblity of respondent forgetfulness	Nontelephone or unlisted homes excluded (unless random digit dialing used)
Fast results	Noncooperation by respondents
Relatively inexpensive	Questions must be brief
	Difficult to obtain detailed responses
	Possibility of interviewer bias (e.g., in wording of questions, recording of responses)
Telephone-recall	
As for telephone-coincidental, except respondent forgetfulness	As for telephone-coincidental. Add possibility of respondent forgetfulness, unless aided-recall used
Personal interview	
More personal than other methods	Respondent may lie
Provides detailed information	Possibility of interviewer bias
With aided-recall, reduces possibility of audience forgetfulness	Time-consuming
	Relatively expensive
Meter	
Records actual set operation and channel	Does not indicate if anyone is watching
Eliminates possibility of human error	Does not provide demographic information (e.g., viewer sex, age)
Avoids interviewer bias	Subject to mechanical failure
Fast results	Relatively expensive

FIGURE 5.6   Advantages and disadvantages of broadcast audience measurement methods.

November, February, May, and July. Some of the larger markets are surveyed seven times a year, through the addition of October, January, and March. These simultaneous surveys are known as "sweeps."

Arbitron conducts continuous measurements in most of the top-100 radio markets and a handful of lower-ranked markets for 48 weeks a year, in four, 12-week cycles. Other markets are measured for 12 weeks twice a year (spring and fall).

In more than 50 large markets, Nielsen uses a household meter to collect TV set usage data (i.e., set on/off, channel tuned) in the preparation of overnight reports. In the top ten markets, it is introducing a different kind of meter, the *local people meter (LPM)*. However, the basic measurement method for television stations in all markets is a diary, which sample households complete for each television set for one week. Each day is broken down into 15-minute periods. Respondents are asked to note the station or channel name, the channel number, and the name of the program or movie to which the set was tuned in each period, together with the age and gender of all family members and visitors viewing and the number of hours each person works per week. VCR recording activity also must be included.

For radio, Arbitron supplies a one-week diary to each member of selected households 12 years of age and older. Respondents enter in the diary (1) the start and stop times of each listening period; (2) station identifiers (e.g., call letters, dial setting, station name, or program name); (3) whether the station was AM or FM; and (4) whether they heard it at home, in a car, at work, or in some other place.

At the end of the week, the completed television or radio diaries are mailed to the respective companies. The information they contain is processed and some of the results published in a local market report, more commonly called a ratings book or, simply, the book. In metered television markets, the set tuning information is augmented at least four months a year with demographic viewing data from a separate sample of diary households.

The television report estimates, by age and gender and for different time periods and programs, the audience for stations in the market. The radio report lists audience trends and current estimates by age and gender for different time periods. It also contains details of listening locations, time spent listening, and the ethnic composition of station audiences.

Market report information prepared by Nielsen and Arbitron is organized according to the geographic area in which viewing or listening took place. The following areas are used in the *Nielsen Station Index* (NSI) report:

Metro area, which generally corresponds to the metropolitan statistical area (MSA), as defined by the U.S. Office of Management and Budget.

Designated market area (DMA), those counties in which commercial stations in the market being surveyed achieve the largest share of the 7:00 A.M. to 1:00 A.M. average quarter-hour household audience.

NSI area, a market's metro and DMA counties, plus other counties necessary to account for approximately 95 percent of the average quarter-hour U.S. audiences of stations in the market.

AUDIENCE MEASUREMENT TERMINOLOGY

To use the market report effectively, the account executive and other members of the sales department staff must understand the information it contains. Understanding begins with knowledge of basic audience measurement terminology. The following are among the terms used most frequently:

Rating   In television, the percentage of all TV households or persons tuned to a specific station:

$$\text{Rating} = \frac{\text{Number of households viewing station}}{\text{Number of TV households in survey area}}$$

Or

$$\frac{\text{Number of viewers to station}}{\text{Total viewer population}}$$

To say that a television program has a household rating of 10 means, therefore, that 10 percent of all TV households in the survey area were watching it.

In radio, rating denotes the percentage of all people in the survey area listening to a specific station:

$$\text{Rating} = \frac{\text{Number of listeners to station}}{\text{Population of survey area}}$$

Households Using Television (HUT)   The percentage of all television households with TV sets in operation at a particular time:

$$\text{HUT} = \frac{\text{Number of TV households with sets on}}{\text{Number of TV households in survey area}}$$

Share   The percentage of HUT or persons using television (PUT) tuned to a specific station:

$$\text{Share} = \frac{\text{Number of TV households viewing station}}{\text{Number of TV households with sets on}}$$

Or

$$\frac{\text{Number of viewers to TV station}}{\text{Number of people viewing TV}}$$

In radio, share represents the percentage of listeners to a station:

$$\text{Share} = \frac{\text{Number of listeners to station}}{\text{Number of listeners to all stations}}$$

Rating, share, and households using television are interrelated, as indicated by the formula used to calculate each:

$$\text{Rating} = \text{Share} \times \text{HUT}$$

$$\text{HUT} = \frac{\text{Rating}}{\text{Share}}$$

$$\text{Share} = \frac{\text{Rating}}{\text{HUT}}$$

Assume that a TV market report gave the following information for the period 6:00 P.M. to 6:30 P.M.:

STATION	DMA HOUSEHOLD RATING
WAAA	15
WBBB	5
WCCC	10
WDDD	8
HUT	60

If you wanted to calculate the share for WCCC, you would merely divide 10 (rating) by 60 (HUT) to give a share of 17 percent. Note that the HUT level is greater than the sum of ratings for stations in the market. That is explained by the fact that some households (22 percent) were viewing cable or satellite services or stations from outside the market.

Similarly, if you knew that 60 percent of households were watching television, and that WCCC had a 17 share, you could figure the station's rating. Simply multiply 17 (share) by .60 (HUT). To determine HUT, divide 10 (rating) by 17 (share).

Other commonly used audience measurement terms include these:

Average quarter-hour (AQH) audience: An estimate of households or persons viewing or listening for at least five minutes during a quarter-hour period.

Cume: Short for *cumulative audience,* an estimate of the number of *different* households or persons viewing or listening for at least five minutes in a specified period.

Gross rating points (GRPs): The total of all rating points achieved for a schedule of commercials.

Gross impressions (*GIs*): The total number of exposures to a schedule of commercials.

Advertisers want to broadcast their messages to people who use, or might use, their products or services, and at a reasonable cost. With an understanding of the terminology in the market report, the account executive can interpret the information it contains and incorporate relevant parts of it in a sales presentation.

The advertiser who is interested only in total numbers of people, or people with certain age or gender characteristics, may be impressed by ratings converted to numbers of households or persons. The account executive can go further and use share information to show that the station reaches more of the advertiser's clientele than the competition, or cumes to indicate how many different people would be exposed to the commercial.

Advertisers also are concerned with the efficiency of their advertising buys, or what it costs them to reach target audiences. Often, this is calculated on the basis of *cost-per-thousand* (*CPM*) households or persons:

$$\text{CPM} = \frac{\text{Cost of spot or advertising schedule}}{\text{Number of households or persons reached}} \times 1000$$

183

For example, if a spot costs $300 and is aired in a program seen in 20,000 households, the household CPM is $15 (300 divided by 20,000 and multiplied by 1000).

Another measure of efficiency is *cost-per-rating point* (*CPP*), which is calculated by dividing the cost of a spot by the rating for the period or program in which it was broadcast. If a spot costs $300 and the rating is 5, the CPP is $60. For an advertising schedule, the cost is determined by dividing the cost of the schedule by the GRPs, or the sum of ratings, obtained.

Audience measurement estimates are important tools for advertising agencies and station rep companies as well. Agency time buyers use them to select markets and stations on which to place their clients' advertising.

The station rep uses the market report in much the same way as the station's account executives: to persuade advertisers and agencies that they can achieve their objectives effectively and efficiently by purchasing schedules on the represented station. Acting in an advisory capacity, the rep can use the report to support recommendations for changes in the station's price structure.

The market report provides essential information for station and rep account executives and advertising agencies. However, much of the data collected is not contained in it, including such key details as reach and frequency. To obtain that and other information, stations often purchase additional services from the audience measurement companies.

Traditionally, audience research has focused on quantitative data of the kinds described. As competition for advertising dollars has intensified, many stations have sought information that goes beyond the age and gender of audience members. Income, home ownership, occupation, educational level, and other characteristics provide important pointers to consumer motivations. They help the station to develop a more complete profile of listeners or viewers. They also permit the sales department to incorporate qualitative data in presentations and to give the client or advertising agency more precise details on which to base media buying decisions.

Such information is available from many sources, including Arbitron and Nielsen. Arbitron offers three different qualitative data services to reflect the demographic, socioeconomic, lifestyle, and purchasing characteristics of consumers in more than 260 large, medium, and smaller (100+) markets. Nielsen has teamed with Scarborough Research to produce the *NSI Profiler*, which describes shopping patterns, demographics, media usage, and lifestyle activities in 75 leading markets. Griffin Media Research provides similar local market information in its radio and television reports. In several dozen markets, Leigh Stowell & Company and Marshall Marketing and Communications research purchasing habits, demographics, psychographics, and media behavior. Mediamark Research Inc. (MRI) surveys the demographics, product usage, and media exposure of the adult population in the 48 contiguous states. Claritas Corporation breaks down the country into zip codes to develop profiles of the people who live there.

WHAT'S AHEAD?

184

If financial forecasters are correct, station sales departments can contemplate a future that is rosier than the past few years.

Total spending on broadcast television advertising is projected to increase at a compound annual rate of 5.6 percent through 2008.[4]

For radio, the predicted growth is 7.9 percent annually.[5] However, that includes both advertiser and consumer spending on satellite radio, a source of increasing competition for radio stations. By mid-2005, the number of subscribers to the two national satellite services was fewer than six million, but both were registering impressive percentage gains.[6]

Television stations will continue to face competition from wired cable and direct broadcast satellite, which are likely to contribute to further audience fragmentation.

The Internet will make additional inroads into the audiences of both radio and television stations. Between 2000 and 2004, the monthly Internet audio and video audience doubled to reach 51 million consumers.[7] The radio audience was about 38 million a month and the average consumer spent about five hours a week with the medium.[8] Nearly one in four Americans have viewed video over the Internet.[9] The percentage that told researchers they had viewed in the past month grew from 7 to 12 percent in the four-year period.[10]

Of course, the Internet also offers significant economic potential for broadcasters. Annual revenues earned by radio and television stations account for merely 3 percent of the $1.65 billion local online advertising market.[11] Many stations have recognized the opportunity and have responded with aggressive campaigns to win dollars from competing media.

A favorite target has been the local newspaper and, especially, its classified advertising revenues. Stations in markets of all sizes have redirected some of those dollars to their balance sheet. Some have achieved that goal by employing classified sales reps.

However, in an era of intensive investor pressure for profits and, for many television network affiliates, decreasing amounts of station compensation, all stations will have to take a serious look at this and other sources of nontraditional revenue.

The sale of classified advertising space on a station Web site is one method of generating additional and, in most cases, new dollars. Examples of classified advertisers that have invested their money with newspapers include companies with employment listings, automobile dealers, and real estate agents. Broadcasters can offer them and other advertisers more attractive options, including combined online and on-air packages and on-air promotions to help drive traffic to their Web sites.

Successful pursuit of classified advertising dollars would be enhanced if broadcasters were to identify additional benefits. For example, they could point to reduced advertiser dependence on the newspaper and increased ability to negotiate better rates.

More stations are entering the online advertising arena, either on their own or as part of a network of Web sites. But many have not yet been persuaded of the economic advantages that it affords.

That is evidenced by the results of the RAB's survey cited earlier in the chapter.[12] It found that fewer than one-half of stations were employing the Internet as a revenue source. Even among users, the monies generated were modest. About 70 percent of stations said they derived 10 percent or less of their total revenues from it.

The apparent lukewarm reception to this potential goldmine may be attributable to some sales managers who do not consider it part of their core business. Others may feel uncomfortable venturing into relatively new and uncharted waters. Whatever the reason, it is clear that many do not place a high priority on it. Only about one-third of respondents to the RAB survey said they include the Internet in training programs for new account executives.

In times of intense competition for advertising dollars, broadcasters will have to ensure that their account executives are knowledgeable and skilled in identifying and capitalizing on all sources of revenue enhancement. That challenge demands adequate and appropriate training. However, in their eagerness to respond to bottom-line pressure from investors, some stations have hired inexperienced personnel and put them to work without any kind of preparation. Failure and dismissal have been the inevitable consequences. Additional turnover has been created by resignations resulting from the absence of station attention to training. One study determined that, among those planning to leave radio, only 36 percent thought that their company was committed to training. In contrast, 61 percent of those intending to stay believed their company supported training for sales personnel.[13]

One factor that may influence sales training activities in television stations is the decision on use of their digital channels. If they opt for multiple program services, each devoted to discrete content, existing account executives will face the challenge of selling in a new and different environment. Adapting to it will require relevant instruction.

Television sales departments also will have to confront adjustments resulting from changes in audience measurement methods. Already, those in the largest markets are experiencing the transition from four-times-a-year sweeps data to daily household and demographic data, courtesy of Nielsen's local people meter. In LPM markets, sales staff will be required to digest and act on information that is more voluminous and current than heretofore.

Another Nielsen innovation will require further adjustments: the measurement of viewing in households with digital video recorders. Timeliness will give way to comprehensiveness, since the information will be provided in three phases. The initial information will record viewing at the time of the program's airing. That will be followed by time-shifted viewing data. Finally, ratings reflecting all viewing will be distributed.

In the more distant future, both radio and television sales departments may confront additional audience measurement challenges. Much depends on the results of tests on Arbitron's portable people meter (PPM). The meter is about the size of a pager and can be carried or worn. It is designed to track listening and viewing wherever they occur by automatically picking up inaudible codes embedded in radio and television programming.

SUMMARY

Broadcast stations generate the majority of their revenue through the sale of time to local, regional, and national advertisers.

Obtaining advertisers is the responsibility of the sales department. It is headed by a general sales manager and includes a national sales manager, local sales manager, and account executives.

The general sales manager develops sales objectives and strategies, prepares and controls the department's budget, and directs and supervises the work of the departmental staff. Knowledge of the financial objectives of the station's owners, broadcast sales and advertising, and the sales activities of competing stations are among the qualities the general sales manager should possess. They should be combined with administrative and sales skills, and with an energetic and competitive personality.

The national sales manager coordinates the sale of time to national advertisers, and the local sales manager supervises the account executives.

Most of the time sold is for 30- or 60-second commercials, or spots. Many stations also sell longer periods of time for the broadcast of complete programs.

The cost of time in different dayparts on a radio station is listed on a rate card. It is influenced by several factors, including supply and demand, the time of day, and the length of the spot. Television stations sell time in, and adjacent to, programs. Rates are determined by supply and demand and spot length.

Instead of accepting money, stations may exchange some of their time for advertiser-provided merchandise or services in a transaction known as a trade or tradeout. Barter programming, co-op, vendor support, and per-inquiry advertising permit advertisers to obtain time at less than rate card prices. Some stations cut their rates or provide bonus spots to attract clients.

Sales and advertising practices are governed by policies the station implements according to its revenue objectives and its notion of responsible operation. However, the government dictates policies on the amount of time that may be sold in children's TV programs and on the use of radio and television stations by candidates for public office.

The effectiveness of the local sales effort is determined largely by the abilities of the account executives. Knowledge of the market, the station, and prospective clients are among the tools necessary for success.

To obtain orders, account executives present custom sales proposals to prospective advertisers and to advertising agencies, emphasizing ways in which the station can assist in attaining client objectives. They are compensated in various ways, and commissions and other incentives usually are employed to encourage effort and productivity.

Sales to national advertisers are accomplished by station representative companies, or station reps, which obtain orders from advertising agencies located in major cities. In addition to selling, most reps offer advice to the station on sales and sales strategy, budget development, programming, research, and promotion.

Market and audience measurement research are important tools of the sales department. Radio and television audiences are measured mostly by diary. Television audiences are measured by meter as well. The research results in estimates of the size and composition of the audience, and enables the station to advise advertisers of the number and kinds of people who hear or see its programs, and the costs of reaching particular demographic categories.

Even though advertising revenues are expected to grow over the next few years, investor pressure and a reduction in TV network compensation will compel many broadcast stations to pursue sources of nontraditional revenue. If they are to reap its benefits, they will have to invest in additional account executive training. Changes in audience measurement methods also will impose training demands on television sales departments.

187

CASE STUDY: RADIO

You are the local sales manager of an all-news station in a large market in the South.

Account executive Cliff Harwell stops by your office. He has just met with Thelma Steel, owner of a local health foods store called Nutrition Works. He has managed her account for five years. Her monthly advertising budget is $3,600 and your station receives all of it. However, Cliff tells you this may be about to end.

Thelma has concluded that she has reached all your listeners and is about to move her entire budget to cable.

During the drive back to the station, Cliff has come up with an idea to retain the account. He calls it "reality radio," and hopes to capitalize on the reality television craze. Here is what he has in mind.

Nutrition Works will hold a contest on the station to pick three people who want to improve their body image. Those selected will be put on a 90-day weight loss and conditioning program using products available at the store. Their photographs will be displayed on the station's Web site at the outset and at 14-day intervals until the program ends. Each will give periodic progress reports in the store's spots. At the end of 90 days, they will record testimonials extolling the ability of Nutrition Works to ensure weight loss and better health.

EXERCISES

1. What are your reactions to Thelma's conclusions about your station's reach and her plan to move to cable?

2. Does Cliff have a salable idea? Explain your response.

3. Do you see any ways in which the idea can be improved? If so, describe them.

CASE STUDY: TELEVISION

You are an account executive with an NBC affiliate in a medium market in the Southeast.

Dorothy Naylor has been one of your clients for nine years. She owns Antiques World, a local antiques store, and spends about $2,000 each month with you. Most of her spots appear in the early-morning local news program.

A month before she is due to renew her contract, she calls to tell you that she plans to move her broadcast advertising to a news/talk radio station. When you ask her the reason, she says that she wants to try something "new and different." The station has offered her sole sponsorship of a 30-minute syndicated antiques program that airs Saturdays at noon. It will also cross-promote the program. She adds that the deal will be less costly than her current television schedule.

Before ending the call, you ask if you may stop by her store and chat with her before she signs with the radio station. She says that won't be a problem.

EXERCISES

1. How will you respond to Dorothy's "new and different" rationale?

2. She appears convinced that the radio program will reach more potential customers than her TV spots. Is she correct? Explain your response.

3. Will you try to counter her cost argument? If so, how?

NOTES

1 *47 CFR* 73.1941(c).

2 *Ibid.*, (d).

3 http://www.rab.com/NTRSURVEY2004.htm.

4 "VSS Forecasts Solid Growth Across All Communications Sectors—First Time in Four Years," http://www.veronissuhler.com/articles/article_080204.html.

5 *Ibid.*

6 http://www.siriusradio.com and http://www.xmradio.com.

7 *Internet and Multimedia 12: The Value of Internet Broadcast Advertising*, p. 4.

8 *Ibid.*, p. 5.

9 *Ibid.*

10 *Ibid.*, p. 6.

11 Peter Krasilovsky, "ISO More Revenue? Try Classifieds," *Broadcasting & Cable*, April 21, 2003, p. 40.

12 http://www.rab.com/NTRSURVEY2004.htm.

13 Vincent M. Ditingo, "The Key to Keep AEs: Training," *Radio World*, April 11, 2001, pp. 42, 45.

ADDITIONAL READINGS

Brady, Frank R., and J. Angel Vasquez. *Direct Response Television: The Authoritative Guide*. Lincolnwood, IL: NTC Publishing Group, 1995.

Eicoff, Alvin, and Anne Knudsen. *Direct Marketing Through Broadcast Media: TV, Radio, Cable, Infomercials, Home Shopping and More*. Lincolnwood, IL: NTC Publishing Group, 1995.

Greenwood, Ken. *High Performance Selling*. West Palm Beach, FL: Streamline Press, 1995.

Herweg, Ashley, and Godfrey Herweg. *Recruiting, Interviewing, Hiring and Developing Superior Salespeople*, 4th ed. Washington, DC: National Association of Broadcasters, 1993.

Herweg, Godfrey, and Ashley Herweg. *Making More Money: Selling Radio Advertising Without Numbers*, 2nd ed. Washington, DC: National Association of Broadcasters, 1995.

Plum, Shyrl L. *Underwriting 101: Selling College Radio*. Mahwah, NJ: Lawrence Erlbaum, 2000.

Schulberg, Pete. *Radio Advertising: The Authoritative Handbook*, 2nd ed. Lincolnwood, IL: NTC Publishing Group, 1996.

Shane, Ed. *Selling Electronic Media*. Boston, MA: Focal Press, 1999.

Warner, Charles, and Joseph Buchman. *Media Selling: Broadcast, Cable, Print and Interactive*, 3rd ed. Ames: Blackwell, 2003.

Webster, James G., Patricia F. Phalen, and Lawrence W. Lichty. *Ratings Analysis: The Theory and Practice of Audience Research*, 2nd ed. Mahwah, NJ: Lawrence Erlbaum, 2000.

Broadcast Promotion and Marketing

This chapter focuses on the promotion and marketing of radio and television stations to audiences and advertisers. It considers

- the responsibilities and qualities of the promotion and marketing director
- the development of a promotion plan
- the goals and methods of effective audience and sales promotion campaigns

Commercial radio and television stations spend considerable time and energy promoting the interests of others directly through advertising and public service announcements. Indirectly, they promote the interests and careers of recording artists and an array of other personalities.

Broadcast promotion and marketing refers to a station's efforts to promote itself, and is directed toward the two groups whose support is necessary to ensure its continued operation: audiences and advertisers.

Without an audience, even the best programs attract little advertiser interest. Through *audience promotion*, a station seeks to persuade people to continue to tune in or to sample its programming.

In the increasingly competitive media marketplace, a station has to fight for its share of advertising dollars. Through *sales promotion*, a station seeks to persuade advertisers and advertising agencies to buy time.

Promotion is so important to success that many stations entrust it to a department headed by a promotion and marketing director, who reports to the general manager.[1] The size of the department varies.[2] It is determined by many factors, including station and market size, the competition, and the importance assigned to promotion by station management. In some stations, the director may have the assistance of only a secretary. In others, the staff may number a dozen or more, and may be organized to reflect the various functions of the department. In markets where a single owner operates multiple stations, the director may be responsible for promoting all of them.

Some stations do not give promotion responsibilities to a separate department. Audience promotion may be carried out by the program department, for example, and sales promotion by the sales department. In small stations, the general manager may play the prominent role in promotion.

Here, emphasis will be on the promotion and marketing director and the promotion functions, no matter who discharges them.

THE PROMOTION AND MARKETING DIRECTOR

RESPONSIBILITIES

The promotion and marketing director is responsible for marketing the station and its programs to audiences, and its audiences to advertisers. In a small department, the director may have to handle all the details. In a large department, specific responsibilities may be assigned to different staff members, with the director supervising their work and carrying out general administrative tasks.

Whether directly involved or acting chiefly in a supervisory capacity, the promotion and marketing director has responsibility for a wide variety of activities. They include

- assisting in the development of a promotion plan
- planning and creating audience and sales promotion campaigns
- implementing campaigns through the preparation and/or coordination of advertising and promotional materials and their scheduling

- evaluating campaigns
- conducting or contracting for research and employing appropriate data in campaign creation, planning, implementation, and evaluation
- planning and overseeing public service activities, unless those duties are handled by a public service director
- coordinating the station's overall graphic look
- maintaining media relations
- administering the activities of the department and coordinating them with other station departments

QUALITIES

The qualities required of an effective promotion and marketing director are as numerous and varied as the responsibilities.

Knowledge   The director should have knowledge of the following:

Marketing, its functions and processes, and their application to audience and sales promotion.

Promotion methods used most frequently, especially (1) advertising— characteristics of all advertising media, media selection, buying, and tradeouts; (2) publicity—available avenues and the cultivation of publicity sources; (3) public relations—role in promotion and the fostering of effective public relations; (4) promotions—vehicles for on-air and off-air promotion and their utilization; (5) public service—ways in which it can assist in the promotional mix.

Research, conducting or contracting for research, and its interpretation and use in promotion.

Professional services, such as those available from printers, advertising and public relations agencies, companies specializing in the production of promotion materials, and from Promax, a professional association of promotion and marketing executives.

Laws and regulations, especially those that apply to advertising, copyright, and contests.

Skills   The promotion and marketing director should display skills in

- planning, creating, implementing, and evaluating promotion campaigns
- planning and coordinating in-house research
- writing advertising and promotion copy, news and feature releases, program listings, and sales promotion materials, such as station and market data sheets, ratings analyses, and program and personality profiles
- producing artwork and layouts for print advertising and promotion, radio and/or television commercials and promos, and graphics for sales presentations

193

- planning and creating content for the station's Web site
- coordinating promotions with other station departments
- maintaining records of departmental personnel, budget, and promotional activities

Personal Qualities   The promotion and marketing director should be

- *alert* to the changing fortunes of the station and its competitors and adaptable in responding to the demands that may be placed on the department as a result
- *creative* in developing and executing promotion ideas
- *communicative* and *cooperative* in contacts with departmental and station personnel and with persons, companies, and organizations outside the station
- *enthusiastic* and *energetic* in approaching and carrying out the varied responsibilities of the position
- *ethical* in dealings with others and in promotion practices

194   THE PROMOTION PLAN

A promotion plan is the product of discussions among the promotion and marketing director, general manager, and the heads of the program and sales departments and, often, the news department. Carrying out the plan is the function of the promotion and marketing director.

Developing and executing the plan is a six-step process:

1. Determine the percentage of the market that is watching or listening to the station's product and that of competitors, together with the audience's demographic and psychographic characteristics.
2. Identify the reasons why listeners and viewers select a station and the reasons they select the station or the competition. Find out, also, why the station's potential audience is not tuning in.
3. Assess the station's strengths and weaknesses and, especially, effectiveness in positioning itself to attract the desired demographics.
4. Having established the strengths, draw up a plan that addresses the weaknesses and how to correct them.
5. Implement the plan.
6. Evaluate the effectiveness of the plan and, if necessary, refine it.

AUDIENCE PROMOTION

The principal goal of audience promotion is to increase audience by maintaining current listeners or viewers and persuading nonlisteners or nonviewers to sample the station's programs. The goal is accomplished through *image promotion* and *program promotion*.

Like the products they advertise, stations must stand out from the competition by winning a place in the public's mind or *positioning* themselves. Image promotion seeks to satisfy that need by establishing, shifting, or solidifying public perceptions of the station.

Traditionally, radio stations have used their format as their image, so that people refer to a station as "the rock station" or "the news station." Stations that air a significant amount of sports programming may project the image of "the sports station." If the station has a heavy schedule of community affairs programming and is closely involved in community activities, the image of "the community station" may be selected.

In today's competitive marketplace, such broad positioning statements often are inadequate. For example, how does "rock" position a station if the community has stations with contemporary rock, album rock, classic rock, and country rock formats?

Because of the similarity of program types on the major broadcast television networks, and the frequent changes in programming, network-affiliated television stations usually have looked to their local programming for image promotion. Often, their efforts center on local news, with themes such as "Eyewitness News" or "Action News." Stations that are affiliated with Fox, The WB, or UPN often position themselves simply by identifying with the network (Figure 6.1).

195

Independent television stations usually turn for their image to competitive programming, such as sports or movies. Some position themselves as "the alternative station," by which they mean that they offer program types different from affiliated stations during certain dayparts.

Again, these general themes do not permit a station to occupy a niche. Remote trucks enable most stations to be "eyewitnesses" to the news. Fox may conjure up many images, from "The Simpsons" to NFL football. In addition, as noted in Chapter 4, "Broadcast Programming," "alternative" programming is insufficient ammunition for an independent competing against an array of alternatives offered by cable and DBS.

FIGURE 6.1   This bus board reflects the practice of many Fox affiliates that position themselves by combining the name of the network with their channel number. (Courtesy WDSI-TV.)

Today, selection of an image must be based on a clear understanding of perceptions of the station and its competitors, the targeted audience, the audience's needs and how the station fulfills them, and of *specific* ways in which the station differs from the competition.

The required understanding should emerge from the research carried out in completing the first three steps of the promotion plan. Focus groups, interviews, and surveys can provide valuable insights into current perceptions of the station and its competitors and suggest an appropriate image. However, the positioning statement must say *exactly* what the station is. "More music" says something, but "More music, 12 in a row" says much more. Research may reveal that a major competitor is perceived as having disc jockeys who talk too much. "Less talk" could be a strong and effective positioner. If technology is determined to be a significant listener benefit, "The all-digital station" may be considered.

Occasionally, research suggests a statement that tells what the station is *not*. One station changed its format to light adult contemporary and wanted to avoid the notion that it was playing elevator music, which, according to focus groups, was the perception held of a competitor. The positioner that resulted was "No hard rock. No elevator music."

The diversity and wide appeal of programming on all television stations make it difficult for a station to develop a positioning statement that sets it apart from the competition. Some stations select an umbrella theme, such as "Making a Difference," and use it as part of all their promotions.

More frequently, stations affiliated with the major television networks try to position themselves through locally programmed dayparts or local programming. Local news plays such a key role in influencing public perceptions that it usually is chosen for image promotion emphasis (see Figure 6.2). Anchors, reporters, technology, comprehensive coverage—all can enhance the station's image. Successful promotion, however, demands that the station identify viewer and nonviewer perceptions and proceed to tackle those that

FIGURE 6.2 The importance of local news promotion to a station affiliated with one of the major TV networks is demonstrated in this billboard bearing the station's slogan. (Courtesy WRCB-TV.)

are important in establishing or reinforcing the image necessary to attract or retain desired demographics.

For instance, a station may view a veteran anchor and the stability of its reporters as major competitive advantages. Research may reveal that viewers perceive as a benefit the fact that the anchor and reporters have worked at the station for a long time, in contrast with the frequent turnover in personnel at other stations. The research may also indicate that certain of the station's newspeople are seen as lacking warmth. That kind of information provides a basis for an image campaign stressing stability and market familiarity, presented in a warm and appealing manner.

Program promotion revolves around a station's efforts to promote its content. In radio, the principal emphasis is on the station's format and personalities. Television stations, on the other hand, draw attention to individual programs or dayparts.

Stations have discovered that effective program promotion requires more than a recitation of format or programs. An important key to success lies in stressing the benefits to the audience by identifying the ways in which the programming is meeting, or could meet, its desires.

News and public affairs programs may meet the desire for information, music for relaxation, entertainment programs for amusement, and so on. Promoting the benefits of tuning in reinforces listening and viewing habits among the current audience and can be a strong motivator for others.

Affiliated television stations can rely on the network to promote network programs. Accordingly, much of the station's promotion effort is directed toward local news or syndicated programs. In theory, independent stations must promote all their programming. In practice, however, most direct their efforts to the promotion of entertainment programs or those for which the station has staked a claim in the marketplace.

Before embarking on an audience promotion campaign, a strategy must be developed. It must take into account several considerations, including the following:

Campaign Purpose

Is the purpose to promote image or programming? If the former, is the concern with establishing, reinforcing, or changing image? If the latter, what element of programming? Are results expected in a short time or over a longer period?

Target Audience

To whom is the campaign to be directed? What kinds of people are most likely to respond?

Audience Benefits

Why should the targeted audience respond? What benefits can they expect?

Promotion Methods

How can the targeted audience be reached? Which medium or media will be used? Will the campaign rely chiefly on one method of promotion or on a combination? What about the time schedule?

197

Content

What kind of content will be most suited to the promotion method or methods selected? Can the content be developed by the station or will outside services be required?

Budget

What kinds of costs will be incurred? Does the purpose justify the costs?

Evaluation

How will the results of the campaign be determined? Will it be necessary for the station to develop an instrument to measure the results? Or will telephone calls, letters, E-mail, ratings, or other feedback indicate the degree of success achieved?

PROMOTION METHODS

The methods by which a station seeks to accomplish its audience promotion goals are limited only by the imagination of those involved in planning the promotion and the available budget. There are four major methods: (1) *advertising*, (2) *publicity* and *public relations*, (3) *on-air* and *off-air promotions*, and (4) *public service*. In most campaigns, a combination of methods is used.

Advertising   Advertising refers to the purchase of time or space. In some cases, stations trade for time or space with other media. Instead of making a payment, they offer to the other media advertising time on their stations that would cost an equivalent amount of money.

Stations may plan, develop, and supervise the advertising themselves or engage the services of an advertising agency.

In audience promotion, the major advantage of advertising is that the station has control over the content as well as when and where it appears. But some stations consider advertising expensive, especially when compared to some of the other available promotion methods.

Among the advertising media that stations use are newspapers, magazines, outdoor, transit, and broadcast.

NEWSPAPERS   Daily or weekly newspapers are published in most communities and reach people who are not regular listeners or viewers. It may be assumed that most readers are interested in being informed. For that reason, many stations use newspapers to advertise news programs, special news features, or other informational programming.

Often, advertisements are placed in the newspaper's TV/radio or entertainment sections. If a program with special appeal is being promoted, an ad may be placed in another section. Advertisements for sports programs, for example, probably will reach more of the interested audience in the sports section. Advertisements for business, travel, and several other kinds of programs will reach the most interested through placement in appropriate sections.

The television supplement published by many newspapers on Sundays represents a valuable vehicle for television stations. It is used by viewers and usually remains around the home for at least a week. An advertisement for a program on a given day may be placed on the page containing program information for that day.

Many stations engage in tradeouts with newspapers, and network-affiliated television stations often participate in co-op advertising with the network, especially at the start of the fall season. The network agrees to pay part of the cost of advertising its programs. The station benefits, since it lists its call letters or channel number and, often, some of its programs in the advertisements.

MAGAZINES Many radio and television stations operate in markets where no general-interest magazine is published. However, large-market stations often have access to the so-called "city magazine" and use it to promote image and format or programs. Additionally, some stations place advertisements on regional pages of nationally circulated magazines, such as *Time* and *Newsweek*.

A very useful magazine for television stations is *TV Guide*, which offers advantages similar to those of the newspaper television supplement. Even though it has discontinued the use of tradeouts, many stations advertise in the publication because of its ability to target viewers directly.

199

OUTDOOR Billboards offer several advantages as an advertising medium. They are available in a variety of sizes, can incorporate special effects, and can be illuminated so that their impact can be felt around the clock. Obviously, they are most useful if they are located in areas with heavy traffic, especially if it is slow-moving.

Many radio stations favor billboard advertisements because they can stimulate drivers to take immediate action by tuning in the station whose frequency is displayed (Figure 6.3). Billboards serve also as useful reminders of television programs, which people can view when they reach home. They have proved valuable to both radio and television stations in promoting the station's slogan and its *logo*, a distinctive symbol that identifies the station and incorporates its call letters and frequency or channel number. Use of the logo is not restricted to billboards, however. It may be employed advantageously in a variety of media (Figure 6.4).

TRANSIT In many cities, buses travel great distances daily, and advertisements on the outside are seen by vehicle drivers, pedestrians, and bus riders. Bus boards come in various sizes and often are displayed on the front, back, and sides of the bus. Advertisements on the inside are seen only by riders, but usually they are read, since they have little competition for attention. Interior cards are available in trains, also, and platform posters are seen by a sizable number of commuters.

Taxicabs operate in most communities, regardless of size. Like buses, they travel many miles each day, and advertisements on the front, rear, or rooftop are seen by vehicle drivers and pedestrians.

Other transit advertising media used by many stations include display cases at airports, the walls of bus shelters, and bus benches.

FIGURE 6.3 A talk station includes its unambiguous positioning statement in all its promotions, including billboard advertising. (Courtesy WGOW-FM.)

200

BROADCAST   Broadcast advertising refers to the use of radio advertising by a television station or television advertising by a radio station. It does not include the use of one's own station, an activity known as *promotion* and discussed later in the chapter. Using audience demographic information for particular television programs or dayparts, a radio station can direct its television advertising to the kinds of people who are most likely to listen to the format or program being promoted. The television medium's combination of sight, sound, color, and motion can be very persuasive and influence people to sample the product.

Many stations avoid television because of what they consider the relatively high cost of producing and airing commercials. However, some stations are reducing the production cost problem by using syndicated spots for their format and a tag line or other device to draw attention to their call letters and frequency.

Radio's mobility means that advertisements on radio can reach people virtually everywhere, no matter what they are doing. Radio stations attract specific demographics, and television stations can reach the sought-after audience by placing advertisements on stations whose formats attract those demographics.

Many television stations consider radio stations particularly effective during the evening drive-time period to advertise their early evening news programs. Some use their anchors to give headlines and invite listeners to view.

The advertising media described above are not the only ones available. Additional outlets or locations include station vehicles, telephone directories, the sides of buildings, malls and shopping centers, shows, displays, conventions, ballparks, time and temperature displays, skywriting, and direct mail.

Publicity and Public Relations   As used here, the term *publicity* refers to space in print publications or air time on other broadcast stations in

FIGURE 6.4 A station's logo may be incorporated in advertisements in all visual media, as shown in this print ad. (Courtesy WSKZ-FM.)

which information about the radio or television station appears and for which the station makes no payment.

In a sense, publicity, advertising, and anything else a station and its personnel do influence perceptions of the station and may be considered *public relations.* Here, the focus is on personal contacts between the station and its various publics.

PUBLICITY   In seeking to gain publicity through other media, broadcast stations recognize that other stations rarely are interested in publicizing their activities. Why should they aid the competition? However, they may be interested if the information is of wide public interest. Usually, such information deals with events or actions that do not reflect well on the station and represent the kind of publicity it could do without.

As a result, most stations concentrate their publicity efforts on the print media, particularly newspapers. Their activities generally center on the preparation of *publicity materials* and the organization of *publicity events*. Among the more common materials are these:

News and Feature Stories

News and feature stories about the station and its employees. Typical examples would include stories about new personnel, awards won by the station or a staff member, and ratings successes.

Photographs

When appropriate, photographs are included with news and feature releases. Sometimes, however, a photograph and caption may be used alone. A photograph of a new transmitter tower, for instance, may be considered an effective publicity device.

Press Kits

When stations wish to publicize special programs or events or, in television, the start of a new season or new program, often they compile a kit for the press. Releases, photographs, and other materials deemed important are included.

Program Listings

Television stations prepare complete broadcast schedules for use by daily newspapers and in the Sunday television supplement. Radio stations do not use listings as extensively. However, many stations list special programs or features, and the guests or subject matter of interview or call-in programs.

Like publicity materials, publicity events are intended to attract the attention of the media, particularly newspapers. It is hoped that, as a result, stories about the station will appear in print. The following are typical of events staged by many stations:

News Conferences

When a station has news that it considers especially significant, it may schedule a news conference and invite reporters and photographers from all media. Usually, the general manager and other appropriate station personnel are in attendance to make the announcement and answer questions. A press kit usually is distributed.

Celebrity Appearances

Radio and television stations try to obtain maximum publicity when celebrities visit their community, particularly if the station has organized the visit or can claim some connection with it. The purpose of the visit, schedule, interests, and personality of the visitor will determine the kinds of publicity opportunities available to the station. A news conference, reception, and appearances in public places are possible publicity vehicles. The celebrity may agree to be interviewed on the station and to record a promotional announcement. Many other events can be arranged with the visitor's cooperation.

Screenings

Many television stations invite newspaper reporters and media critics to view programs before the air date so that they may review them in their publications. Stations hope that the resulting articles will be positive and attract audience. Again, a press kit usually is prepared and distributed to those attending the screening.

Other kinds of events may be organized to capture media attention and publicity. Not all succeed, and that is one of the shortcomings of publicity as a method of audience promotion. The station has no control over the use of promotional materials delivered to the media or over whether reporters and photographers will attend a news conference. Screenings may result in negative comments or reviews and may prove damaging to the station's hopes. Usually, there is media interest in celebrity visits, though the focus of reporters and photographers may be on the celebrity exclusively and the station may not even rate a mention.

Publicity does have several advantages. Program listings are consulted and listening or viewing decisions are made as a result. Stories and photographs about the station in newspapers keep the station's call letters and frequency or channel number before the public. Comments on, or reviews of, programs attract public attention to the station, and the promotional benefits of publicity are achieved at little financial cost to the station.

Occasionally, a station reaps major publicity benefits unexpectedly. That was the case for a Baltimore station after the Baltimore Orioles began the season with ten straight losses. A disc jockey vowed to stay on the air until they won their first game. That happened 258 hours later. During that time, the vigil was covered, and the station mentioned, by the major broadcast TV networks, CNN, ESPN, the wire services, every major radio network, and hundreds of newspapers in this country, and by media around the world. That is the kind of publicity that money cannot buy!

A station can take steps to ensure publicity. At the least, the promotion and marketing director should initiate a media relations program with noncompeting media, especially the local newspaper. Establishing and maintaining contacts with entertainment reporters and with city, business, feature, and lifestyle editors can produce continuing benefits. They will result in a heightened awareness of the reporters' and editors' priorities and information interests and enable the station to satisfy them with news releases and ideas for stories. Joint sponsorship of charity or public service events with another medium provides an additional vehicle for favorable publicity.

PUBLIC RELATIONS   As indicated earlier, the term "public relations" covers essentially everything that affects how people perceive the station. Perceptions may be influenced by something as basic as the way a secretary

203

answers the telephone or the carefully planned involvement of the station and its staff in a community fundraising activity.

The principal publics with which a station tries to develop good relations are listeners or viewers and potential audiences. Influential publics, such as government leaders and leaders of community groups, also are important. Since advertisers also may be listeners or viewers, their perceptions of the station must not be ignored.

In striving to develop relationships with its publics, a station can do much to ensure that it will be regarded as a responsible, trusted, and valuable member of the community. For that reason, all employees must understand their role in the effort and must be encouraged, in all their dealings with the public, to act in ways that reflect well on the station.

At most stations, activities are planned to support the public relations effort. Opportunities abound, but the following are among those used most often:

Speakers' Program

Station executives and other staff members give talks to classes in schools and colleges and to community organizations.

Public Appearances

Station employees, especially radio personalities and television news anchors and reporters, appear at events in the community, such as charity fundraisers, shows, and exhibitions.

Participation in Community Organizations

Many stations encourage their employees to become members of organizations and clubs and to serve as officers. They also support their participation in fundraising or other activities of charitable and service groups.

Open House

The public is invited to visit and tour the station and to meet with members of the staff. Appropriate occasions might include the station's anniversary, an addition to the building, or the installation of new equipment.

Awards

Awards won by the station and its staff are displayed prominently in the station.

Sponsorships

Many stations sponsor student scholarships and awards for citizens who have made significant contributions to the community. Other opportunities for sponsorships include sporting, educational, and cultural activities in the community, such as youth sports teams, children's art exhibitions, and concerts.

The activities described above are indications of the kinds of planned public relations efforts by stations. However, the list is by no means exhaustive. Each station should consider ways in which it can play a role in the life of its community. The result can be a better community and heightened public awareness, as well as enhanced public perceptions of the station.

Promotions Promotions refer to efforts by the station to promote itself to the public directly rather than through other mass media. When a station uses its own air to promote its image or programming, it is engaging in what is known as *on-air promotion*. *Off-air promotion* describes those promotion activities carried out directly with the public off the air, such as through the distribution of giveaways and advertising specialties on which the station's logo is displayed.

ON-AIR: RADIO   Since a radio station determines how it will use its air time, promotional announcements, called *promos*, and other on-air promotions may be scheduled frequently, and may cover a wide range of programs, personalities, or station activities and achievements.

Format is a major factor in on-air promotion. Most stations with a music format draw attention to music content and personalities. Stations with a news format are likely to stress the range of news and information services provided. A talk station may emphasize personalities and issues.

Through its on-air promotions, a radio station strives to keep its call letters and frequency in the forefront of the listener's mind, to remind regular listeners and inform those sampling the station of its programming, and to point to the benefits of listening. Most stations also use their air extensively to promote their image through image promotion announcements or by including their slogan with other promotional announcements. The following are examples of ways in which radio stations use announcements to promote themselves on the air:

Identification Announcements

The Federal Communications Commission (FCC) requires stations to identify themselves hourly by call letters and city of license. Stations may include promotional material in their ID announcements, and frequently they do so with a musical jingle.

Slogan

Stations that have a slogan often use it in their FCC-required station identification announcements and with other promotional announcements during appropriate programs. A station whose slogan emphasizes its community role, for example, may use it with time checks, traffic and weather reports, and with news and sports programs.

Format

Station format promos are useful in identifying for listeners ways in which the station fulfills their desires, and may be scheduled at any time.

Programs

Individual program announcements permit the station to promote programs, as opposed to format. Stations may use them for the program of a

205

particular personality, a special, or a sports or interview program, for example.

News

Obviously, news is programming. For some stations it is the format. However, stations with a music format often separate news from other promotion. In addition to emphasizing the news programs themselves, many announcements draw attention to the news team, the speed and accuracy of their news gathering and reporting, and their awards.

Personalities

People, as well as programs, are a part of most stations' promotion efforts. Station personalities, such as disc jockeys, interviewers, and sports anchors, are among those who may be promoted.

CONTESTS Many stations have concluded that one of the most effective ways of attracting attention and listeners is through contests. Their conclusion is not surprising, in view of the lengths to which some people will go to win a prize.

Contestants have eaten live worms and a precooked leather football for Super Bowl tickets, and goldfish for concert tickets. They have buried themselves underground and changed their names legally for cash. At a marriage ceremony on a busy street corner, the groom dressed as a prisoner, complete with ball and chain, and the bride wore a police uniform to show who would be boss in the union. Why? That is what they said they would do if they won a station's "How Far Would You Go for a Trip to Jamaica?" contest.

The large number of stations that conduct contests suggests that they are a very effective promotional tool. However, not every contest idea will lead to a surge in audience. Some never move beyond the idea stage because further consideration shows that they are lotteries, and the broadcasting of lottery information is a criminal offense in many states.

There are three elements of a lottery, and all three must be present if a promotion is to be considered an offense. They are *prize, chance,* and *consideration.* Obviously a prize is anything of value that a contestant may win. Cash, merchandise, trips, and services are examples of the prize element. Chance exists if the winners or the value of the prizes are determined, in whole or in part, by chance or lot. It is not a factor if the outcome rests on the skill of contestants or on the use of subjective standards, as in a beauty or talent contest. Of all the elements, consideration is the most difficult to define. Basically, it is the price a contestant must pay to take part, such as an entry fee or possession of an item for which payment had to be made. It also covers the expenditure of substantial time and effort by the contestant, such as listening to a long sales pitch or taking a test drive. To complicate the problem further, the interpretation of "substantial" differs from state to state.

The federal ban on the broadcasting of many kinds of lottery information, including promotions, was lifted by the Charity Games Advertising Clarification Act of 1988, which took effect in 1990. However, the act did not override state and local lottery regulations, and the promotion and marketing director must be familiar with those regulations before embarking on any contest that contains the three elements described.

Assuming that the contest idea raises no legal problems, consideration focuses on whether it has possibilities. Among the questions to be asked are these:

- Is it simple? In other words, will the rules be understood easily and will it be easy for people to participate?

- Is it involving? Does it have the potential to excite people and provide enjoyment directly for participants and indirectly for those not taking part?

- How will it affect programming? Can it be conducted without detracting from programs? Is it compatible with the station's sound?

- Is it appealing? Is the targeted audience likely to be attracted to the contest and the prizes to be won?

- How frequently must it be scheduled and how long must it last to attract the number of participants to make it worthwhile?

- What will it cost? What kinds of expenses will the station incur and will they be justified?

If a decision is taken to proceed, rules must be established and prizes determined and obtained. At this stage, FCC rules on licensee-conducted contests take effect.[3] They require that the licensee "shall fully and accurately disclose the material terms of the contest, and shall conduct the contest substantially as announced or advertised. No contest description shall be false, misleading or deceptive with respect to any material term."[4]

Although the material terms vary with the nature of the contest, they generally include the following:

How to Enter or Participate

The station must let people know exactly what they must do to be considered entrants. The contest rules should be stated in easily understood language and should be free of ambiguities. The airing of contest information on the station or its inclusion on the Web site can provide regular listeners or users with the necessary details. If one of the aims is to boost audience, infrequent listeners and nonlisteners must be alerted and encouraged to tune in. Presumably, additional information vehicles will be required, and decisions will have to be made on which of them will reach targeted contestants most effectively and efficiently.

Eligibility

Who will and who will not be allowed to enter? Many stations routinely exclude employees and their families. The station may decide that others will not be eligible. For instance, if the grand prize is an automobile, persons who do not have a driver's license may be declared ineligible.

Entry Deadline

Deadline dates for the receipt of entries must be clear. This is particularly important if participants are required to mail them. Will they be dated by postmark or arrival at the station?

207

Prizes

The rules must indicate whether prizes can be won, when they can be won, the extent, nature, and value of the prizes, and the basis for their valuation. Prizes should not only be attractive but numerous enough to encourage participation. The station may provide them or arrange trade-outs for some or all of them with area businesses. Whatever their source, they must be described fairly and realistically. It would be hard to argue that "space available" plane tickets are part of a "dream vacation" or that "keys to a new car" is an accurate description if the car itself is not to be awarded. One of the biggest complaints from contest participants is the time they often have to wait to receive prizes. Accordingly, they should be available at the time winners are selected or shortly thereafter.

Selection of Winners

The rules must set forth when and how winners will be chosen. If entrants must telephone the station within a fixed period of time, attempts must be made to ensure that an open line will be available during that period. If the contest is designed to last for a designated period, care must be taken to avoid a premature end. This could happen, for instance, if the winner is the first person to submit the correct answer. If a tie is possible, a decision must be taken on a tie-breaking procedure.

The station should assign an employee to supervise the contest and to ensure that it runs smoothly. The person selected also will be responsible for guaranteeing compliance with the FCC's rules and other applicable regulations and laws. One station landed itself in trouble when it organized a "Roll in the Dough" contest. Scantily clad, honey-drenched contestants were required to roll around in 100,000 one-dollar bills to win the number that stuck to them. A total of $7,000 was awarded, but the station had to answer to the government for violating federal laws prohibiting the defacing of the currency.

The supervisor also should be charged with keeping contest records. This is especially important if individual prizes worth more than $600 are awarded, since details of the winners must be reported to the Internal Revenue Service.

ON-AIR: TELEVISION   Like radio, television on-air promotion seeks to remind or inform the audience about the station to which they are tuned, the programs available, and the benefits to be gained. But there is an important difference.

By their emphasis on format and personalities, radio stations attempt to encourage listeners to stay tuned for considerable periods of time. Television stations would like to believe that people will switch to them and stay there. In reality, they tend to be attracted to specific programs. Accordingly, much of the effort is directed toward promoting individual programs or series and, for that reason, the scheduling of promos is important.

If the announcements are to be successful, they must reach those people who are most likely to view the programs being promoted. Since viewer tastes usually reflect preferences for types of programs, it is common to promote news or information programs before, during, or after similar programs. The same goes for reality programs, situation comedies, game shows, dramas, and other program types.

The frequency of program promos is also important. The goal should be to ensure that all those who might tune in are exposed to the announcement at least once.

Among the most common methods used by television stations to promote their image or programs are the following:

Identification Announcements

Stations may identify themselves aurally or visually at the required hourly intervals. In practice, of course, most announcements regularly combine audio and video and often link call letters and city of license with the station's logo or slogan.

Slogan

Use of the slogan can be an effective way of promoting the station's image, whether used alone or in combination with other program promos. Some network-affiliated stations adopt the network slogan and add their call letters and channel number.

Programs

209

Entertainment: The most common method of promoting entertainment programs is with a film or tape clip. Use of a *specific promo*, one that comprises a scene from the next program in a series, is more effective than a *generic promo*, which emphasizes the series rather than any single program.

Movies: Use of clips is a common device to promote movies. Stations usually look for the strengths of individual movies for the promotional emphasis. Stars, the plot, awards won by the movie, or the comments of critics are among the items that may be promoted.

Information: Clips from films or taped information programs may be especially desirable if they include a clash of opinion or a heated exchange. If a well-known person is to be interviewed, the emphasis may be on the personality rather than the content.

Local News: Local news is a major element in the budget of most television stations and may be the only locally produced program broadcast daily. It also plays a major role in the community's perceptions of the station. For these reasons, most stations place high priority on local news promotion. Among the emphases of news are generic promos, such as the anchors and reporters, the speed and accuracy of the station's news gathering and reporting, awards won for news coverage, and a slogan used by the news department. Specific promos are used to highlight stories that will be included in a particular newscast.

Many stations air audio promos under the closing credits of programs, urging viewers to stay tuned for the program that follows or to join the station again for a program with similar appeal later that day or on following days. The major networks often use a split screen at the conclusion of their prime-time programs to permit affiliates to promote their late news.

A station's own air has the potential to be a most valuable promotional tool. Its potential will not be realized, however, if the promotion department has access only to those times that cannot be sold to advertisers. Station management must make a commitment to use air time in the same way clients use it: to sell something. In this case, the station is selling its image and programs.

Since promos must be scheduled to reach targeted demographics, the department must request *fixed-position promotions*, which, by definition, cannot be bumped. A contract is signed with the sales department listing promo length and the specific time or daypart in which it will air. For internal accounting purposes, the promotion department is billed like any other client. Of course, times that have not been sold to clients still may be available for use by the department at no charge.

Obviously, all programs cannot be promoted on a regular basis. Priorities must be established, and that is done in consultation with the general manager, program and/or news director, and sales manager. As noted earlier, news has an ongoing priority at most stations affiliated with the major networks because of its dominant impact on the station's image. At both affiliated and independent stations, high-cost syndicated programs must be given preference if they are to attract enough viewers to justify the price charged to advertisers to recoup the investment and generate a profit. Finally, scheduling should permit the kind of rotation that ensures adequate exposure without the kind of repetition that would prove annoying to viewers.

OFF-AIR PROMOTIONS   On-air promotions permit radio and television stations to reach people who happen to be listening or viewing. Off-air promotions can draw the attention of a wide range of people to the station.

Stations use a variety of means to promote themselves directly to the public off the air. Some, such as remote broadcasts and event sponsorships, are used intermittently. Many, however, are carried out on a continuing basis in both radio and television. They include the following:

Bumper Stickers

Size limitations are more than offset by the fact that stickers are seen daily by large numbers of people. Usually, they contain call letters or other station identifier and logo. Often, they include the station's slogan or promotion for a particular program.

Advertising Specialties

This term refers to a wide range of items bearing the station's logo and any other promotional material the station feels appropriate. Included in this category are pens, pencils, ashtrays, coffee mugs, T-shirts, and a host of similar items that are used regularly and are likely to be seen by persons other than the user.

Mail

Direct-mail promotions occasionally are used for special programs, though the cost is a deterrent to many stations. Some stations eliminate the mailing costs by including the promotion with bills, statements, or advertising matter sent out by companies sponsoring the programs.

Plastic Cards

Cards, similar to credit cards, are distributed by many stations and permit holders to enjoy special buying or use privileges with area merchants.

Record Sheets

Many radio stations publish weekly compilations of the top-selling recordings in their format and distribute them through music stores.

Station Publications

Many stations publish magazines and/or newsletters. In most instances, they use them both as a promotional and a sales vehicle. The articles promote the station, its projects, and its personnel. The ads that are included enable the station to satisfy advertisers' desire for a print ad, as well as a broadcast ad.

Station Web Site

The newest off-air method, the Web site offers round-the-clock promotion opportunities. It permits wide dissemination of a variety of information about the station, its programming and other activities, and access to and interaction with its personnel. Many stations provide multimedia content that combines text, graphics, audio, photographs, and moving video.

The Web site may be used to promote both image and programming. Successful image promotion requires consistency with other promotion methods in both the appearance and content of the station logo and theme. Program details and opportunities for users to sample representative program content can stimulate interest in tuning to the on-air product.

Stations have discovered that effective sites encourage return visits and lead to more frequent listening or viewing. Among the ingredients are pages that are visually pleasing, ease in locating desired information, and content that is appealing and updated regularly.

A study of television station Web sites revealed that banner ads for programming were most common. They were followed by news banner ads and online contests and sweepstakes.[5] Promotional content included most frequently on radio Web sites is information about the disc jockeys, concerts, and station events.

To maximize the potential of the site, stations should familiarize themselves with the rewards that visitors expect and respond to them, when feasible. Often, they go well beyond the acquisition of information. One study found that the top feature sought on radio sites was the ability to listen to the station.[6] Other features that were ranked highly pointed to the desire for interactivity. They included opportunities to enter contests, vote on the music, and contact the DJs and personalities.[7]

Regular listeners and viewers may be encouraged to visit the site by on-air references to it. To attract others, stations should list the address in all their printed materials and include it in all their nonprint advertising and promotion pursuits.

211

Public Service As noted in Chapter 4, "Broadcast Programming," a station should foster good relationships with the public. One of the most effective ways of attaining that goal is through public service. Conscientious effort will be rewarded with community gratitude and awards, favorable publicity, and the perception of the station as a responsible corporate citizen.

Success is achieved to a large extent by employee and station involvement in community activities. However, a station can enhance its identity by a commitment to public service on the air. Using air time for promotions designed to raise funds or goods for the needy, to encourage traffic safety, or to combat adult illiteracy are examples of ways in which service can be rendered.

Stations regularly carry public service announcements for nonprofit agencies. Their broadcast does not lead, necessarily, to a public perception of the station as a concerned member of the community. But combining them with a serious commitment to public affairs programming may produce the desired results. The programs must deal with issues of community concern or meet a community need, and must be aired at times when they are likely to be heard or seen by a significant number of people. Many stations satisfy the first requirement, but not the second.

212

SALES PROMOTION

Sales promotion seeks to encourage the purchase of time on the station by advertisers and advertising agencies, and often involves the promotion of the broadcast media, as well as the station, for advertising.

Advertisers are interested in getting their messages to the people most likely to use their products or services, and in the most economical way. Accordingly, sales promotion places heavy emphasis on the broadcast media's ability to reach targeted demographics at a competitive cost.

The strengths of the station may be promoted in terms of the *quantity* or *quality* of the audience. Quantity refers to the number of listeners or viewers, while quality denotes characteristics of the audience, such as age, gender, and socioeconomic status. The station may point to quantitative or qualitative strengths over its entire schedule, during periods of the day, or in particular programs.

The element of cost is used in comparison with competing stations as well as other media. The aim is to persuade the advertiser that the station can deliver the number or kinds of people desired in a cost-efficient manner. An effective sales promotion campaign is the result of careful planning based on the following considerations:

Campaign Purpose

Is the primary purpose to project station image or sell time? If the former, will it be attractive to the targeted advertisers? If the latter, will the focus be on particular programs or dayparts? What about the financial expectations?

Target Clients

Will the campaign be directed toward existing advertisers and time-buyers, potential new clients, or both?

Client Benefits

What benefits will the campaign stress? Demographics and the cost of reaching them? Exposure to potential new customers? Other benefits?

Promotion Methods

Which medium or media will be used to reach the clients? Will the station's own air or Web site be used? What about the possibility of a joint promotion with an advertiser or advertisers?

Content

What content will be suited best to the medium or media selected? Can it be prepared by station staff or will outside services be required?

Budget

What costs will be incurred? Can they be justified by anticipated new business?

213

Scheduling

During which quarter of the year will the campaign benefit the station most? Will that period match advertisers' needs?

Program Impact

Can the campaign be used to draw additional listeners or viewers to the station? Will it detract from programming?

Evaluation

Will the campaign be evaluated on the basis of dollars generated or will other criteria be used, also?

PROMOTION METHODS

The targets of sales promotion efforts are those persons who make decisions about the purchase of advertising time. For the most part, that means advertisers themselves and media buyers in advertising agencies. The emphasis is on what the station can accomplish for the advertiser. The methods are the same as those used for audience promotion.

Advertising The broadcast and advertising trade press is an effective means of reaching those who are influential in making time-buying decisions, and includes publications such as *B&C Broadcasting & Cable*, *Advertising Age*, *R&R (Radio & Records)*, and *Daily Variety*. Often, stations place additional advertisements in the trade publications of other professions so that they may directly reach decision-makers in businesses that advertise, or may be persuaded to advertise, on radio or television.

The content of the advertisements is determined by the purpose of the campaign. Some attempt to project the station's image. Others seek to sell time on the station. It is hoped that success with the first will influence decisions on the second. The important point is that all advertisements should attract the interest of the decision-makers and be tailored to meet their needs.

The purpose of the advertising will suggest those characteristics of the station to be highlighted. Image advertising may place particular emphasis on community involvement and resulting recognition received by the station through community awards. The theme of market leadership may be projected through ratings and station facilities.

Advertisements geared directly to the sale of time often point to ratings for particular programs. Ratings dominance in certain dayparts and with key demographics also may be stressed. Additional characteristics may include the station's coverage area, personalities, and merchandising plans.

Direct-mail advertising can be targeted to advertisers of particular kinds of products or services and draw attention to the station's strengths for those advertisers. Additionally, direct mail offers great flexibility in the number and format of sales promotion materials that can be distributed.

Trade press and direct-mail advertising permit stations to reach directly those who make decisions on the purchase of advertising time and reduce the amount of waste circulation. Other advertising vehicles, such as newspapers, billboards, and displays, are used to promote sales, even though the audience for them is not limited to time-buyers.

Publicity and Public Relations   The focus of sales publicity in newspapers and magazines is on those station activities and achievements likely to impress advertisers. Stories about ratings successes, awards won by the station or staff members, and favorable reviews of programs are examples of information that can be useful.

Public relations activity concentrates on personal contacts between station executives and sales personnel with the business community. Many stations require or urge membership in appropriate community and professional organizations and participation in community activities. A speakers' program allows station personnel to make presentations at meetings attended by people involved in business.

Promotions   One of the most basic and effective tools is the sales kit used by the local sales staff, the station representative, and advertising agencies. It provides information on the market and the station, and may be left behind after a sales call or mailed to potential clients.

With some modifications, many of the off-air promotions used in audience promotion can be beneficial in sales promotion. Bumper stickers can point to the station's advertising effectiveness. Advertising specialties can be selected from among those used most frequently by business persons. Ashtrays, coffee mugs, pens, pencils, calendars, and memo pads are examples.

Mailings or E-mails to actual and potential time-buyers could include information on station sales activity, advertising news, explanations of advertising legislation, and a calendar of forthcoming special programs or events that the station will air or sponsor. Other examples are expressions of thanks for business placed with the station and details of forthcoming advertising opportunities.

The Web site lends itself to the distribution of much of the content of mailings. Relevant audience data and listener or viewer profiles could be added to the list.

On a more personal level, station sales staff promote sales by entertaining clients at meals or at sports, social, or cultural events. Many stations organize, especially for clients, sports or recreation activities such as golf or tennis tournaments. Television stations often arrange a party for advertisers to see excerpts from the fall season's program schedule.

Increasingly, the impetus for promotions is coming from the client, who teams with the station in a joint effort. Many advertising agencies make such activities a condition of the buy. In these so-called *value-added promotions*, the client receives from the station marketing assistance that exceeds the value of the spots purchased. However, these promotions can produce benefits for the station—and for the consumer, too.

Plastic cards are an example. The station produces and distributes the cards and airs announcements promoting their use to obtain discounts at the client's business. The client makes a spot buy in an amount that matches the value of the promotional time and offers the discounts. As a result, the station obtains revenue from the sale; the advertiser receives exposure beyond the time purchased and the improved in-store traffic that should result; and the card holders enjoy the discounts. Such promotions impress participating clients with the station's advertising effectiveness, and can be used as a persuasive tool with other clients or potential clients.

Mutual benefits can be achieved, also, through radio remote broadcasts from stores, malls, and other places of business. The joint sponsorship of events by stations and advertisers is another example, and appearances by radio and TV personalities at places of business can have similarly beneficial results.

Many other joint ventures are possible. However, they should be chosen carefully, and with an eye to their value as sales promotion tools.

A value-added promotion method practiced by some stations is *merchandising*. It involves services by the station to assist the advertiser, but the station receives no income, apart from that for the air time purchased.

In effect, the station is donating those services to the advertiser. For that reason, many stations reject merchandising entirely, but some stations use it to promote sales, especially if they are seeking a competitive edge against other stations or if their ratings are so low that additional sales incentives are necessary.

Among the more common methods of merchandising are these:

Point-of-sale signs, supplied by the station and located in the advertiser's store or place of business.

Displays in stores and shops. Again, the materials are provided by the station.

Newspaper and billboard advertisements for a program that the advertiser sponsors. The advertiser is named in the ads, but does not pay any of the advertising costs.

Appearances by station personalities at the advertiser's place of business, at no cost to the advertiser.

Remote radio broadcasts from the advertiser's business, with the station meeting the costs involved.

Public Service A station's dedication to public service is no less important to its sales promotion than to its audience promotion efforts. The station that is perceived by advertisers as an important member of the community can reap financial benefits. Whether that perception is based on the involvement of the station and its staff in community activities or on its commitment to public affairs programming, the sales department has an important stake in the station's public service endeavors.

WHAT'S AHEAD?

The role of the promotion and marketing director has always been important. As competition for audiences and advertisers continues to intensify, it will become pivotal to the station's success in projecting an identifiable image that differentiates it from other stations and other media.

In this new environment, branding will assume even greater significance. If listeners and viewers are to be attracted to the station, they must have a clear and unambiguous perception of what its product is, to whom it is directed, and the benefits it offers.

The branding imperative coincides with an era of reductions in audience size, especially for television stations, lessening the impact of on-air promotions.

Their diminished influence also will be felt by radio stations. Listeners have limited tolerance for nonprogram content. Why should they suffer clutter when they can program their own listening experiences, courtesy of the Internet and the iPod?

To avoid clutter, stations will be compelled to place heavier reliance on alternative promotional methods. One that will undoubtedly grow in importance is the Internet. Webcasting, the Web site, and E-mail will continue to offer unprecedented opportunities to forge stronger bonds with existing audiences and to attract new ones.

The benefits of the Internet to stations of all sizes and in all markets are many. The online medium is more affordable and cost-effective than traditional off-air media. Its permanent accessibility and its capacity to offer detailed and tailored content permit the station to expand its range of services. It also facilitates database building and market research.

Another existing off-air method that may become more important is billboard advertising. Its use will add to promotion and marketing costs. However, as noted earlier in the chapter, billboards offer many advantages, especially with longer commuting times in many markets. Of course, one way of deriving benefits and minimizing expenses is to use suitably painted station vehicles as roaming billboards. When they are not being used for remotes, they may be parked in high-traffic locations.

Like radio, television can enjoy the benefits of the Internet. In fact, many stations use their Web site chiefly as a promotional tool. Even so, some TV promotion directors worry that driving audiences to the site may be accompanied by the risk of losing them as viewers.

A much greater challenge looms for them. It grows out of decisions about how the station will use its digital bandwidth. Theoretically, the transition from analog to digital offers additional promotional platforms. Capitalizing on them, of course, rests on the way in which they are programmed. In turn, that will pose branding considerations and inevitable dilemmas. Will the existing brand be expanded and reinforced? Will a new brand, or brands, have to be introduced? If so, what will be the impact on viewers who are already bombarded with brands?

The new age will demand new strategies. The threats to stations are many. Fortunately, so are the opportunities.

SUMMARY

Broadcast promotion and marketing refers to those activities through which a radio or television station attempts to promote its own interests. In many stations, the task is assigned to a promotion and marketing department, headed by a director who answers directly to the general manager.

The director assists in the development of a promotion plan, which identifies the station's competitive strengths and weaknesses, and sets forth a course of action to capitalize on strengths and correct weaknesses. Carrying out the plan is the director's responsibility and involves the planning, creation, implementation, and evaluation of audience and sales promotion campaigns.

The promotion and marketing director should have knowledge of marketing, promotion methods, research, professional services, and applicable laws and regulations. Professional skills in writing and production and in planning and evaluating promotion campaigns are also desirable. Adaptability, cooperation, and creativity are among the necessary personal qualities, and they should be combined with the administrative ability to run the department.

Audience promotion seeks to maintain and increase the station's audience. Usually this is accomplished by projecting to listeners or viewers an image of the station (image promotion) and by promoting the station's content (program promotion).

Sales promotion is targeted toward those who make decisions on the purchase of advertising time, usually advertisers themselves and media buyers in advertising agencies. Promotion activities may be designed to project the station's image or to sell time to clients.

Even though the targets and goals of audience and sales promotion may differ, most stations use four principal methods for both: advertising, publicity and public relations, promotions, and public service.

The most commonly used advertising media for audience promotion are newspapers, outdoor, transit, and broadcast. Sales promotion relies more heavily on trade press and direct-mail advertising, though other media are used.

Many stations consider publicity to be "free" advertising, since they receive promotional benefits at little or no financial cost. Accordingly, they provide newspapers with news releases, photographs, press kits, and program listings for possible use. Publicity events, such as news conferences and TV program screenings, also are organized for coverage by other media.

Public relations is a broad term covering essentially anything that may influence people's perceptions of a station. Most stations attempt to influence perceptions through planned efforts. Speeches, public appearances, participation in community organizations, awards, and sponsorships are examples of audience promotion activities. In sales promotion, the public relations effort focuses most frequently on personal contacts between station executives and sales staff and members of the business community.

Promotions are attempts to promote the station directly to audiences and advertisers both on and off the air. Typical radio on-air audience promotions include ID announcements, format, program, news and personality promos, and contests. Television on-air promotions are characterized by promos for individual programs or series. In both radio and television, the station's Web site is an increasingly important means of off-air promotion. Others include bumper stickers, advertising specialties, and direct mail.

Sales promotions include the sales kit, mailings to advertisers, and advertising specialties. Entertaining clients and potential clients is a widespread practice. Increasingly, stations are engaging in joint marketing efforts with advertisers in value-added promotions.

Public service is important both in audience and sales promotion. In general, it is characterized by close identification with the community through station and staff involvement in community activities and through relevant public service promotions and announcements and public affairs programming.

Radio promotion directors will have to find new ways of attracting audiences if they are to avoid on-air clutter. For their television counterparts, the introduction of digital offers new promotional opportunities, and many resultant challenges.

CASE STUDY: RADIO

You are promotion director of an FM oldies station in a medium market in the Southeast.

Account executive Kevin Steel stops by your office. He handles the Crofton Outlet Mall account and tells you that the mall—a major client—will be celebrating its tenth anniversary in November. He has an idea for a joint promotion to mark the event.

The station's traffic reporter will fly his plane over the mall on the anniversary date and drop "Crofton Cash" books on the parking lot. The books will contain fake dollar bills to be used like cash at mall stores.

The mall will make a $10,000 advertising buy on the station. The station will air promos and do a live remote from the mall on the "drop" day.

EXERCISES

1. What promotional benefits does Kevin's idea have for the station?

2. Are there any shortcomings? Can they be removed?

3. Do you anticipate any problems in executing the idea? If so, describe them.

CASE STUDY: TELEVISION

You are promotion and marketing director of a CBS affiliate in a major market in the Northeast.

Your 5:30 P.M. newscast ranks fourth in its time slot. You show some improvement at 6:00 P.M., but not enough to move beyond third place against competing newscasts on the ABC and NBC affiliates.

Your Monday 5:30 P.M. broadcast includes a "Home Sweet Home" segment with tips on residential property maintenance and repair. It is sponsored by a homebuilder. You approach her about a joint promotion. Here is how it will work.

Every Monday segment will contain the answer to a question to be posed in the Tuesday newscast. Viewers will be invited to submit the answer to the station by email. Every Wednesday, a correct answer will be drawn and the winner's name announced in the broadcast.

The promotion will run for 12 weeks. At the end of that time, a grand prize winner will be selected from the 12, weekly winners.

The prize will be a new, three-bedroom house, constructed by the builder at her expense.

The builder will agree to continue sponsorship of "Home Sweet Home" for three years beyond the expiration of her current contract. The station will air a schedule of promos in its three, early-evening local newscasts during the promotion period.

EXERCISES

1. Is the promotion a contest or a lottery? Explain.

2. What impact is it likely to have on the ratings for the 5:30 P.M. newscast? Why?

3. Are there potential problems with the promotion? What are they? Can they be overcome?

NOTES

[1] Different titles are used for the head of the department responsible for promotion and marketing. They include promotion manager, marketing director, director of creative services, and director of advertising, promotion, and publicity.

[2] Just as the title of the head of the department differs from station to station, so does the name of the department.

[3] The FCC defines a contest as a "scheme in which a prize is offered or awarded, based upon chance, diligence, knowledge or skill, to members of the public."

[4] 47 CFR 73.1216.

[5] Sylvia M. Chan-Olmstead and Jung Suk Park, "From On-Air to Online World: Examining the Content and Structures of Broadcast TV Stations' Web Sites," *Journalism & Mass Communication Quarterly*, Vol. 77, No. 2 (Summer 2000), pp. 321–339.

[6] *Radio Station Web Site Content: An In-Depth Look*, p. 10.

[7] *Ibid.*

ADDITIONAL READINGS

Bobeck, Ann. *Casinos, Lotteries & Contests*, 2nd ed. Washington, DC: National Association of Broadcasters, 2003.

Eastman, Susan Tyler (ed.). *Research in Media Promotion*. Mahwah, NJ: Lawrence Erlbaum, 2000.

Eastman, Susan Tyler, Douglas A. Ferguson, and Robert Klein (eds.). *Promotion and Marketing for Broadcasting, Cable & the Web*, 4th ed. Boston, MA: Focal Press, 2001.

Money Makers II: Sales Promotions from the Hundred Plus Television Markets, 2nd ed. Washington, DC: National Association of Broadcasters, 1996.

Todreas, Timothy M. *Value Creation and Branding in Television's Digital Age*. Westport, CT: Quorum Books, 1999.

Broadcast Regulations 7

This chapter surveys broadcast regulations and focuses on

- modifications of the 1996 Telecommunications Act regulatory framework

- FCC licensing and reporting requirements

- FCC policies pertaining to ownership, programming, announcements, commercials, and operating requirements

- FCC regulations on indecency, violence, contests, hoaxes, and political campaigns

Historically, broadcasting has been the most heavily regulated mass medium. Broadcast regulation was based upon concepts of "public interest" and scarcity, which meant, simply, that there were more applicants for licenses than there were available frequencies. In the 1980s, a deregulation frenzy swept the federal government, and the "scarcity" rationale for regulation was declared by the Federal Communications Commission (FCC) to be no longer valid.

In the early 1990s, the relaxation of formal broadcast regulation continued. Ownership rules were changed in 1991 to permit duopoly, the common ownership of more than one station in the same class of service in the same market. Deregulation casualties of the 1980s and 1990s included long-standing FCC rules, such as the Financial Interest and Syndication Rules (Fin-Syn), the Prime-Time Access Rule (PTAR), the Fairness Doctrine, the Personal Attack Rule, and the Political Editorial Rules. In February 1996, the Congress enacted, and the President signed, the Telecommunications Act of 1996.[1]

This new law was a sweeping revision of the 1934 Communications Act. However, its principal long-term impact has been on the ownership face of the industry. The law should more appropriately be called the "Consolidation Act of 1996," because it has permitted concentration of electronic media ownership at the national and local levels. And that consolidation theme has been continued and expanded since passage of the act.[2]

BACKGROUND

During the early days of broadcasting, there were very few rules to follow. Anyone who wanted to transmit a broadcast signal on any frequency could do so, thus creating a jamming effect on frequencies carrying more than one station.

After years of discussion and compromise among all factions involved in this growing industry, Congress passed the Radio Act of 1927. The act provided for the formation of a Federal Radio Commission (FRC), comprising five persons appointed by the President, one of whom would be selected as chairman. The FRC was to oversee broadcasting on a trial basis for one year. At the end of the year, its term was extended and it continued in effect until 1934.

It soon became apparent that broadcasting needed a new and more comprehensive regulatory agency. In February 1934, President Franklin D. Roosevelt sent to Congress a proposal to create an agency to be known as the Federal Communications Commission (FCC) and to bring all means of electronic communication under the jurisdiction of this one agency. The Commission would be composed of seven members appointed by the President, with the advice and consent of the Senate. One member would be designated as chairman by the President.

Today, the FCC is a five-member body, but that is not the only change. Under Chairman Mark Fowler (1981–1987), the FCC embarked on a program of industry deregulation. His successor, Dennis Patrick (1987-1989), accelerated the trend, culminating with the elimination of the Fairness Doctrine.[3] That decision put the FCC into bad standing with Congress, which had already been legislating to fill the regulatory void caused by the agency's policy changes.

After George Herbert Walker Bush became president in 1989, he appointed as FCC chairman Alfred Sikes, former head of the National Telecommunications and Information Administration. Sikes successfully mended congressional fences. He worked to revise certain archaic rules, such as those on financial interest and syndication and, at the same time, pioneered new concepts, like the entry of telephone companies into video. Sikes also undertook some technology-based initiatives, such as high-definition television (HDTV) and digital audio broadcasting (DAB). He was an activist chairman who perpetuated marketplace regulation and charted many new waters. Sikes resigned on January 19, 1993, one day before Bill Clinton assumed office.

President Clinton appointed Commissioner James Quello as acting chairman. He served until Clinton nominee Reed Hundt was sworn in as chairman later that year. Chairman Hundt's FCC was often bogged down in internal conflict. He did initiate efforts to reintroduce some elements of licensee responsibility in the wake of deregulation. One of his successful undertakings was in the area of children's television content and reporting rules. Early in President Clinton's second term, Hundt resigned and was replaced by former FCC General Counsel William Kennard.

In 2001, another Bush, George W., became president. He appointed Michael Powell, son of Secretary of State Colin Powell, as FCC chairman.

223

He attempted to accelerate media consolidation[4] and wrestled with the questions of indecency, violence, and localism. The FCC is a political body and has regular changes in leadership and membership. That is evidenced by Powell's resignation in 2005 and his replacement by Kevin Martin.

THE ROLE OF BROADCAST REGULATIONS

THE FCC, THE BROADCASTER, AND THE PUBLIC INTEREST

When broadcasting emerged, it was recognized as having an obligation to serve "the public interest." This phrase, along with "convenience and necessity," was included in the Communications Act for specific reasons, not the least of which was to give the FCC maximum latitude to use its own judgment in matters relating to commercial broadcasting. Section 303 of the Communications Act, for example, begins: "Except as otherwise provided in this Act, the Commission from time to time, as public convenience, interest or necessity requires shall . . . ." This section goes on to list 19 functions, ranging from the power to classify radio stations to the power to make whatever rules and regulations the FCC needs to carry out the provisions of the act. The term "public interest" similarly occurs in the crucially important sections dealing with granting, renewing, and transferring licenses.

The public interest has been discussed and defined by Congress, the courts, broadcasters, and the public for so long that its meaning has become whatever a person wants it to be. This is especially true of broadcasters, since they are ultimately the ones who determine what the public interest means, at least for their audiences. The real burden of definition must come from the FCC, but even the FCC has granted leeway to licensees, since they are in daily contact with their audiences and obtain feedback from them, thereby being able to gauge what is in their best interests. The FCC does believe that it is in the public interest for stations to carry programs dealing with community issues and problems. The whole topic of what is and what is not public interest is once again under review.

Following the Red Lion Supreme Court decision in 1969[5] upholding the constitutionality of the Fairness Doctrine, many broadcast regulations were based upon the scarcity rationale. It was scarcity that allowed for different First Amendment standards for the print and electronic media businesses. In its 1987 decision eliminating the doctrine, the FCC decided that scarcity of viewpoint sources no longer existed, which left only the concept of public interest as a basis for regulations. In the future, decisions on the public interest would be made on a case-by-case basis.

OTHER REGULATORY AGENCIES

Broadcast regulation does not come entirely from the FCC. Of all the regulatory agencies, probably the one that has the greatest impact on broadcasting, other than the FCC, is the Federal Trade Commission (FTC).

Deregulation by the FCC has further enhanced the importance of that agency. In 1986, the FCC eliminated many of its rules on station business practices, including fraudulent billing and contests. The terminated regulations were characterized as "unnecessary regulatory underbrush," which duplicated other federal and state laws. Much of the responsibility abdicated by the FCC was absorbed by the FTC.

The FTC is the federal government's primary agent for advertising regulation. Its general mandate is to guard against unfair and deceptive advertising in all media. Broadcasters, or rather the companies that advertise on broadcast facilities, are the main targets of this agency, since the broadcast media are a mass-advertising funnel that reaches out to almost the entire population. Because the agency was created under the authority of Congress to regulate interstate commerce, products or services must be sold in interstate commerce, or the advertising medium must be somehow affected by interstate commerce, before the FTC can intervene. Since it is charged with policing unfair or deceptive advertising, the terminology needs to be defined.

Deceptive Advertising   There are four considerations in deciding whether an advertisement is deceptive:

- The meaning of the advertisement must be determined. In other words, what promise is made?

- The truth of the message must be determined.

- When only a part of the advertisement is false, it must be determined whether the false part is a material aspect of the advertisement; that is, is it capable of affecting the purchasing decision of the consumer?

- The level of understanding and experience of the audience to which the advertisement is directed must be determined.[6]

Two cases will help explain these concepts. In the early 1970s, a spokesman for Chevron F-310 gasoline additive in advertisements claimed he was standing in front of the Standard Oil Research Laboratories when, in fact, he was standing in front of a county courthouse. Was this deceptive advertising? The FTC said no—that the location of a spokesman is irrelevant to a consumer making a purchasing decision.[7]

On the other hand, Standard Oil of California was ordered to stop claiming that its Chevron gasolines with F-310 produce pollution-free exhaust. The Commission banned television and print advertisements in which the company claimed that just six tankfuls of Chevron will clean up a car's exhaust to the point that it is almost free of exhaust-emission pollutants.[8]

Other agencies, both state and federal, also are involved in the regulation of advertising. The advertising industry itself has industry-sponsored groups that are active in resolving complaints against advertisers. The National Advertising Division (NAD) of the Council of Better Business Bureaus is an example.

Consumers, as a whole, have little or no influence when it comes to policing false advertising. For the most part, all they can do is report it to the regulatory agencies.

Besides the FTC, the advertising business is touched by at least 32 federal statutes, including the Federal Food, Drug, and Cosmetic Act; Consumer Credit Protection Act; Copyright Ac; and Consumer Product Safety Act.

225

The FTC's ascendancy to fill the regulatory void left by the FCC has not been limited to advertising matters. In a significant decision on FCC must-carry rules, a federal court adopted an FTC report that concluded that the absence of the rules would not be harmful to local broadcasting.[9]

Other federal agencies and executive departments have also stepped into the power vacuum left by FCC deregulation actions. One such example is the Department of Justice. It has become especially active since passage of the 1996 Telecommunications Act. As noted above, the act allowed expanded electronic media ownership consolidation nationally and locally. Since then, the department has been investigating on a case-by-case basis the extent to which legally permitted consolidation also concentrates on radio advertising revenue. Such examinations have extended to situations where in-market concentration leads to dominance in a particular format. Transactions subject to review before transfer are said to have been "red flagged." Still another federal agency stepping into the power vacuum is the National Telecommunications and Information Administration (NTIA), which is located in the Commerce Department and is the White House policy office on telecommunications. The NTIA is principally a policy agency and its initiatives often show up in the FCC's agenda.

THE ROLE OF FCC COUNSEL

While it is theoretically possible to navigate the requirements and regulations of the FCC without professional assistance, it is a bad idea. Most electronic media companies opt for qualified legal representation.

Professional counsel keeps the client abreast of the many FCC deadlines (Figure 7.1) and provides a vehicle for commenting on rules and regulations changes that the FCC is considering. Available FCC firms range from the sole practitioner to the midsize boutique communications specialty firms to the mega worldwide firms.

For purposes of illustration, the authors have selected a Washington, DC, boutique firm, Cohn & Marks. This is a smaller specialty firm of about ten attorneys. Figure 7.2 profiles the firm's experience, services, and illustrative clientele.

DEADLINES TO WATCH

License Renewal, FCC Reports & Public Inspection Files

Jan. 1, 2004 & Jan. 16, 2004	Radio stations in **Arkansas, Louisiana** and **Mississippi** broadcast pre-filing announcements regarding license renewal applications. Radio stations in **Alabama** and **Georgia** broadcast post-filing announcements regarding license renewal applications.
Jan. 10, 2004	Filing deadline for quarterly Children's Television Programming Reports for all commercial television stations.
Jan. 10, 2004	Place Issues/Programs List for October–December quarter in public inspection file for all full-service radio and television stations and Class A TV stations.
Feb. 2, 2004	Filing deadline for license renewal applications for radio stations in **Arkansas, Louisiana** and **Mississippi**.
Feb. 2, 2004	Deadline to file biennial Ownership Report and to place EEO Public File Report in public inspection file and on internet web site for all radio and television stations in **Arkansas, Kansas, Louisiana, Mississippi, Nebraska, New Jersey, New York** and **Oklahoma**.
Feb. 2, 2004 & Feb. 16, 2004	Radio stations in **Indiana, Kentucky** and **Tennessee** broadcast pre-filing announcements regarding license renewal applications. Radio stations in **Alabama, Arkansas, Georgia, Louisiana,** and **Mississippi** broadcast post-filing announcements regarding license renewal applications.

Deadlines for Comments in FCC Proceedings

Docket	Comments	Reply Comments
Docket 00-230; FNPRM Secondary Sprectrum Market		Jan. 5
CSR 6257 Request for Exemption from Closed Captioning Rules for Paul Gaudino Family Fitness Show	Jan. 8	Jan. 28
Docket 00-248; FNPRM Streamlining Rules for Satellites and Satellite Earth Stations		Jan. 10
Request for Exemption from Closed Captioning Rules for John Aukerberg Show	Jan. 21	Feb. 10
Report No. SPB-196 Proposals to Reduce Spacing Between Director Broadcast Satellites	Jan. 23	Feb. 13
Docket 03-185; NPRM Digital LPTV		Jan. 26
Docket 97-80; 2dFNPRM Consumer Equipment and Digital Compatibility	Feb. 13	Mar. 15
Docket 03-237; NOI/NPRM Interference Temperature	(1)	(2)
Docket 03-254; NPRM Coordination of Satellite and Broadcast Auxilary Shared Use	(3)	(4)
Docket 03-108; NPRM Development of Smart Radios	TBA	TBA

(1) Comments due 75 days after publication in Federal Register.
(2) Reply comments due 105 days after publication in Federal Register.
(3) Comments due 30 days after publication in Federal Register.
(4) Reply Comments due 45 days publication in Federal Register.

Commercial FM Allotments

The FCC has recently allotted the following commercial FM channels to the communities indicated below. The filing deadlines for these allotments will be announced in accord with the procedures for broadcast spectrum auctions. This is a listing only of the allotments that have been announced during recent weeks. Other channels have been allotted previously which will also be subject to the auction rules.

Community	Channel	MHz	Filing Deadline
Ash Fork, AZ	267A	101.3	TBA
Fredonia, AZ	278C1	103.5	TBA
Peach Springs, AZ	285C3	104.9	TBA
Hartington, NE	232C2	94.3	TBA
Carrington, NM	261C2	100.1	TBA
Leedey, OK	297A	107.3	TBA
Centerville, TX	274A	102.7	TBA
Memphis, TX	297A	107.3	TBA
Presido, TX	292C1	106.3	TBA
Silverton, TX	252A	98.3	TBA
Beaver, UT	246A	97.1	TBA
Salina, UT	233C	94.5	TBA

Cut-Off Date for Low Power FM Applications

The FCC has accepted for filing applications for new low power FM stations as indicated below. The deadline for filing a petition to deny against any of these applications is indicated below. Informal objections may be filed any time prior to grant of the application.

Community	Channel	MHz	Filing Deadline
Springfield, IL	241	96.1	Jan. 7
Springfield, IL	240	95.9	Jan. 7
Springfield, IL	240	95.9	Jan. 7
Springfield, IL	240	95.9	Jan. 7
Beavercreek, OH	248	97.5	Jan. 7
Bowling Green, OH	249	97.7	Jan. 7
Springfield, OH	248	97.5	Jan. 7
Yellow Springs, OH	248	97.5	Jan. 7
Guerneville, CA	236	95.1	Jan. 12
Round Lake Hgts. IL	268	101.5	Jan. 12
Jackson, TN	254	98.7	Jan. 12
Knoxville, TN	266	101.1	Jan. 12
Merritt Island, FL	238	95.5	Jan. 20
Sarasota, FL	243	96.5	Jan. 20
Hobbs, NM	290	105.9	Jan. 20
Midland, TX	231	94.1	Jan. 20
Fargo, ND	290	105.9	Jan. 20
Fenwick, WV	269	101.7	Jan. 21
Corning, NY	298	107.5	Jan. 22

FIGURE 7.1 FCC deadlines. (Source: Drinker Biddle & Reath, LLP. Used with permission.)

Cohn and Marks LPP provides specialized legal representation to national and international communications and media-related businesses. It has a strong general litigation and lobbying capability, and represents a wide variety of national businesses, trade associations, and local entities in regulated and other aspects of their operations.

Experience

The reach and complexity of modern communications systems and technology have led to the development of related practice areas. In addition to the Federal Communications Commission, members of the firm are also experienced in dealing with the following government entities:

-- United States Federal courts, including the United States Supreme Court

-- State Courts

-- United States Congress and State Legislatures

-- Department of Commerce

-- Department of State

-- Federal Trade Commission

-- Department of Justice

-- United States Copyright Office

-- Copyright Arbitration Royalty Panel

-- Patent and Trademark Office

-- Equal Employment Opportunity Commission

Services

The firm's communications legal services include:

Providing advice and counsel on business and regulatory aspects of mergers, acquisitions and other transactions subject to government approval;

Prosecuting and, when necessary, litigating issues concerning the acquisition and renewal of broadcast stations, cable television, and common carrier licenses and franchises and providing regulatory analysis regarding ongoing operational matters;

Providing advice, counsel and litigation services on all related aspects of a client's business, including antitrust and trade regulation, copyright and trademark, hiring, firing, and employment discrimination issues, and drafting and reviewing contracts necessary to business activities.

Advising clients on and litigating on their behalf First Amendment issues such as libel and slander (including prepublication review), access to government information (FOIA) and Privacy Act concerns, and protection of confidential press sources.

Services

The firm's communications legal services include:

Providing advice and counsel on business and regulatory aspects of mergers, acquisitions and other transactions subject to government approval;

FIGURE 7.2 Profile of the experience, services, and clientele of the Washington, DC firm Cohn and Marks, LLP. (Source: Cohn and Marks, LLP. Used with permission.)

Prosecuting and, when necessary, litigating issues concerning the acquisition and renewal of broadcast stations, cable television, and common carrier licenses and franchises and providing regulatory analysis regarding ongoing operational matters;

Providing advice, counsel and litigation services on all related aspects of a client's business, including antitrust and trade regulation, copyright and trademark, hiring, firing, and employment discrimination issues, and drafting and reviewing contracts necessary to business activities.

Advising clients on and litigating on their behalf First Amendment issues such as libel and slander (including prepublication review), access to government information (FOIA) and Privacy Act concerns, and protection of confidential press sources.

<u>Clientele</u>

Based in Washington, DC, the firm's core practice is devoted to representation of companies that are subject to the jurisdiction of the Federal Communications Commission, or whose activities are affected by other state and federal rules and policies. The diverse communications clients represented by Cohn and Marks LLP include:

-- Major Commercial and Noncommercial Radio and Television Stations and Networks

-- Radio and Television program producers

-- Cable Television Systems and Networks

-- Newspapers

-- Trade Associations representing media interests

-- Telecommunications Providers and Customers

-- Internet Service Providers

-- Internet Publishers

-- Authors, Entertainers and Athletes

Cohn and Marks LLP, founded in 1946, is distinguished by a specialized, collegial practice that emphasizes close personal attorney/client relationships and delivery of quality services. The firm's partners and staff include individuals with legal teaching experience and outstanding academic backgrounds. The firm's expertise is enhanced by insight gained in government service by a number of partners who have held key legal and policy-making positions at the Federal Communications Commission, the U.S. Information Agency, and the Department of Stare.

The firm often works with other professionals and legal counsel involving such matters as securities or tax issues while largely confining its efforts to those areas where its unique skills are needed. This approach has enabled the firm to deliver what it knows best and to build a stable organization of specialized professionals. In this way, it has met the legal needs of the largest companies in the world as well as those of smaller enterprises, a number of whom it continues to serve into the third generation of family owners.

FIGURE 7.2 *Continued.*

APPLICATION AND REPORTING REQUIREMENTS

One day, perhaps, both federal income tax and broadcast station forms will be simplified. Until that happens, the forms will continue to be cumbersome. The broadcast industry is full of forms: for a construction permit to build a radio or television station, for a broadcast license renewal, and so on.

To begin the process of establishing a new broadcast station, an individual, partnership, or corporation must meet certain criteria. They include the following:

- The licensee must be a U.S. citizen.

- The licensee must be of good character.

- The licensee must have substantial financial resources to establish and maintain the station.

- The licensee must have the technical ability to operate the station according to FCC regulations.[10]

Applicants requesting to construct a new facility or make changes in an existing AM, FM or TV facility must use FCC Form 301 (Figure 10.13). FCC facility construction permits are issued for a period of three years. They are no longer subject to extension as they once were.

Once the construction is completed, it is necessary to apply for a license using FCC Form 302. Applicants must show compliance with all terms, conditions, and obligations set forth in the original application and construction permit. Upon completion of the construction, the permittee may begin program tests upon sending a notice to the FCC.

During the period of operation, all stations were required to file with the FCC an annual employment report form, FCC 395-B, on or before May 31 of each year. The employment data filed were to reflect figures from any one payroll period in January, February, or March. The same payroll period had to be used each year. The FCC used the reported data to monitor compliance with its equal employement opportunity (EEO) regulations.[11]

In addition, stations had to file at license renewal time an EEO report form, FCC 396. The report was required to determine whether or not the station's personnel composition reflected that of the community of license. Stations with fewer than five employees were exempt from filing the form.

In 1998, the FCC suspended the requirement that stations file the two forms in the wake of a court ruling that threw out the FCC's broadcast affirmative action requirements.[12] Chairman Kennard announced that a proposal for new rules would be issued, and he urged broadcasters to voluntarily file EEO data with the FCC. Subsequently, the FCC adopted a new EEO plan. A detailed discussion of the commission's EEO reporting regulations appears in Chapter 3, "Human Resource Management."

The FCC requires each commercial broadcast licensee to file an ownership report, FCC Form 323, once a year, on the anniversary of the date that its renewal application must be filed.

Sports and network affiliation agreements must be in writing, and single copies of all local, regional, and national network agreements must be filed with the FCC within 30 days of execution.

Deregulation has ended the need to file with the FCC notification of radio and television station programming changes. To replace previous program ascertainment requirements, the FCC requires only that stations place in their public file quarterly a list of five issues and programming related to those issues. The quarterly lists must be in the file by January 10, April 10, July 10, and October 10, respectively, each year. See Figure 7.3 for an illustration of what a

ISSUES/PROGRAMS LIST
STATION XXXX
[COMMUNITY OF LICENSE]
(MONTH), 20XX – (MONTH), 20XX

Issue	Program Title	Brief Description	Date/Time of Broadcast
Energy	Community Dialogue	Interview with John Smith, President, Local Gasoline Station Owner's Association, concerning gasoline allocations and rationing.	August 12, 20XX 8:30 – 9:00 p.m.
	Issues and Answers	Interview with Joe Blow, Secretary, Department of Energy.	July 18, 20XX 11:30 – 12:00 p.m.
	Focus	Interview with Roger Dalton, President, Chamber of Commerce, concerning loss of tourist revenue because of gasoline shortage.	August 6, 20XX 9:00 – 10:00 a.m.
Crime	Community Dialogue	Discussion with representatives from county police departments Pertaining to rise in suburban crime rate and prevention methods.	September 3, 20XX 8:30 – 9:00 p.m. and September 10, 20XX and 8:30 – 9:00 p.m.
Education	Community Dialogue	Interviews with members of School Board with respect to goals and objectives for academic year.	September 6, 20XX 8:30 – 9:00 p.m.
	Focus	Debate between Janice Jones, Chairperson, United Teachers Local 18, and Thomas Johnson, President of School Board, regarding to strike. the right of teachers (Special hour-long program also included call-in segment with comments from the community.)	September 24, 20XX 9:00 – 10:00 a.m.
	Superintendent's Scrapbook	Weekly program prepared by the Office of Superintendent of Public Schools. Program topics Included:	
		Evaluation of annual standardized testing results;	July 10, 20XX 10:00 – 10:15 a.m.
		Report on closing of certain neighborhood elementary schools;	July 17, 20XX 10:00 – 10:15 a.m.
		Report on expansion of school library facilities necessary for continuation of accreditation.	August 28, 20XX 10:00 – 10:15 a.m.

[Other listings for issues and responsive programs would be reflected in similar fashion]

FIGURE 7.3 Sample quarterly issues/programs list. (Source: Cohn and Marks, LLP. Used with permission.)

typical station quarterly issues/programs list might look like. Note that the list should reflect the station's "most significant programming treatment" of community issues and needs. The programming need not be locally produced.

Broadcast licenses are not issued on a permanent basis and must be renewed on a regular timetable. All licensees, except those TV and noncommercial stations selected to complete the long-form audit, must file the simplified renewal application form, FCC 303-S (Figure 7.4). It must be filed every eight years by television and radio stations, on or before the first business day of the fourth month prior to the expiration of the existing license.[13]

Federal Communications Commission
Washington, D. C. 20554

OMB 3060-0110
July 2004

FOR FCC USE ONLY

FCC 303-S

APPLICATION FOR
RENEWAL OF BROADCAST STATION
LICENSE

FOR COMMISSION USE ONLY
FILE NO.

Section I - General Information- TO BE COMPLETED BY ALL APPLICANTS

1. Legal Name of Licensee

Mailing Address

City	State or Country (if foreign address)	ZIP Code

Telephone Number (include area code)	E-Mail Address (if available)

FCC Registration Number	Call Sign	Facility Identifier

2. Contact Representative | Firm or Company Name

Mailing Address

City	State or Country (if foreign address)	ZIP Code

Telephone Number (include area code)	E-Mail Address (if available)

3. If this application has been submitted without a fee, indicate reason for fee exemption (see 47 C.F.R. Section 1.1114):

☐ Governmental Entity ☐ Noncommercial Educational Licensee ☐ Other ____________

FCC 303-S
July 2004

FIGURE 7.4 Excerpt from FCC Form 303-S.

4. **Purpose of Application.**

☐ Renewal of license

☐ Amendment to pending renewal application
If an amendment, submit as an exhibit a listing by Section and Item
Number the portions of the pending application that are being revised.

Exhibit

5. **Facility Information:** ☐ Commercial ☐ Noncommercial Educational

6. **Service and Community of License**

a. ☐ AM ☐ FM ☐ TV ☐ FM Translator ☐ LPFM

☐ TV Translator ☐ Low Power TV ☐ Class A TV

Community of License/Area to be Served	
City	State

b. Does this application include one or more FM translator station(s), or TV translator
station(s), LPTV station(s), in addition to the station listed in Section I, Question 1?
(The callsign(s) of any associated FM translators, TV translators or LPTVs will be
requested in Section V).   ☐ Yes   ☐ No

7. **Other Authorizations.** List call signs, facility identifiers and location(s) of any FM
booster or TV booster station(s) for which renewal of license is also requested.

Exhibit No.	☐ N/A

FCC 303-S (Page 2)
July 2004

FIGURE 7.4 *Continued.*

The short-form renewal was a product of deregulation and consisted of only eight questions. However, the simplicity has begun to fade, and the "postcard" form has grown from its original 1 page to 29 pages. In response to the Children's Television Act of 1990,[14] the FCC added a ninth question for all television renewal applicants. It requires a summary of the applicant's children's programming activity and its compliance with commercial content restrictions. Other questions have been added since then.

Licenses that are in good standing may be sold and transferred by licensees to third parties with the consent of the FCC. To obtain consent,

NOTE: In addition to the information called for in Sections II, III, IV and V, an explanatory exhibit providing full particulars must be submitted for each item for which a "No" response is provided.

Section II - Legal -TO BE COMPLETED BY ALL APPLICANTS

1. **Certification.** Licensee certifies that it has answered each question in this application based on its review of the application instructions and worksheets. Licensee further certifies that where it has made an affirmative certification below, this certification constitutes its representation that the application satisfies each of the pertinent standards and criteria set forth in the application, instructions, and worksheets. ☐ Yes ☐ No

2. **Character Issues.** Licensee certifies that neither the licensee nor any party to the application has or has had any interest in, or connection with:

    a. any broadcast application in any proceeding where character issues were left unresolved or were resolved adversely against the applicant or any party to the application; or ☐ Yes ☐ No | See Explanation in Exhibit No.

    b. any pending broadcast application in which character issues have been raised. ☐ Yes ☐ No | See Explanation in Exhibit No.

3. **Adverse Findings.** Licensee certifies that, with respect to the licensee and each party to the application, no adverse finding has been made, nor has an adverse final action been taken by any court or administrative body in a civil or criminal proceeding brought under the provisions of any laws related to the following: any felony; mass media-related antitrust or unfair competition; fraudulent statements to another governmental unit; or discrimination. ☐ Yes ☐ No | See Explanation in Exhibit No.

4. **FCC Violations during the Preceding License Term.** Licensee certifies that, with respect to the station(s) for which renewal is requested, there have been no violations by the licensee of the Communications Act of 1934, as amended, or the rules or regulations of the Commission during the preceding license term. If No, the licensee must submit an explanatory exhibit providing complete descriptions of all violations. ☐ Yes ☐ No | See Explanation in Exhibit No.

5. **Alien Ownership and Control.** Licensee certifies that it complies with the provisions of Section 310 of the Communications Act of 1934, as amended, relating to interests of aliens and foreign governments. ☐ Yes ☐ No | See Explanation in Exhibit No.

6. **Anti-Drug Abuse Act Certification.** Licensee certifies that neither licensee nor any party to the application is subject to denial of federal benefits pursuant to Section 5301 of the Anti-Drug Abuse Act of 1988, 21 U.S.C. Section 862. ☐ Yes ☐ No

I certify that the statements in this application are true, complete, and correct to the best of my knowledge and belief, and are made in good faith. I acknowledge that all certifications and attached Exhibits are considered material representations. I hereby waive any claim to the use of any particular frequency as against the regulatory power of the United States because of the previous use of the same, whether by license or otherwise, and request an authorization in accordance with this application. (See Section 304 of the Communications Act of 1934, as amended.)

Typed or Printed Name of Person Signing	Typed or Printed Title of Person Signing
Signature	Date

WILLFUL FALSE STATEMENTS ON THIS FORM ARE PUNISHABLE BY FINE AND/OR IMPRISONMENT (U.S. CODE, TITLE 18, SECTION 1001), AND/OR REVOCATION OF ANY STATION LICENSE OR CONSTRUCTION PERMIT (U.S. CODE, TITLE 47, SECTION 312(a)(1)), AND/OR FORFEITURE (U.S. CODE, TITLE 47, SECTION 503).

FCC 303-S (Page 3)
July 2004

233

FIGURE 7.4 *Continued.*

the seller and buyer must file with the FCC's Media Bureau FCC Form 314 (see Figure 10.11).

OWNERSHIP POLICIES

Simply put, the ownership rules govern who can own what, and where. They include limitations on numbers and kinds of stations that can be commonly owned in a market and on the total number that can be owned in the country as a whole by a single person or entity.

Another ownership consideration has to do with the length of time a station must be held by an owner before it can be sold. Cross-ownership rules exist for newspaper-broadcast combinations.

Deregulation's largest impact on changing the face of the broadcast industry has resulted from the relaxation of the ownership rules. The oldest and best known was the duopoly rule, which was designed to prevent a single person or entity from owning more than one station in a market providing the same class of service. Consequently, no individual or company could own more than one AM, one FM, or one TV station in the same service area. This media-concentration rule served its purpose for many years. But the decline of AM's competitive position in particular, and of radio's profitability in general, led to its reexamination.

THE PROGRESSION TO CONSOLIDATION, 1992–1996

On September 16, 1992, a new duopoly rule became effective. The change allowed a single party to have up to three radio stations in the same market in markets with fewer than 15 stations. However, the three commonly owned stations could not exceed 50 percent of the total number of stations in the market. No more than two of the three stations could be the same class of service (AM or FM). In markets with 15 or more stations, a single entity could own up to four stations, no more than two of which could be AM or FM. In those markets, there was an additional requirement: the combined audience share of the commonly owned stations could not exceed 25 percent.

Before the implementation of the new local ownership rules, many operators who were experiencing financial or competitive strain had entered into local marketing agreements (LMAs). Under an LMA, a station sells all or some of its weekly broadcast schedule to another station in the market, which uses the air time to broadcast content, including commercials, over the selling station. When the new duopoly regulations were adopted, they were accompanied by a new LMA requirement. It said that if an LMA exceeded 15 percent of the selling station's weekly broadcast schedule, that station had to be counted as an owned station for the station buying the time. For example, if FM station A bought more than 15 percent of the time of FM station B, FM station A could own no other FM station in the market because two was the limit in the same class of service.

The ownership rule changes also affected the limits for the number of stations that could be owned nationwide by a single party. The 1992 multiple ownership rules increased the radio levels to 18 AM and 18 FM stations, and a further increase to 20 AM and 20 FM stations was permitted thereafter.

The television multiple-ownership limit of 12 was unaffected by the 1992 changes. However, the television rule depended upon the percentage of TV households reached nationally by commonly owned stations, with the upper limit being 25 percent. Therefore, if a company owned five television stations that covered 25 percent of the television households in the United States, it could not own any more. Special variations of the rule allowed

UHF stations to count for only one-half of television market households in calculating the 25 percent.

THE 1996 TELECOM ACT: CONSOLIDATION ACCELERATED

The change in local ownership rules continued in the 1996 Telecommunications Act. Now, the changes became dramatic.

Multiple ownership limits for radio nationwide were eliminated completely. By 1998, there were publicly traded companies that owned hundreds of commercial radio stations each. Such companies included Clear Channel, Cumulus, and Infinity.

The local-level ownership rules for radio changed as well. Limits were set according to market size and class of service. The 1996 local radio ownership concentration rules are as follows:

Commercial Stations in Market	Single Owner Limit (Own, Operate, or Control)
45 plus	Up to 8, no more than 5 in the same class of service
30–44	Up to 7, no more than 4 in the same class of service
15–29	Up to 6, no more than 4 in the same class of service
14 and less	Up to 5, no more than 3 in the same class of service—but a single owner cannot own more than 50 percent of the total number of commercial stations in the market[15]

The television rules were changed more modestly under the 1996 act. National ownership levels were removed, as they were in radio. However, there was a cap of coverage of 35 percent of U.S. TV households. Once that limit was reached, no additional stations could be purchased, whatever the number of stations currently owned.

The 1996 law permitted the FCC to issue waivers to allow common ownership of radio and television stations in the same market. The prohibition on duopoly ownership of TV stations in the same market remained, but the 1996 law ordered the FCC to study the matter. Existing restrictions against daily newspaper ownership of electronic media servicing all or part of the same market continued, but were under FCC review.

Prior to the 1996 law, the FCC eliminated what was known as the "three-year rule." It had required broadcasters who acquired a station to operate it for three years before being allowed to sell it. Now, there is no holding period for existing stations. The end of the rule led to a flurry of station transactions and brought new investors and new types of financing into the industry.

The combination of the changes in the ownership rules and the abolition of the three-year rule resulted in innumerable mergers, corporate takeovers, and leveraged buyouts.

Ownership Rules Changes Post-1996

The 1996 law mandated that the FCC conduct an ownership rule review every two years. The purpose was to ascertain if the rules were still necessary in the public interest as a result of competition.[16]

One such review resulted in FCC adoption of new rules on media concentration in June 2003.[17] The proposed new rules allowed ownership of more than one TV station in a market depending on the number of TV stations in the market. For example, a company could own two stations in a market with five or more stations.

The national limits on TV station ownership were increased from a household penetration of 35 percent to a maximum of 45 percent. However, in January 2004, Congress reduced the national level to stations that reach 39 percent of total TV households. The new rules maintained the "UHF discount."

The local radio limits remained the same as set in the 1996 Telecomm Act, but the FCC replaced its signal contour method of defining radio markets with a geographic market approach designed by Arbitron. The national limit on radio station ownership remained unlimited.

Cross-ownership was permitted among TV, radio, and newspapers. The FCC restated its commitment to localism.

The new rules were challenged immediately in the federal courts and stayed. In June 2004, the rules were sent back to the FCC by a federal court of appeals for reexamination. The stay against implementing the rules continued.

The FCC petitioned the court for a rehearing on that portion of its ruling pertaining to media ownership. The June 2003 proposed ownership rules were adopted on a 3-2 party-line vote. Commissioners and chairpersons often change in the wake of a presidential election, even if the ruling party remains in office. For that reason, the future of the 2003 rules changes now on remand to the FCC is not certain. However, in September 2004, the court did allow the FCC to implement the rule that the number of stations permitted in a market would be based on the Arbitron definition of a market.

Localism

The proposed ownership rule changes in June 2003 resulted in an FCC examination into whether or not the ownership concentration triggered by the 1996 act had diminished the dedication to localism.

In September 2003, Chairman Powell announced a localism initiative.[18] It had three parts: (1) a localism task force; (2) accelerating activation of low-power stations; and (3) notice of inquiry.[19]

Powell appointed a localism task force that conducted hearings around the country. Further, the FCC opened a filing window to resolve conflicts among low-power FM applicants. The commission believes that LPFM epitomizes local broadcasting. Finally, the FCC issued a notice of inquiry to collect comments on whether localism-based rules are effective or need to be changed or supplemented.

PROGRAMMING POLICIES

Programming policies cover a broad area of station activity. Here, the focus is on those of particular significance to station management.

POLITICAL BROADCASTS

Enforcement of federal laws and FCC regulations pertaining to political advertising has become a particular emphasis with the FCC. There is obviously a great deal of interest in this topic by office holders and office seekers. Congressional pressure has led to political rate audits, and the Commission is authorized to levy fines for violations of the political rules. Former candidates have also sued broadcast stations for alleged overcharges. Who is allowed access to the airwaves, when, and at what rate are critical questions. Ignorance or informed noncompliance can be expensive and career-ending. FCC attorneys advise their clients to issue political advertising policy statements and to maintain a station political advertising checklist (Figure 7.5). Now, on to the specifics of the laws and regulations.

The "equal opportunities" provision of Section 315 of the Communications Act is commonly (and incorrectly) referred to as the "equal time" provision. It allows broadcasters to permit a legally qualified candidate for public office to "use" a station's facilities, but they must afford equal opportunities to all other opposing legally qualified candidates for that office, provided a request for equal opportunities is made within seven days of the first prior use.

The use of a broadcast facility by a candidate is defined as any appearance on the air by a legally qualified candidate for public office, where the candidate either is identified or is readily identifiable by the listening or viewing audience. Appearances by candidates in the following types of broadcasts are not considered "uses" and are exempt from the provision:

- bona-fide newscasts
- bona-fide news interviews
- bona-fide news documentaries (if the appearance of the candidate is incidental to the presentation of the subject or subjects covered by the news documentary)
- on-the-spot coverage of bona-fide news events (including but not limited to political conventions and activities incidental thereto)

In response to petitions from the National Association of Broadcasters (NAB) and others, the FCC authorized broadcasters to sponsor political debates. In 1987, the debate exemption was expanded to cover candidate-sponsored debates.[20] In both cases, even if all competing candidates do not appear in the debate, the broadcast will be exempt from the equal opportunities requirements, provided the debate has genuine news value and is not used to advance the candidacy of any particular individual. Also, taped debates need not be aired within 24 hours of their occurrence to qualify for exemptions, as long as they are broadcast currently enough so that they are still bona-fide news.

237

POLITICAL ADVERTISING CHECKLIST

Name of Candidate:_____

Name of Corporation, Labor Union or Public Interest Group Sponsoring Natural Issues Ads:
_____

Person Ordering Advertising:_____

Relationship to Candidate:_____

Person to Whom Disclosure Is Given:_____

Date	Item
---	Candidate has been determined to be "legally qualified."
---	Candidate's announcement constitutes a "use," i.e., candidate personally appears on the spot and is identifiable.
---	Candidate's announcement contains proper sponsorship identification.
---	Candidate has provided NAB form or other written statement of agency authorization to place advertising on behalf of candidate.
---	Candidate has been provided with:
--	XXXX-TV Statement of Policy on Political Advertising; and
--	XXXX-TV Station Rate Information
---	Campaign Committee has provided list of officers and directors.
---	Appropriate candidate tag line and visuals when spot makes direct reference to another candidate for the same office.

_____   _____
Date   Salesperson

FIGURE 7.5 Sample political advertising checklist. (Source: Cohn and Marks, LLP. Used with permission.)

Specifically, licensees now may air in-studio debates featuring only the most significant candidates. Minor candidates are not entitled to request other air time if they are not invited to appear.

In 1991, the Section 315(a) (4) exemption was expanded to include a situation in which a local television station dedicated an hour of time to be shared equally by the two major presidential candidates for separate 30-minute presentations. Although not technically a debate, it did qualify for the use exclusion.[21]

If a broadcast constitutes a "use" of a station by a legally qualified candidate for public office, Section 315 of the Communications Act prohibits a station from censoring the broadcast content, directly or indirectly. This "no censorship" provision bans a station from refusing to broadcast a "use" by a candidate or any person connected with the content or format of the broadcast. Thus, even if the proposed broadcast contains libelous statements, the station is prohibited from rejecting it. For this reason, the U.S. Supreme Court has exempted broadcasters from liability under state libel and slander laws for any defamatory material contained in such a broadcast use.

Under Section 312(a)(7) of the Communications Act, broadcasters are required to allow "reasonable access to or to permit purchase of reasonable amounts of time for the use of a broadcasting station by a legally qualified candidate for Federal elective office on behalf of his candidacy." In 1971, the FCC ruled that each licensee has a public interest obligation to make the facilities of its station "effectively available" to all candidates for public office. It was assumed that this rule would be considered in a case-by-case manner.

Comparisons between the requirements of Sections 315 and 312(a)(7) always seem to cause confusion. It can best be avoided by remembering that, under Section 315, a broadcaster has no obligation to political candidates unless one of them has been allowed to use the broadcast facility. Section 312(a)(7), on the other hand, requires a broadcaster to provide time to candidates for federal elective office. Section 315(b)(1) and (2) of the 1934 act set standards for rates to be charged to political candidates. The following paragraphs summarize the rate advice one law firm provides to its clients:

Pre-election Period and Lowest Unit Charge

For "uses" broadcast during the forty-five days before a primary or primary runoff election and sixty days before a general election (including election day), you may charge candidates no more than your "lowest unit charge" for the same class (rate category) of advertisement, the same length of spot, and the same time period (daypart or program). The candidate must be sold spots at the lowest charge you give to your most favored advertiser for the same class, length of spot and time period. If your lowest unit charge is commissionable to an agency, you must sell to candidates who buy direct at a rate equal to what the station would net from the agency buy. This agency rule does not apply to spots sold by a station's national rep firm.

Candidates get the benefit of any volume discounts you offer to other advertisers even if they purchase only one spot. Thus, if you charge $20 for a single one-minute spot and $150 for ten one-minute advertisements (or $15 per ad), you may charge a candidate only $15 for a one-minute ad even if the candidate buys only one spot. However, you can offer legally qualified candidates an additional volume discount from the lowest unit charge for purchases that do not qualify for the volume discount, but you must make the volume discount available on a non-discriminatory basis to all candidates.

Any station practices that enhance the value of advertising spots must be disclosed, and must be made available to candidates. These include, but are not limited to, discount privileges that affect the value of the advertising, such as bonus spots, time-sensitive make goods, preemption priorities, and other factors that enhance the value of the advertisement. Under the rules, if you have provided any commercial advertiser with even a single time-sensitive make-good for the same class of spot during the preceding year, you must provide time-sensitive make goods for all candidates before the election.

Who Is Entitled to the Lowest Unit Charge?

Only "uses" by legally qualified candidates for public office are entitled to the lowest unit charge. The candidate must appear personally in the spot by voice or image, and the appearance must be in connection with his or her campaign. If the owner of the general store runs for sheriff, he or she is not entitled to the lowest unit charge for spots promoting the store's weekly specials.

A demand for equal opportunities can change this. A candidate making a valid equal opportunity claim in response to his or her competitor's spots will be entitled to the same rate the competitor paid, and may use the time any way he or she sees fit. If the candidate he or she is responding to got the lowest unit charge, he or she gets it too, by operation of the equal opportunities provision.[22]

In addition to all the other requirements, broadcasters have an affirmative obligation to discover who is behind the nominal sponsoring organization of political advertising.

All of these matters, including "issues" advertisements, are now subject to Congressional and Department of Justice examination.

BIPARTISAN CAMPAIGN REFORM ACT OF 2002 (BCRA)

This law, also known as the Campaign Spending Law, amended Section 315 of the 1934 Communications Act.

As noted earlier, candidates for federal elective office receive the lowest unit rate 45 days before a primary or 60 days before a general election. BCRA requires that federal candidates must do something additional to qualify for the lowest unit rate. At the time of purchase of lowest unit rate spots, the candidate or the authorized committee must certify in writing that the candidate will not make any direct reference to another candidate for the same office unless the political spot contains, for radio, a personal audio statement voiced by the candidate and identifying the candidate and the office being sought and announcing that the candidate has approved the broadcast.

For television and cable, a clearly identifiable photograph or similar image of the candidate must be shown for at least four seconds and a simultaneously displayed printed statement must identify the candidate and advise that the candidate approved the broadcast and that the candidate or the candidate's authorized committee paid for the broadcast.

BCRA was to be the law that outlawed the unregulated and unrestricted use of soft money. It was to be replaced by third-party issue ads. Third-party issue ad organizations are called 527s.In the 2004 presidential campaign, such organizations generated much controversy.

As to third-party issue ads (i.e., political ads that advocate the election or defeat of federal candidates or solicit any political contributions, but are not authorized by a federal candidate or the candidate's authorized campaign committee), the ad must state that it is not authorized by any federal candidate and identify the name of the responsible political party, committee, person and/or connected organization paying for the broadcast. For television and cable, this statement is required to be made with an unobscured, full-screen view of a representative of such committee or other person in voice-over. It must also appear for at least four seconds in a clearly readable manner with a reasonable degree of contrast between the background and the printed statement. Surely, you have seen or heard these announcements. Now, you know why.

BCRA also imposed some new public file requirements. They are set out later in the chapter.

FAIRNESS DOCTRINE

The Fairness Doctrine required broadcasters to devote time to coverage of "controversial issues of public importance" and to make sure that such coverage was not grossly out of balance. In other words, reasonable opportunity was to be afforded for presentation of contrasting views. It was left to broadcasters to decide what issues were controversial and how to treat them on the air.

After calling the Fairness Doctrine the *sine qua non* for broadcast license renewal in 1974, the FCC declared it unconstitutional and essentially unenforceable in 1987.[23] Subsequent to its repeal, Congress each session, until 1993, annually passed a law to codify the doctrine. Since the Republicans took over Congress in 1995, there has been no such effort and the FCC has shown little interest.

In 2000, the FCC repealed its personal attack and political editorial rules, both corollaries of the Fairness Doctrine. That action would seem to have sealed its fate.

However, the FCC's media ownership rules may give it life again. The objections to the perceived loss of localism as a consequence of ownership concentration in local markets may revive the doctrine's corpse. Localism is intertwined inextricably with Fairness Doctrine concerns.

CHILDREN'S PROGRAMMING

The FCC began a study of children's television programming in the early 1970s. In 1974, it issued a Children's Television Report and Policy Statement. The Commission stated that television stations would be expected to provide diversified programming designed to meet the varied needs and interests of the child audience. It said that television stations should provide a "reasonable amount" of programming designed for children, intended to educate and inform, not simply to entertain.

On December 22, 1983, the FCC adopted a report and order terminating its 13-year inquiry into this kind of programming. While reaffirming the obligations of all commercial broadcast television stations to serve the special needs of children, it rejected the option of mandatory programming requirements for children's television by a three-to-one vote. As a result, broadcasters could justify their inattention to such programming based on alternate children's programming available in the market on public television or cable.

Citizens' groups were outraged by the perceived FCC abandonment of the licensee's obligation to children's programming. Their unhappiness was intensified by the FCC's 1984 elimination of commercial guidelines for children's programming.

In 1990, activists succeeded in their efforts to restore commercial limits and licensee program obligations for children, and the Children's Television Act passed. President Bush (the elder) signed the law and, in 1991, the FCC adopted regulations implementing the act. They went into effect in 1992.[24]

As administered by the FCC, the act no longer allows broadcasters to satisfy their children's programming obligation by relying on what is available on cable and public television. Children's programming was defined as those "programs originally produced and broadcast primarily for an audience of 12 years old and under."[25] Broadcasters' compliance with the program requirements would be examined at license renewal time. The law also reimposed limitations on commercials in children's programming: 12 minutes per hour on weekdays and 10.5 minutes on weekends.

Under regulations adopted by the FCC to implement the 1992 law, television stations had to report quarterly in their public inspection file their compliance with the commercial limits requirements. In addition, TV stations were to keep an annual list of programming and other efforts geared to meet the educational and informational needs of children.

FCC experience under the new regulations was not good. Fines for exceeding the commercial limits were sizable and frequent. The anticipated children's programming upgrade and improvement did not occur.

After four years of experimentation under the Children's Television Act, the FCC in 1996 issued new rules and new reporting requirements. The Telecommunications Act required TV stations to air at least three hours per week of "core" children's programming, which is defined as programming designed to educate and inform children. It must air on a regularly scheduled basis weekly during the hours of 7:00 A.M. to 10:00 P.M. Such programming must be at least 30 minutes in length.

To monitor compliance with its new rules, the FCC also introduced FCC Form 398, which television stations must complete on a quarterly and annual basis. It requires the reporting television station to have a named children's programming liaison and to report performance for the quarter just ended and plans for the quarter coming up. The station must also notify the public of the existence of Form 398 and collect public comments on its children's programming.

OBSCENITY, INDECENCY, AND PROFANITY

The U.S. Criminal Code forbids the utterance of "any obscene, indecent, or profane language by means of radio communication."[26] The problem, as it pertains to programming, is the definition of what is obscene or indecent.

The prevailing standard for obscenity was adopted by the U.S. Supreme Court in its 1973 resolution of Miller v. California. The Court's three-part test is: (1) whether the average person, applying contemporary community standards, would find that the work, taken as a whole, appeals to prurient interests; (2) whether the work depicts or describes in a patently offensive way sexual conduct specifically defined by applicable state law; and (3) whether the work lacks serious literary, artistic, political, or scientific value.

After the Miller case, the FCC standard for indecency was the "seven dirty words" test announced in the Pacifica case involving George Carlin.[27] That changed in 1987, when the FCC issued a new indecency standard.[28] It is now defined as "language or material that depicts or describes, in terms patently offensive as measured by contemporary community standards for the broadcast medium, sexual or excretory activities or organs." Contemporary community standards, said the FCC, were meant to be those of the average broadcast viewer or listener.

The 1987 indecency standard has been a problem from its inception. There have been three major points of contention: What was prohibited? When was it prohibited? How much would violations cost? The standard itself has been upheld by court decisions in the face of claims that it is vague and indefinite.[29]

Enforcement hours have been another story. Originally, the FCC proposed a "safe harbor" when adult programming might be broadcast. That time period was identified as the hours of midnight to 6:00 A.M. For a time, under a congressional mandate, the FCC extended the coverage of its indecency rule to 24 hours a day. However, the courts repeatedly refused to allow the FCC limitations. The issue was finally resolved in 1995 when the U.S. Court of Appeals for the D.C. Circuit ruled that the FCC could permit the broadcasting of indecent material between the hours of 10:00 P.M. and 6:00 A.M. [30]

In addition to establishing safe harbor hours for adult content, the FCC, as noted in Chapter 4, "Broadcast Programming," has approved a voluntary ratings system to alert viewers to adult content, indecency, and violence in television programming.

Another major enforcement wrinkle is the amount of an FCC fine. Under current forfeiture schedules, the basic one-time indecency fine is $7,000, with statutory discretion based on circumstances to raise that to a maximum of $27,500. In June 2004, the FCC adjusted its maximum forfeiture penalties to reflect inflation. The new rates for indecency are $32,500 per violation or per day of a continuing violation with the amount of continuing violation not to exceed $325,000.[31] Many of the cash penalties imposed so far have been against New York "shock jock" Howard Stern. His show is syndicated nationally, and the FCC has been fining both the originating and carrying stations.

Clear Channel Communications carried Stern in six markets and it was fined $175,000 by the FCC in 2004.[32] The company agreed to the fine and told Congress it was cleaning up its act. "Zero tolerance" is the term it uses to describe its indecency policy.[33] Major broadcasting companies are trying to pass through indecency fines to talent. In some instances, talent has been fired and, like Stern, may be heading for the unregulated satellite skies.[34]

The frenzy over indecency was triggered by a television show and not a radio show. In February 2004, singer Janet Jackson had an on-the-air "wardrobe malfunction" during the Super Bowl halftime show with Justin Timberlake.[35] In September 2004, the FCC fined CBS, the offending network, $550,000 for the incident.

Consequently, congressmen and senators outdid each other in their zeal to raise the indecency fine.[36] So as not to miss the boat, the FCC began consideration of a requirement that broadcasters record and archive their programs for possible indecency compliance issues.[37]

Indecency has been, and will be, a major initiative for the FCC. Litigation is costly, and broadcasters who cannot afford to fight for perceived First Amendment principles would be well advised to be cautious in observing a less-than-definite standard. The only real definition we had from the FCC on indecency pertains to the "F word." It is bad, anywhere and anytime,[38] even at the 2004 Democratic National Convention on CNN.[39]

243

VIOLENCE

Violence is, and has been, an area of industry self-regulation. While threatening regulation, the FCC knows very well, given its problems with indecency, that program content regulations are difficult to enforce. From time to time, members of Congress, like the late Senator Paul Simon, have threatened legislation. However, each time the industry has escaped.

One serious threat was resolved when the FCC adopted a table of voluntary program ratings (see Appendix A, "TV Parental Guidelines") designed to alert viewers to program content. Compliance with the ratings by program exhibitors has not been universal.

In addition to the ratings initiative, there was also an agreement by the television networks to pay for an ongoing independent study of the level of violence in television programming. The agreement followed threats of FCC regulation and congressional legislation.

However, the wolf is at the door again. A motivated FCC, in the company of some powerful U.S. senators, has opened a new notice of inquiry into violent programming. Part of this incentive comes from the 2004 indecency frenzy. There has been an effort in Congress to exile violent programming to the safe harbor established for indecency.[40] Time will tell.

244

RACIAL SLURS

Shock jocks are not new to the airwaves, but the audience fragmentation of the 1990s and the success of Howard Stern have led to a shock jock breakout from East to West. More and more on-air hosts are pushing the envelope of acceptable standards for program content. Complaints about problem content are no longer limited to indecency. The 1990s saw an increasing number of allegations of racism.[41]

The FCC has been confronted with the problem of racial comments in the past. Its policy has been to rely on industry self-regulation, and it has no fine or forfeiture for such comments. The FCC's position is that federal law does not prohibit them. Indeed, the U.S. Supreme Court has decided that hate speech is protected First Amendment activity.[42]

In one case, the FCC was asked to halt the sale of a Washington, DC, radio station to a company that employed a disc jockey who allegedly made racially insensitive comments on the air. In a petition filed to block the sale, the African American Business Association said that the sale would create a hostile environment for Blacks working at the station.[43]

While a search is under way to find a solution to this emerging problem at the national level, the current remedial approach appears to rely on the amount of pressure that can be brought against management by community groups. In one instance, community pressure was joined by a withdrawal of advertising support for the offending program, and station management elected to suspend and then fire the disc jockeys.[44] In 1998, five years after their dismissal, the disc jockeys were hosting a successful nationally syndicated morning show in the same market. Where dictates of good taste do not govern an air host's behavior, perhaps concern about occupational longevity would be an appropriate guiding principle. But, obviously, it does not always work.

ON-THE-AIR HOAXES

The electronic media industry has a legacy of spoofs and hoaxes dating back to the famous 1938 "War of the Worlds" broadcast by Orson Welles. His elaborate radio production describing an invasion from Mars caused a panic.

The late 1980s and early 1990s saw a new rash of incidents, perhaps another by-product of audience fragmentation. One, in St. Louis, resulted in a substantial FCC fine. In that case, a disc jockey for KSHE-FM aired a Civil Defense alert for impending nuclear attack.[45] The fact that it occurred in the midst of the Gulf War only intensified audience reaction.

Responding to this and other complaints, many involving false reports of crimes, the FCC issued a new hoax rule in 1992. It forbids the broadcast of false information concerning a crime or catastrophe if (1) the information is known to be false; (2) it is foreseeable that the broadcast will cause substantial public harm; and (3) broadcast of the information does, in fact, directly cause substantial harm.[46] The basic FCC one-time fine for knowingly broadcasting a hoax is $7,000.

LOTTERIES

There has been a long-time FCC requirement that prohibits stations from broadcasting any advertisement or information concerning a lottery. As noted in Chapter 6, "Broadcast Promotion and Marketing," there are three elements to a lottery: prize, chance, and consideration. The prize must consist of something of value. Chance means that skill will not improve a player's chance of winning. Consideration means that the contestant has to provide something of value to participate. Listen- or watch-to-win requirements by many stations are not deemed to be consideration.

245

Many states have lotteries that use the electronic media to promote and disseminate information, but there was some concern that the FCC lottery prohibition would prevent broadcasters from airing lottery spots and news. To remedy the situation, Congress passed a law stating that the lottery rule should not apply to "an advertisement, list of prizes, or information concerning a lottery conducted by a state . . . broadcast by a . . . station licensed to a location in that state or adjacent state which has a lottery."[47]

Congress revisited the lottery question in 1988 when it passed the Charity Games Advertising and Clarification Act. The FCC implemented the law in 1990.[48] In essence, the new rules created further exemptions to the general lottery prohibition. Basically, lotteries for tax-exempt charities, governmental organizations, and commercial establishments running an occasional lottery may be advertised now. To qualify, however, the lottery and its advertising must be legal under state law.

The FCC does have a fine for noncompliance with the lottery rule: $4,000 per occurrence. This is one area in which broadcasters may need local legal advice before proceeding.

In recent years, questions have arisen about the ability of broadcasters to carry commercials for casinos that have sprung up around the country. Initially, the FCC reasoned that, under the lottery prohibition of the United

States Code,[49] they could not. There has been a series of cases on the topic and, in 1998, the Supreme Court refused to review a decision of the Ninth Circuit U.S. Court of Appeals that found the FCC's gambling prohibition unconstitutional.[50]

The FCC has said that it will enforce its gambling casino advertising prohibition in those states not affected by the decision, absent a court order. Apparently, gambling advertising will be legally contested state-by-state.

OTHER REGULATIONS

The deregulation era has seen the termination of many regulations, some of long standing. Most were eliminated in the FCC's "regulatory underbrush" proceedings in the 1980s, which allowed other federal agencies, like the FTC, to enter the regulatory void. Among the FCC regulations discontinued were those pertaining to

- double billing
- distortion of audience ratings
- distortion of signal coverage maps
- network clipping
- false, misleading, or deceptive advertising
- promotion of nonbroadcast business of a station[51]

Obviously, many rules remain in effect. Two that bear mention are rules regarding contests and phone conversations. The FCC has a strict contest rule.[52] As noted in Chapter 6, "Broadcast Promotion and Marketing," it requires the following:

- A station must fully and accurately disclose the material terms of the contest (prizes, eligibility, entry terms, etc.).
- The contest must be conducted substantially as advertised.
- Material terms of the contest may not be false, misleading, or deceptive.

As applied by the FCC, failure to mention a relevant fact can be as serious as making a false statement. For example, advertising a resort stay as a contest prize must include information that transportation is not included, if it is not.

FCC phone conversation rules also survived the "underbrush" proceedings. Simply stated, persons answering the phone must grant permission before their voice is put on the air live or prior to recording it for later broadcast.

ANNOUNCEMENTS

As used in broadcasting, the word "announcement" has a multitude of meanings and just as many regulations to cover them.

If a broadcast station or network airs a program that relates to an element of time that is significant, or if an effort is made by the program content to create the impression it is live, an announcement must be made stating that the program is either taped, filmed, or recorded.

A good example might be ABC-TV's "The Day After," which dealt with the time in which we live and the fear of World War III and a nuclear holocaust. The program was done in such a way that it seemed that the action was taking place live. The producers included messages at the beginning and end of the program that it was a taped dramatization.

Broadcast stations are required to identify themselves at the beginning of daily operations and at the end of operations for that day. In other words, stations must start and end their broadcast day with station identification announcements. They are also required to air a station identification hourly, as close to the hour as feasible at a natural break in the programming. Television stations may make their station identifications either visually or aurally.

When a station broadcasts any material for which it receives compensation, it must identify the person or group sponsoring the broadcast. Compensation refers to money, services, or other valuable consideration. Sponsorship identification remains a problem, particularly in children's shows where the station receives the program from a distributor in exchange for air time.

247

Disregarding the sponsorship identification rule has landed some stations in trouble for *payola*, the practice whereby recording company representatives have secretly rewarded disc jockeys for playing and plugging certain records. Payola is one FCC policy that has not been a casualty of deregulation.

Similarly, the sponsorship identification rule also applies to *plugola*. That is the on-the-air promotion of goods or services in which someone selecting the material broadcast has an undisclosed financial interest.

In broadcasting, there is a type of announcement referred to as a "teaser" or "come-on" spot. This announcement may consist of catchwords, slogans, symbols, and so forth. The intent is to arouse the curiosity of the public as to the identity of the advertiser or product to be revealed in subsequent announcements. The FCC has ruled that, even though the final advertisement in a campaign fully identifies the sponsor, the law requires that each teaser announcement reveal the identity of the sponsor.

When concert promotions are carried on a station and it receives some type of valuable consideration in return, the station must make this fact known. Concert-promotion television announcements for which consideration has been received must be logged as commercial announcements.

Finally, there are public service announcements. These are announcements aired by the station without charge and include spots that promote programs, activities, or services of federal, state, or local governments (e.g., sales of savings bonds), or the programs, activities, or services of nonprofit organizations (e.g., Red Cross, United Way), or any other announcements regarded as servicing community interests. Here, the station must identify the group on whose behalf the PSA is being aired.

COMMERCIAL POLICIES

Commercial broadcasting in the United States operates in a free-enterprise system. Profit is the motivating factor, and it comes from a station's success in generating revenue from advertisers.

The public interest should be the primary consideration in program selection. However, as part of the deregulation of radio and television, the FCC has eliminated all program-length commercial restrictions. The rationale is the belief that audience selection and other marketplace forces will be more effective in determining advertising policies that best serve the public.

On the other hand, the FCC continues to prohibit the intermixture of commercial and programming matter. Its basic concern is whether a licensee has subordinated programming in the public interest to commercial programming, in the interest of salability. The selection of program matter that appears designed primarily to promote the product of the sponsor, rather than to serve the public, will raise serious questions as to the licensee's purpose. But the fact that a commercial entity sponsors a program that includes content related to the sponsor's products does not, in and of itself, make a program entirely commercial.

If the program content promotes an advertiser's product or service, one key question the FCC will ask is on what basis the program material was selected. If the licensee reviews a proposed program in advance and makes a good-faith determination that the broadcast of the program will serve the public interest and that its information or entertainment value is not incidental to the promotion of an advertiser's product or service, the program will not be viewed as a program-length commercial. To avoid any possible questions by the FCC, care should be taken to separate completely the program's content and the sponsor's sales messages.

Another commercial policy deals with "subliminal perception." Briefly, this pertains to the practice of flashing on a television screen a statement so quickly that it does not register with the viewer at a conscious level, but does make an imprint on the subconscious. For instance, if a station or network were to flash on the screen the words "Buy Coke" every ten seconds throughout a program, in all probability the viewer would have a strong desire to buy a Coke by the end of the program. It is quite obvious why this type of advertising is illegal.

For years, radio and television broadcasters have been accused of "cranking up the gain," so to speak, on their commercials. Whether the commercials are louder than the program itself has to be determined on an individual basis. The FCC requires that stations take appropriate measures to eliminate the broadcast of objectionably loud commercials.

The sale of commercial time is the lifeblood of the broadcasting industry. However, there may be times when a licensee does not want to sell time to an individual or group. The courts have held that broadcast stations are not common carriers and may refuse time for products or services they find objectionable. The licensee also may refuse to do business with anyone whose credit is bad.

Whether stations should be required to sell time for opinion or editorial advertising was an open question until 1973, when the Supreme Court upheld the principle of licensee discretion. Care should be taken to note the

248

exceptions to the general rule. First, it is obvious that stations cannot refuse to sell time to a political candidate in response to a valid Section 315 equal opportunities request. Second, the antitrust laws make it illegal for a station to refuse advertising if the purpose of the refusal is to monopolize trade or if the refusal is part of a conspiracy to restrain trade.

Prior to the FCC's "postcard renewal" and deregulation proceedings, license renewal applicants were required to state the maximum amount of commercial matter they proposed to allow in any 60-minute period. Currently, there is no rule that limits the amount of commercial material that may be broadcast in a given period of time.

Restrictions placed on commercials in children's programs included commercial limits, separation of program and commercial matter, excessive promotion of brand names, and false advertising. The FCC had eliminated commercial limits in its deregulation of television, but a federal court found that it had inadequate justification to do so. As noted earlier, the Children's Television Act of 1990 reimposed commercial limits of 12 minutes per hour on weekdays and 10.5 minutes per hour on weekends. The act also directed the FCC to reexamine the question of program-length commercials with respect to children's programming. In a 1992 proceeding convened to implement the act, the Commission defined such a commercial as a "program associated with a product in which commercials for that product aired."

249

OTHER POLICIES

PUBLIC INSPECTION FILE

All broadcast stations must keep certain documents and information open to public inspection at "the main studio of the station, or any accessible place" in the community of license during regular business hours. Public inspection file content must now be retained for the entire license term of eight years. In addition to permitting on-site inspection, stations must make photocopies of public file contents available upon receiving telephone requests for such contents. Under public file rules adopted by the FCC in mid-1998 and by Congress in the Bipartisan Campaign Reform Act of 2002, stations may maintain all or part of their public file in a computer database rather than in paper files.

Set forth below is a summary of the contents of the public inspection file required under the new rules. Except where noted, the requirements apply to both commercial and noncommercial stations.

Authorizations: A station's current authorization (license and/or construction permit) and any documents that reflect a modification of or condition on the authorization.

Applications: All applications filed with the FCC and related materials, including information about any petitions to deny the application served on the applicant. These are retained as described above.

Citizen Agreements: All written agreements with citizens groups, which must be retained for the duration of the agreement, including any renewals or extensions.

Contour Maps: A copy of any service contour maps submitted with any application filed with the FCC, together with other information in the application showing service contours, main studio, and transmitter site locations. This information is retained as long as it is current and accurate.

Ownership Reports: The most recent complete ownership report filed with the FCC, any statements filed with the FCC certifying that the current report is accurate, plus any related material. Copies of the contracts listed in the report or an up-to-date list of those contracts are also required. Copies of contracts must be made available within seven days if the latter option is chosen.

Political File: The requirements were changed by the Bipartisan Campaign Reform Act of 2002. This law imposes supplemental public file requirements for certain issue ads that are not subject to the access, equal opportunities, and lowest unit rate rules applicable to candidate ads. The new requirements apply not only to ads placed by candidates for federal elective office, but also to national issue ads purchased by corporations, labor unions, public interest groups, PACs, etc., to present messages support or oppose any federal law, regulation or policy, or that support or oppose any change in such federal requirements.

On issues relating to any "political matter of national importance," broadcasters and cable systems must retain in their public inspection file the following:

1. a record of each request to buy time
2. a note as to whether the request was accepted or rejected
3. the rate charged, if it was accepted
4. air dates and times
5. the class of time purchased
6. the issue involved
7. if applicable, the name of the candidate and election/office
8. the name of the purchaser and contact person and a list of the chief executive officer/board of directors

All requests for time that a station receives from a candidate for public office, and a description of how the station responded to the request, are retained for two years.

Annual Employment Reports: A copy of all annual employment reports filed with the FCC and related material. These are retained for the entire license term.

The Public and Broadcasting: A copy of the revised manual (when it becomes available).

Public Correspondence: A copy of all written comments and suggestions received from the public, including E-mail communications, regarding the station's operation, unless the writer requests the correspondence not be made public, or the licensee believes that it should be excluded from the file based on its content (for example, defamatory or obscene letters). E-mail correspondence may be retained as described above. (Note that this requirement does not generally apply to noncommercial stations, but such stations may choose to retain letters from the public regarding violent programming. All TV stations are required to file with their license renewal applications summaries of any letters received regarding violent programming.)

Material Related to an FCC Investigation or Complaint: Material that has a substantial bearing on a matter that is the subject of an FCC investigation or a complaint to the FCC about which the applicant, permittee, or licensee has been advised. This is retained until the FCC provides written notification that the material may be discarded.

Issues/Programs Lists: The quarterly list of programs that have provided the station's most significant treatment of community issues during the preceding three-month period. Each list should include a brief narrative describing the issues to which the station devoted significant treatment and the programs (or program segments) that provided this treatment, including the program's (or segment's) title, time, date, and duration. These are due on January 10, April 10, July 10, and October 10 of each year and must be retained for the entire license term.

251

Children's Commercial Limits: For commercial TV stations, quarterly records sufficient to substantiate the station's certification in its renewal application that it has complied with the commercial limits on children's programming. The records for each calendar quarter must be placed in the file no later than the tenth day of the succeeding calendar quarter (e.g., January 10, April 10, etc.). These are retained for the entire license term.

Children's Television Programming Reports: For commercial TV stations, the quarterly Children's Television Programming Report on FCC Form 398 showing efforts during the preceding quarter and plans for the next quarter to serve the educational and informational needs of children. This must be placed in the file no later than the tenth day of the succeeding calendar quarter (see above). These reports are kept separate from other materials in the public file and are retained for the entire license term.

License Renewal Local Public Notice Announcement: Statements certifying compliance with the local public notice requirements before and after the filing of the station's license renewal application. These are retained for the same period as the related license renewal application.

Radio Time Brokerage Agreements: For commercial radio stations, a copy of each time brokerage agreement related to the licensee's station or involving programming of another station in the same market by the licensee. Confidential or proprietary information may be redacted where appropriate. These are retained for as long as the agreement is in effect.

Must-Carry/Retransmission Consent Election: For TV stations, a statement of the station's election with respect to either must-carry or retransmission consent. In the case of noncommercial stations, a copy of any request for mandatory carriage on any cable system and related correspondence. These are retained for the duration of the period for which the statement or request applies.

Donors' Lists: For noncommercial stations only, a list of donors supporting specific programs. This is retained for two years.

OPERATING REQUIREMENTS

The legal guidelines for operation comprise one of the most important policies for a broadcaster. In the early days of radio, broadcasting stations went on the air when they pleased and where they pleased. Adhering to an assigned frequency was of no concern. With the passage of the Communications Act of 1934, broadcasting became highly regulated. Despite deregulation of many areas of station activity, the FCC continues to monitor technical operations very closely.

When licensees are allocated a channel for broadcast purposes, in effect they have entered into a contract. They must keep their signal on that channel and at the power allotted to them at all times. They are also required to run checks on their entire transmitting system and to note and retain the information gathered.

Licensees must observe FCC rules on the painting and lighting of towers, whether they own them or not. The FCC is now emphasizing observation of these rules and has an authorized $10,000 fine to deal with those who do not adhere to them. A similar initiative has been under way to ensure that all stations have Emergency Alert System equipment in operational order. The fine for a deviation is $8,000. Those stations with directional patterns must keep them within prescribed limits or be subject to a $7,000 fine.

Inspectors from one of the various FCC field offices arrive unannounced and inspect the station for violation of the FCC's engineering standards and other rules. After the inspection, the licensee will receive either (1) no notice at all, if the inspector determines that no violation exists; (2) a letter alerting the station that a problem does exist that could, if continued, result in a violation or prevent the station from performing effectively; or (3) an official notice of violation.

An important fact for all managers of broadcast stations to keep in mind is that, no matter how good their programs are, no matter how grandiose their facility may be, or how efficient their sales staff is, everything within their command is just as good as the technical staff that keeps the station on the air.

FINES AND FORFEITURES

Sections 503(b)(1) and (2) of the 1934 act authorize the FCC to levy monetary fines and forfeitures for violations of its regulations or certain federal statutes. For a review of the violation classifications and the base fine for each, see Section 1.80(b) of the Commission's Rules.[53]

REGULATORY FEES

The Omnibus Budget Reconciliation Act of 1993 requires the FCC to assess annual regulatory fees. These "user fees" are separate and distinct from application fees, which were authorized in 1987. Collection commenced on April 1, 1994, and the FCC may levy a late fee of up to 25 percent.

Regulatory fees for radio are determined by class and market size and range from $350 to $8,775. Fees also are imposed on AM and FM construction permits. Television fees vary with VHF or UHF allocation and market size. Again, construction permit fees are assessed.

DEALING WITH COMPLAINTS

For the most part, stations only receive complaints when an individual or group is angry about a program, a news report, a commercial, an editorial, or something technical like "your darn station is coming in on my toaster."

However, some people complain not only to stations, but also to the FCC. It disposes of most complaints by sending a letter to the complainant without ever contacting the broadcast station in question. For complaints involving political broadcasts or questions of access, the Commission encourages good-faith negotiations between licensees and persons who seek broadcast time or have related questions. In the past, such negotiations often have led to a disposition of the request or questions in a manner that is agreeable to all parties.

In general, the FCC limits its interpretive rulings or advisory opinions to cases in which the specific facts in controversy are before it for decision.

Written complaints to local stations must be kept in the public file, and management should act or react to the complainant as soon as possible. Radio and television station operators are in a business where the image of the station must be a positive one or the audience may simply turn the dial or shut the TV or radio off. Good public relations are important ingredients in the management of any electronic media system.

253

WHAT'S AHEAD?

With deregulation and some of the controversies that have ensued, the question now is what further changes, if any, will take place in the regulations and the agencies that enforce them. If the broadcast industry accepts the responsibility of self-regulation, deregulation may continue.

Accordingly, deregulation brings additional responsibilities for the broadcast manager. Some management decisions, especially in the area of programming, will have to be looked at in a different light without the federal regulations to guide the industry. If the industry does not take advantage of deregulation, it will find the old regulations being imposed once again. It is going to take time to determine whether or not broadcasters are willing to seize the opportunity to function in an environment similar to that of the print media. Responsible management will be the key.

SUMMARY

Traditionally, broadcast regulation has been based on the principles of the public interest and scarcity. The public interest remains intact. However, the FCC has effectively removed scarcity as a rationale.

The FCC was established by the Communications Act of 1934. It is the agency charged with regulating the electronic media but, in recent years, embarked on a program of industry deregulation. The Telecommunications Act of 1996 escalated further deregulation and electronic media consolidation. The law increased the participation of other arms of the federal government, like the Department of Justice, in communication regulation. Another agency, the Federal Trade Commission, polices advertising in broadcasting and other media.

Would-be and actual station licensees are required to file a large quantity of information with the FCC. Forms must be submitted to request authorization to construct a station and to obtain a license to operate. The FCC also requires submission of ownership reports and license renewal forms, among others.

Despite deregulation, the FCC retains and continues to enforce many policies. There are restrictions on the numbers and kinds of stations that can be owned by one person or entity in a single community and nationwide. Programming policies cover, among other content, political broadcasts, and the use of obscenity, indecency, and profanity.

Stations are required to maintain for public inspection a file containing copies of all applications to the FCC, ownership and employment reports, details of programs broadcast in response to community issues, and other information. They also must comply with operating requirements set forth in their license.

In this new era, broadcasters must show that they can operate responsibly without close regulation. If they do not, a reimposition of at least some of the terminated policies is likely. In fact, there is evidence of that now in the FCC's localism initiative, the indecency zero tolerance, industry reaction to stiff fines, and in a reexamination of violence in programming.

CASE STUDY

WPOL-TV is the local news ratings leader in a presidential election battleground state. It is an open election, with no incumbent. The presidential aspirants and their supporters have beaten a path to WPOL's door to buy time.

You are a salesperson at the station. Sitting across from you is a representative of something called "Swift Tanks for Truth." This group, known as a 527 under the Bipartisan Campaign Reform Act of 2002, wants to buy news program spots. The spot will feature a presidential candidate that Swift Tanks opposes. It will contain visual footage of their villain and will have voice-over audio suggesting that the candidate's tank triumphs are not what he represents them to be.

EXERCISES

1. Before you go any further with this client, what must you have him do?

2. What must you give the potential client?

3. Are there any special tag-line requirements for the spot under the BCRA of 2002?

4. If Swift Tanks decides not to buy time, are your statutory responsibilities at an end?

CASE STUDY

Bob "The Love Sponge" has been your ratings king at KLUV-FM for the last ten years. The show has always been a little on the edge, but that is why it has been so popular. However, each ratings period, it becomes a little harder to come up with something more shocking than in the previous period.

It is now the fall book, most important for the new annual advertising budgets.

Bob has a brain malfunction that results in the KLUV "Please call in when you are having sex" contest. Unfortunately, Bob has not consulted management and simply springs it one morning in drive time, beginning at 5 A.M.

The calls come pouring in and the two-way conversations often are more than mere innuendo. By 6 A.M., the mayor is on the phone to the general manager. It seems he listened for an hour to make sure he was not hearing things.

Listeners swamped the FCC with complaints. The FCC issued a notice of apparent liability for violation of the FCC's indecency rules. The show lasted one day.

You are the GM trying to analyze the situation.

255

EXERCISES

1. Since the show began at 5 A.M., during the FCC indecency "safe harbor," can that be used as a defense?

2. Would the program concept in itself violate the FCC's 1987 indecency definition?

3. Is the station absolved because Bob did not consult with management before the start of the contest?

4. If the FCC concludes that an indecency violation has occurred, what will the fine be?

5. Can the station collect the fine from Bob?

6. Is the station required to fire Bob?

NOTES

[1] Telecommunications Act of 1996, Pub. L. 104–104, Feb. 8, 1996, 110 Stat. 56.

[2] "FCC Sets Limits on Media Concentration," *FCC News*, June 2, 2003, (http://www.fcc.gov.)

[3] Syracuse Peace Council, 2 FCC Rcd. 5043, 1987.

[4] "FCC Sets Limits on Media Concentration."

[5] Red Lion Broadcasting Co. v. Federal Communications Commission, 395 U.S. 367, 1969.

[6] Don R. Pember, *Mass Media Law*, p. 471.

[7] Pember, *op. cit.*, p. 470.

[8] Pember, *op. cit.*, p. 476.

[9] Century Communications Corporation v. Federal Communications Commission, 835 F2d 292, 1987.

[10] 47 *USC* 308(b).

[11] 47 *CFR* 73.2080 (b) and (c).

[12] Lutheran Church-Missouri Synod v. FCC, D.C. Cir. No. 97–116 (April 14, 1998).

[13] The 1996 Telecommunications Act changed the license term to eight years for both radio and television stations. Prior to that, the television term was five years and the radio term was seven years.

[14] 47 *USC* 303(a), 303(b), and 394.

[15] 47 *CFR* 73.3555.

[16] "FCC Sets Limits on Media Concentration."

[17] *Ibid.*

[18] *Antenna*, Drinker, Biddle & Reath, LLP, September 2003, pp. 1–2.

[19] FCC Docket 04–233, Notice of Inquiry, Broadcast Localism Proceeding, (http://www.fcc.gov).

[20] WCVB-TV, 63 RR 2d 665, 1987.

[21] In King Broadcasting Co., 6 FCC Rcd. 4998, 1991.

[22] *Political Broadcasting Advisory*, Fisher Wayland Cooper Leader & Zaragoza, LLP, January 1998, p. 7.

[23] Meredith Corp. v. Federal Communications Commission, 809 F2d 863, 1987; Syracuse Peace Council, 2 FCC Rcd. 5043, 1987.

[24] In the Matter of Policies and Rules Concerning Children's Television Programming, 6 FCC Rcd. 2111, 1991.

[25] *Ibid.*

[26] 18 *USC* 1464.

[27] Federal Communications Commission v. Pacifica Foundation, 438 U.S. 726, 1978.

[28] New Indecency Enforcement Standards to Be Applied to All Broadcast and Amateur Radio Licenses, 2 FCC Rcd. 2726.

[29] Action for Children's Television v. Federal Communications Commission, 852 F2d 1332, 1988.

[30] Action for Children's Television v. Federal Communications Commission, 58 F3d 654.

[31] "FCC Adjusts Maximum Forfeiture Penalties to Reflect Inflation," *FCC News*, June 18, 2004 (http://www.fcc.gov.)

[32] *Inside Radio*, February 26, 2004, p. 1; August 13, 2004, p. 1.

[33] "Assume the Position," *Broadcasting & Cable*, March 31, 2004, pp. 2–3.

[34] *Inside Radio*, August 5, 2004, p. 2.

[35] "Sexy Half-time Stunt," *Broadcasting & Cable*, February 9, 2004, pp. 6, 37.

[36] *Inside Radio*, June 24, 2004, p. 1.

[37] *Inside Radio*, August 18, 2004, p. 2.

[38] "FCC's Got a Brand New Bad," *Broadcasting & Cable*, March 22, 2004, p. 6; see also, *Inside Radio*, July 30, 2004, p. 1.

[39] *Inside Radio*, July 30, 2004, p. 1.

[40] "Congress and the FCC Take Aim," *Broadcasting & Cable*, May 31, 2004, pp. 1, 4.

[41] "Disc Jockeys Air Racial Diatribe," *St. Louis Post-Dispatch*, May 11, 1993, p. 1.

[42] R.A.V. v. City of St. Paul, Minnesota, 112 S. Ct. 2538, 1992.

[43] "Infinity, Stern Hit with Racism Complaint," *Broadcasting & Cable*, November 22, 1993, p. 36.

[44] "Steve & D.C. Suspended," *St. Louis Post-Dispatch*, May 13, 1993, p. 1.

[45] Letter to KSHE-FM, 6 FCC Rcd. 2289.

[46] *Broadcast Hoaxes*, 70 RR 2d 1383, 1992.

[47] 18 USC 1307(a) (2).

[48] Broadcast of Lottery Information (Charity Games), 67 RR 2d 996, 1990.

[49] 18 USC 1304.

[50] Valley Broadcasting Co. v. United States, 107 F. 32. 1328 (9th Cir. 1997).

[51] T. Barton Carter, Marc A. Franklin, and Jay B. Wright, *The First Amendment and the Fifth Estate*, pp. 393–394.

[52] 47 CFR 73.1216.

[53] 47 CFR 1.80(b)(4).

ADDITIONAL READINGS

Creech, Kenneth C. *Electronic Media Law and Regulation*, 4th ed. Boston: Focal Press, 2003.

Green, Bill. *NAB Legal Guide to Broadcast Law and Regulation Update*. Washington, DC: National Association of Broadcasters, 1998.

Middleton, Kent R., William E. Lee, and Bill F. Chamberlin. *The Law of Public Communication*, 7th ed. Boston: Allyn and Bacon, 2005.

Overbeck, Wayne G. *Major Principles of Media Law, 2006 Edition.* Belmont, CA: Thomson Wadsworth, 2006.

Sadler, Roger L. *Electronic Media Law.* Thousand Oaks, CA: Sage, 2005.

Zelezny, John D. *Cases in Communications Law: Liberties, Restraints, and the Modern Media,* 4th ed. Belmont, CA: Thomson Wadsworth, 2004.

Managing the Cable Television System

8

This chapter considers cable TV management by examining

- franchising and refranchising procedures
- managerial functions and responsibilities, with special attention to programming, economics, marketing and promotion
- revenue enhancement, and the role of digital products and services
- the regulatory environment in which cable systems operate

While Guglielmo Marconi was working toward his dream of a telegraph system without wires, he would have laughed at the irony that, less than a century later, telecommunications *with* wires would again be all the rage. To Marconi and other electrical tinkerers of the early twentieth century, it was a great goal to one day be able to send messages over long distances without the need of wires. These electronic pioneers brought us radio and, later, television. All the while, the fact remained that many more messages could be sent—much more clearly—through cable than could be broadcast over the airwaves.

Marconi might have laughed. But broadcasters are not amused. Cable is a major competitor, siphoning off audiences, revenues, and programming from conventional terrestrial television services. Into the new century, the ultimate irony is that hard-wired cable is itself under attack from wireless-to-home satellite transmission.

More than 8,800 cable systems pass 97 percent of the nation's 109 million television households. Cable penetration totals almost 67 percent of those homes, yielding more than 73 million subscribers. Of that number, 50 million also subscribe to pay-cable services.[1]

Cable viewing shares have surged since the mid-1980s. In the 2003–2004 television season (September–May), more than 50 percent of all prime-time television viewers watched ad-supported cable networks. This was the first time that cable surpassed all seven terrestrial broadcast networks.[2] Cable had won the total day shares viewing five years earlier.

Cable's audience growth has been accompanied by vigorous subscriber services and advertising revenue growth. Annual revenue in 2004 was $57.6 billion.[3] It included advertising, video, Internet, phone, pay-per-view (PPV), video-on-demand(VOD), and other services provided by the nation's cable systems.

Systems generate significant ad revenue, both local and national. Local spot revenue is growing quickly and was expected to rise to $6 billion in 2005. National spot at the local level runs about 20 percent of the local spot. That would put it at about $1.2 billion in 2005. Percentage compounded annual growth of cable ad revenue is in the mid-teens.

National advertiser-supported cable networks also generate significant advertising revenue. It was projected at $14.5 billion for 2005.

As they look to the future, cable companies are contemplating ways of consolidating their profitability. As indicated above, many have already begun the process of transforming themselves from program purveyors to suppliers of a full range of communications services. Subscriber growth will be limited because cable passes almost all TV households and satellite TV has become a real subscriber competitor. So, cable television must increase its sales of current and new products to an existing base of subscribers.

THE FRANCHISING PROCESS

Anyone considering a career in cable television should be familiar with the basis of cable operation: *franchising*. The franchise agreement provides the cable system with authorization to utilize public rights-of-way in conducting business, and establishes the terms and conditions under which this can be done. The franchise is to cable what the license is to broadcast stations.

From the beginning, the process was an area of shared responsibility between local and federal governments. Local governments issued the franchise because of the uses cable systems made of city streets and other rights-of-way. The Federal Communications Commission set standards for the provisions franchise agreements should include.

This structure of dual responsibility was confusing and ripe for abuse. Revenue-starved cities placed many demands on potential cable operators as preconditions to franchise issuance. This was true, particularly, when an exclusive franchise was at stake. In their zeal to win, competing companies made promises that were neither practical nor affordable. Bribery of officials to obtain lucrative franchises was not unknown. No one was happy—neither the local governments nor the operators.

It was in this climate that Congress enacted the Cable Communications Policy Act of 1984. The act continued the requirement that operators obtain a franchise. Franchising authority remained with local governments, and they determined the franchise term.

However, limitations were imposed on what a government could demand before granting a franchise. Cities could require franchisees to offer broad categories of programming (e.g., for children), but were not permitted to specify carriage of particular networks or services to satisfy the requirement. They could also include in the franchise agreement a provision that channel space be allocated for public, educational, or governmental access, so-called "PEG" channels. Systems with 36 or more channels had to provide space for *commercial leased access*; in other words, channels available for lease by persons unrelated to the cable company.

The 1984 law provided that the franchise authority might grant one or more franchises within its jurisdiction. Companies that overpromised in their eagerness to obtain a franchise could receive relief upon adequate showing of an inability to comply. Cities were entitled to collect a franchise fee from cable operators. However, it could not exceed 5 percent of the cable system's gross revenue for any 12-month period. The act also freed systems from franchise authority rate regulation.

The history of experience under the 1984 act was not one of success. Basic provisions of the law were challenged in court by the cable industry itself. One such provision was that which allowed franchise authorities to award exclusive franchises.[4] Deregulated cable rates exploded. The twin pressures of litigation and consumer reaction forced Congress to reexamine cable regulation. It did so, and passed the Cable Television Consumer Protection and Competition Act of 1992. The major impact of the new law on franchise requirements was a prohibition on the granting of exclusive franchises. The law imposed many new obligations on franchisees and ended the "deregulation" of cable.

Four years later, Congress passed the Telecommunications Act of 1996. This was a major electronic media deregulatory law that also impacted cable television.

Basic requirements of the various laws are reviewed in the regulation section later in the chapter.

FRANCHISE RENEWAL

As noted earlier, cable franchises are issued by local governments, not the FCC. Unlike broadcast licenses, cable franchises have no universally fixed term. Each local authority sets the term of the franchise or franchises within its jurisdiction. Before 1984, there were no universal rules for the procedure or for criteria to be applied in franchise renewals. Cable operators wanted the security that the FCC license afforded broadcasters. Broadcast licensees had a "renewal expectancy." In other words, if they had rendered "substantial past meritorious service to the public" during their license term, they expected that the license would be renewed. On the other hand, the absence of renewal standards in the cable industry had become an impediment to investment.

The Cable Communications Policy Act of 1984 addressed cable operator renewal concerns. The act set national renewal standards, but left the administration of those standards to local franchise authorities. It also established specific timetables and criteria for renewal. Cable operators may initiate the renewal procedure by submitting written notice to their franchise authority. Any operator seeking renewal is entitled to a public hearing at which its past performance can be evaluated and the future cable-related needs of the community considered. The hearing must be held within a 6-month period, beginning no later than 30 months before the expiration of the franchise. At the conclusion of this evaluation, an operator may submit a renewal proposal. The franchise authority has a fixed period within which to accept it, or indicate its preliminary determination that the franchise should not be renewed.[5]

Denial of a renewal proposal must be based on one or more of the four factors examined at such a proceeding, which considers whether

- the cable operator has substantially complied with the material terms of the existing franchise and with applicable law;

- the quality of the operator's service, including signal quality, response to consumer complaints, and billing practices, but without regard to the mix or quality of cable services or other services provided over the system, has been reasonable in light of community needs;

- the operator has the financial, legal, and technical ability to provide the services, facilities, and equipment as set forth in the operator's proposal; and

- the operator's proposal is reasonable to meet the future cable-related community needs and interests, taking into account the cost of meeting such needs and interests.[6]

The relative security afforded a cable operator by the law should not lead to laxity about the renewal process, however. Even though most franchises are granted for 10 to 15 years, many operators recommend an early start on preparing the new proposal.

If the franchisee has performed well during the franchise term, the task of obtaining renewal may not be too difficult. Nonetheless, the need to plan is extremely important. It should include identifying and resolving potential problems, striving to respond to community needs and desires for programming, and determining whether or not the system should be upgraded or expanded. With an eye toward renewal, many systems operated by multiple system operators (MSOs) sample customer attitudes in their monthly program guide.

Sensitivity to subscribers' needs is essential. An operator who is not prepared will run into difficulties during the refranchising procedures. It is important to let the public know what has been accomplished and what is planned.

Presentations before the local governmental authority must be professional. Information must be accurate and displayed in a form that can be read and understood easily. Keeping files on complaints, no matter how minute, as well as complimentary correspondence, also will be of value.

Once the franchise has been renewed, full attention returns to day-to-day operations.

ORGANIZATION

Like a broadcast station, a cable television system is organized according to the major functions that must be carried out to ensure successful operation. While differences exist in organizational structure, the functions are similar and are allocated to departments. As new products and services are added to the menu, such as digital subscriber line service (DSL), high-speed Internet, digital tiers, and telephone services, supervision of these functions is assigned to existing organizational units. In the instances cited above, responsibility for developing these add-on products and services most likely would be assigned to the marketing director, with the assistance of the technical operations director. The following departments are found in many systems:

263

Government Affairs and Community Relations

These activities are often performed by only one person, with the title of director. Government affairs revolves around contacts with federal, state, and local elected officials, especially those who make up the franchising authority. The planning and execution of public relations campaigns designed to create and maintain a favorable image in the franchise area are the focus of community relations.

Human Resources

A manager may be the only person charged with human resource responsibilities. They include recruiting and interviewing job applicants, orienting new employees, developing and implementing employee training and evaluation programs, and processing benefits.

Business Operations

A director supervises the work of personnel in this department, which has responsibility for recording revenues and expenditures, handling collections, and computer operations.

Advertising Sales

The sale of local availabilities in advertiser-supported networks is a major responsibility of this department, headed by a manager. Many systems also sell classified advertising and spots on local origination channels. Cable television systems used to outsource this function. However, spot sales have become such an important revenue stream that almost all systems execute this function in-house.

Technical Operations

A director is charged with responsibility for this department, which engages in a variety of tasks. They include maintenance and operation of the head-end (i.e., the facility that receives, processes, and converts video signals for transmission on the cable) and trunk and feeder cables; maintenance of the standby power supply; testing and adjustment of signal strength; installation and repair of drop cables and hookups to cable boxes and videocassette recorders; planning and construction of extensions to the cable system in new subdivisions and apartment complexes; and the dispatch of technicians. As noted earlier, some responsibility for installation and maintaining new products and services may be assigned to the department as well. The director is assisted by supervisors with expertise in the different operational areas.

Marketing

A marketing director heads this department. Its major responsibilities are the sale of the system's program services and products to subscribers, and the planning and execution of advertising and promotion campaigns in furtherance of those goals. The department engages in market analyses to assess customer preferences and potential, and determines the packaging of new and old services and their price structure. The department also conducts door-to-door, direct mail, and telemarketing sales campaigns. Services and products also are promoted on the system.

Customer Service

This department, headed by a director, deals with all customer service and repair calls, inquiries, and complaints. This is an important function. Inattention to customer service in cable's "build-out" years gave cable an image problem and stimulated national regulatory initiatives. Failure to service the customer promptly and efficiently can lead to *churn*, or customer turnover. As the rapid growth of satellite TV has demonstrated, customers do have a place to go and an inclination to do so if they are dissatisfied.

The number and organization of employees is influenced by the size of the system and by its status as a single entity or part of a multiple system operation. Management preferences also play a role, and scores of variations exist. Figure 8.1 shows how a system may be organized. It is headed by a general manager (GM).

The GM directs and coordinates all system activities to ensure efficient and profitable operation within the framework established by federal law and the local franchise agreement. In particular, the general manager

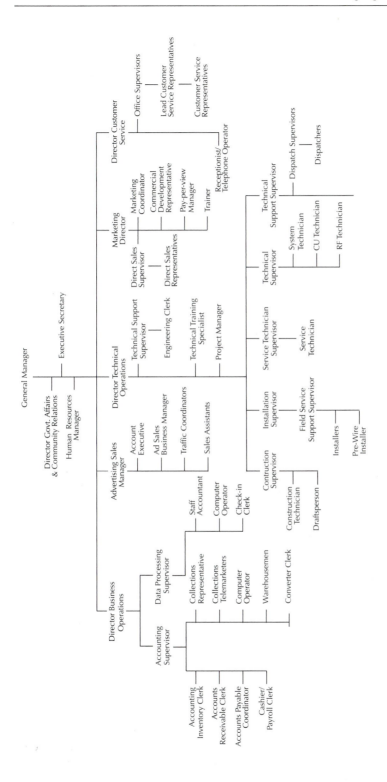

FIGURE 8.1 Organization of a cable television system.

- supervises and coordinates, directly or through subordinates, all personnel
- directs, through subordinates, employee compliance with established administrative policies and procedures, safety rules, and governmental regulations
- examines, analyzes, and establishes system directions and goals
- prepares and directs procedures designed to increase efficiency and revenues and to lower costs
- prepares, implements, and controls the budget
- approves requisitions for equipment, materials, and supplies, and all invoices
- represents the system to local government, business, the media, and other groups
- interfaces with the corporate office should the system be part of an MSO

+As in a broadcast station, each department is unique. However, there are major differences. The cable company sends its signals through wires; the broadcast station through the airwaves. In broadcast, advertisers are the primary market. In cable, the audience is the market and the system's financial success is tied closely to the number of subscribers it can attract and the number of services and products they purchase.

These realities impose on cable managers an obligation to ensure that the technical quality of the signal is of the highest caliber. Viewers will continue to subscribe as long as they feel they are receiving value for their money. If they do not, the system will experience subscriber disconnects. Accordingly, the marketing and technical staffs must cooperate closely, since the retention and addition of subscribers depend heavily on a signal that is technically acceptable when delivered to the home. The system manager must pay close and constant attention to those two areas of activity. They are the very foundation upon which the company survives.

The general manager must know what is happening in every department. This can be accomplished through regular meetings with department heads. Such meetings also provide an effective method of solving problems before they become crises.

Cable managers must be sensitive to the needs of their employees. Getting to know the staff, being receptive to their problems and ideas, and keeping an open-door policy will be beneficial in the smooth and effective running of the operation. Apathy and discontent also may be avoided as a result.

PROGRAMMING

The programming challenge for cable system operators has never been greater. The explosion of available program services has continued unabated. New federal laws require operators to carry certain local broadcast stations.[7] Old federal laws permit or require that channels be provided for mandatory access, like PEG, and for lease by third parties. Franchise agreements may require still other channel dedication for services such as local origination.

266

And stiff competition has arrived in the form of satellite TV companies with digital capability and a large universe of program offerings.

In addition, technological advances, including video compression and fiber optics, are rapidly expanding program choices and channel capacity. Video-on-demand, pay-per-view, and digital channels and tiers are now part of the program mix.

So, there are marketplace demands for channels and franchise and regulatory demands for channels.

It is a misconception to think that every cable television system in the United States has the capacity to be part of the 500-channel universe. In fact, about 53 percent of systems have channel capacity of between 30 and 53 channels and about another 25 percent between 54 and 90 channels. Systems with fewer than 90 channels account for more than 90 percent of cable TV subscribers.[8] Marketplace and other demands fill those limited channels quickly.

Management must make program selections that satisfy subscribers' demands for choice and value while maximizing system revenue.

Essentially, system programming is of two types: *voluntary* and *involuntary*. Voluntary operator program choices include distant broadcast signals, advertiser-supported networks, premium services, and special programming, such as PPV and VOD. Involuntary programming may include local broadcast stations under the must-carry rules, PEG mandatory access, leased access, and local origination.

Once chosen, programming must be paid for. Most voluntary programming requires payment; most involuntary programming does not. System operators pay for programming in two ways. The first is a requirement of federal law. In 1976, Congress enacted a comprehensive copyright law that required cable systems to pay semiannual fees for the carriage of some television stations. Copyright fees are not owed for carriage of local stations under must-carry. However, a compulsory fee set by law is required to carry distant commercial stations, including superstations.

In addition to the copyright payment, most voluntary program selections involve a payment directly to the program supplier. Such payments normally are calculated on a per-subscriber basis and are influenced by system size, since volume discounts are offered. There may be surcharges for some networks, especially those that offer professional sports, such as ESPN and TNT. In those instances, the programmer passes along to the cable system part of the substantial rights fee for such programming. However, many advertiser-supported cable networks allow systems to sell local advertising in network programming. This local revenue generation helps to offset the programming cost. As noted earlier, local ad sales are becoming significant.

Costs for noncommercial premium channels, like HBO, are far different. Payments are also set on a monthly, per-subscriber basis, but the amounts are much higher than for commercial, advertiser-supported networks. Again, volume discounts are offered. Obviously, no commercial offset for local system revenue generation is possible. Consequently, subscriber charges for premium channels are also much higher than those for basic sources.

Some program decisions result in payments to the cable system. Home shopping networks, for example, pay local systems a percentage of gross product sales generated in the system's franchise area. New networks often provide systems with financial marketing support to assist their launch in the community. However, the sums are not large.

It has been emphasized that the audience is the major customer of cable television and provides its principal financial support. For that reason, an important economic consideration in all programming decisions is the anticipated impact on subscriptions. A major goal in program selection is the addition of subscribers and the minimizing of disconnects. Decisions to accomplish those goals will rely on the operator's familiarity with the composition and program preferences of the community and of subscribers and nonsubscribers.

The operator's expertise in program selection is very important. It was noted earlier that cable systems pass 97 percent of the nation's television households, but that only about 67 percent of those homes subscribe. Attractive program choices must be available to convert some of the nonsubscribing homes to subscribers.

Recognizing the potential and limitations of the system's technology, legal obligations contained in federal law and the franchise agreement, and the need to maximize audience appeal and ensure a profit, the operator proceeds to program the available channels. Typically, the services provided include the following:

Local Origination and Access Channels

Many systems are required by the franchise agreement to produce programs for carriage on local origination, or community, channels. Time, temperature, and newswire displays, round-table discussions, and local sports are examples. Some also use the channel for community bulletin boards and program previews. In all cases, operators control the content.

The agreement also may require that channels be reserved for public, educational, and governmental access. This programming is produced by persons outside the cable company and often includes discussions, credit and noncredit courses, and meetings of local government bodies.

As noted earlier, some systems are required to offer leased access to individuals or groups. The content varies widely, reflecting the interests and goals of the leasing parties.

Most systems add audio to the service mix. Local radio stations are an example. Many also carry digital audio programming with several dozen channels of specialized music.

Local, Over-the-Air Broadcast Stations

The 1992 Cable Consumer Protection and Competition Act reimposed must-carry rules on the cable industry.[9] Simply put, "must-carry" requires a cable system to carry the commercial and noncommercial stations in its area. Under the law, broadcasters were required to choose between must-carry or retransmission consent before October 6, 1993. Retransmission consent is a legal alternative to must-carry. If a station elected retransmission consent, that amounted to a must-carry waiver. Under retransmission consent, broadcast stations could not be carried on a cable system without their consent. If a station and system could not reach a retransmission agreement, the system was free to drop the station in question.

The 1992 law considerably reduces programming discretion by a cable operator with respect to local television stations. More details on the specifics of must-carry may be found in the regulation section later in the chapter.

Distant Broadcast Stations

So-called "superstations," such as WGN (Chicago) and WTBS (Atlanta), offer entertainment and sports programming that may not be available from other sources. The system pays to the stations a small, monthly subscriber fee.

Basic Cable Networks

Operators have a large universe of basic networks from which to choose. Some target a narrow audience with specialized content, while others seek a broader audience with more diverse programming (Figure 8.2). Together,

Name	Content
A&E Network	Original series and movies, documentaries, biographies, dramatic specials, feature films, contemporary performances
ABC Family Channel	Original movies, series, specials
AMC	Popular movies, original series, documentaries, specials
CNN	Breaking news, business, weather, sports, entertainment, health, science, interviews
C-SPAN	Live coverage of the House of Representatives, National Press Club speeches, Congressional hearings, federal judiciary, call-in
Discovery Channel	Science and technology, exploration, adventure, history, lifestyle, how-to
FOX News Channel	News of the day's events
Lifetime Television	Entertainment and information, issues affecting women and their families
MTV: Music Television	Contemporary music, music specials, documentaries, news
Nick at Nite	Hit sitcoms, original shows
TLC	Nonfiction entertainment
USA Network	Original series and movies, sports, off-network shows, theatrical films
VH-1 (Music First)	Music, artists, pop culture
Weather Channel, The	Local, regional, and national weather, severe weather coverage, travel, original series

FIGURE 8.2 Selected basic cable networks and their content.

the networks provide a range of programming, and their selection will reflect the operator's perceptions of the interests and needs of the community and its subgroups. Compensation arrangements for system carriage of these mostly advertiser-supported networks were reviewed earlier in the chapter.

Pay-Cable Networks

These networks (Figure 8.3) offer commercial-free entertainment for a monthly subscriber fee, part of which is retained by the cable company. As a result, these so-called "premium" channels are a high economic priority for operators.

Some systems are using channel space for their own newscasts and for system-purchased syndicated programming, previously the exclusive domain of network affiliates and independents. Those with the necessary technology are reserving channels for PPVprogramming, which permits subscribers to select special programs, such as sports or entertainment specials, for which they are billed separately. Individual systems may contract for the rights to carry a pay-PPV event or to acquire programs from one of several national PPV services. For an example of a PPV marketing piece, see Figure 8.4.

Still other channels are being dedicated to the emerging video-on-demand market, which has become a significant revenue source. Vidieo-on-Demand provider iN DEMAND reported that, starting around June 2004, Movie-on-Demand orders exceeded those for PPV by more than two-to-one.[10]

Programming is a key contributor to successful operation. Without appealing programs, there would be no subscribers. Without subscribers, there would be no system. Providing a balanced program service at an acceptable cost is a continuing challenge.

Name	Content
Cinemax	First-run movies and premieres
FLIX	Classic movies from the 1970s, 1980s, and 1990s, first-run theatricals
HBO (Home Box Office)	Original movies, comedy, documentaries, series, music, family shows, sports specials, world championship boxing
Movie Channel, The (TMC)	Top Hollywood movies, movie trivia, celebrity interviews, behind-the-scenes looks at movie sets
Showtime	Hollywood hits, award-winning original pictures, series, championship boxing
STARZ	New hit movies
Sundance Channel	Feature films, shorts, documentaries, world cinema, animation

FIGURE 8.3 Selected pay-cable networks and their content.

FIGURE 8.4 Excerpt from a PPV marketing piece. (Source: Charter Communications. Used with permission.)

TIERING

Once the operator has made all the programming choices, attention will turn to marketing the selected products. Historically, cable systems have bundled certain categories of programming together for sale to potential subscribers. That practice is known as *tiering*. Typically, the subscribers' fee structure is tied to the tiers, and the total monthly charge depends on the options chosen.

There has always been a relationship between tier structure and government regulation, both federal and local. The best current example of the relationship is the massive change in tiering that resulted from the Cable Television Consumer Protection and Competition Act of 1992. The law required cable systems to establish a separate *basic tier* and specified what must be included in it.[11] The minimum requirements include all must-carry stations, distant television stations carried by the system, excluding superstations, home shopping stations,[12] and mandatory access channels. Most systems call this "basic" or "limited basic." Rates for this government-mandated tier are regulated by the local franchise authority. Details of rate regulation appear later in the chapter.

The basic tier requirement, and the rate control that went with it, caused a significant realignment of the structures that existed before the 1992 law.

Operators had to create a new home for those program sources that were subject to price increases or surcharges. Because of government-imposed basic rate control, operators could no longer easily pass along to subscribers program costs for existing sources or for new sources.

As a consequence, most of the nation's almost 9,000 systems have established some form of expanded basic tier. *Expanded basic*, or *expanded service*, as some call it, usually includes the nonmust-carry, nonpremium services that existed previously in the old basic tier, which are found primarily the advertiser-supported networks. Typical expanded basic offerings would include CNN, USA, MTV, and A&E, for example.

The new tiering plans also have premium levels beyond the expanded basic service. This is where digital has had a big impact. Digital cable is in more than 30 percent of cable homes and increasing rapidly, from 6 million to 25 million since 2000.[13] MSOs create program tiers by genre, such as sports, music, movies, family, and Spanish programming. For an example, see Figure 8.5.

Whether the system is analog or digital, beyond expanded basic are positioned the standard, premium noncommercial program services. Such offerings might include HBO, Showtime, Cinemax, The Movie Channel, and The Disney Channel. These premium channels may be subscribed to on an individual or package basis.

ECONOMICS

The new century has seen an end to cable's build-out phase. With virtually all TV households passed by cable and satellite gaining new subscribers every day, cable's revenue growth no longer will come principally from adding new subscribers. Emphasis now is on digital conversion and the addition of new services.

Cable enters this stage with more than 73 million basic subscribers and 50 million premium subscribers. In addition to subscriber revenue, cable adds income from digital music channels, DSL, high-speed Internet, telephone, and the sale of advertising time.

REVENUES

It is the responsibility of the system's marketing department to recruit subscribers. Figure 8.6 illustrates how the marketing process works for the program services listed in Figure 8.5.

Note that the limited basic tier listed on the top of the channel lineup in Figure 8.5 is not listed on the price sheet in Figure 8.6. It is included in Cox Standard, which is really expanded basic. After that, the marketing effort focuses on the program genre tiers noted above. The "Supersize" is "Digital Deluxe," where customers get it all for a discount, $53.01.

One technique formerly employed by cable system marketers is no longer available. Before the 1992 cable law, subscribers were required to buy through one tier to get to the next. For example, they had to purchase expanded basic

272

CHANNEL LINE UP
(225) 615-1000

Cox Standard

Limited Basic

2	CSPAN
3	WVLA / NBC
4	Cox4
5	WBRZ / ABC
6	WGMB / FOX
7	WAFB / CBS
8	QVC
9	News 9
10	WBRL / WB
11	LPB Kids & You
12	WLPB / PBS
13	KZUP
14	PAX
15	Catholic Life Channel
16	WBXH / UPN
17	WLFT
18	WBRZ Wx
19	WBTR
20	Local Religious Programming
21	Governmental Access
22	KPBN
23	WGN

Expanded Basic

24	Disney Channel
25	f/x
26	Lifetime
27	USA
28	TNT
29	American Movie Classics
30	Nickelodeon
31	TBS
32	ABC Family
33	Cartoon Network
34	CNN
35	ESPN
36	ESPN 2
37	Cox Sports Television
38	Fox Sports Southwest
39	A&E
40	E!
41	Spike TV
42	Fox News Channel
43	VH-1
44	CNBC
45	Headline News
46	Discovery Channel
47	History Channel
48	The Learning Channel
49	Shop At Home
50	Bravo
51	Court TV
52	Animal Planet
53	Food Network
54	HGTV
55	The Weather Channel

56	Country Music Television
57	TV Guide Channel
58	BET
59	Sci Fi
60	Comedy Central
61	Discovery Health
62	ShopNBC
63	Home Shopping Network
64	MSNBC
65	Oxygen
66	TV Land
67	Travel Channel
68	CSPAN 2
69	TBN
70	Univision
71	Hallmark Channel
72	MTV
73	MTV 2

Cox Digital Cable

Digital Gateway

100	Discovery Kids
101	The Science Channel
102	Discovery Home
103	Discovery Times
104	Discovery Wings
105	Outdoor Life
106	Speed Channel
107	Noggin
197	NBA Preview
198	ESPNow
199	Pay-Per-View Previews

Digital Movie Tier

201	Independent Film Channel
202	Sundance Channel
203	Encore
204	Encore Westerns
205	Encore Love Stories
206	Encore Mystery
207	Encore Action
208	Encore True Stories
209	Lifetime Movie Network
210	Turner Classic Movies

Digital Variety Tier

219	NickToons TV
220	Nick GAS
221	Game Show Network
222	Toon Disney
223	Encore Wam
225	BBC America
226	Good Life TV
227	Women's Entertainment
228	Soap Net
229	MBC
230	DIY
231	Fine Living

Premium channels must be purchased separately. VERSION 7/04

232	MTV Hits
233	VH1 Mega Hits
234	VH1 Classic Rock
235	MTV Jams
236	VH1 Soul
237	VH1 Country
238	Fuse
239	Great American Country
240	BET on Jazz

Digital Sports/Info Tier

241	ESPNow
242	NBA TV
243	Fox Sports World
244	ESPNews
245	ESPN Classic Sports
246	Fox Sports en Español
247	Outdoor Channel
248	TVG
249	The Tennis Channel
250	The Golf Channel
261	CNN fn
262	Bloomberg
263	G4tech TV
264	Biography Channel
265	History International
266	International Channel
267	Inspirational Life
268	EWTN

273

FIGURE 8.5 Cable tiers. (Source: Cox Communications. Used with permission.)

FIGURE 8.6 Tier pricing. (Source: Cox Communications. Used with permission.)

274

to obtain premium services. The law prohibits buy-through requirements, except for the government-mandated basic channels.

A cable system's revenues are not limited to regular video program services. Pay-per-view and digital audio also contribute to an operator's gross revenue. Installation, reconnect, and change of service charges, together with equipment rental (e.g., remote controls, addressable converters), add incremental income.

If revenues are to be enhanced, cable managers must continue to pay close attention to subscriber needs and provide prompt, efficient, and courteous service. One study of almost 1,800 subscribers and nonsubscribers concluded that good service equates with good value and poor service with poor value, regardless of the rates charged.[14]

Many systems have installed telephone automatic response units (ARUs) so that questions may be channeled directly to the appropriate information source. Allied with computers, the units permit subscribers to check their account balance and the date and amount of their last payment, order special movies or events, report a service problem, confirm or reschedule a service or installation appointment, and receive general information.

Important as technology is, its contribution may be limited by the personnel assigned to it. Accordingly, customer service representatives (CSRs) must be trained in its use and must understand the importance of customer satisfaction. A dissatisfied customer may mean one fewer subscriber and a lost revenue source. Telemarketing assistants must be informed, but not aggressive and dictatorial.

Similarly, company employees who come face-to-face with customers and prospective customers must be knowledgeable and skilled in human relations. Installers and service technicians must be aware of the subscriber's needs, take appropriate steps to avoid damage to property, and be tolerant in explaining and responding to questions about the operation of cable in the home. Door-to-door sales representatives must be suitably dressed and act in a professional manner.

The importance of cable to subscribers is exemplified when a storm or other event interferes with service. Typically, the system's telephone lines are jammed with calls and the temperament of the CSRs is put to the test. Patience and a sympathetic attitude can do much to disarm customers' annoyance and to reassure them that the problems are being resolved. On such occasions, however, frankness is mandatory. Only realistic estimates of service resumption time should be given. If wild and unsubstantiated guesses are made and not fulfilled, annoyance will grow into anger and, possibly, more lost customers and revenue.

Advertising is becoming an increasingly significant revenue source. As noted earlier, local spot was expected to reach $6 billion in 2005. Multiple system operators have been especially aggressive in developing this source. Often, they interconnect individual systems in contiguous geographic areas to deliver more homes to advertisers. Some large metropolitan systems owned by different operators may interconnect for the purpose of marketing local and spot announcements.

Cable has several advantages for advertisers. It attracts audiences that are characterized as better-educated and more affluent than the average TV viewer. The special-appeal programming of many basic networks permits the targeting of specific demographics, much like radio. In addition, time is less costly than on a broadcast television station. However, the quality of ads produced only for cable often is inferior, and the automated hardware to run them is expensive and often unreliable.

Time is sold on local origination channels and on many expanded basic networks. The majority of networks make available time for local sale. Figure 8.7 shows the rate card for a system operated by Charter Communications.

The knowledge, skills, and personal qualities of the advertising sales manager and the account executives, and the sales tools necessary for success, are similar to those required of their broadcast counterparts, described in Chapter 5, "Broadcast Sales."

Historically, cable systems have not been preoccupied with ratings. What was important was that subscribers signed up and enjoyed their viewing experiences enough to continue their subscription. Now that advertising is becoming a more important revenue source, systems are more ratings-conscious. To

Charter Media.

Northshore Rate Card

Approximately 49,000 Households in St. Tammany Parish

Abita Springs 70420, Covington 70433, Covington 70435, Lacombe 70445, Madisonville 70445, Madisonville 70447,
Mandeville 70448, Mandeville 70471, Pearl River 70452, Slidell 70458, Slidell 70460, Slidell 70461

Network		24-hr	6am-Mid	6am-6pm	5pm-Mid	6pm-10pm	Fixed*
Lifetime		$10	$20	$15	$40	$50	$65

	Network	24-hr	6am-Mid	6am-6pm	5pm-Mid	6pm-10pm	Fixed*
GROUP 1	Discovery	$10	$17	$14	$30	$42	$50
	ESPN						
	Fox News						
	HGTV						
	TBS						
	TLC						
	USA						
GROUP 2	A&E	$10	$15	$12	$28	$40	$48
	CNN						
	ESPN2						
	Food						
	History						
	Nickelodeon						
	Spike TV						
	TNT						
GROUP 3	ABC Family	$8	$12	$10	$24	$35	$42
	BET						
	FX						
	Headline News						
	Travel						
	Weather						
GROUP 4	AMC	$7	$11	$9	$20	$30	$35
	CNBC						
	Court TV						
	E! TV						
	Fox Sports SW						
	MSNBC						
	MTV						
	TV Land						
	VH-1						
	WE						
GROUP 5	Animal Planet	$4	$8	$6	$15	$25	$30
	Bravo						
	Cartoon						
	CMT						
	Comedy Central						
	National Geographic						
	Outdoor Life						
	Sci-Fi						
GRP 6	Hallmark	$3	$6	$5	$12	$22	$25
	Golf						
	SoapNet						
	Speed						

Each rate is the cost to air one :30 second spot on a specific network within the group. Production is not included.
*Fixed position is a 2-hour or smaller window; This does not include special events like NFL, NBA, College Football
College Basketball, NASCAR, Professional Wrestling, etc. Special package prices are available for these events.

FIGURE 8.7 Local spot rate card. (Source: Charter Communications. Used with permission.)

assist them, Nielsen has developed the Nielsen Homevideo Index (NHI), which measures audiences for basic and pay services. The company also undertakes specially commissioned studies for operators.

Reliable audience information is a necessity if local ad sales are to continue their growth and operators are to make informed decisions in selecting programs with appeal to audiences and to the advertisers that seek them.

High-speed Internet Access   Many cable systems provide high-speed Internet service to compete with the DSL provided by some telephone companies, such as BellSouth, Qwest, and Verizon. Cable enjoys the competitive advantage: its service is faster than DSL.

Cable has about twice the number of high-speed Internet access customers than DSL providers. Since cable high-speed Internet service penetration is only about 27 percent of cable homes, it has a lot of room to grow. See Figure 8.8 for an example of how a high-speed Internet provider markets the service.

Telephone Service Cable is offering circuit-switched telephony services to both residential and business subscribers. This business is in its infancy for cable companies and has significant growth potential. Further, cable is

- Up to 100x faster than dial-up
- Up to twice as fast as most DSL connections
- No long term contracts
- Always on and never a busy signal
- No need for a second phone line ever

Charter High-Speed Internet

3 Mbps - $39.99
- Up to 3 Mbps downstream/256 kbps upstream

384 Kbs - $29.99
- Up to 384 Kbs downstream/128 kbps upstream

Fastest Internet Service

Charter High Speed™ Internet, up to 3 MB

DSL, up to 1.5 MB

Dial-Up, up to 28K

© Charter Communications 2004. Special offer good at time of installation, service call or visit to a front lobby. Offer good on new service upgrades only. Services, packages, prices and Internet speeds may not be available in all areas and prices may vary by market. Residential customers only. Charter On Demand, PPV and other non-recurring subscription services extra. A cable modem and network card may be required at installation of high-speed Internet service. Modem rental is extra and depends on Internet service level. Franchise fees, taxes and other fees not included, with the actual amount depending on location and service ordered. Digital programming on additional TVs, does require a digital receiver for an extra monthly rate. An HDTV receiver is required to receive HDTV service, additional fee may apply. 30-day money back guarantee stipulations: New Charter residential customers (those who have not been Charter customers for 180 days prior to subscribing) qualify to have all levels of subscription service refunded/credited if not fully satisfied with the service. Current customers adding a new level of subscription service qualify to receive a refund/credit on those newly added subscription services only. Valid for customers who pay for their first month of new or upgraded monthly recurring subscription services including video and/or high speed Internet service, hardware purchased or leased, and installation (when customer paid for installation). PPV and other non-recurring subscription purchases are not refundable. Limited to one refund or credit per subscription per household. Refunds/credits will be given only when request for cancellation of service is received by Charter within 45 days of installation of service (30 days subscribing to the service, plus 15 day grace period for formal request of refund/credit). Any equipment associated with the new subscription must be returned prior to release of refund/credit by Charter. Local and state taxes, franchise fees and any other fees or charges may apply and are the responsibility of the customer and will not be refunded or credited.

Figure 8.8 Excerpt from a high-speed Internet marketing piece. (Source: Charter Communications. Used with permission.)

277

experimenting with voice-over Internet protocol (VOIP). This service has unlimited local and long-distance service, caller ID, call waiting, call return, three-way calling, call forwarding, and emergency 911 service. The service is priced modestly on a trial basis, $34.95 in the New York City area, and also has development potential.

Music Services   Access to licensed music, such as ASCAP, BMI, and SESAC, has become another revenue source for cable TV systems. An example is Real Networks' Rhapsody Jukebox subscription service. It provides access to over 30,000 albums produced by the 5 largest music companies and 200 smaller labels.

Digital Video Recorders   Cable also markets products. One example is the successful launch of digital video recorders (DVRs). This product empowers the subscriber to record programming onto a hard drive. The technology enables the viewer to pause live programs and fast-forward recorded content. Customer appetite appears to be strong, and Time-Warner has deployed DVR service nationwide.

EXPENSES

In addition to paying regular taxes, cable television systems are required to hand over to the franchising authority up to 5 percent of their revenues and, in some cases, channel capacity for public, educational, and governmental use.

The cost of laying cable, converting to digital, and adding new services is a substantial investment for a business that must share its revenues with the community. The investment becomes even larger if the cable company has agreed in its franchise to originate local programming and has to equip a production facility.

Many of the system's operating expenses are similar to those of a broadcast station: salaries, commissions, employee benefits, payroll taxes, utilities, supplies, programming, travel, and communication. Major differences are the franchise fees described above, maintenance and repair of miles of cable and associated equipment, and pole rental. Principal expense items are listed in Figure 8.9.

Like the broadcast manager, the cable manager faces a difficult task in trying to increase revenues and control costs in a very competitive marketplace. With the advent of direct broadcast satellite (DBS) competition and the conversion to digital cable, operators' programming expenses have exploded. Annual increases are far ahead of the inflation rate. Since 1992, they have increased almost four-fold. Consumers have many options in spending their entertainment and information dollars. Likewise, advertisers have a choice of vehicles for marketing their products and services. Careful attention to the needs of both groups, and appealing and economically attractive responses, are imperative.

Technical salaries	Utilities
Technical overtime	Vehicles
Office salaries	Equipment repairs
Office overtime	Production
Marketing salaries	Advertising and marketing
Marketing commissions	Office supplies
Contract labor—marketing	Postage
Employee training	Telephone—base rate
Employee benefits	Telephone—long distance
Payroll taxes	Insurance
Installations	Legal and consulting
Contract labor—technical	Publications and subscriptions
Maintenance	Travel
Operating supplies	Bad debt
Converter maintenance	Janitorial / building
Pole rental	Property and general taxes
Basic programming	Data processing
Pay-cable programming	Franchise fees
Pay-per-view	Copyright fees
Program guide	Charitable contributions
Subscriber billings	Association dues

FIGURE 8.9 Cable TV system expense items.

PROMOTION

Cable promotion has begun to reflect the maturity of the business itself. The original elements are still there, to be sure. Systems continue to use direct mail, door-to-door, and on-the-air solicitations. Most systems have a dedicated program-listing channel. Other techniques are being employed as well. Principal among them is over-the-air television. Local TV stations once were reluctant to accept cable advertising, since the two were seen to be in direct competition for audiences. For the most part, that reluctance is gone and systems, individually or as part of an area marketing group, use broadcast television extensively. The results are impressive. People who watch television are, after all, a logical market for cable systems.

Radio is attractive, too. It is cost-effective, and advertising can be targeted to the unique formats and demographics of stations.

Newspaper is used successfully, particularly to feature coupons for a premium service at an introductory rate and with no installation cost. Program listings in the newspaper's television program supplement, in cable guides, and in *TV Guide* also are forms of valuable promotion.

Many systems use a monthly program guide to carry listings and interest subscribers in upgrading their service. Some employ a basic channel, called a *barker channel*, to promote premium services and pay-per-view.

Promotion costs can sometimes be offset by co-op money from the national cable networks, and system managers need to know how to access such funds.

Promotion sophistication for the system will increase as the battle for subscribers and advertisers continues to intensify. As a result, it will become a critical skill for cable management.

There are professional organizations that can assist. One is the Cable & Telecommunications Association for Marketing (CTAM).

REGULATION

Since its inception, cable has been an irritant to the FCC. To begin with, it was not an area of federal prerogative. Regulatory responsibility has always been shared with local authorities, whose streets and rights-of-way are essential for a cable system's operation.

The giant cable industry of today was not even contemplated when the 1934 Communications Act was written. Consequently, federal regulation of cable was done on an as-needed basis by the FCC. Courts and the FCC, alike, wrestled with rationales for tying regulation into the framework of the act. The commission's jurisdiction was confined to system operational matters; franchising was left to local authorities.

Historically, the principal motivation for regulation of cable was its status as an unregulated monopoly with no effective competition. With today's strong competition from DBS and other multichannel video providers, that rationale has largely faded. Cable now seeks protection from competition. For example, the industry is striving for relief from an FCC rule that requires operators to offer uniform pricing throughout a franchise area. Cable asserts that, since DBS has significant household penetration, effective competition now exists. Accordingly, it should be freed from pricing regulation that was justified on the grounds that it was a monopoly.[15] Regulators' attitudes toward cable today are quite different from the initial reaction.

The initial FCC cable regulatory motivation was to protect licensed television broadcasters from the perceived threat of cable. The threat took two forms: first, cable's ability to reduce locally licensed stations' audiences and revenues by importing out-of-market signals; and second, its retransmission of expensive local broadcasters' programming without compensation.

As noted previously, the FCC first attempted to deal with its cable concerns under imputed authority derived from the 1934 act. By 1984, cable had grown to the point that it was able to demand, and receive, explicit regulatory status from Congress. That law was the Cable Communications Policy Act of 1984, which deregulated cable. However, industry stewardship of its deregulated status was not successful in the eyes of many consumers and Congress.

In response, Congress passed the Cable Television Consumer Protection and Competition Act of 1992.

To combat the first threat, the importation of out-of-market signals, the FCC enacted signal carriage rules. They took three forms: *must carry, network nonduplication,* and *syndicated exclusivity*. The second problem, noncompensation to local broadcasters, was addressed to some degree by Congress in the Copyright Act of 1976 and in the 1992 Cable Consumer Protection and Competition Act.

All the signal carriage rules of the FCC have had many reincarnations, but none more than the must-carry rules. As noted earlier, must-carry requires a cable system to carry the commercial and noncommercial television stations in its area. These long-standing rules were struck down on First Amendment grounds in two court decisions in the mid-1980s. Broadcasters' attempts to restore them were finally achieved in the 1992 Act, but they were challenged in the courts. In 1997, however, the Supreme Court upheld their constitutionality in a 5-4 decision.

The 1992 must-carry rules apply to carriage of both commercial and noncommercial television stations. The principal requirements are as follows:

- Systems with more than 12 channels must set aside up to one-third of their channel capacity for local signals.

- Home shopping stations are entitled to must-carry, as are qualified low-power television (LPTV) stations.

- Systems with 12 or fewer channels must carry 1 local noncommercial station; systems with 13 to 36 channels may be required to carry up to 3 local noncommercial stations; and systems with more than 36 channels may be required to carry more than 3 local noncommercial stations, if the programming of the additional stations does not substantially duplicate the content of the other stations.

It was noted earlier that the 1992 law allows stations to select a retransmission consent option in lieu of must-carry. Stations that opt for retransmission consent must negotiate with local cable systems for channel position and compensation. If the negotiations are unsuccessful, a local station might end up with no system carriage at all for three years.

A second FCC signal carriage rule is network nonduplication, or network exclusivity. It prohibits a cable system from carrying an imported network affiliate's offering of a network program at the same time it is being aired by a local affiliate.

The third significant carriage rule involves syndicated program exclusivity, known as *syndex*. Prior to 1980, the FCC protected a local station's syndicated programs against duplication in the market from distant signals imported by cable systems. In 1988, the FCC reinstituted the rule, but delayed its implementation until January 1, 1990. The rule allows a local station with an exclusivity provision in its syndicated program contract to notify local cable systems of its program ownership. Once notified, the system is required to protect the station against duplication from imported signals, including those of pay and nonpay cable networks.

The other principal FCC concern about the emerging cable industry was the question of compensation of broadcasters for retransmission of their signals by cable. The controversy finally was resolved in 1976, when a new copyright law was passed. Under the law, cable TV was to pay royalties for transmission of copyrighted works. These revenues were in the form of a compulsory license paid to the Registrar of Copyrights for distribution to copyright owners.

According to the provisions of the law, cable operators must pay a copyright royalty fee, for which they receive a compulsory license to retransmit radio and television signals. The fee for each cable system is based on the system's gross revenues from the carriage of broadcast signals and the number of *distant signal equivalents*, a term identifying non-network programming from distant television stations carried by the system.

The law requires a cable operator to file semiannually a statement of accounts. Information in this report includes the system's revenue and signal carriage, as well as the royalty fee payment.

The law also established a now-abolished Copyright Royalty Tribunal (CRT), composed of five commissioners, to distribute the royalty fees and resolve disputes among copyright owners and to review the fee schedule in 1980 and every five years thereafter. The CRT administered three funds: (1) the basic royalty fund; (2) the 3.75 percent fund established to compensate copyright owners for distant signals added after June 24, 1981; and (3) the syndex fund. Changes in the funds administered and the amounts collected have occurred as the FCC and Congress have altered the signal carriage rules. The abolition of the CRT had no effect on copyright fees owed, or on cable system reporting requirements.

The 1992 cable law did much more than restore must-carry. Essentially, it reregulated cable. Of special significance was the act's reintroduction of rate regulation, which had been abolished in 1986. The period of deregulation saw an explosion of system rates, with resulting pressure on Congress by angry subscribers. Rate regulation ended with the Telecommunications Act of 1996. It contained a sunset provision for rate regulation in 1999.

WHAT'S AHEAD?

The future of cable can be summed up in one word: competition. It has arrived—DBS, wireless cable, telephone and utility companies, and others. Indeed, any business with a fiber network in place may emerge to challenge cable systems that formerly enjoyed a virtual monopoly (Figure 8.10).

DBS has become an especially strong foe. Attracted by low-cost dishes and local station carriage, DBS households increased ten-fold between 1993 and 2003, to 19.5 million and a market penetration of 23.51 percent. The number of subscribers continues to rise and, by mid-2005, had reached more than 25 million. In the face of this intense competition, cable percentage penetration of the video provider market is no longer growing.

Cable television operators have not thrown up their hands, however. In fact, media investment analysts correctly anticipated continuing cable prosperity into the early years of the twenty-first century, sparked by some of the

MVPD Service Provider	Customers (in Millions)	Percent of MVPD Market
DBS	23.97	24.34%
C-Band	0.30	0.30%
MMDS	0.10	0.10%
SMATV	1.10	1.12%
Broadband Competitors	1.40	1.42%
Total Non-Cable	26.87	27.29%
Cable	71.60	72.71%
TOTALS	98.47	100.00%

FIGURE 8.10 Analysis of multichannel video program distributors (MVPDs). (Source: *2004 Year-End Industry Overview*, p. 21. http://www.ncta.com. Used with permission.)

same technologies that have resulted in the intensified competitive environment in which the industry finds itself. Cable has found and is developing new services and products. The industry has just scratched the surface of high-speed Internet, telephone, digital tiering, DVRs, and music channels.

With all this has come a quantum increase in cable's program performance with audiences and acceptability by advertisers. Statistical analysis suggests that these trends are likely to continue. And with all that will come continuing revenue and profitability growth.

The cable industry is largely consolidated now. Eight multiple system operators have 75 percent of subscribers. The build-out and consolidation phase is largely over.

Cable has demonstrated its ability to thrive in a world of intense competition. It emphasizes the market advantages it possesses. Digital conversion and the development of new products and services indicate that the industry's best years are ahead. With its energies spent on business development and not on responses to angry regulation, cable is on the high-speed digital path to increased success.

SUMMARY

Cable is hardwired and requires rights-of-way over and under city streets to gain access to viewers' homes. Because of this unique requirement, cable systems are licensed by local governments. The licenses are called franchises, and they have to be renewed at intervals set forth in the franchise agreement.

Cable television systems are run by general managers, who answer to ownership. Reporting to the general manager are the heads of departments with clearly identified responsibilities. Usually, they include government affairs and community relations, human resources, business operations, advertising sales, technical operations, marketing, and customer service.

Programming decisions take into account technological, legal, and audience-appeal and associated economic factors. Program sources include local origination and access channels, local and distant over-the-air television stations, and basic and pay-cable networks. Many systems also offer special programs on a PPV and VOD basis. Typically, program services are bundled into tiers and are priced accordingly.

Initially, cable revenues consisted almost entirely of monthly subscriber fees. As the industry has matured, it has developed other revenue sources, including the sale of local advertising, and digital and other devices, such as high-speed Internet, telephone, music channels and DVRs. Pay-per-view and VOD also contribute to revenue enhancement. Operating expenses are similar to those of broadcast stations, but with some notable differences. Systems must pay to the local franchise authority a franchise fee of up to 5 percent of their gross revenues. They are also required to meet the cost of maintaining and repairing miles of cable and allied equipment, and of renting poles on which to string the cable.

Promoting the varied program services available is a high priority in attracting and retaining subscribers. Among the most effective promotional tools are door-to-door and direct-mail marketing, local television and radio stations, newspapers (especially the television program supplement), and the system's own channels. Successful managers should be involved in professional promotion and marketing organizations like CTAM.

Cable systems are required to carry, or obtain retransmission consent from, local commercial and noncommercial television stations. Many systems also have to provide PEG mandatory access and/or local origination channels. New competitors are entering the video distribution marketplace, and they pose major challenges to the cable industry. In turn, cable operators have attracted subscribers to a range of new communication services.

CASE STUDY

James Dean has inherited a 90-channel analog cable TV system from a favorite uncle. Uncle Dean had begun the system in 1968 after graduation in electronics from Bayou University in Thibodaux, Louisiana. The old man was interested mostly in electronics and technology. As a consequence, he was on top of industry trends but not adept at marketing his system. At the time of his death, Dean the elder had signed a contract to convert to a digital system and had funds in the bank to begin construction.

James wanted to be a movie star but gave up the idea and was looking for a career. He had received a degree in telecommunications before his acting misadventure in Los Angeles. He would like to develop his inherited cable business but is nervous about its spotty revenue and profit history. As he gazes out of his late uncle's office window after the funeral, he notices that a DBS sales office has opened in part of the telephone building next to its new DSL service directly across the street.

He faces a dilemma: should he retain the system or would he be better off if he were to sell it and take the money to the bank?

EXERCISES

1. What pro-active actions could James take to develop the business and enhance revenue and profits?

2. What personal activities could James undertake to enhance his ability to succeed if he retains the business?

3. Is continued operation of the business just too risky given the new competition across the street in the form of a new DSL business by the phone company and the new multichannel video company in the form of DBS?

4. Should James go back to attempting to make movies and distribute them on the cable system to attract subscribers?

NOTES

285

[1] *Industry Statistics*, http://www.ncta.com.

[2] *2004 Year-End Industry Overview*, p. 13, http://www.ncta.com.

[3] *Industry Statistics*, http://www.ncta.com.

[4] City of Los Angeles v. Preferred Communications, 106 S.Ct. 2034, 1986.

[5] 47 USC 546.

[6] 47 USC 546(c)(1)(A–D).

[7] 47 USC 534, 535.

[8] *Television and Cable Factbook* 2003, p. F-2.

[9] 47 USC 534, 535.

[10] *2004 Year-End Industry Overview*, p. 7, http://www.ncta.com.

[11] 47 USC 543.

[12] Kim McAvoy, "Home Shopping Gets Must Carry," *Broadcasting & Cable*, July 5, 1993, p. 8.

[13] *Industry Statistics*, http://www.ncta.com.

[14] "Service Showing," *Broadcasting*, February 5, 1990, p. 86.

[15] "Capital Watch," *Broadcasting & Cable*, September 20, 2004, p. 26.

ADDITIONAL READINGS

Bartlett, Eugene. *Cable Communications: Building the Information Infrastructure.* New York: McGraw-Hill, 1995.

Covington, William G., Jr. *Creativity in TV & Cable Managing and Producing.* Lanham, MD: University Press of America, 1999.

Crandall, Robert W., and Harold Furchgott-Roth. *Cable TV: Regulation or Competition?* Washington, DC: Brookings Institution, 1996.

Creech, Kenneth C. *Electronic Media Law and Regulation*, 4th ed. Boston: Focal Press, 2003.

Eastman, Susan Tyler, and Douglas A. Ferguson. *Media Programming: Strategies and Practices*, 7th ed. Belmont, CA: Thomson Wadsworth, 2006.

Eastman, Susan Tyler, Douglas A. Ferguson, and Robert Klein (eds.). *Promotion and Marketing for Broadcasting, Cable and the Web*, 4th ed. Boston, MA: Focal Press, 2001.

Parsons, Patrick R., and Robert M. Frieden. *The Cable and Satellite Television Industries*. Boston: Allyn and Bacon, 1998.

Understanding Broadcast and Cable Finance: A Handbook for the Non-Financial Manager. Northfield, IL: BCFM Press, 1994.

Warner, Charles, and Joseph Buchman. *Media Selling: Broadcast, Cable, Print and Interactive*, 3rd ed. Ames: Blackwell, 2003.

Public Broadcast Station Management

This chapter is devoted primarily to that area of noncommercial broadcasting known as public broadcasting. It examines

- the organization and framework of public broadcasting in the United States
- the major management functions performed by public broadcast station executives
- the challenges facing public broadcasting and the management tools available to meet them
- the differences and similarities in operations between commercial broadcasting and public broadcasting

Noncommercial educational broadcasting accounts for about 19 percent of all radio stations and 22 percent of full-power television stations licensed in the United States.[1] Despite these significant percentages, most broadcast professionals and broadcast students know little about the intricacies of educational broadcasting.

Within the category of noncommercial broadcasting there is a subcategory known as "public broadcasting." It encompasses those broadcasters who meet the minimum operating requirements established by the Corporation for Public Broadcasting (CPB) to qualify for federal funding.

Public broadcasting represents a specialized area of over-the-air broadcasting with its own concepts and principles. In public television, for example, unlike its commercial counterpart, the emphasis is not on generating mass audience numbers per program, but on the cumulative weekly audience. That is true because programs seek to respond to the content preferences of diverse audiences. Accordingly, calculation of the number of different people or households viewing over the course of a week is a more realistic measure of program appeal than the number tuned to a particular offering. Public radio is largely format-based, as is commercial radio. However, public radio formats are somewhat different in that they possess more limited audience appeal. The emphasis is to increase time spent listening (TSL) by the audience. Commercial broadcasting sells the audience to advertisers; advertisers are the market. In public broadcasting, the audience is the market and, increasingly, public stations depend on direct audience financial support. It follows that revenue sources for public broadcasting and commercial broadcasting are very different. So are expenses.

There is one major similarity between public and commercial broadcasting, however. That is the bottomline. Commercial stations operate for profit and must be expense- and revenue-conscious. Public stations, while nonprofit in nature, are financially accountable and must conform expenses to anticipated revenue generation. This is especially true in these days of significantly diminished governmental funding.

THE STRUCTURE OF PUBLIC BROADCASTING

The origins of the current structure in public broadcasting date to the 1967 report of the Carnegie Commission on Educational Television. Many of its recommendations to enhance the viability of noncommercial educational broadcasting were enacted into law that same year by the Public Broadcasting Act, which created the CPB.

Distribution services for programs were added in 1969 to 1970, when the CPB and some noncommercial stations formed membership corporations. The television vehicle was named Public Broadcasting Service (PBS) and the radio organization was called National Public Radio (NPR). Both of these entities provide member stations with various program options and services, which will be discussed in greater detail later in the chapter.

As a result of these developments, a three-level structure emerged:

1. local noncommercial educational radio and television stations licensed by the Federal Communications Commission (FCC)

2. the CPB, which is primarily a funding mechanism

3. PBS and NPR, membership corporations

TELEVISION

In 2005, 379 noncommercial television stations were licensed, of which 126 were VHF and 253 UHF.[2] Of these, 169 licensees, operating 348 stations, belonged to the Public Broadcasting Service.[3] The licensees, some of which operate more than one station, may be divided into four distinct categories:

Community organizations are nonprofit corporations created to build and run stations. Most are located in large cities and have a significant dependence upon community support. Some are major program production centers. There are 86 such organizations.

Colleges/universities, which have relied less on viewer support than community organizations. Some operate as program origination sources for other public stations. They are the second largest group of licensees, numbering 57.

State authorities have been created by law in about half of the states to operate statewide networks of public stations that are heavily involved in program production, both for instruction and for general audiences. Twenty licensees operate the largest number of noncommercial television stations in the United States.

Local educational or municipal authorities place a heavy emphasis on instruction. They rely on the audience for some degree of financial support. The number of licensees has declined over the years and totals six.[4]

ORGANIZATION AND PERSONNEL

The size and structure of a public television station depend on market size, the type of licensee, and the programming it offers to the public. Stations are organized into various departments performing specific functions. Figure 9.1 depicts the structure of a community corporation, WYES-TV, which operates a television station in New Orleans. Note that community corporations may be organized somewhat differently from other licensees because of their generally larger size and, in some instances, their role as national production centers.

The level to which the general manager reports varies according to the type of licensee operating the station. Community stations generally have a broad-based board of directors to which the manager is responsible. In college/university stations, the manager usually reports to a designated administrator. The upper-level structure in state-operated stations is an entity created

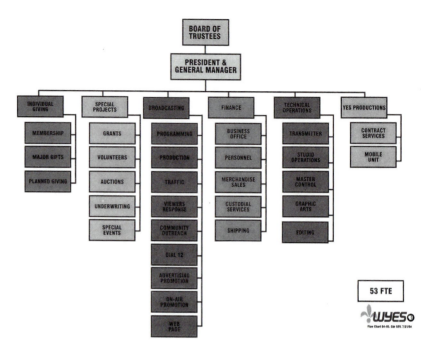

FIGURE 9.1 Organizational chart of a community corporation licensee, WYES-TV, New Orleans. (Used with permission.)

by state law. Public school station managers deal with the superintendent of schools or the school board. Whatever the nature of the licensee or structure, the manager is accountable to a higher authority, and that authority determines the degree of autonomy exercised by the local manager.

MANAGEMENT TASKS

The responsibilities of the public broadcast manager are concentrated in eight primary areas. An examination of each will permit an appreciation of the challenges the public television executive faces and the tools available to meet them. It will also offer an opportunity to compare and contrast public and commercial television.

The main management functions of the public television executive are as follows:

- fund-raising and expense control
- programming
- promotion
- research
- cable relations
- community outreach

- engineering
- administration

Fund-raising and Expense Control   If there is a top priority for public broadcast management, it is revenue. For years, the base of financial support for public television licensees had been governmental. In the mid-1990s, the reliability of that support came into question. In 1995, the Republican Party replaced the Democratic Party as the Congressional majority in the House of Representatives and the Senate. It was the first time in 40 years that both houses of Congress had been in Republican hands.

The Republicans had several marquee issues on their 1995 agenda, one of which was the elimination or reduction of federal financial support for noncommercial public radio and television.

This legislative initiative triggered an intense grassroots lobbying effort on behalf of public broadcasting. Federal financial support, though reduced, was not eliminated.

The crisis could not have come at a worse time, because the 1990s also saw increased competition for audiences and funds. In the late 1990s, a new financial problem appeared in the form of the FCC-mandated conversion to DTV.

Public television stations need funds to operate. Since they are noncommercial, the sale of time to advertisers is precluded. Principal sources of funding are

- federal government
- state and local governments
- audience
- underwriting
- other

FEDERAL GOVERNMENT   The financial underpinning of America's public television stations rests on three corners: its members, state governments, and CPB/federal grants and contracts. The public has assumed, mistakenly, that federal funds form the base. They do not. Despite their importance, 84 percent of public television's money comes from other sources.

Federal funding to most public TV stations comes principally from an annual Community Service Grant (CSG) from the CPB. Only one CSG is permitted per licensee. To qualify for a grant, each public station must file an annual Certification of Eligibility. Basic requirements are that the station be full-power with a noncommercial educational license; that it operate at least 3,000 broadcast hours per year; that it have a minimum full-time professional staff of ten; and that it have nonfederal financial support of at least $900,000 a year. Stations must also file an annual financial report, a Station Activities Survey, and an Offer and Acceptance with the CPB

After receiving the certification, the CPB determines the amount of the grant per station and assigns a CSG factor to the station. The factor is also used to calculate PBS membership and regional network fees.

The CPB also disburses other, specialized funds. They are designed for specific activities, such as the production of topical programs, the stimulation of audience expansion, and the involvement of the audience in national TV programs. An example of program production is "America at the Crossroads," whose goal is to stimulate the national dialogue about post–9/11 America. The Program Challenge Fund has as its purpose the creation of prime-time limited series and specials for the national PBS schedule. The fund was responsible for the production of "The Commanding Heights" and "American Family." An Interconnection Grant seeks to broaden the reach of public television services. Funds assist the establishment and development of interconnection systems for the distribution of public telecommunications services. The Outreach Fund for National TV Programs aids innovative community outreach and citizen engagement projects supporting national, public television broadcasts.[5]

Stations may also apply to the National Telecommunications and Information Administration (NTIA) for support in purchasing equipment.[6] In this case, a formal grant application must be submitted to the NTIA, and the station must be able to raise matching funds from nonfederal sources. The CPB may exclude any nonfederal funds raised for equipment purchases supported by the NTIA from the calculation of nonfederal funds required to support the qualification for a Community Service Grant.

STATE AND LOCAL GOVERNMENTS   These institutions are the second-largest source of public television station revenue. States may fund local licensees directly, as in the case of universities and community corporations or, indirectly, as when states fund agencies or commissions that operate state networks. In some states, the funding is calculated by using the CSG factor. Local governmental entities fund public school stations. Whatever the type of licensee, public station management must comply with the appropriate state or local procedures in a timely manner to ensure continued financial support.

AUDIENCE   Audience membership and related activities are the primary source of revenue for public television stations. No matter what level of viewer financial support a public station enjoys today, it is certain that all categories of licensees will have a greater need for it in the future. Historically, community stations, out of necessity, have better developed this method of raising funds than the other types of public television licensees. However, with traditional funding sources retrenching, many stations are discovering audience support.

For the novice fund-raiser, there are tried and proven methods to be employed, and there is outside assistance available. Public Broadcasting Service has a division in its development department called Station Independence Program (SIP). It is user-supported and offers fund-raising assistance to stations, particularly in local pledge drives and auctions. One of its significant functions is to provide stations with programs that perform well as fund-raisers.

The principal fund-raising activities for most television stations are pledge or membership drives, usually built around a PBS-sponsored fund-raising, which is supported with national promotion and programming. It is conducted three times a year, and stations may participate in all, some, or none. Many stations take part more than once a year. However, multiple annual fund-raisers do cause a fatigue factor in the audience. As a result, some stations are experimenting with a plan that drops one of the extended on-the-air drives in favor of spot announcements emphasizing the value of public station programming and the need for public support. If a station chooses to be involved in only one, it is usually the multiday winter event. To tie in with the fund-raising activity, a station builds a set and assembles a group of fund-raising appeals to be used during breaks in the specially selected programming. Timing, structure, and copy for the breaks are art forms in themselves.[7] The use of local celebrities is recommended, either to make appeals for funds or to take phoned-in pledges on camera. In areas without access to celebrities, videotapes of personalities making appeals are available from PBS. Stations often award premiums or gifts to viewers who call in pledges, their value determined by the amount of the pledge. For example, WYES-TV in New Orleans offers a MemberCard, which entitles the bearer to two-for-one meals at more than 200 restaurants on the Louisiana–Mississippi Gulf coast (see Figure 9.2). Additionally, the card provides members with a continuing reminder of the sustaining value of their public station commitment.

Then, there are entrepreneurial activities. One such established fund-raising activity is the auction. Very simply, goods and services donated by area businesses and organizations are auctioned on the air to the highest bidder. Many stations also offer items donated by sports figures or celebrities. Auctions are expensive to produce and cause the preemption of regularly scheduled programs. However, they are an important source of funds. Some licensees are experimenting with concepts like four-day weekend auctions to lessen the negative impact on programming. Others are studying the possibility of doing half-hour to one-hour auctions regularly throughout the year. Still others conduct auctions as nonbroadcast community events.

293

WYES MemberCard

For your gift of $~~75~~ *$50* or more, you'll receive the WYES MemberCard, entitling you to 2-for-1 dining at over 200 great restaurants throughout Louisiana and the Mississippi Gulf Coast ... plus thousands nationwide.

A directory will highlight the names, locations and phone numbers of participating restaurants, lodging establishments and cultural attractions nearest to you.

FIGURE 9.2 Examples of a premium offered by WYES-TV, New Orleans. (Used with permission.)

Auctions also may be specialized. WYES-TV in New Orleans organizes an annual auction called "Art Collection Twelve." This two-day, weekend, on-the-air event features the works of local and national artists. Audience members act as volunteers (Figure 9.3).

WYES-TV also mounts a wine auction each October and a "Showboat" auction in the spring.

Art Collection Twelve
October 1-3 & 8-10, 2004

ART COLLECTION TWELVE spans two weekends in October and offers our viewing audience the opportunity to bid on beautiful works of art by local and national artists. Volunteers help to make Art Collection Twelve a success! A partial list of auction job descriptions follows. We hope that one appeals to you! Please contact WYES' Volunteer Coordinator, Anita Hedgepeth, at 587-9490 to discuss the volunteer opportunities that interest you.

VOLUNTEERS

PRE-AUCTION JOBS

ART COLLECTOR Contacts donors in person or by phone to obtain donations. Picks up donations and delivers to WYES.

PROCESSING Helps inventory art before and during auction. Processes all paperwork.

WRITERS Writes descriptions of all art donations for publication in the **ART COLLECTION TWELVE** catalog.

TYPIST Types descriptions of all art donations for publication in the **ART COLLECTION TWELVE** catalog.

OFFICE WORK Helps with mailings, paperwork from auction office committees, answering phones, addressing thank you letters, and many other duties.

AUCTION JOBS

TBT **Telephone bid takers.** Volunteers answer telephones during on-air auction and write bids from the viewers. Good hearing and legible handwriting are a must! Training session is **mandatory** and volunteers must arrive 30 minutes prior to shift.

AA **Auctioneer Assistant.** Must be responsible & reliable. Assist auctioneer as items are being sold. Record bids as they are received. On-air position.

PADDLE DESK Assign paddles and paddle numbers to in-house bidders.

IN-HOUSE BIDDING Stationed in the studio audience area to record all in-house bids.

CONFIRMATION Telephone high bidders to confirm address, name, phone and type of payment.

DISPLAY Arrange and hang auction items for on-air viewing.

FIGURE 9.3 Volunteer jobs at Art Collection Twelve. (Source: WYES-TV, New Orleans. Used with permission.)

Special events are an additional source of funds. One example is the annual wine-and-cheese party conducted by KETC-TV at a major downtown hotel in St. Louis. The event is open to the public, with special discount admission available to members who have previously contributed in pledge drives. Another type of event involves bringing in PBS talent for a local appearance. Funds are raised through admission prices or donations that enable participation in cocktail parties or dinners attended by the talent. There is no limit to the kinds of events that might be carried out, save the lack of imagination. Contacts with other PBS members and station executives are useful ways to collect information on fund-raising ideas that work.

UNDERWRITING   Underwriting is a mechanism used to develop or present programs by securing grants from foundations, corporations, or businesses.

Stations that are also production centers may seek underwriting from major corporations or foundations to develop programs. The objective for the station and the underwriter is to have the production selected for distribution by the PBS and use by other stations. For the funding sources, this provides visibility and enhances image. Achieving the objective does the same for the producing station.

Stations also obtain underwriting to present programs of local origination or programs obtained from other sources. The underwriter, in effect, sponsors the programs.

295

This type of local underwriting raises day-to-day operating funds for the station. It is also the kind of local revenue development that is most similar to the sale of spot announcements by commercial stations. However, public stations are somewhat restricted in what can be shown or said in an underwriting credit (i.e., identification of the funding source or sources), due to their essential noncommercial nature.

The pricing of underwriting credits is critical. Some public stations have written guidelines, similar to a commercial broadcaster's rate card. Whatever structure is employed, a public television broadcaster should market a program without limiting the underwriting announcement cost to that of the program itself. Stations that are hard-pressed for support are learning to ask for the value the marketplace puts on the program offered. Such value may well be in excess of the cost.

The PBS regularly issues revised guidelines on the permissible limits in underwriting announcements. The underwriting rules were first "enhanced," or made more flexible, by the FCC in 1982,[8] following a failed18-month experiment allowing certain public stations to sell advertising. FCC policy statements, rulings, advisory opinions, and letters applying its rules and policies to specific underwriting announcements have cautioned against the use of certain types of language, phrases, and visuals, that it deems promotional. They include the following:

- Call to action (e.g., "Come in today and take a test drive")
- Superlative description or quantitative claim about a company, its products or services (e.g., "The most intelligent car ever built")
- Direct comparison with the products or services of other companies

- Price or value information (e.g., "Only $160 down and $160 per month"; "7.7 percent interest now"; "Affordable"; "Discount"; or "Free")

Current rules allow the presentation in donor underwriting credits of the following:

- logograms or slogans that identify and do not promote
- location
- value-neutral descriptions of product line or service listing
- brand and trade names and product or service listings[9]

The underwriting guidelines are a serious matter, and the FCC has shown an increasing willingness to entertain complaints brought against public stations alleged to have exceeded the limits.

Like audience support, underwriting must be developed for public television to survive. However, the noncommercial aspect is one of the appeals of public television, and this type of support could ultimately become counterproductive if the audience begins to perceive excessive commercialism.

OTHER   Public television stations of the twenty-first century have had to become more than program purveyors to survive in the multimedia world. Stations are offering, or are learning to offer, a range of services beyond the traditional broadcast program model to remain competitive. They call them "entrepreneurial activities." The objective is to generate support to augment that provided by government entities and the audience.

One example is for-profit services. Some stations, particularly community corporation licensees in large markets, have developed this alternative service into a significant revenue item. Entities engaging in this activity organize a for-profit subsidiary corporation to avoid charges of unfair competition from their commercial counterparts.

WYES-TV has done this. It rents two mobile units for everything from NBA basketball with the New Orleans Hornets to movie production to use by the national commercial television networks.

Other possible ancillary revenue sources include the sale of advertising in the membership publication. Selling editorial space to other community arts and educational organizations should be explored, especially with those organizations that are unable to support financially an independent publication. Some public television stations rent tower space.

In sum, management should always be alert to the development of potential revenue-generating opportunities in our expanding multimedia world. Figure 9.4 illustrates the mix and proportion of the support elements that make up the revenue of a community corporation television licensee.

For public television, the budget battle will continue. New funding sources need to be identified and developed as old ones fade out. It is necessary for the public electronic media manager to stay abreast of trends. One way to monitor developments is by reviewing the quarterly and annual revenue reports distributed by the Station Independence Program. Another, as mentioned earlier, is ongoing communication with associates in the industry.

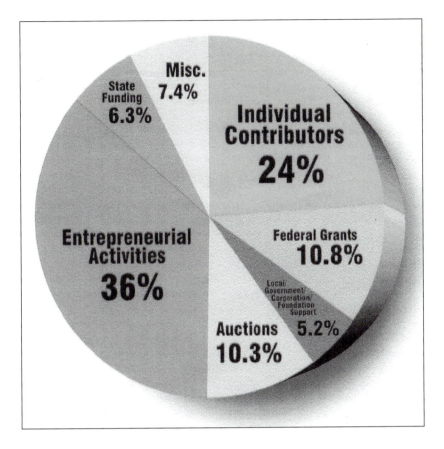

FIGURE 9.4 Support elements for WYES-TV, a community corporation licensee in New Orleans. (Used with permission.)

297

Expense control is a critical management function. Because of operational variables resulting from the different types of licensees and market sizes, it is difficult here to make more than general statements about expenses. However, specific comparative information is available from the CPB and the Association of Public Television Stations (APTS).[10] Utilization of the CPB and APTS data makes it possible for the station manager to compare local expense results with those of other public stations of similar type and size around the country. Judgments can then be made about the appropriateness of expense levels at the local station.

The largest single expense item for public television stations is programming. Prices of all programming are increasing, and competition for popular commercial syndicated product, in particular, has made its cost almost prohibitive for the budget-pressed public station. Cable networks—such as A&E and The Discovery Channel—are also competing for programming that was previously the exclusive prerogative of PBS and individual public stations.

Local origination is so expensive that many stations do little of it. Those operated by universities have an edge here by using qualified students, but this resource has not been fully developed on most campuses. With more viewing choices available to audiences than ever before, local identity demands some local origination, and the problem will have to be dealt with. Some local origination is also necessary to satisfy FCC license obligations.

Personnel costs are always a pressure point, particularly in stations largely dependent upon governmental support. Many stations are unionized. To some degree, that impacts management's efforts to deal with the budget. Elected officials who make funding decisions for many public stations are susceptible to pressure applied by employees and their representatives.

The low inflation trend of the late 1990s continued into the new century. When those inflation patterns begin to rise—as they inevitably will—labor costs will rise with them, further straining already stretched resources.

Another major expense item is development, really fund-raising. As noted above, it is responsible for generating audience financial support, securing underwriting, and conducting auctions and other events. As government support becomes more problematic and operating costs continue to rise, development costs also will grow.

Capital costs are a continuing problem. Technology developments are escalating rapidly. Government requirements, such as those associated with DTV, threaten to exacerbate capital demands. Some public stations have been successful at fully funding annual depreciation. Others are exploring the possibilities of capital-giving campaigns to remain competitive and develop the teleplex concept. WYES is doing that in New Orleans, in conjunction with the University of New Orleans and other stations.

For an example of the distribution spread of a community corporation licensee's expense dollar, see Figure 9.5.

Programming Programming is a critical area of management responsibility. It is an axiom in public television that "without audience there is no support, and without support there is no audience." In this era of deregulation and fragmented audiences, management must focus on the three essential programming elements: *strategy, acquisition,* and *scheduling.* Only through a masterful management of all three can a public television station build the cumulative audience required for success.

STRATEGY Most public television stations have program directors or managers who must develop the program strategy in cooperation with senior management. Strategy is determined by the nature of the licensee, the needs and interests of the community, the requirements for fund-raising from the audience and, increasingly, by ratings. Public television executives for years have dismissed ratings as a game the commercial stations play. Since, so the reasoning went, public TV had a superior product for an audience other than the "lowest common denominator," so there was no reason to be concerned about audience shares. However, public stations must have significant audience financial support to survive. And so the quantity and frequency of viewers may matter to public television after all.

The basic direction of program strategy depends upon the type of licensee. A community licensee puts emphasis on presenting entertainment and cultural programs. The college/university, public school, and state networks may

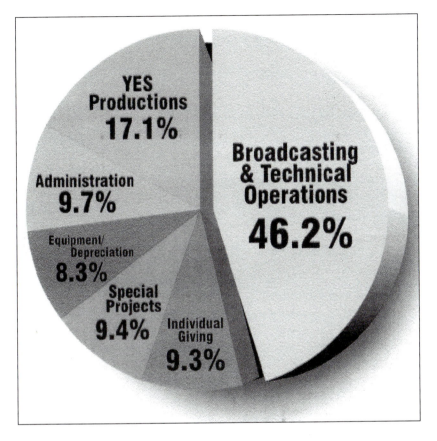

FIGURE 9.5 Expense dollar distribution for WYES-TV, a community corporation licensee in New Orleans. (Used with permission.)

have as their thrust more instructional or educational programs. Instructional programs were important in keeping public stations on cable systems before the return of the must-carry rule requiring cable carriage of local television stations. It was resurrected by the Cable Television Consumer Protection and Competition Act of 1992 and survived a Supreme Court challenge. Aside from its possible value as a cable carriage mechanism, however, instructional programming is also a revenue source. Most public television stations carry some instructional programming.

Paying attention to community needs and interests distinguishes a public station from the many choices, including other public stations, now available to viewers over-the air or through cable and DBS. For an example of how a station can originate specialty local programming in a market with two public television outlets, see the local origination section below.

Another factor in program strategy is the need to generate viewer financial support. Again, that varies with the type of licensee and location. Stations licensed to community corporations depend primarily on audience support. However, in these days of uncertain governmental funding, all stations must rely on it more and more. Hand-in-hand with this factor is the reality that, to some extent, public broadcasting has succeeded because it is unique. It presents something that the public cannot obtain elsewhere. Public television must remain unique, even though the wide range of viewing options available to audiences makes that a difficult objective.

Obviously, the amount of financial support required today cannot be supplied by a minuscule core of loyal viewers. Public television's audience base must be broadened. Ratings may not mean mass program numbers, as required in commercial television, but they do mean adequate weekly cumulative household totals. To some extent, this need for larger ratings may be in conflict with the need to remain unique. A balance between ratings and uniqueness is a goal for management to achieve.

ACQUISITION Having determined program strategy, management must next identify sources from which to secure the desired programming. There are five major sources. Together, they account for almost 95 percent of a public television station's total broadcast hours:

- Public Broadcasting Service
- regional networks
- instructional
- commercial syndication
- local origination

PUBLIC BROADCASTING SERVICE On the average, public stations obtain a majority of their programming from PBS. It can be acquired in one of two ways. The first method is *full-service*. Under this plan, the station pays a program assessment and is entitled to all of the programming that PBS provides. This includes the traditional popular children's programs, such as "Mister Rogers' Neighborhood," "Barney," and "Sesame Street," and the news and public affairs offerings, like "The NewsHour with Jim Lehrer" and "Washington Week in Review." It also embraces entertainment programming, such as "Mystery!" and "Masterpiece Theater," and science and nature programming like "Nova." Concerts, such as "Evening at Pops," specials, and documentaries developed by PBS also are part of the plan.

A second method of acquiring PBS programming is through the Program Diversity Fund (PDF). This method is used for stations in multistation markets. Stations using the fund are limited to PBS programming purchases up to 25 percent of the PBS schedule.

PBS now operates under the "chief program executive model." In other words, programs are commissioned and selected by one PBS executive, resulting in greater flexibility and freedom than was possible under the committee approach used formerly.

REGIONAL NETWORKS The regional networks have declined as a major program supplier to public broadcasting stations. Some are no longer in existence and others have had new incarnations.

INSTRUCTIONAL Instructional programming plays a role in public television. How much of the schedule it occupies depends upon the type of licensee. Among the many sources for instructional programming are Western Instructional Television, TV Ontario, Central Educational Network, and Great Plains National (GPN).

COMMERCIAL SYNDICATION   Budget constraints and program strategy considerations formerly resulted in the infrequent use by public television stations of product supplied by commercial syndicators. In recent years, however, efforts to broaden the membership base have led to its increased use. Some large-market community stations have programmed off-network series successfully. Highly regarded offerings, such as *St. Elsewhere* and *Hill Street Blues*, have been purchased. PBS itself has resorted to this tactic. In the mid-1990s, it acquired *I'll Fly Away* from a national commercial network for prime-time broadcast. Commercial syndicators, like Wolper Productions and Granada TV, have become regular sources for public television stations.

LOCAL ORIGINATION   The level of local origination depends upon the type of licensee and the location. Community stations in large cities do more than the other types of stations. Local programming is expensive, but it does provide identity and distinguishes public television stations from their commercial competitors and one another.

WYES-TV has differentiated itself from a second PBS station through its local programming. In a city of parades, the station has a parade of local programming. Representative titles are self-explanatory. They include "Seafood Celebration 2," "The Nightlife That Was," "German New Orleans," "Stay Tuned: New Orleans Classic Commercials," and "Steppin' Out: It's Carnival Time." To control the costs associated with local origination, some stations have experimented with hiring independent contractors on a per-program basis. Such arrangements avoid the expense of maintaining a large, on-site staff for program production.

SCHEDULING   Management can have a good program strategy and acquire excellent programming, but fail on scheduling. If the program schedule is not built properly, the desired goals will not be achieved.

There are as many opinions on how to schedule as there are stations in the country. While there is no absolute right or wrong, there are some general guidelines. Most public television stations observe the 1997 nonbinding Common Carriage Agreement, which has as its objective the airing by local stations of the PBS core schedule on the night and in the order fed during prime time. This common carriage is important to program underwriters, to promotional efforts, and to establishment of a ratings position.

After making a decision on the core schedule, management should examine its commitment to, or requirement for, instructional programming. These programs usually are aired in daytime and may be a source of revenue. In many instances, stations now deliver instructional programming overnight via broadcast on a batch basis for later classroom use. This development frees up more daytime hours for programming.

With the two "must" parts of the schedule in place, allocation of the rest of the time is somewhat discretionary. Public stations do have constituencies that must be considered, including minorities and special interest groups. To those must be added the needs and interests of the community as a whole and the demands to raise financial support from the audience.

Whatever program choices are made, for whatever reasons, scheduling decisions must also be guided by the principles of audience flow and counter-programming. As noted in Chapter 4, "Broadcast Programming," audience flow is simply the movement of the audience from one program to the next and results from the placement of similar type programs back to back. Whenever possible, dissimilar programs should be separated. As indicated earlier, counter-programming is scheduling against the competition a program that will serve a segment of the audience whose interests or needs are not being met. Difference is the key to counter-programming, whereas similarity is encouraged for audience flow.

Special scheduling considerations come into play during fund-raising when, for example, emotional or special appeal programs produce the best results. Different considerations also may be a factor during ratings periods. Such periods are increasingly important, and the competition stacks the schedule with their best product at those times. Local licensee philosophy may prohibit ratings period schedule strategy, but management needs to consider it, at least.

Promotion   Historically, the role of promotion in public television was neglected. Perhaps that resulted from the erroneous belief that ratings were not important, or possibly promotion was thought not to be important because public programming was unique and would sell itself. Whatever the reason, there is an increased awareness of its significance, and many public stations spend 5 percent or more of their budget on promotional activities.

There are many ways to promote, but the cheapest and most available is the station's own air. However, it has its limitations. The average household has the television set turned on about eight hours a day, but that set is tuned to public television only one to two hours per week. Therefore, the task is complicated. On-the-air promotion must be effective. That means that it causes the viewers of one program to sample other programs offered by the station. A viewer who watches "The NewsHour with Jim Lehrer" is a candidate for "Washington Week in Review." On-the-air promos for a program should be run during similar programs that are likely to attract the same audience. A "Frontline" audience is probably not given to watching "Sesame Street." It is a truism of audiences today that they watch programs and not stations. Accordingly, it makes good sense to promote in the program being aired other programs that that audience is likely to view.

On-the-air promotion must also be well produced. Promo production is an art form in the commercial world and needs to become such in public television. Promos should be attention-getting and not stereotyped. Station IDs should be alive and colorful. Public stations gradually have begun to recognize the importance of creative promos, and that trend must continue. Too often, management overlooks the role of effective, well-produced, and properly placed program and station promos.

On-the-air promotion reaches only the audience the station already has. Usually, so does a station's monthly program guide. For this reason, the program guide can be a limited promotional vehicle. But it does not have to be. The WYES-TV guide, for example, is published monthly in a slick, glossy, local, and popular publication called *New Orleans*. This tactic assumes that the station's program fare will become known to members and not-yet members each month. It is a clever and very efficient means of promotion (Figure 9.6).

More typically, it is an in-house publication that is circulated to viewers pledging financial support and carries listings of regular and special programs. Stations that depend solely on on-the-air promotion and program guides limit their opportunities to broaden their audience and increase their financial support.

FIGURE 9.6 Cover of *New Orleans* magazine, which contains the monthly program guide for WYES-TV. (Used with permission.)

New viewers must be attracted. The most commonly used method of broadening the public television audience has been newspapers, especially Sunday television sections, which may be more widely consulted than *TV Guide*. Newspapers are valuable for promoting image, news, and special series. However, their readership is declining, and newspaper demographics are older than the target audience public television needs to attract. Hence, newspapers should not be relied upon to the exclusion of other media choices available.

Radio can be used to supplement other promotion. It is economical and can be targeted to the desired audience. For example, "The NewsHour with Jim Lehrer" can be promoted on news and talk stations. "Masterpiece Theater" and "Mystery!" spots can be run on adult contemporary stations.

Another potential promotional tool is cable television. While cable presents a financial and audience challenge to public television, it can be used effectively. Cable systems have local advertising time available in national, advertiser-supported networks. Cable spots are relatively inexpensive, often cheaper than radio, and certainly less expensive than commercial television. In addition, they can be targeted toward a specific audience. More and more stations are dedicating cash to the purchase of ad time in local system availabilities on basic cable networks. These campaigns are designed to attract viewers aged 25 to 44 and to change perceptions about public television. The networks used include A&E, ESPN, CNN, TNT, USA, MTV, Lifetime, and Nickelodeon.

Periodicals such as *TV Guide* and local market life and leisure-type publications should also be considered as promotional vehicles. Other possibilities are outdoor, transit, and taxicab advertising.

In recent years, an exciting new promotional vehicle has emerged for public stations: the Internet. Stations can now display their programming on Web sites and promote to an audience that largely consists of the demographics desired by public television.

For the promotion-minded public broadcast executive, budget will be a problem. However, in this multiple-choice viewing world, promotion is essential. Management must know what promotion options are available and how to use them. The promotion function in public television now is of critical importance and, in many stations, is combined with the fund-raising function. For that reason, the promotion manager is often called the *development director*.

Research   Research provides the road map for a station's programming and promotional strategies. Its importance cannot be over-emphasized. Research provides insights into what genre of programs should be considered for airing and into program placement in the schedule and in relation to other programs. It also provides guidance on what programs should be promoted to the public, both on the air and in outside media.

Research can be developed from routinely available sources or can be specially commissioned. The former include standard quarterly ratings reports provided to subscribing stations by Nielsen. In addition, specialized reports can be ordered. One example is the county coverage survey, which provides management with details of the relative strengths and weaknesses of a station in each county of the survey area.

Additional ratings information is available to PBS members in the *Station Audience Report*, issued at the end of each sweep period in November, February, May, and July. PBS also issues annual Designated Market Area (DMA) profiles. These research reports provide household demographic characteristics, sex/age demographics, and general market information for each of Nielsen's DMAs. Individual markets may have characteristics that require special consideration in programming and promotion. The *DMA Market Profile* is one source of such data.

Station management may utilize other methods of obtaining research information. One technique is to place a questionnaire in the monthly program guide, seeking the program preferences and attitudes of the audience, which presumably consists of confirmed viewers. Such input is important because of the necessity of satisfying this financially supportive core audience. Program guide surveys are augmented by mail and telephone calls to the station, usually from committed viewers.

To broaden its information base, a public station may commission special research among viewers in the market who may not be part of its current audience. In-depth special research may suggest program and promotional changes that could result in a broadening of the station's viewership.

Many private companies provide such services. For example, The Gallup Organization will work with a station to design a questionnaire, complete the field research, and issue a report. Companies charge a fee and, for some stations, the cost is prohibitive. An alternative is to commission a local college or university to undertake the work. Public broadcast stations operated by college/university licensees are particularly well positioned to avail themselves of that opportunity.

Fund-raising efforts also are a research tool. Programs that produce the largest viewer pledges often are a good indication of what the audience wants. Comments made by viewers while calling in pledges also provide useful insights.

Stations also collect information when they call viewers. Outside the on-air campaigns, many stations conduct telemarketing membership renewal campaigns, during which they compile audience program preference data.

To complement this local information, management should determine audience strategies that have worked well in other markets. Contacts with other public station managers can provide valuable data.

In the current fragmented, competitive viewer market, research is an important and ongoing function of the public television station executive.

Cable Relations   Initially, the emergence of the cable industry was a favorable development for public television. Many stations operate on UHF channels and experience coverage and signal-quality problems. Cable systems enhanced their coverage area and improved the reception quality for many viewers. Because public television relies heavily on viewers for financial support, the benefits to be derived from cable carriage are obvious.

It was noted in Chapter 8, "Managing the Cable Television System," that court decisions in the mid-1980s eliminated the FCC must-carry rule requiring cable systems to carry local broadcast stations.[11] However, the rule was

305

restored by the Cable Television Consumer Protection and Competition Act of 1992 and upheld by the United States Supreme Court.[12] Under this law, a system's obligation to carry noncommercial educational stations depends on its channel capacity. Systems with 12 or fewer channels must carry one local noncommercial station. Those with 13 to 36 channels must carry all local noncommercial educational stations up to a maximum of three, while systems with more than 36 channels must carry all local noncommercial educational stations.[13] If a system operates in a market with no noncommercial educational stations, it must import one.

Good relations with cable systems in the station's DMA are important. Public station managers must appreciate the need to maintain contact with them to lobby for the uniqueness of their product. A growing number of stations designate a person to handle relations. The cable operator must be told of specials and schedule changes. If the station will be off the air for any reason, the cable system must be informed, since service interruptions result in telephone calls to the system. If adequately advised, cable operators may be able to avoid the calls by displaying information pertaining to the schedule change or transmission difficulties.

Problems with cable systems should be reported to the Washington-based APTS, which works with policy makers on questions of vital concern to the public television industry. Cable regulation is certainly one.

306

Community Outreach   Any entity that relies on governmental support as much as public television needs to be image-conscious and to maintain good community relations. Station and staff involvement in community life through participation in local activities and organizations can be helpful.

Beyond that, the traditional ways to promote community outreach are through on-the-air public service announcements and community events calendars. Requests for this kind of publicity assistance are frequent and should be accommodated whenever possible.

The concept of community relations also should be kept in mind when planning local origination of programs of a continuing nature, such as news or public affairs and documentaries.

However, outreach has become a specialized art and it is now probably the second most important management task behind fund-raising. It seeks to promote community engagement through public television. A national center for outreach has been established in Madison, Wisconsin. Its goals are to provide revenues, training, and funding for public television stations, to promote meaningful outreach at the local level, and to expand the presence of outreach within public broadcasting.

The center provides the following:

- information clearinghouse
- catalyst for action
- outreach pipeline
- grants
- training[14]

An example can explain the center's role. Public stations air educational children's programming. WYES-TV in New Orleans does this. Then, it uses "outreach" to extend the programming beyond the screen by using workshops for parents, teachers, and caregivers. The station distributes program guides, activity sheets, and media literacy information. It also offers a "First Book" program to distribute books to disadvantaged children.

A final consideration is license renewal. Every television station must apply for renewal every eight years. If citizens or citizen groups do not believe that the station has been operated in the public interest, they can file a petition to deny renewal. This has happened to some public stations, most often because of the station's failure to address the needs of some constituency, such as an ethnic group.[15] Good community relations can identify a problem like this before it matures to a denial petition.

Engineering   Engineering, which has always been a big problem for PBS stations, has become a bigger one with digital. As before, equipment must be purchased and maintained. Even the best programming is not worth much if the audience cannot receive a quality signal. But quality costs money. Capital costs are a significant ongoing expense. Most managers do not have engineering backgrounds to evaluate technical options effectively. However, it is important to devote the time required to stay abreast of these matters. The on-the-air look and sound are critical to the station's success.

As noted earlier, the expense of equipment acquisition may be offset by grants from the National Telecommunications and Information Administration. The station applicant must support the purchase with some of its own funds, usually up to 50 percent of the total amount.

Digital television is the major engineering challenge in the early years of the twenty-first century. High-definition television (HDTV) is a reality and PBS has taken a leadership role. Its HD Channel offers original high-definition programming.

At the local level, digital has provided stations with 19.4 Mbps for broadcast. This means that stations can provide multicasting or other on-air services beyond their normal program schedule. How this extra spectrum is used is left to the station. In New Orleans, WYES-TV operates HDTV from 7 P.M. to 6:30 A.M. From 6:30 A.M. until 7 P.M., it operates four channels of standard-definition programming (see Figure 9.7).

Administration   Having identified the component parts of public television, let us now turn to the administrative function. Quite simply, it involves integrating the parts into a smoothly operating station that delivers the desired product to an aware audience. It includes managing employee benefits, relations, and conflicts. It is negotiating—for acquisition of program product, for equipment, and union contracts. It also involves the presentation for approval of the operating budget to the supervising authority, be it a board, official, commission, or agency. It is paper work, such as the preparation of grant applications, the CPB Certification of Eligibility, and program schedules for *TV Guide*, newspapers, and ratings services. In reality, it is managing people and deadlines.

FIGURE 9.7 How WYES-TV, New Orleans, uses its 19.4 Mbps of digital spectrum. (Used with permission.)

Administration is the management function where a lot of executives fail. If attention to detail is missing, the component parts, as good as they may be, will not matter. It is the least inspiring but most important aspect of public electronic media management. For it is here that it all does, or does not, come together.

RADIO

A total of 2,551 noncommercial radio stations are licensed in the United States.[16] Among those, nearly 800 are funded by the CPB[17] and broadcast NPR and Public Radio International (PRI) programming. Still others, mainly community corporations, receive CPB grants and do not air NPR or PRI programming. Like public television stations, public radio stations are divided into four licensee categories: community organizations, colleges/universities, state authorities, and local educational or municipal authorities.

ORGANIZATION AND PERSONNEL

The staff size and organizational structure of a public radio station depend on the market, type of licensee, and format. Normally, a station has a general manager or station manager, who reports to a supervising authority. As in public television, the composition of the upper-level governing authority depends on the type of licensee.

Reporting to the general manager or station manager are various departments. Structures and titles vary widely. Figure 9.8 presents the organizational

309

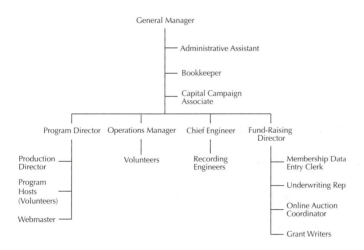

FIGURE 9.8 Organizational chart, WWOZ-FM, New Orleans. (Used with permission.)

chart of a community corporation licensee in New Orleans. The station is CPB-funded but carries no NPR or PRI programming. It has a small paid staff and 450 volunteers. The station employs an eclectic format that features blues, jazz, Cajun, zydeco, gospel, Brazilian, and Caribbean. It is a national program producer and broadcasts live from the annual New Orleans Jazz & Heritage Festival each year. On-air hosts program their own music.

The station generates a weekly cumulative audience of 50,000. Its motto is "More platter, less chatter." It programs no news or public affairs. However, at every odd hour of the day, it airs the *Livewire,* which lists that night's events in area clubs. For additional information about the station, visit http://www.wwoz.org.

MANAGEMENT TASKS

Public radio managers exercise responsibility over seven principal station activities. A review of each of these management tasks will reveal the evolving nature of public radio and the problems it faces in the current fragmented, competitive marketplace. It will also allow an examination of the management tools and techniques to meet the challenges and an opportunity to contrast public radio with its commercial brethren. The tasks are as follows:

- fund-raising and expense control
- programming
- promotion
- research
- community outreach
- engineering
- administration

Fund-Raising and Expense Control   Many of the comments about public television budgets made earlier in this chapter also apply to radio.

Formerly, program production was concentrated at the national level. Today, CPB radio programming funds are paid directly to qualified stations. In addition, NPR has "unbundled" its programming. In other words, member stations now may take all or part of the NPR program offerings. These changes obviously have had an impact on the financial management of public stations.

Public radio is noncommercial. Unlike commercial radio, it does not have advertisers as a principal source of operating funds. Therefore, it has looked to alternative funding sources. The four principal sources are

- federal government
- state government
- audience
- underwriting

FEDERAL GOVERNMENT Public radio relies upon two principal kinds of federal funding, both of which emanate from the CPB. The first is the Community Service Grant. To qualify, a station must demonstrate that the station has adequate power to provide a minimum designated signal over the station's city of license, that it has at least five full-time employees, and that it operates a minimum of 18 hours per day on a minimum nonfederal income of $100,000.

The Corporation for Public Broadcasting's second method of distributing federal funds is via National Program Production and Acquisition Grants. They are a result of the 1987 CPB decision to fund program production at the local station level rather than through NPR.

Neither grant requires station matching funds. However, CPB does provide grants for many local station activities, some of which do require station funds.

It is important for management to know the many kinds of grants available and how to obtain them. Some of them will be discussed later in the chapter.

Equipment purchase support is available through the NTIA. To qualify for NTIA funds, stations must submit a detailed written proposal and be able to generate matching funds.

Federal funding is important to local public radio. Even though it usually accounts for less than 20 percent of revenues generated, attention to the details and procedures necessary to ensure the station's continuing qualification for federal monies is a management priority task.

STATE GOVERNMENT A second key ingredient in public radio finances is the support of state governments. States may fund some licensees directly through annual appropriation, as in the case of public radio stations operated by colleges or universities. Some states operate statewide public radio networks that are funded, in part, by state legislatures.

The future public radio manager should simply be aware that significant state financial resources are available and that complying with state procedures and deadlines is a major management function.

AUDIENCE All public radio stations rely upon their audiences, to some degree, to meet their budgets. For many stations, this source of funding is now the most important single revenue item, more so for community corporation licensees than for other licensee categories. WWOZ-FM in New Orleans derives 66 percent of its annual revenue from membership pledge drives and related activities. Generally, this audience outreach takes the form of one or more on-the-air pledge or membership drives. Spring and fall are favored times of the year for such activities. That is how WWOZ-FM does it.

Memberships are available at various levels. The higher the dollar amount, the better the premium that accompanies the pledge. WWOZ's premiums tie into the lifestyle of its members. They include passes to popular nightspots, such as House of Blues, Rock 'N' Bowl, and Tipitina's.

As noted earlier, WWOZ is a national program production station. Part of its CPB Program Acquisition and Support Grant supports the production of compact disks (CDs) cut at live performance venues. The CDs are used, in part, as pledge drive premiums. The station's average annual membership pledge is $180, compared to the national average of $73.22.[18]

The design of the fund-raising drive is in the hands of the local station. For NPR stations, there is also a national fund-raising framework. Special versions of popular programs are presented. For a producer's manual for the WWOZ spring membership drive, please see Appendix B, "Excerpt from Membership Drive Producer's Manuals."

Most stations prefer not to break the existing format during fund drives. Instead, special editions or encore presentations of programs are presented in their regular time periods. During fund-raising, a station might use a Garrison Keillor special, for example. Such programming is then interspersed with on-the-air appeals to the audience. Premiums might be anything, but the more successful ones are books, such as *Go Public*, which features coverage maps and format information on public radio stations across the country, and coffee mugs displaying the names of popular programs. Phone-in pledges are taken by volunteers, usually community leaders and members of community organizations. Where possible, involvement of local sports or entertainment celebrities is desirable.

Public radio stations do engage in other kinds of fund-raising. Music stations often mount performance events for revenue. WWOZ, for example, organizes a series of *Piano Night* concerts. The station also arranges an annual *Mangold Freeze*. These two events generate $75,000 in net annual revenue for a station whose annual revenue is $1.4 million.

Some public radio stations produce auctions. However, this fund-raising method is difficult because radio lacks the visual element. Special events, with personalities from national programs carried by the station, are another type.

New methods of audience fund-raising are developing and evolving. It is important to be aware of ideas and success stories from stations around the country. This can be done by direct contact with other public stations or by membership in selected organizations. Other development and fund-raising information is available on the Internet.[19]

UNDERWRITING   This revenue source is used either to develop or present programs. As a rule, public radio stations are more active than television stations in program development. Stations involved in program production may submit grant applications to large corporations or foundations to secure funds.

Stations not engaged in program development still may rely on underwriting to defray some of the costs of presenting programs. To secure presentation underwriting, a representative of the station offers to a local business sponsorship identification during the program in exchange for a monetary contribution. To preserve noncommercial integrity, close attention must be paid to the preparation of underwriting copy.

Product identification is acceptable. Price information, product comparisons, and customer motivational language are not. Comments made earlier in the chapter about the specific guidelines are relevant here.

Since underwriting is one of the few realistic revenue sources available to public radio, management should provide sufficient personnel and support to develop it.

For a summary of the principal sources of revenue for a public radio station, please see Figure 9.9.

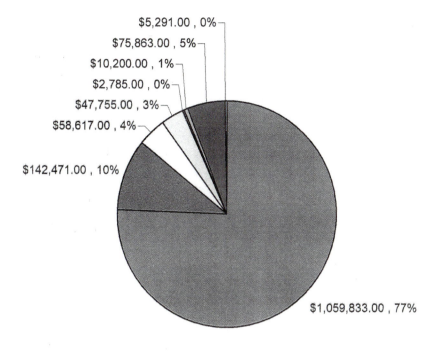

$5,291.00 , 0%

$75,863.00 , 5%

$10,200.00 , 1%

$2,785.00 , 0%

$47,755.00 , 3%

$58,617.00 , 4%

$142,471.00 , 10%

$1,059,833.00 , 77%

313

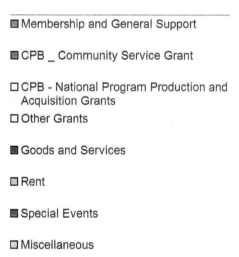

■ Membership and General Support

■ CPB _ Community Service Grant

□ CPB - National Program Production and
  Acquisition Grants
□ Other Grants

■ Goods and Services

□ Rent

■ Special Events

□ Miscellaneous

FIGURE 9.9 Revenue distribution for WWOZ-FM, New Orleans, a community corporation licensee. (Used with permission.)

In these times of decreased resources and increased competition, expense control for public radio management is as important as revenue enhancement.

The largest public radio expense items are programming and staff. Public radio stations tend to originate more programming than public television stations. Many stations also maintain a local news presence, and that is expensive.

Purchased programming is also expensive. The unbundling of NPR programming has not led to the predicted cost reduction for stations. As a result, many member stations have defected and spent their money with competitors, like Public Radio International. Loss of member dollars for NPR programming only further increases the cost for those who use it.

Public radio is not as equipment-intensive as public television. However, the quality of on-the-air product and signal are affected by technological developments and their accompanying expense. Digital audio broadcasting (DAB) is an example of a likely future expense in this category. Digital analog is here in the form of IBOC. Digital multichannel radio is progressing. When fully deployed, it will result in noncommercial FM radio having additional spectrum available for separate program streams from the main channel. The implementation of digital will require raising capital funds to buy it and having the engineering expertise to install and operate it.

Promotion is becoming a greater expense item. Deregulation has led to an increased number of radio stations with more varied formats. As a result, the public station will have to spend more on promotion to stay positioned as an attractive media alternative.

Specific expense comparisons can be made with similar public radio stations in other markets by consulting annual expense data compiled by the CPB. Management should examine such information as part of the continuing effort to allocate and control expense dollars.

For an example of public radio station expense distribution, please see Figure 9.10.

Programming   The measurement of a successful program strategy in public television is cumulative audience. In public radio, however, it is TSL, or how long listeners are tuned in, and that requires a different program approach. The goal is to select a format that will retain the audience for extended periods of time. Usually, a public radio station plays to one constituency, whereas a public television station plays to many in order to build audience.

Public radio is format-based. In that respect, its programming is similar to that of its commercial counterparts. However, public formats are specialized, with narrower audience appeal. For that reason, most of them would not be commercially viable. Public stations provide an important function by servicing what would otherwise be unserved portions of the radio audience.

FORMAT SELECTION   To succeed in public radio today, a niche in the fragmented radio spectrum must be identified and a format developed to fill it. Historically, management has had six recognized formats from which to select:

> *Classical and fine arts* consists of recorded music and, at times, live concerts. Additional programming to support this format is available from NPR and other sources.

314

Jazz is mainly recorded music and live concerts. Supplemental programming is obtainable from NPR.

News and public affairs is a format that can be partly local and partly national. National programming support is available from NPR and from PRI, which carries the BBC World Service.

Community service and public access is primarily a locally originated format designed to provide information to, and a forum for, those who may be neglected by the programming of other radio stations in the market.

Eclectic is the format used by most stations. It offers something for everyone, but does not generate the high TSL now considered desirable.

Dual format is a program concept featuring news and a certain type of music, usually classical or jazz.

315

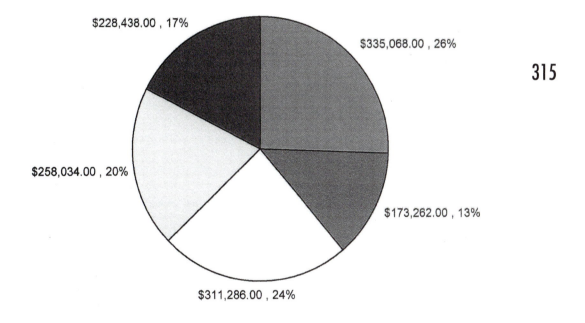

FIGURE 9.10 Expense distribution for community corporation licensee WWOZ-FM, New Orleans. (Used with permission.)

In addition to these six recognized formats, another public radio format has developed. It is known as the *Adult Acoustic Alternative (AAA)*. This experimental concept represents an attempt to attract younger demographics by offering contemporary music, and it appears to be having some success.

Like public television, public radio has had to rely more on audience support due to decreased government funding. Commercial services to assist public radio in increasing its audience have been developed. An example is "Classical 24," a service that selects classical music that will appeal to the NPR news listener.[20]

The format ultimately selected will be dictated by the type of licensee operating the station, the needs and interests of the community, and the positioning of other radio alternatives in the market.

NATIONAL AFFILIATION   Having selected a basic format, the public radio program director must now decide how to augment it with a national service or services. At present, two primary services are available.

The oldest, and best known, is National Public Radio, or NPR, a private, nonprofit membership corporation that produces and distributes programs. National Public Radio programs via satellite to more than 780 stations in all 50 states.[21] The programming it provides can be purchased in its entirety or in units. In recent years, NPR has tended to make more individual programs available. Major program blocks include the Morning News Service, the Afternoon News Service, and Performance Programming.

The morning service features a program called *Morning Edition*, and the afternoon service's main offering is *All Things Considered*. They are now the most listened-to public radio programs in the United States. Nationa Public Radio's weekly audience has doubled in the last ten years to 26 million persons.[22] Performance programming comprises a variety of content, including music (classical, jazz, and folk), drama, and comedy. Popular features are *Car Talk* and *Talk of the Nation*. National Public Radio also offers as a major feed *Performance Today*, which includes occasional features in a classical music context.

National Public Radio members pay for the programming they use and for transmission costs, as well as the basic station membership fee.

In addition to its programming services, NPR also provides program-producing stations with distribution services. The Extended Program Service enables stations to send their programs to other stations via the Public Radio Satellite System, which maintains uplinks and downlinks throughout the country.

The other national service is Public Radio International, or PRI. Originated in 1982, this nonprofit corporation provides an alternative to NPR, and many stations subscribe to both. Instead of membership fees, public stations pay affiliation fees, the amount of which depends on market size.

Public Radio International's programs originate with local stations and independent producers. Funding for program acquisition is provided by foundations, corporations, and station program fees.

Initially, Public Radio International did not offer as full a range of programs as NPR. However, its program offerings have expanded considerably. It distributes news and special programs, some of which, like *Prairie Home*

Companion and *Michael Feldman's Whad 'Ya Know?*, have enjoyed significant followings. Other popular programs include *This American Life* and *Studio 360*. As noted earlier, PRI also carries the BBC World Service.

Unlike NPR, PRI does provide some programming for the basic affiliation fee. It is an important program source for public radio program directors, and affiliation with it does not preclude association with other sources. Public Radio International's program schedule is available on the Internet.[23]

National Public Radio's program pricing policies have led to the rise of independent program producers seeking to capitalize on the programming void and develop a new market for their products.

Some major market public radio stations also have become program producers. Examples are WGBH, Boston, and WCLV, Cleveland, which operates as Seaway Productions. WFMT, Chicago, offers the WFMT Radio Network. Another example is WWOZ, New Orleans, which produces recordings of live jazz concerts for distribution to stations around the country.

Program directors have an ever-increasing selection of content sources. To stay in touch with what is happening, they should consider membership in the Public Radio Program Directors Association (PRPD),[24] which makes information available to its members through a newsletter. Staying current is a continuing challenge for public radio management, and industry associations are one way to do it.

Promotion   Radio is more competitive and fragmented than ever. As more stations go on the air, as more are allowed to upgrade their power, and as contour overlap is reduced, the situation will intensify. In this climate, public radio management must promote. Gone are the days when programming promoted itself through its uniqueness. The number one way to promote is on the station's own air. The goals are to persuade existing listeners to tune into some of the station's other programs and to increase the TSL.

Outside promotion in public radio is conducted in a variety of ways. The most traditional has been the program guide, which appears in all shapes and sizes, from simple one-sheets to elaborate magazine-style monthly publications, such as Minnesota Public Radio's *Minnesota Monthly*. Some stations have foregone the monthly publications altogether. Instead, they rely on their Web site and other forms of advertising. As noted earlier in this chapter, promotion is one of the larger expense items.

Newspaper has also been a traditional public radio promotional vehicle. It is suitable for image promotion and can be employed to promote news, programs, and series.

There is a realization in public radio that promotion methods must change to adapt to the new competitive environment. While research shows that public radio listeners are above-average newspaper readers, many development directors now utilize television. Television is expensive and may be cost-prohibitive. However, some public radio stations have been successful at playing TV spots as public service announcements on commercial TV stations. While broadcast TV is expensive, cable TV is not. Local spots in national, advertiser-supported cable networks carried by cable systems are affordable and effective. Announcements on CNN, A&E, The Discovery Channel, and

317

The Weather Channel are examples for news and public affairs formats. Bravo, MTV, BET, and VH1 may be more appropriate for music formats.

New forms of outside promotion for public radio are emerging. Borders, a national bookstore chain, promotes public radio with in-store kiosks. National Public Radio and many of its member stations maintain Web sites. The Internet allows the station to display its program schedule, features, and special events, and even to attempt to recruit new members.

The CPB has recognized the importance of promotion and makes available to stations promotional Tune-In Grants. To qualify, stations must apply for them, but they are fairly automatic. There is a matching funds requirement, as well as a requirement to file a final report once the promotion campaign is over.

National Public Radio also develops promotions for its news programs, and promotional ideas are found in the NPR monthly memo to managers.

Peer contact is always valuable for insights into promotional concepts that have worked for others.

While some promotional techniques of commercial radio are inappropriate for public radio, there are many that can be used. Among those are bumper stickers, T-shirts, and some kinds of contests. On-the-air contests do build quarter-hour audience and do increase critical time spent listening. On-the-air promotion is an element of the total promotion concept.

318

Development directors for public radio are also frequently the promotion managers. The promotion aspect of the job should be given as high a priority as the fund-raising aspect.

Research   Public radio management must regularly identify the constantly changing program needs and interests of the audience. A good place to begin is with a review of reports provided to subscribing stations by the national ratings service, Arbitron. The frequency of the report depends on the size of the market. Because public radio stations do not have access to the kind of ratings information provided by PBS to television stations, management should consider subscribing to a service that is available and affordable.

As an alternative, a public radio station may choose to develop its own data through specially commissioned research. WWOZ-FM in New Orleans contracts for proprietary research with a company called Audigraphics,[25] which analyzes Arbitron data for the station. The analysis provides station management with strategic planning information, such as the appeal of the station and the loyalty of its audience compared to certain competitors. For specifics of the station's listening demographics, please see Figure 9.11.

Many public stations operated by colleges or universities are in a unique position to undertake audience research.

Other useful information comes from mail and telephone calls to the station. Talk shows featured on many public radio stations are an effective means of sampling audience attitudes. Station fund-raising also often yields valuable insights into listener likes and dislikes.

Finally, through the CPB, it is possible for a public radio station to secure financial assistance for research. The CPB offers grants for research development. Stations must submit detailed written proposals to qualify. Competition is quite intense, but the effort may prove worthwhile.

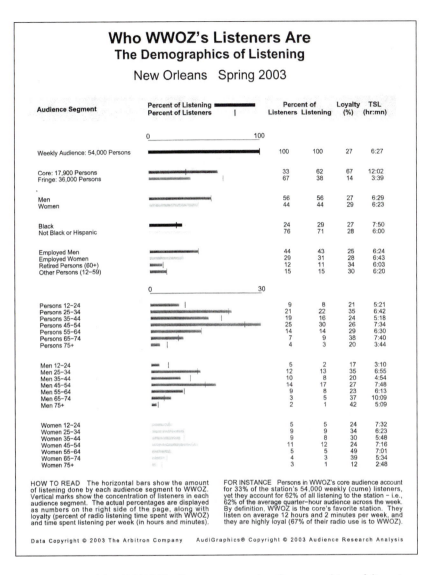

Who WWOZ's Listeners Are
The Demographics of Listening

New Orleans   Spring 2003

Audience Segment	Percent of Listening ▬▬ / Percent of Listeners │	Percent of Listeners	Listening	Loyalty (%)	TSL (hr:mn)
0 — 100					
Weekly Audience: 54,000 Persons		100	100	27	6:27
Core: 17,900 Persons		33	62	67	12:02
Fringe: 36,000 Persons		67	38	14	3:39
Men		56	56	27	6:29
Women		44	44	29	6:23
Black		24	29	27	7:50
Not Black or Hispanic		76	71	28	6:00
Employed Men		44	43	25	6:24
Employed Women		29	31	28	6:43
Retired Persons (60+)		12	11	34	6:03
Other Persons (12–59)		15	15	30	6:20
0 — 30					
Persons 12–24		9	8	21	5:21
Persons 25–34		21	22	35	6:42
Persons 35–44		19	16	24	5:18
Persons 45–54		25	30	26	7:34
Persons 55–64		14	14	29	6:30
Persons 65–74		7	9	38	7:40
Persons 75+		4	3	20	3:44
Men 12–24		5	2	17	3:10
Men 25–34		12	13	35	6:55
Men 35–44		10	8	20	4:54
Men 45–54		14	17	27	7:48
Men 55–64		9	8	23	6:13
Men 65–74		3	5	37	10:09
Men 75+		2	1	42	5:09
Women 12–24		5	5	24	7:32
Women 25–34		9	9	34	6:23
Women 35–44		9	8	30	5:48
Women 45–54		11	12	24	7:16
Women 55–64		5	5	49	7:01
Women 65–74		4	3	39	5:34
Women 75+		3	1	12	2:48

HOW TO READ The horizontal bars show the amount of listening done by each audience segment to WWOZ. Vertical marks show the concentration of listeners in each audience segment. The actual percentages are displayed as numbers on the right side of the page, along with loyalty (percent of radio listening time spent with WWOZ) and time spent listening per week (in hours and minutes).

FOR INSTANCE Persons in WWOZ's core audience account for 33% of the station's 54,000 weekly (cume) listeners, yet they account for 62% of all listening to the station – i.e., 62% of the average quarter-hour audience across the week. By definition, WWOZ is the core's favorite station. They listen on average 12 hours and 2 minutes per week, and they are highly loyal (67% of their radio use is to WWOZ).

FIGURE 9.11 Who WWOZ's listeners are: the demographics of listening. (Source: WWOZ-FM, New Orleans. Used with permission.)

Community Outreach   Community outreach is as critical to public radio stations as it is to public television stations. The paramount reasons are the level of governmental support and the license renewal, which occurs every eight years. Over the years, there have been occasional cases in which the licenses of some stations have not been renewed. Often, the reason lay in offenses to community sensibilities by the stations.[26]

To enhance community outreach, a public radio station can, of course, utilize public service announcements and involve itself in local civic and charitable activities. Depending on the format, the station may have legitimate visible personalities. Talk shows have become America's town meetings. Stations with host talent should consider instituting a speakers' bureau to provide guest speakers for civic organizations, charities, and schools. Similarly, invitations to community leaders to appear on interview programs will assist in maintaining good community relations.

There is more local programming in public radio than in public television. Hence, there are more opportunities to develop community relations. WWOZ does it by going into the live music venues in New Orleans where it broadcasts and records.

Engineering   Observations made earlier about the importance of engineering in public television are equally applicable to public radio. Equipment must be bought and maintained to provide the quality signal necessary to retain and build an audience. As already noted, management should be aware of the grant assistance available from NTIA for equipment acquisition.

Administration   Most of the comments made earlier in the chapter about public television administration also pertain to public radio. However, some additional comments are necessary.

320

Because radio budgets are tighter, fund-raising more difficult, and staff sizes smaller, public radio managers are under more pressure to administer expertly their more limited resources. Employing personnel who can perform multiple functions well is a real management challenge. Local program origination is a bigger factor than in television, and that poses its own problems. Coupled with that is the need for adequate supervision of on-the-air programming and talent. Some public stations have offended public sensibilities with programs, music, or comments by talent. Regulatory officials and lawmakers are taking a tougher, more rigid position on indecency and obscenity, as evidenced by the promulgation and implementation of the 1987 FCC's indecency standard (see Chapter 7, "Broadcast Regulations"). Public managers and program executives need to be vigilant. Apart from the equities of a case, the cost of defending an FCC indecency complaint can destroy the budget of even the best financially positioned station.

Stations that belong to NPR do have some administrative assistance. National Public Radio as representation and distribution divisions. The representation division attempts to protect the position of public stations on critical issues before various governmental bodies. It also acts as a mediator in disputes between NPR and member stations. The responsibility of the distribution division is the NPR satellite system, which is important to many stations that produce programs. National Public Radio also provides a monthly memo that keeps management abreast of current issues and opportunities.

Management should also maintain contact with management at other stations for advice and ideas. A listing of stations and executives can be found in the *Public Broadcasting Directory*, published annually by the CPB.

LOW-POWER FM RADIO

In 2000, the FCC authorized a new noncommercial service called low-power FM (LPFM). Stations are limited to 100 watts of power and an antenna height of 100 feet above average terrain.[27] They are not available for licensing to individuals and are dedicated to noncommercial educational entities and public safety or transportation organizations.

The average range of LPFM is thought to be 3.5 miles. In practice, it seems to be a bit more. There has been a raging controversy over interference issues arising from LPFMs and a battle over an FCC plan to issue more such licenses.

Advocates assert that these entities are restoring some of the "localism" that, they argue, has been lost to consolidated radio and its profit quest.

NONCOMMERCIAL LICENSING PROCESS

As noted in Chapter 10, "Entry into the Electronic Media Business," the FCC uses an auction to award licenses for new commercial station facilities. The process for granting new spectrum for noncommercial licensees is not the same.

Where there are two or more applicants for a noncommercial new build, the FCC had historically used a point system to award licenses. The system was challenged unsuccessfully in the federal court of appeals for the Washington, DC, circuit.[28] The court-sanctioned points are as follows:

- two points for "local diversity"
- one or two points for the best technical proposal
- three points for the best-established "local entities"
- two points for being a "statewide" educational network (alternative to local diversity)[29]

WHAT'S AHEAD?

Public broadcasting has grown considerably in the last ten years. Audiences have increased. So has funding, to some extent. A Roper poll commissioned by PBS placed the network second to defense as a value expenditure. And then there was the trust factor. Public Broadcasting Service bested Congress, the federal government, the courts, commercial broadcast networks, newspaper publishers, and cable TV.[30]

Notwithstanding the impressive survey results, the fight for the soul of public broadcasting will continue. Some who work in it and consider it unique will have difficulty adjusting to the fragmentation of audiences. Purists in the audience will be offended by the increased number of underwriting credits and the growing amount of mainstream, entertainment programming.

Financial stability will be the ever-elusive goal to be satisfied. In 2004, then-PBS chief Pat Mitchell advanced a plan to free the organization from federal funding. She proposed that the federal government pay $5 billion to PBS and nothing thereafter. The money would be offset by public stations giving back analog spectrum early so that the FCC could auction it off. Public Broadcasting Service has been trying to get out from under the sometimes fickle U.S. Congress since the 1960s. This payment would make it more stable and more competitive, she argued.[31] Who knows what will happen to this proposal?

In the future, public broadcasting will become more performance-driven to survive. In that respect, it will not be unlike its commercial counterparts. Local origination will probably decline, due to cost. College and university licensees may be an exception, since they can receive assistance from students in exchange for academic credit. Syndicated programming will become more dominant in both radio and television.

The Congress and public broadcasting are in a truce over funding at the moment. But soon the issue will be faced again.

The role of the Internet in the future of public broadcasting also must be considered. A marriage of television and the Internet will occur and lead to a situation where viewers watch programs selected from a menu. Established delivery systems, such as the current, over-the-air commercial and noncommercial networks, may have had their best days.

It will be important for the future that those aspiring to a public broadcasting career keep upgrading their professional qualifications through on-the-job experience and continuing education. Events in the new century are moving at a rapid pace, and the places and types of employment will probably be significantly different from those of the past.

SUMMARY

Noncommercial broadcasting evolved into public broadcasting with the passage of the Public Broadcasting Act of 1967. A three-tiered structure now exists: (1) local stations funded in part by (2) the CPB Broadcasting, with program distribution provided by (3) nonprofit membership corporations—PBS for television and NPR for radio.

Public television stations are operated by four types of licensees: community organizations, colleges/universities, state authorities, and local educational or municipal authorities. Organization of the local station depends to some extent on licensee type. Some stations are more active in programming for general audiences and others in instructional television.

Absent any specialized activity, the major management tasks in public television stations can be classified fairly uniformly into eight categories: fund-raising and expense control, programming, promotion, research, cable relations, community outreach, engineering, and administration. Budget considerations have become paramount, because continued significant governmental funding is no longer assured. As a result of the necessity of raising nongovernmental funds, public television has become more ratings-conscious and pays special attention to weekly audience cumulative numbers, as opposed to program numbers. Increased competition from many sources has led to a need to attach more importance to programming concepts and promotion. The reality of cable television must also be dealt with, particularly since many stations depend on cable's reach to deliver programs to areas not covered by their over-the-air signals.

The future will be demanding for public television. Management will have to refine and develop skills to contend with the opportunities and problems of the evolving competitive marketplace.

While there are more than 2,500 noncommercial radio licensees in the United States, fewer than 800 meet the eligibility requirements for funding by the CPB and, thus, are classified as "public." National Public Radio provides programming and distribution services for these stations. However, the growth of alternative program sources has reduced the reliance that stations once had on NPR.

Basically, public radio management has seven major functions: fund raising and expense control, programming, promotion, research, community outreach, engineering, and administration.

Public radio also has had to make fund-raising a priority. Accordingly, developing ratings is important. Ratings in public radio mean TSL, not cumulative audience. Fragmented markets have also led to a new emphasis on promotion.

Most stations use one of seven recognized and evolving formats: classical, jazz, news, access, eclectic, dual, and adult acoustic alternative (AAA). Many produce programs for distribution to other stations.

Strategy for the new century requires the public radio manager to achieve results in a more crowded marketplace and with fewer resources.

323

CASE STUDY: TELEVISION

KTWO-TV is slated to become the second public television station in a mid-sized market in the Southeast. There already is a generic PBS affiliate in the community. It is a tape and celluloid operation. This station, KBAD-TV, carries whatever PBS offers. The only thing that is live at the station is the guard dog.

KTWO-TV is a community corporation at the moment. The president, Can Do, is a wealthy car dealer who has contributed $700,000 to get things going. He has hired you to bring his plan to life. The goal is to be the best that he can be with someone else's money. The station will be a full-power facility, with 15 fulltime staff and broadcasting 3,000 hours a year.

Mr. Do has gone back to the dealership. He expects you to secure the rest of the funding, programming, and anything else that might be required.

EXERCISES

1. Your first thought is to secure federal funding. What must you file for and with whom?

2. Will you be successful?

3. What are your other potential sources of funding?

4. You want to buy certain PBS programs for KTWO's debut. These selections amount to about 50 percent of the total PBS schedule and include the common carriage schedule. What do you apply for with PBS? Will you be successful?

5. Mr. Do wants to underwrite programming on the station for his car lots. His sample copy says, in part, "Tow it in or ride it in to get the best price on the best cars in the city." Will you air the copy? Why or why not?

CASE STUDY: RADIO

KTUN-FM is an all-music station in an all-music Southern city. It airs no news, public affairs, or sports. The station broadcasts 24 hours a day with five fulltime employees. The signal is very competitive in the market and has a strong audience base from which it derives 80 percent of its annual revenue. However, this is not quite enough.

The station needs new equipment—some digital—and needs to rehab its studios and offices. It distributes an expensive monthly publication, which is a premium for members. The staff is afraid to discontinue it, even though the cost savings would be sizable.

You have been retained as an outside consultant to address the problems.

EXERCISES

1. As of now, KTUN-FM has no CSG from the CPB. Can it qualify for one?

2. It does not buy, and does not intend to buy, any NPR or PRI programming. Does this fact change your answer to number 1?

3. Is there any grant that can be applied for to provide funds for needed equipment?

4. Suggest an alternative to the expensive monthly program guide.

5. Does the advent of digital radio offer any revenue answers not currently available?

6. Can any radio station, especially a public station, operate without any news and public affairs?

7. If KTUN were an LPFM, could it qualify for CPB funding?

NOTES

1. http://www.fcc.gov.

2. *Ibid.*

3. http://www.pbs.org.

4. *Ibid.*

5. http://www.cpb.org.

6. The NTIA is part of the Department of Commerce and is the telecommunications policy office for the executive branch of government.

7. For what to do and what not to do in membership drive break structuring, see Susan T. Eastman and Robert Klein, *Promotion and Marketing for Broadcasting and Cable*, 2nd ed., pp. 249–279.

8. T. Barton Carter, Marc A. Franklin, and Jay B. Wright, *The First Amendment and the Fifth Estate: Regulation of Electronic Mass Media*, 3rd ed., p. 352.

9. *Ibid.*

10. Public stations file annual financial reports with the CPB, which issues station revenue and expense profiles. The data are categorized according to the type of licensee and the size of the operating budget. Comparative financial data are also available through the APTS (http://www.apts.org).

11. Quincy Cable TV, Inc. v. Federal Communications Commission, 768 F2d, 1434, 1985; Century Communications Corporation v. Federal Communications Commission, 835 F2d, 292, 1987.

12. Turner Broadcasting System, Inc. v. Federal Communications Commission, 114 S. Ct. 2445.

13. 47 USC 535.

14. http://www.nationaloutreach.org.

15. Alabama Educational Television Commission, 50 FCC 2d 461.

16. http://www.fcc.gov.

17. http://www.cpb.org.

18. *Ibid.*

19. http://www.aranet.com.

20. http://music.minnesota.publicradio.org.

21. http://www.npr.org.

22. *Ibid.*

23. http://www.pri.org.

24. http://www.prpd.org.

25. http://www.aranet.com.

26. In Trustees of the University of Pennsylvania, 69 FCC 2d 1394.

27. http://www.fcc.gov.

28. American Family Association et al. v. FCC, 2004.

29. *Antenna*, Drinker Biddle & Reath, June 2004, pp. 1, 3.

30. John Eggerton, "In PBS We Trust, According to PBS Survey," *Broadcasting & Cable*, February 9, 2004, p. 11.

[31] Bill McConnell, "A $5 Billion Proposal," *Broadcasting & Cable*, June 14, 2004, p. 16.

ADDITIONAL READINGS

Keith, Michael C. *The Radio Station*, 6th ed. Boston: Focal Press, 2003.

McCauley, Michael P., Eric E. Peterson, B. Lee Artz, and DeeDee Halleck (eds.). *Public Broadcasting and the Public Interest*. Armonk, NY: M. E. Sharpe, 2003.

Public Television, a Program for Action: The Report and Recommendations of the Carnegie Commission on Educational Television. New York: Harper & Row, 1967.

A Public Trust: The Report of the Carnegie Commission on the Future of Public Broadcasting. New York: Bantam Books, 1979.

Witherspoon, John, Roselle Kovitz, Rober K. Avery, and Alan G. Stavitsky. *A History of Public Broadcasting*, rev. ed. Washington, DC: Educational Broadcasting Corp., 2000.

Entry into the Electronic Media Business

This chapter examines the methods of achieving a management position or ownership by focusing on

- how to identify and secure employment in a managerial capacity or a capacity that may lead to management

- how to buy an existing station, by exploring methods of finding the property, financing the acquisition, and executing legal and other procedures to consummate the transaction

- how to build a new station or cable system, by identifying methods of locating open frequencies and franchises, obtaining financing, and complying with governmental requirements

Many college and university students pursuing the electronic media curriculum have as their ultimate goal either station management or ownership. Some use the first as a steppingstone to the second. However, as noted in Chapter 1, "Broadcast Station Management," managers operate at various levels, and the aspirations of some students may stop short of those goals.

There is no precise formula for reaching management or ownership status, but more than 80 years of broadcast history and experience provide directions to the promised land. The purpose of this chapter is to journey down that road and point out the landmarks along the way. This chapter is, in fact, a road map of some of the methods and procedures utilized by successful broadcasters. All the detail required to reach the destination would require at least a separate book, maybe more.

Students wishing to pursue the ownership option, in particular, are encouraged to take other courses to augment their broadcast education while they are still undergraduates. Prominent among courses that might be suggested are basic introductions to business financing and accounting. Some understanding of the complexities and terminology of finance and accounting is critical to the realization of a person's ownership goals. This is even more important since the Telecommunications Act of 1996, because the places, numbers, and kinds of existing stations available for purchase have changed significantly (see Chapter 2, "Financial Management").

EMPLOYMENT

Employment is the most traditional and common means of entering the electronic media business. Those professionals who have no present ownership goals may view increasingly challenging managerial positions as ends in themselves. Individuals with ownership aspirations also generally work in the industry for some time, because some personal resources are necessary, and because lenders and investors simply do not finance new owners without some demonstrable track record, which means experience. Even those few and fortunate individuals possessing extensive funds are better served by a working apprenticeship in the industry, given the competitive, specialized nature of media markets.

In all but rare cases, students enter the industry through employment. Despite possession of a degree, most college graduates will start on their career journey at the bottom, in an entry-level position.

Even at that level, competition for jobs is intense. Hundreds of colleges and universities graduate thousands of electronic media students annually. The edge will go to those who have used their college years wisely. That means high academic performance. It also means participation in relevant activities outside the classroom and laboratory. Internships completed and a demonstrated ability to write are especially helpful. The importance of such pursuits should not be minimized, since taking the first step is the most challenging part of the career journey. Academic achievement, combined with professionally related experience, are what most employers expect. Students who are serious about employment will not disappoint them.

There are several ways of accumulating experience before graduation. Volunteer or paid employment often is available to those who enroll in colleges and universities that operate radio or television stations or provide programming for cable television systems. Internships offer the chance to develop hands-on experience in commercial and noncommercial stations, cable systems, and allied operations, such as recording studios, production houses, commercial radio and television networks, advertising and public relations departments and agencies, and station representative companies. These opportunities have an added advantage: They provide interns with a valuable means of displaying their abilities to those engaged in the hiring of personnel. More and more schools have organized internship programs, in part through the efforts of alumni working in the industry. The College of Mass Communications and Media Arts at Southern Illinois University, for example, has such programs in Hollywood and Chicago. Internships are becoming a significant employment source as more and more companies hire interns for starting positions. Many employers also seek out part-time employees, especially for weekend and vacation work.

Some new graduates set their sights on entry-level positions in large markets. That is probably unrealistic, and it is not necessarily the wisest course, since the level of competition is likely to be extremely high. In addition, it is too easy to become super-specialized or lost in the crowd, both of which may prove to be impediments to advancement.

329

Learning how to wear multiple hats in a smaller market may actually be a qualification advantage for the future. However, it should be noted that post-1996 industry consolidation has led to the possibility of entry-level positions in larger markets, which offer upward mobility in consolidated companies.

Small markets, as noted above, offer several advantages. Competition for jobs is not as keen. Opportunities are more numerous. There are fewer unions. Most significantly, perhaps, employees are expected to perform a broader range of responsibilities. The immediate reaction may be one of shock at the volume and variety of work required. However, those feelings will turn to appreciation later with the realization of the wealth of knowledge and experience acquired.

The details of many of the managerial functions performed in the electronic media were discussed in earlier chapters. However, it may be useful here to identify examples of typical paths to career advancement.

A beginning position in radio as a disc jockey may lead to promotion to music director or production director and, ultimately, to program director. In time, a reporter may assume greater responsibility as public affairs director, en route to a news director's slot. The aspiring general sales manager may start out as a sales trainee and move in stages from small to larger accounts and into the local sales manager's chair before attaining the ultimate goal. From program director, promotion and marketing director, news director, or general sales manager, a step up to general manager (GM) may be the next move. Promotion to GM typically requires significant sales experience, however.

A starting camera operator in a television station may advance to a management position as program director, production director, or operations manager by achieving success, in turn, as a floor manager, production assistant, assistant producer/director, and producer/director. A general assignment reporter may progress to a beat reporter before advancing to assignment editor, news producer, assistant news director, and, finally, news director. Initial employment as an assistant in traffic, continuity, or promotion and marketing may pave the way for an upward move to traffic, continuity, or promotion and marketing director. Again, if the desired destination is a GM's post, the final step may be taken comfortably from one of several department head positions.

A beginning producer/director in a cable television system may be advanced to director of local origination, a sales representative to sales manager, and then to marketing director. A technician may progress to chief technician or chief engineer, and a customer service representative to office manager and, subsequently, to accountant or bookkeeper and business manager. The top management position as system manager may result after advancement through the ranks to head of marketing, engineering, or business.

Upward movement in all electronic media careers often occurs through promotion in a station, system, or group. In such cases, identifying appropriate vacancies presents no problem, since they are publicized to existing employees. However, if advancement is possible only through a move to another station in the market or to another market, the search for positions is more challenging. A similar challenge faces those who are about to embark on a career.

Among the best sources for locating positions are *B&C Broadcasting & Cable, R&R (Radio & Records), Inside Radio,* and *M Street Journal.* Another would be *Radio Business Report.* They list openings in markets of all sizes and in all areas of commercial and noncommercial station activity, from entry-level positions of all types to general management (Figures 10.1 through 10.4). Those with a special interest in public broadcasting will find *Current*

JOIN RADIO ONE INC.

Are you looking for a new opportunity in radio sales? Interested in joining a growing and diverse company?

We have positions available in our markets for new AE's and seasoned sellers!! We also have the following sales management positions available:

✓ **General Sales Manager**
Houston
✓ **General Sales Manager**
Louisville
✓ **General Sales Manager**
Boston
✓ **TV Sales Manager**
Indianapolis

For other sales opportunites with Radio One, view our open positions at www.radio-one.com. Let us hear from you! Send your resume to our VP of HR at sgolsch@radio-one.com or fax to (301) 918-9274. Inquiries will be kept confidential.

FIGURE 10.1 Ad for an entry-level radio account executive. (Source: *Inside Radio.* Used with permission.)

Must have 10+ years experience managing complex technical field operations in the cable industry, strong grasp of regulatory and plant maintenance issues, mastery of technical concepts like DOCSIS and HFC Technology, understanding of impact of field operation on business strategy, and strong communications skills. Engineering background a plus. Highly competitive salary and benefits package. Send resumes to Executivena@aol.com.

FIGURE 10.2 Cable television help wanted ad. (Source: *Broadcasting & Cable.* Used with permission.)

TWO OPENINGS

KFSN-TV, the ABC owned station in Fresno, CA, has two current job openings: PRODUCER (Job# BC04-08) - Ideal candidate must have the following skills: great news judgment, excellent writing, ability to create compelling teases and use pre-production elements to create an impactful newscast. REPORTER (Job#BC04-09) - Ideal candidate must have great live shot skills and the proven ability to establish sources and break big enterprise stories. Two years experience and college degree preferred for each position. Please send resume and non-returnable tape with position and job number to: KFSN-TV, Human Resources, 1777 G Street, Fresno, CA 93706. ABC, Inc. is an EEO Employer. (No phone calls please)

331

PRODUCER

WYFF, Hearst-Argyle Television is looking for an aggressive high-energy newscast producer. College degree and one year of experience required. Tape/resume to Andy Still, News Director, WYFF-TV, 505 Rutherford Street, Greenville, SC 29609. EEO

FIGURE 10.3 Television help-wanted ads. (Source: *Broadcasting & Cable.* Used with permission.)

RADIO JOBS
800-640-8852
ads@insideradio.com

Management Positions

Business Manager - St. Louis
Big League Broadcasting has an immediate opening in
St. Louis for a **Business Manager**.

General Manager - San Antonio
Salem Communications seeks proven,
sales-focused leader.

Corporate Vice President of Sales
Clear Channel of Columbia, SC seeks an
experienced **Business Manager** to join our
6-station cluster.

332

General Manager
KeyMarket of Ohio/PA is searching for General Managers
and GSM's.

Affiliate Relations Executive
A Connecticut company, focusing on producing radio
programming and promotions, seeks an Affiliate
Relations Executive.

FIGURE 10.4 Jobs hotline for subscribers to *Inside Radio*. (Source: *Inside Radio*. Used with permission.)

magazine helpful, while a publication such as *Multichannel News* will provide useful information on cable television openings.

There are several commercial publications, such as *Entertainment Employment Journal*, that list positions in all fields and at all levels. Related national and state or regional professional associations also provide information on job openings in their publications.

Several organizations, including the National Association of Broadcasters (NAB), operate clearinghouses.[1]

National station representative firms, such as Blair Television and The Interrep Radio Store, are often asked by client stations to identify candidates, especially for management positions. Many trade publications run "situations wanted" ads, and associations do likewise in their newsletters. Some, like the Radio-Television News Directors Association (RTNDA), maintain a telephone line dedicated to job openings. The fee for use of the service is nominal.[2]

Specialty firms have emerged for some employment classifications. One, MediaRecruiter, assists those seeking sales careers.[3]

Another method of taking the initiative in the job search is through registration with specialized employment placement firms, more commonly known as "head hunters." Many companies provide such services, and a partial listing can be found in the "Professional Services" section of *Broadcasting & Cable Yearbook*.[4] Typically, an applicant files a résumé with the firm, which attempts to match qualifications with the needs of an electronic media employer. Sometimes, fees are paid by the employer.

The final method worthy of mention is networking. There is an old adage that it is not what you know but who you know that counts. Relationships should be developed with industry professionals during internships. Most colleges and universities maintain active contact with their electronic media alumni. Of special interest to minority students is Howard University's Annual Communication Job Fair in Washington, DC. Representatives of many of the most important electronic media companies in the United States attend to meet and interview students who are seeking employment.

Job seekers looking for their first full-time position or advancement must convince employers of their skills and potential contributions. To that end, a letter of application must be accompanied by a résumé and, where appropriate, an audiotape or videotape. Tapes are not just for on-the-air positions. They may also demonstrate other skills, such as production, promotion, and copywriting.

There was a time when broadcasters were skeptical of the relevance of a broadcast education, but in this age of fragmented audiences and increased competition, electronic media executives have come to appreciate the need for a formal education in the field. Consequently, it may be beneficial to highlight the management, programming, sales, promotion and marketing, and audience research courses completed in college. Information on related courses and hands-on experience also should be set forth. In some instances, it can be beneficial to list equipment competence, such as with AVID and other digital editing systems. Any experience, skill, or talent possessed by the applicant that eases the transition from school to work for the potential employer should be given special emphasis.

If the ultimate goal is ownership rather than management, the employment search may be conducted somewhat differently. There is no "best way" to go about it, but there are some tips and techniques that are often productive.

First, the market in which the applicant has an interest in ownership must be identified. Note the stations and/or cable systems serving the market. A listing of stations may be compiled from *Broadcasting & Cable Yearbook*, which contains information on station ownership, management, formats, technical facilities, addresses, and telephone numbers.

To evaluate station desirability within a market, ratings and revenue information on each station may be acquired by reviewing the contents of BIA's *Investing in Radio* and *Investing in Television*.[5]

333

After completing this audition process of markets and stations, it is time to address letters or telephone calls to the management at the target stations. If a group owner is preferred over an individual station, the group offices should be contacted.[6] With the expansion of the limits on multiple ownership, group operators account for an increasing percentage of station licensees.

Should there be an interest in cable, *Television and Cable Factbook*[7] provides telephone numbers, addresses, ownership, management, and system information. Data on multiple system operators (MSOs) and cable networks, such as HBO, USA, and CNN, are also included.

There is no right or wrong way to identify and secure employment. However, any approach must begin with facts. The information provided in this section should be adequate to initiate the process.

OWNERSHIP

The second method of entry into the electronic media business is through ownership, which can be accomplished in one of two ways: (1) purchase of an existing facility or (2) construction of a new facility.

PURCHASE OF AN EXISTING FACILITY

In the United States today, there are almost 11,000 commercial radio stations, more than 1,300 commercial television stations, and about 8,900 cable systems, and permits outstanding to build additional radio and television stations.[8] The decision to purchase an existing facility will provide a far greater number of choices in more varied locations than are available when constructing a new facility. Purchase offers the additional advantage of being able to examine the performance record of a facility already operating. The job of financing the purchase of an existing station is substantially less difficult than that of a new build or start-up. The disadvantage of purchasing is that attractive existing operations are in demand.

Through the late 1990s, market demand for existing facilities was especially strong. The market hangover of the late 1980s and early 1990s—caused by the Federal Communication Commission's (FCC) liberal licensing policies of the 1980s, station debt defaults due to exorbitant prices of that decade, and the 1989–1993 recession—came to an end. In addition to the removal of these three negative factors, two positive factors occurred.

The first was the 1996 Telecommunications Act. As noted in Chapter 7, "Broadcast Regulations," it eliminated national ownership limits for radio and increased them for television. The law, implemented by the FCC, also allowed companies or persons to own up to eight radio stations in a single market. The relaxation or, in some instances, elimination of ownership rules occurred in the most favorable economic climate in this country in over a generation, and maybe since the postwar boom of the 1950s. In New York, the stock markets posted double-digit annual growth. Electronic media companies had record sales in the high employment, high consumer-confidence economy. Existing media companies and some new ones were quick to seize the opportunities offered by liberalized ownership rules and a surging stock market and economy.

All this created substantial demand for existing facilities. As a result, cash-flow multiples began to rise again from their 1991 lows. It was noted in Chapter 2, "Financial Management," that cash flow, or the amount of cash generated, determines the value of an electronic media property. Large-market radio multiples ranged from 14 to 20 (i.e., stations were valued at 14 to 20 times their cash flow). In middle markets, the range was 10 to 14 and, in smaller markets, 8 to 10. Television multiples averaged 8 to 8.5. The dollar value of all sales of existing radio and television facilities shot up from the 1992 level of $1 billion.

At the start of the new century, external events altered the momentum generated by the Telecommunications Act and a booming economy. In 2001, the United States was hit by a devastating terrorist attack on September 11 and a receding economy. It was suddenly a new and different country with a new president and new priorities.

The effects on the station trading market are best reflected in the volume of broadcast station transactions. In 2002, sales of radio and television stations totaled $7.9 billion.[9] The following year, the number dropped to $2.7 billion.[10] More than 70 percent of transactions in each year were attributable to radio sales. For the first six months of 2004, sales were estimated at $1.28 billion. A new factor had emerged: the war in Iraq.

In June 2003, the FCC tried to loosen the ownership rules yet again (see Chapter 7, " Broadcast Regulations"). The action was blocked by the courts. However, should the FCC ultimately prevail, we may expect to see renewed stimulation in station trading. With it may come new opportunities for start-up companies as the consolidators are forced to divest some of their holdings. The change of the measurement standard for local radio markets (see Chapter 7) will force some large operators to trim what they have in some markets.

To understand what consolidation has done to existing radio station ownership concentration, see Figure 10.5 for a listing of the top 35 radio groups and their holdings. These numbers have changed almost weekly since the 1996 Telecommunications Act became effective.

The market interest in existing operations also extended to cable systems. Cable rates, as noted in Chapter 8, "Managing the Cable Television System," were reregulated in 1992, and the Telecommunications Act ended cable rate regulation in 1999. Cable systems also sell on multiples of cash flow, typically 11 to 12. However, most are priced on a per-subscriber basis. Prices vary, but the typical system was historically in the range of $2,000 to $2,200 per subscriber. By late 2004, however, per subscriber sales had risen to $3,000.

While the regulatory impact on cable valuation seems to have lessened, now there is the looming Direct Broadcast Satellite (DBS) challenge. Direct Broadcast Satellite is only about 10 years old as an industry. Cable, on the other hand, is more than 50 years old and passes more than 90 percent of the 109 million TV households in the country. Its future revenue and profit growth will have to come from other sources than new subscribers.

The basic consolidation now going on in radio and TV occurred in the cable industry years ago. This activity is best seen in the number of cable systems in the country. Between 1999 and 2004, it declined from 11,500 to fewer

Rank	Owner	No. of Stations
1	Clear Channel	1,204
2	Cumulus	305
3	Citadel	215
4	Infinity	186
5	Entercom	107
6	American Family	105
7	Salem	99
8	EMF	96
9	Saga	83
10	Cox	76
11	Regent	75
12	ABC/Disney	73
13	Univision	72
14	Radio One	67
15	NextMedia	65
16	Entravision	53
17	Multicultural Radio	47
18	Triad	46
19	Beasley Broadcast	44
20	Nassau	44
21	Three Eagles	44
22	Waitt	43
23	Family Stations	41
24	Journal Communications	38
25	New Northwest	37
26	Midwest Communications	36
27	Bonneville	35
28	Susquehanna Radio	34
29	Minnesota Public Radio	34
30	Cherry Creek	32
31	Forever Broadcasting	32
32	Max Media	32
33	MCC Radio	32
34	American General Media	31
35	Quantum	31

336

FIGURE 10.5 Top 35 radio groups by stations. (Source: Patrick Communications. Used with permission.)

than 9,000. The major trading activity tends to be mergers. However, there are still small systems held by companies and individuals.

Finding the Station or System   What is for sale, and how does one locate it? Finding a station or cable system to purchase can be accomplished in two principal ways: (1) through direct contact with the station or system owner and (2) through the use of an intermediary, most often a media broker.

DIRECT CONTACT   One way to initiate direct contact is to select markets that are of interest and then list the stations and cable systems in the markets. Two good sources for these data are *Broadcasting & Cable Yearbook* and *Television and Cable Factbook*. These publications give the ownership of each station or system, which may be an individual, a partnership, a corporation, or a broadcast group. Owners sometimes operate stations, but often they are nonoperating investors.

Owners and managers are very sensitive to sale rumors and inquiries, because these are disruptive and destabilizing. For that reason, inquiry to a station or system owner should be discreet and direct, not through secretaries or other employees. Because of the delicacy of the subject, an owner, even when properly contacted by someone unknown, may not want to confirm the availability of the property for sale. Occasionally, an owner may tell an unknown inquiring party outright that the station is for sale. A more likely answer is, "No, it is not for sale" or, in some cases, "Anything is for sale for the right price."

For these reasons, the direct approach may be time-consuming and, in the end, unproductive. If successful, however, it is probably going to be cheaper than other methods of purchasing a property.

USE OF A MEDIA BROKER   The most efficient and productive search for a property is conducted through the use of a media broker, who generates income by listing stations or systems for sale and then locating qualified buyers for the properties. Brokers are known to media owners and are sympathetic to their concerns about confidentiality. Media brokers compete actively among themselves to obtain listings. For a profile of a media broker, see Figure 10.6.

When obtained, the listings may be *exclusive* or *nonexclusive*. Exclusive means that only one broker has a listing for a designated period, while nonexclusive means that more than one broker has the same listing. The kind of listing may become important to the prospective buyer. For example, a would-be purchaser, who is about to make an offer on a station after expenditure of time and money to investigate, may be shocked to learn that the broker had a nonexclusive listing and that another broker has completed the deal. Accordingly, the broker should be asked exactly what kind of listing it is. For an illustration of an exclusive listing agreement, see Figure 10.7.

As mentioned earlier, brokers are paid for what they do. Fees vary, but a standard fee is 5 percent on the first $3 million or less, 2 percent on the next $7 million, and 1 percent on amounts over $10 million. Fees on very large transactions usually are negotiated and generally are not calculated by this formula. Whatever the fee, it does add to the cost, and the buyer will pay it through a higher price or through a direct agreement to pay some or all of it.

337

Profile of a Media Broker: Patrick Communications

A media broker represents Sellers and Buyers of radio and television stations. A brokerage company may also arrange financing for a transaction and write valuation appraisals of stations needed for tax reasons, estate settlements or the distribution of partnership interests. One leading media broker with more than 350 station sales worth over $3.0 billion in recent years is Patrick Communications.

The Patrick firm is based in suburban Maryland between Washington, D.C. and Baltimore, Maryland. The company has four media brokers and four support personnel. This is a typical size of many media brokerage companies. In fact, some brokers work alone and operate from home offices. Patrick Communications has been in business for over 20 years but began focusing on media brokerage exclusively in the early 1990's.

Like most brokers, the Patrick brokers prefer to represent Sellers of stations. That way they control the sale process and will be paid regardless of who buys the station. The goal is to create a private auction atmosphere among multiple Buyers for a station or group. That tends of drive up the price of the property. Transaction size for the firm ranges from deals under $1.0 million to well over $100.0 million. The brokers earn a commission on each sale and are paid by their client when the transaction closes and the new owner takes over the station. These commissions range from five percent on small deals to one percent on the largest deals. In some cases, the client will tack on an incentive bonus for the brokers for achieving a particularly large sale price. The average broker in the Patrick firm will earn $1.0 million or more per year.

Clients come from a network of friends in the industry who consistently use the Patrick brokers, from clients generated through direct mail and telephone solicitation, from call-ins generated by the more than $500,000 in trade press advertising sponsored by the firm each year and by referrals from attorneys, bankers, engineers and others who often suggest that their clients use the Patrick firm to handle a sale. The firm also hosts large suites at the two major industry conventions each year as well as receptions and other industry sponsorships designed to keep its name in front of the owners in the industry. One of the most effective means of doing that is to announce a steady stream of deals–large and small–in the trade press throughout the year.

The principals of Patrick Communications are husband and wife, Larry and Susan Patrick. Larry is a former college professor who has owned 29 stations himself and managed a large radio-television-cable group. He was also formerly Senior Vice President of the National Association of Broadcasters. Larry holds both a Ph.D. in communications and management as well as a law degree. Susan started as a financial analyst and then became a broker. She has more than 20 years of experience. She holds a B.A. in communications and a M.B.A. in finance. Together the Patrick also operate 17 small market radio stations under a different company name, Legend Communications..

The other two brokers are Greg Guy and Summer Marcum. Greg holds a B.A. and M.A. in communications. He started with the firm as an analyst helping prepare materials on stations that the

FIGURE 10.6 Profile of a media broker. (Source: Patrick Communications. Used with permission.)

firm was selling. He quickly learned how to sell stations and today sells 20 or more stations worth tens of millions of dollars every year. The newest broker for the firm is Summer Marcum, a recent college graduate who is doing some of the analyst work but has already begun selling stations in her first year with the firm. She holds a B.A. but is now working on her M.B.A. The support people at the firm handle administrative details, the firm's advertising, travel arrangements and a host of other duties that make things run smoothly.

The keys for any successful media brokerage firm like Patrick Communications is first and foremost a reputation for industry knowledge and contacts as well as a track record of honesty. Brokers jealously guard their reputations and must often negotiate difficult situations between Sellers and Buyers. The broker must remain calm, focused on the objective and treat everyone with respect and fairness. Deals involve people's lives, big money and often opposing views of what a station is worth. Brokers must be superb negotiators who are calm and can find solutions for any problem.

Patrick Communications has achieved a reputation for honesty and success. As a result, the Patrick brokers are often asked to speak to state broadcasting association conventions and other industry events. Many large broadcasting companies will also invite the brokers to attend their annual management meetings to update their management team on the value of stations and what the market for buying and selling stations is currently. Because of their expertise, the brokers are also often requested to testify at trials and arbitration hearings on the value of stations as expert witnesses.

For the brokers at Patrick Communications, work is like playing Monopoly every day for real and with big money. They live to help their clients either realize the value of their properties when they sell or to help them grow their companies through acquisitions. Life as a broker is often hectic with a great deal of travel to stations, constantly balancing ten or more different assignments at one time and the pressure of large dollar transactions. It is a highly rewarding career, both personally and financially, and is ideal for someone with a good analytical mind, great people skills and an ambition to work very hard for the clients.

339

FIGURE 10.6 *Continued.*

Despite the negatives, use of a media broker probably is the best way to proceed in acquiring a station or system. A listing of media brokers can be found in the "Professional Services" section of *Broadcasting & Cable Yearbook* and in the "Brokerage and Financing" section of *Television and Cable Factbook*. Brokers also run ads in trade publications such as *Radio Business Report* and issue press releases and announcements on transactions they have completed or stations they have listed. An example appears in Figure 10.8.

Brokers may be national in scope, such as Media Services Group, Inc. and Blackburn and Company, or regional, like The Exline Company. Some brokers provide more than sales assistance. Patrick Communications, for instance, also offers financing help.

Having identified a broker, the prospective purchaser must choose the method of working with the broker. One way is to register by completing the broker's buyer information form. The data facilitate the matching of the buyer's geographical interest, the type of facility desired (AM, FM, TV, or

January 8, 2002

PERSONAL & CONFIDENTIAL

Mr. Jack Siegal
President
Chagal Communications
501 Santa Monica Boulevard
Suite 301
Santa Monica, California 90401-2430

Re: <u>Engagement Agreement for KFOX-AM, Torrance, CA</u>

Dear Jack:

This letter shall serve to confirm our agreement with regard to Patrick Communications, LLC ("Broker") and the brokerage commission due Broker should Chagal Communications ("Seller") consummate a transaction to sell KFOX-AM, Torrance, California (the "Station") to a Buyer delivered by Broker. The target price for this Station is Thirty Million Dollars ($30,000,000).

This is an exclusive agreement and Broker acknowledges that Seller alone can accept or reject offers at its discretion for the sale of its Station as well as set the terms for the transaction. Seller agrees to provide Broker with all leads or contacts concerning the sale of the Stations. There are no excluded parties to this Engagement Agreement.

All materials provided to Broker by Seller shall remain proprietary and confidential to Seller. In the event of termination of this Agreement, Broker shall return all materials on the Station to Seller without retaining any copies.

This engagement agreement shall remain in effect for one year from the date this letter is executed by Seller. The agreement may be canceled with thirty (30) days written notice from Seller to Broker sent certified mail return receipt requested. In the event of cancellation or expiration of the agreement, Seller agrees to protect Broker for any Buyers produced by

FIGURE 10.7 Exclusive listing agreement. (Source: Patrick Communications. Used with permission.)

cable), and the financial capability with the broker's listings. The buyer will be contacted by the broker as ownership opportunities develop. This procedure enables the broker to preclear the client as a qualified buyer so that immediate action can be taken when an especially good property comes along.

A second way of working with a media broker is to respond to a specific ad about a station or cable system. This amounts to a case-by-case use of a broker's services and does not necessarily lead to the close working relationship that could make one a favored client who is called first on a very special deal.

Mr. Jack Siegal
Chagal Communications
January 8, 2002
Page 2

Broker for consideration by Seller for a period of one (1) year. Upon cancellation or termination, Broker shall provide within 15 days a written list of parties contacted by Broker to Seller and shall be protected as to these parties.

Upon the sale of the Station to a Buyer produced by Broker, Seller agrees to pay Broker a commission of five percent (5%) on the first Three Million Dollars ($3,000,000) of consideration received for the Stations and two percent (2%) on all amounts received above Three Million Dollars ($3,000,000). In the event that the Station sells for Thirty-five Million Dollars ($35,000,000) or more, Broker shall be entitled to a bonus payment of Five Hundred Thousand Dollars ($500,000).

The total consideration for the Station shall include all monies that a Buyer pays to Seller, whether in cash, promissory notes, assumed obligations, covenants not to compete or consulting agreements and also will include any payment made for assets owned by a related party to this transaction but transferred to the Buyer in connection with this sale. Payment is also due whether the purchase is of assets or stock interests. This commission shall be paid in full by cashier's check or wire transfer of first available funds upon the Closing of the transaction, regardless of when the payments are made by the Buyer to the Seller.

In the event that a Buyer shall default and forfeit an escrow deposit, Broker shall be entitled additionally to twenty-five percent (25%) of the forfeited amount in addition to any commission owed from a subsequent sale of the station.

The parties agree that Broker may issue a press release on the day that any transaction is filed with the Federal Communications Commission. No other releases shall be made prior to this date. All other discussions with prospective Buyers shall remain confidential throughout the term of this Agreement.

Broker is an independent contractor under the terms of this Agreement. Seller is not responsible for any federal or state tax withholding on any payments made by Seller to Broker. In the event that Broker is required to pursue legal action to collect any monies due it under the terms of this Agreement, Broker will be entitled to all costs of collection, including reasonable attorney's fees. In the event of a dispute between the Seller and Broker, the parties agree that this Agreement will be governed by the laws of the State of Maryland with venue in Howard County, Maryland.

341

FIGURE 10.7 *Continued.*

The receipt of information on available properties leads to the next stage of the acquisition process—station evaluation.

Station Evaluation   Once the acquisition candidate has been identified, it must be analyzed. Before analyzing the reasonableness of the price, the buyer should review the status of the market and its competition. Finance sources will expect the buyer to be fully versed on these topics. Rarely does a

Mr. Jack Siegal
Chagal Communications
January 8, 2002
Page 3

Both parties, by signing below, acknowledge their authority to execute this Agreement. The parties also agree that this Agreement may be executed in counterpart,

Agreed and Accepted by:

SELLER: **Chagal Communications**

_____   _____
Name: Jack Siegal   Date
Title: President

BROKER: Patrick Communications, LLC

_____   _____
Name: W. Lawrence Patrick   Date
Title: President

342

FIGURE 10.7 *Continued.*

good price cure a bad market. Analyzing the market will be a key element in analyzing price.

ANALYZING MARKET AND COMPETITION   Cash flow and capital appreciation of a station will depend in no small way upon the condition of the market and the number of existing and potential competitors. Market data can be obtained from local chambers of commerce or from BIA's *Investing in Radio* or *Investing in Television*, which provide information on rates, rev-

Cumulus Broadcasting, Inc.
Lew Dickey, Jr., President, Chairman and CEO

has agreed to acquire

A nine station group in Sioux Falls, South Dakota and Rochester, Minnesota

for **$65,000,000 for stock** *from*

Southern Minnesota Broadcasting Company
Greg Gentling, President

PATRICK COMMUNICATIONS
is proud to have served as the broker in this transaction

(410) 740-0250, www.patcomm.com

343

FIGURE 10.8 Media broker's announcement of a completed transaction. (Source: Patrick Communications. Used with permission.)

enues, formats, ratings, facilities, and the market. Statistics to analyze include population, retail sales, and employment trends. Is there explosive growth, stable growth, or no growth? Markets with no upside or, worse yet, with only a downside should only be considered if the price is substantially discounted or if some major economic development is scheduled for the area.

Market size determines the number of national advertising dollars spent in the market. The top-100 markets command more of those dollars than the 100+ markets. Whether or not a market is about to move into or out of the top 100 is a significant valuation consideration.

Retail sales also are important, because they are a reliable predictor of electronic media revenue available in a market. Generally, electronic media dollars equate to .0035 percent of retail sales for radio and between 1 percent and 2 percent of retail sales for television. Comparisons can be made to other markets to evaluate the relative strength of electronic media overall and the vitality of a market's radio and television components. For markets not covered by *Investing in Radio* or *Investing in Television*, prospective buyers can make their own calculations.

If a station already has a high percentage of total revenue available, it may have peaked, which means it may have no upside revenue potential. Another market evaluation benchmark is data on employment. Who are the largest employers and in what businesses are they engaged? The departure or closing of a large employer can depress a market. State governments, insurance companies, universities, and federal facilities are normally stable. Some caution is advised in the case of military bases and defense plants in the post–Cold War period. The Pentagon maintains a base closure list, which should be consulted if the target market has a military installation. Are any major plants about to be constructed or expanded? The market's employment base and stability should be examined.

After checking the vital signs of the market, the prospective buyer should examine the competition. Some markets have too many stations. It is not just the signals licensed to the community, but also those from outside the market that get in, that are competitive factors. Data on competition can be gathered from sources like *Investing in Radio* and *Investing in Television* and from national ratings services, such as Arbitron for radio and Nielsen for television. Determine how much of the audience is attributable to "below the line" or outside-the-market stations. The broker or station owner should provide the ratings service's reports.

Not all the competition information may be readily apparent. In the 1980s, the FCC aggressively authorized new stations in a proceeding known as Docket 80–90[11] and permitted the upgrade of existing stations to new tower heights and power. In still other cases, FCC rules allowed stations licensed to small communities to "move in" to larger ones. Any one of these developments could immediately diminish the attractiveness of a proposed investment.

In a new initiative in 2004, the FCC began to sell FM spectrum to the highest bidder in 288 markets. The auction list should be consulted, since the FCC will conduct follow-on auctions.[12] Communications attorneys stay current on these developments, as do consulting engineers. Analysis of the competitive environment is not complete until the status of potential new or modified signals that might affect the market is known.

Review of competition should not be limited merely to the number of stations. Station comparisons should also be made of power and antenna heights. Selection of a station with inadequate transmission capabilities when compared with the competition might lead to the purchase of a permanent, second-class station. Such purchase errors are difficult, if not impossible, to correct.

The competitive analysis should not be confined to a comparison of technical facilities. A prospective purchaser also should examine competitors' formats. The best discovery would be that a significant format was not being offered in the market at all. The presence of a "niche" opening satisfies an important investment criterion. If, however, there are no obvious format holes, research may reveal that a competitor already in the market with an established format is not executing it well. That may present enough of an opportunity, assuming everything else checks out, to justify going ahead. However, prospective purchasers must remember that the cost of head-to-head competition is always more. Even if success is achieved in such a battle, the return on investment will be less than can be achieved in markets where an open niche exists.

In television acquisition, it is wise to pay attention to network affiliation. Obviously, an affiliate with a strong network may command a better price than one with a weak network. Those stations that have an underperforming network parent have to do more locally to maintain market position. Probably, that will mean higher operating costs for programming, promotion, and personnel, especially news talent. Higher costs mean lower cash flow and lower valuation. Translated, that means the upside may be limited.

Television stations with no affiliation, or independents, are to be left to the sophisticated television investor. With the success of Fox, UPN, and The WB, those remaining true independents will have a very hard time making ends meet.

Assuming that the evaluation of the market and the competition is satisfactory, it is now time to evaluate the price.

ANALYZING PRICE   Stations and cable systems are usually offered for sale at a price rather than on a "best offer" basis. That price can be firm, which means that the seller will not take less, or an asking price, which is negotiable.

The reasonableness of the price must be evaluated. The most common and generally accepted criteria for judging prices are multiples of *cash flow*. Cash flow is a station's operating income before charges for depreciation, interest, amortization, and taxes. Stated another way, it is net revenue minus operating expenses, that is, general and administrative, program, sales, and technical. In some situations, cash flow may be increased by adding back on a pro forma basis certain expenses the current owner has that the new owner will not. Examples are extraordinary legal, telephone, or travel, or even an excessive compensation arrangement. How cash flow is defined is important, because it is the base number from which price computations emanate. Some lenders and investment bankers also use the term *trailing cash flow*, which means simply the cash flow as previously defined for the most recent 12–month period available. This is a different concept from that of calendar year or fiscal year. Trailing cash flow analysis ensures that the financial performance of the station used to determine price will reflect the most current cash flow, along with any positive or negative trends that might be at work.

Once cash flow is determined, multiples are applied to calculate price. As noted earlier in the chapter, the late 1990s through 2002 were marked by a resurgence of station and system trading activity. Multiples paid for radio stations depend on the market size. In larger markets, or those where consolidation trading was under way, the FM multiples range was between 14 and the 20s. In middle markets, the range was between 10 and 14. For smaller markets, the yardsticks were between 8 and 10. AM radio multiples were 1.25 to 1.50 times net cash billing. Normally, they do not involve cash flow. Like FM radio, television multiples are related to cash flow, and they were in the 8 to 8.5 range. Except for AM radio, multiples in the late 1990s were in an upward trend. Multiples in this consolidation age have exceeded the last trading frenzy of the pre-1989 period.

345

Prices paid for cable television systems are commonly calculated on a per-subscriber basis, with current levels in the $3,000 neighborhood per subscriber. As in broadcasting, an alternate method of cable system valuation depends on multiples of cash flow, usually ranging between 11 and 12.

Standard multiples are not absolute, however. Adjustments to the multiple depend on the size of the market and the station's place in it. Small markets do not justify the full multiple, nor do markets with depressed economies. Stations with declining sales and audience do not bring full price. Network affiliate prices have declined because of the erosion of audience shares and concerns about prospects for the future.

There are situations where multiples do not apply at all. A station may have no earnings and, in that instance, a determination has to be made on what a license in that market is worth. Some guidance can be found in calculating the property's probable revenues by applying a multiple to the retail sales. One method applies a multiple to retail sales in the market to derive the electronic media revenue for the market, and then divides that figure by the number of stations in the market. That number yields possible station revenue and provides a basis to predict cash flow. Buying a station with no earnings is an art form and should be reserved for the sophisticated buyer.

Financing   At this point, the prospective buyer has evaluated the market and the station and has decided to make an offer. However, before the offer is submitted, the financing to complete the transaction must be in place. There are numerous sources of financing, depending upon the buyer's circumstances. Among the principal sources are:

- banks
- venture capital
- investment banks
- funds for minority acquisition
- seller financing
- governmental agencies
- nontraditional financing

BANKS   The most traditional source of funds is the commercial bank. Banks have established criteria for lending that must be met. For example, they require the applicant to have some money of their own to invest, which means that a percentage of the purchase price and operating funds required comes from the applicant's own resources. There is no fixed rule, but a minimum of 20 percent is not uncommon. Banks also closely examine the operating statements of the facility to be purchased and will lend a multiple of the operating cash flow for the most recent 12-month period. Midway through the first decade of the new century, banks were using a multiple range between five and six times trailing broadcast cash flow to determine what they will lend. They also want statements of historical financial results and projections of future performance of up to five years. A pro forma balance sheet will also be required.

The multiple will vary depending on the bank and is different for AM, FM, affiliate television, independent television, and cable. The multiple applied by a bank for loan purposes is less than the multiple used to evaluate the price of a station. Most banks have no standard for independent television and AM radio, because they do not view them as desirable lending opportunities. Cable systems command a multiple of seven to eight times trailing cash flow with large banks and are viewed somewhat as utilities. For FM and affiliate television, the multiple now used by most money center banks is five times trailing cash flow.

To illustrate, consider the purchase for $8 million of an FM station cash flowing $800,000 per year, a ten-multiple purchase price. To establish the loan amount, the bank multiplies trailing cash flow ($800,000) by five, resulting in a $4 million loan for the purchase. The down payment and working capital would have to be provided by the buyer. In this example, the equity required would equal 50 percent of the purchase price.

For the first-time buyer without significant personal funds or a substantial partner, bank financing is difficult to achieve. Banks will require experience in the business, as well as equity.

Another limitation with banks is that electronic media lending is an area of specialization, and many do not feel that they have the expertise to evaluate such transactions. Consequently, it may be difficult to find the right bank. Examples of commercial banks active in electronic media lending are Bank One and Bank of America Illinois.[13] Note, however, that large money center banks consider only multimillion dollar, multistation transactions. For small, single-station purchases, banks in local communities likely will be the best source if one can be found that is willing to commit itself. If a station has no profit history, bank financing will not be available without a substantial personal guarantee.

VENTURE CAPITAL   There are venture capital firms that assist and, in effect, become partners with the prospective entrepreneur to acquire a property. Unlike banks, venture capital firms are high-risk lenders. Such companies often will invest in stations or management that have potential but no proven track record.

For example, there may be a station with good facilities that has never made any money. A venture capital firm might take a chance if it becomes convinced that a new format and new management can turn the station around. Most banks would never do a "turn around" without guarantees from investors with substantial capital. Similarly, a venture capital firm might invest with a manager who was successful for an owner but who has not yet been an owner, or who does not have adequate personal capital to become an owner.

Venture capital companies are often called "vulture capital companies." The name is derived from the price one has to pay to become a partner with one of these firms. While the venture capital fund may provide all or part of the necessary financing, the firm usually demands a significant ownership— often a majority position—in the acquired property. These investors will back proven management with capital, with the expectation of making money on increased value over time of that station and any additional stations that may be acquired. In most such arrangements, the buyer will be giving up control of the enterprise to the venture capital firm, and performance will have to satisfy the provider of the funds. Examples of venture capital firms are Alta Communications of Boston and Bain Capital, also of Boston.

INVESTMENT BANKS   Many institutions have been very active in raising funds for the electronic media industry in recent times. Typically, an investment bank will agree to raise funds from public or private sources for a purchase. Their activities may be *guaranteed* or on a *best efforts* basis. Guaranteed means that, on the day it is time to pay for the purchase, the investment banker will be there with the funds. Best efforts means that the firm will attempt to raise the money, but it is not committed to the buyer if it does not.

For their services, investment bankers charge a fee, which is usually a percentage of the money raised. These companies prefer multimillion dollar transactions involving multiple stations and, normally, are not a source for a first-time buyer. Investment bankers are most often employed by small, intermediate, or large companies seeking to grow larger by acquisition or merger. Morgan Stanley and Company in New York is an example.

FUNDS FOR MINORITY ACQUISITION   Government policy has attempted to encourage the development of minority ownership in the electronic media. Consequently, there are specialized financing sources available to minority buyers. Perhaps the most prominent of these is Broadcap, whose offices are located in Washington, DC.

SELLER FINANCING   Sometimes, the seller becomes the financing source. To facilitate a sale or to avoid immediate tax consequences, a seller may extend terms to the buyer. The seller, in effect, becomes the lender and "carries the paper." Seller financing arrangements are attractive, because they might require less equity or down payment than a bank or other source. The seller might also be willing to have the debt bear a fixed rate of interest, as opposed to the floating rate over prime that most commercial banks use. Where this type of financing does occur, the seller takes a collateral position in the assets of the station. However, this interest of the seller in the station means the buyer cannot use the assets to secure any additional borrowing without the seller's permission. Seller financing is a good approach for the first-time buyer. However, due to the consolidation occasioned by the Telecommunications Act of 1996, most deals today are cash or publicly traded stock.

GOVERNMENTAL AGENCIES   Principal in this category is the Small Business Administration (SBA). For qualified applicants, this federal agency will guarantee up to 90 percent of a loan at a commercial participating bank, or it may make a loan directly from its own funds. As a threshold requirement, the applicant must demonstrate in writing rejections by at least two commercial banks. The negative in this case is the time it takes to get such a loan approved. It may be difficult to persuade a seller to wait for an extended period during which there is no guarantee of success. In addition, these are times of reduced circumstances for government spending, and there are concerns about the availability of such fund guarantees and even the future of the SBA.

NON-TRADITIONAL FINANCING   As one of the case studies at the end of the chapter demonstrates, nontraditional financing may be just about anything. For example, taking a second mortgage on property that a prospective station buyer has, or has access to, provides cash for a down payment to be used with seller paper or a bank.

There is more qualified assistance available for prospective purchasers than there was before the dawn of the electronic media deregulation decade in 1979. Most media brokers now provide financing services and can help select a source and assist in the written presentation. Fees are charged for such services, and they vary, depending upon whether the broker secures equity, senior debt, or junior debt. However, media brokers do know where electronic media financing is, and they have a substantial interest in securing it for their clients, since they do not collect the commission for the sale of a property unless the financing for the buyer is complete.

Among the publications available to introduce the novice to financial concepts and methods is BCFM's *Understanding Broadcast and Cable Finance: A Handbook for the Non-Financial Manager.*[14]

Submitting an Offer   With the financing in place, it is now time to formalize the offer, which must be submitted in writing for consideration by the seller. The media broker, if one is being utilized, will prepare a written offer for the prospective buyer to review carefully and sign. This offer most often takes the form of a letter of intent (Figure 10.9). It is wise at this stage to hire an attorney to originate or examine the offer, since it is a legally binding document. Terms and conditions must be clearly written to avoid misunderstanding and even litigation. Attached to the offer should be a check for the deposit. Again, deposit amounts vary, but 5 percent of the total purchase price is the norm. This deposit assures the seller that the buyer is serious and will forfeit the deposit if the buyer does not complete the transaction as agreed. The offer should be written to expire at a certain time—72 hours, for example. This will prevent the seller from shopping the offer in an attempt to get a higher price from another purchaser.

349

The offer may provide for an inspection period (most often 30 days) during which the buyer may examine facilities and financial records. This is called the *due diligence* period. Now, the buyer focuses on the station or system like a laser for the final audition. For an example of the due diligence checklist used by an acquisition company, see Figure 10.10.

If the inspection is unsatisfactory, the buyer may withdraw without penalty. However, with the expiration of the inspection period, all contingencies are removed and the transaction is firm. Risk has now been attached. That is, the buyer must now appear at the closing with funds in hand. Should that not happen, the escrow deposit will be lost. In other words, risk of losing the deposit by failure to close in a timely manner has now attached to the offer.

Letter of Intent, Contract, and Transfer Application
Following acceptance of the letter of intent by the seller, attorneys for both sides set to work on more formal documents. The letter of intent is a recitation of the principal terms and responsibilities of both parties. Major topics in

LEGEND|COMMUNICATIONS

5074 DORSEY HALL DRIVE, SUITE 205
ELLICOTT CITY, MD 21042
(410) 740-0250, (410) 740-7222 FAX

December 13, 2000

Mr. Douglas Olson
Quality Communications, Inc.
First Entertainment Holding Corporation
5495 Marion Street
Denver, Colorado 80216

Re: Purchase of KGWY-FM, Gillette, Wyoming

Dear Doug:

This letter will serve as an Offer Letter concerning Legend Communications of Wyoming, LLC's intent to purchase the assets of KGWY-FM, Gillette, Wyoming, from your company. This offer will be outlined in further detail in a formal Asset Purchase Agreement which will be drafted and delivered to your counsel within 45 days. You agree to provide Legend with all of the requested due diligence materials relating to this sale and purchase within 15 days of the date of acceptance of this agreement.

The purchase price for the assets of the station, excluding the studio and office building and the real estate on which it sits, is as follows:

- A total purchase price of $1,600,000.

- $1,100,000 in cash at closing.

- $500,000 in a five-year consulting agreement paid quarterly to your company in arrears beginning at the end of the first full quarter following the Closing of the transaction.

- This consulting agreement will be backed by both the corporate guaranty of Legend.

- The Seller would retain the cash on hand and accounts receivable of the stations. Legend would collect and remit those accounts receivable to the Seller every 30

FIGURE 10.9 Letter of intent. (Source: Patrick Communications. Used with permission.)

the letter are price, method of payment (which means cash or terms), and assets to be sold. The prorating of expenses is also often covered. This category includes the responsibility for accrued vacation time of employees and adjustments for annual expenses already paid, such as insurance and taxes. Parties must also provide for the payment of the accounts receivable owned by the station. Are they, too, included in the purchase price, or will they be collected by the buyer and remitted to the seller after a period of time, usually 90 days? Often stations have balances of air time owed to clients who

Mr. Douglas Olson
Quality Communications, Inc.
December 13, 2000
Page 2

days for 120 days. The uncollected balances would be returned to Seller for collection at the end of the 120 day period.

- Legend would post $80,000 as an Escrow Deposit concurrent with the execution of the Asset Purchase Agreement with a mutually-acceptable Escrow Agent.

- Legend will have the right to review and accept all leases and contracts between the Seller's station and third parties. Likewise, Legend shall have the right to accept or reject any personal service agreements with employees.

- Seller will warrant that all station asset are in good working condition and will be delivered to Legend in compliance with all Federal Communications Commission standards.

- There shall also be no adverse material change in the business condition, prospects, technical operations or financial performance of the station between the execution of this letter and closing of the transaction.

- Seller will attempt to retain the employees of the station between execution of this letter and the closing of the transaction and will not adjust the compensation, duties or status of any employee without the express, written permission of the Legend.

- All transfer and filing fees would be shared equally by the parties.

- The parties agree that the studio and office building may be purchased separately by Legend or its assigns. The price of the building shall not exceed $300,000 but shall be determined by an appraisal of the property to be conducted by a licensed Wyoming real estate appraiser. The parties agree to negotiate in good faith to establish the final value of this separate real estate purchase.

Seller agrees that for a period of 90 days from its acceptance of this letter that it will not negotiate with, offer for sale or have any discussions concerning the sale of either its assets or stock with any party other than Legend Communications of Wyoming, LLC.

If after delivery of all of the due diligence materials and drafting of the contract, a formal application for transfer of the broadcast license is not submitted to the Federal Communications

FIGURE 10.9 *Continued.*

provided goods or services. As noted earlier, these transactions are known in the industry as trade or barter, and adjustments to the accounts of buyer and seller may be in order here.

The letter of intent is followed by a formal purchase contract, which is a complete legal document that addresses all aspects of the transaction, major and minor. The contract outlines responsibilities, timetables, and place and time of the closing. It provides for everything, from transfer of title to real estate to accrued vacation time of employees, and may even provide a mechanism

Mr. Douglas Olson
Quality Communications, Inc.
December 13, 2000
Page 3

Commission by February 15, 2001, the parties agree that either party can terminate this transaction by delivering a certified letter of termination, return receipt requested, to the other party so long as the delivering party is not in breach of its responsibilities under this agreement.

The parties agree that each will approve any press release that may be issued by either party and will cooperate in the approval of same. The parties also agree to use their best faith efforts to complete this transaction, file an application to transfer the license of KGWY-FM with the Federal Communications Commission in a timely manner and close this transaction.

Each party signing this letter also acknowledges his or her authority to execute this document on behalf of their respective companies. This letter may be executed in counterpart.

Agreed and accepted by:

Seller:

Quality Communications, Inc.

By: Douglas Olson	Date
Title: Vice-President	

Buyer:

Legend Communications of Wyoming, LLC

By: Nicki Williams	Date
Chief Financial Officer	

352

FIGURE 10.9 *Continued.*

for dealing with disputes, such as binding arbitration or mediation. Questions frequently arise over handling of accounts receivable and accounts payable, for example. Once executed, the purchase contract must be filed with the FCC within 30 days.

Subsequent to the filing of the purchase document, a transfer application, FCC Form 314 (Figure 10.11), must be filed with the commission. It requests the FCC to assign the license for the station from the selling to the acquiring entity.

INITIAL DUE DILIGENCE REQUEST LIST

We reserve the right to make additional requests based upon our review of the information provided. It is requested that you furnish all requested information and documents in one transmittal tabbed to correspond to the list below and indicating "none" or "not applicable" where appropriate.

A.   FINANCIAL AND CORPORATE

☐   1.   Any audit, review or compilation reports for the last three years.

☐   2.   Monthly and year-to-date Balance Sheets, Income Statements and Cash Flow Statements, to extent available (for three-year period plus current year-to-date).

☐   3.   Monthly revenues by station, by income type (direct, local agency, national, network, NTR, etc.) for 1999, 2000, 2001 and current year-to-date. Please note accounting method (calendar or broadcast).

☐   4.   Bank statements, deposit slips and bank reconciliations for last two years.

☐   5.   Accounts Receivable Aging (including reconciliations to G/L) December 2000, December 2001, and March/June/September 2002.

☐   6.   Accounts Payable Aging (including reconciliations to G/L) December 2000, December 2001 and September 2002.

☐   7.   General ledgers, 2000 and 2001 and most recently-closed month (9/02).

☐   8.   Y/E payroll register, 2000, 2001 and YTD 2002.

☐   9.   Budgets for 2001 and 2002 in detail.

☐   10.   Bad debts/write-offs detail for last two years and current year-to-date, at minimum.

☐   11.   Barter transactions – revenues, expenses and current balances.

☐   12.   Latest ASCAP and BMI annual reports and monthly statements.

☐   13.   Credit application form and policies.

☐   14.   Summary of capital expenditures during the current YTD and budget for 2002.

☐   15.   Copies of all loan agreements and related documents, including security agreements, notes, pledges, and guaranties for all current loans and loans paid or refinanced within the last three years.

☐   16.   Copies of all organizational and corporate operating documents of the licensee(s) and parents, subsidiaries, and affiliates, including:

- Articles of Incorporation (corporation), Certificate of Co-Partnership (Partnerships), Certificate of Formation (Delaware LLC), or Articles of Organization (Non-Delaware LLC)
- Bylaws, Partnership Agreement, LLC Operating Agreement
- Investors and Buy-Sell Agreements
- Capitalization Summary listing all equity holders, including holders of options or warrants, or securities convertible into equity
- Minute Books
- Stock Transfer Ledger

B.   SALES

☐   1.   Sales projections/pacing reports – latest available.

☐   2.   Market revenue reports, monthly for last two years, if applicable.

☐   3.   National rep agreements.

☐   4.   Billings by customer – 2001 and YTD 2002

☐   5.   Commission rates – direct, agency, national (if any) – on billings or on collections?

☐   6.   Any house accounts?

☐   7.   Summary of significant non-spot revenue for the last calendar year and the current year-to-date.

C.   PROGRAMMING

☐   1.   Ratings information for last three years by key demos by station.

☐   2.   Programming rights agreements, consulting agreements.

353

FIGURE 10.10 Acquisition company due diligence checklist. (Source: Delta Starr Broadcasting, LLC. Used with permission.)

☐	3.	Network affiliations contracts.
☐	4.	Copies of all research done within the last two (2) calendar years and the current year-to-date.

D. EMPLOYEES

☐	1.	Listing of employees: name, position, date of hire, current salary, and bonus arrangements.
☐	2.	Copies of all employment contracts.
☐	3.	Resumes of department heads.
☐	4.	Employee handbook.
☐	5.	Any non-compete agreements with employees?
☐	6.	Employee benefit plans including medical, dental, lift, 401(k), etc.
☐	7.	Please include a summary of health premiums, employee contributions, 401(k) employer match, etc.

E. TAX

☐	1.	Federal, state and local income tax returns for 2000 and 2001.
☐	2.	Any federal or state examinations completed, ongoing or scheduled.
☐	3.	Any issues that have been raised during the course of any audit or examination.
☐	4.	Property tax bills.
☐	5.	Form 941 for 2000 and 2001, and latest Form 941 and state quarterly filings.

F. FIXED ASSETS

☐	1.	Most recent fixed asset listing, and those listed under capitalized leases.
☐	2.	Real estate legal description, existing surveys, existing title insurance policies, appraisals, if any, phase I or phase II environmental reports, for all properties, owned or leased, including tower sites.
☐	3.	Fixed asset amortization methods and remaining life.
☐	4.	Copies of all appraisals, engineering studies and environmental reports conducted during the last three years.
☐	5.	For all broadcast towers, whether owned or leased, all engineering reports, tower stress studies, FAA reports and communications and any engineering studies relating to tower coordinates or broadcast performance.

G. CONTRACTS

☐	1.	All contracts and leases not listed elsewhere, including any broadcast tower tenants.
☐	2.	Insurance agreements, premiums and binders.

H. OTHER

☐	1.	Any litigation or administrative proceedings that are open, threatened, or have occurred in last two years.
☐	2.	FCC licenses – provide copy.
☐	3.	Summary of all copyrights, trademark and trade name registrations under federal or state law.
☐	4.	Copies of coverage maps for the stations showing both daytime and nighttime signals, if different.

FIGURE 10.10 *Continued.*

The FCC or, to be specific, the FCC's Media Bureau, may not act on the transfer application until 30 days after it has been accepted for filing. In the intervening period, notices of the impending transaction are run on the air of the station and in the local newspaper. The purpose of this public notice is to give members of the community an opportunity to comment on the proposed transaction. Assuming no objections, and assuming the seller is in good standing with the FCC, the transfer will be approved.

Federal Communications Commission
Washington, D. C. 20554

Approved by OMB
3060-0031

FOR
FCC
USE
ONLY

FCC 314

**APPLICATION FOR CONSENT TO
ASSIGNMENT OF BROADCAST STATION
CONSTRUCTION PERMIT OR LICENSE**

FOR COMMISSION USE ONLY
FILE NO.

Section I - General Information

1. Legal Name of the Licensee/Permittee

   Mailing Address

   City | State or Country (if foreign address) | ZIP Code

   Telephone Number (include area code) | E-Mail Address (if available)

   FCC Registration Number | Call Sign | Facility ID Number

2. Contact Representative (if other than licensee/permittee) | Firm or Company Name

   Mailing Address

   City | State or Country (if foreign address) | ZIP Code

   Telephone Number (include area code) | E-Mail Address (if available)

3. Legal Name of the Assignee

   Mailing Address

   City | State or Country (if foreign address) | ZIP Code

   FCC Registration Number | Telephone Number (include area code) | E-Mail Address (if available)

4. Contact Representative (if other than assignee) | Firm or Company Name

   Mailing Address

   City | State or Country (if foreign address) | ZIP Code

   Telephone Number (include area code) | E-Mail Address (if available)

All previous editions obsolete.

FCC Form 314
September 2004

FIGURE 10.11 Excerpt from FCC Form 314: Application for consent to assignment of broadcast station construction permit or license.

The time required for FCC approval depends upon the volume of transfers pending. Once approved, the FCC transfer order does not become final for 40 days. During that time, the proposed transfer is still susceptible to challenge. However, at this advanced stage, it is only the FCC itself that can initiate the action. For example, information may come to the FCC's attention reflecting on the character of, or on the integrity of, the filing representations made by parties seeking the assignment. Problems rarely occur in this "waiting period," but occasionally they do.

5. If this application has been submitted without a fee, indicate reason for fee exemption (see 47 C.F.R. Section 1.1114):

☐ Governmental Entity   ☐ Noncommercial Educational Licensee/Permittee   ☐ Other _____

6. **Purpose of Application:**

☐ Assignment of license

☐ Assignment of construction permit

☐ Amendment to pending application

File Number of pending application:_____

If an amendment, **submit as an Exhibit** a listing by Section and Question Number of the portions of the pending application that are being revised.

Exhibit No.

7. Were any of the authorizations that are the subject of this application obtained through the Commission's competitive bidding procedures (see 47 C.F.R. Sections 1.2111(a) and 73.5001)?   ☐ Yes ☐ No

If yes, list pertinent authorizations in an Exhibit.

Exhibit No.

8. a. Were any of the authorizations that are the subject of this application obtained through the Commission's point system for reserved channel noncommercial educational stations (see 47 C.F.R. Sections 73.7001 and 73.7003)?   ☐ Yes ☐ No

b. If yes to 8(a), have all such stations operated for at least 4 years with a minimum operating schedule since grant pursuant to the point system?   ☐ Yes ☐ No

If no, list pertinent authorizations in an Exhibit and include in the Exhibit a showing that the transaction is consistent with the holding period requirements of 47 C.F.R. Section 73.7005(a).

Exhibit No.

FCC Form 314 (Page 2)
September 2004

356

FIGURE 10.11 *Continued.*

The procedure for acquisition of a cable system is much the same: offer, deposit, letter of intent, and contract. However, notification to, and approval by, the regulatory body is another matter. There is no central federal regulatory body for licenses of cable as there is for broadcast. Cable franchising, or licensing, authority has been specifically reserved for local governments by federal law.

Even though franchising has been left to local governments, the federal government may still impose franchise requirements. The Cable Television

Consumer Protection and Competition Act of 1992, for instance, requires that once an existing system is acquired in a purchase, it must be held by the purchaser for three years before it can be sold again.[15]

Most often, franchising authorities are cities, but some states have cable commissions. Consequently, each cable system has its own licensing authority, which, in turn, has its own procedures. It is impossible to generalize such requirements, except to say that most franchise agreements have some language about notification of a sale to the governmental body. The proposed buyer must obtain competent advice on the local procedures and comply with them.

The parties now meet a final time for the closing. Documents are signed and funds transferred. The seller goes to Bermuda, and the buyer goes to work.

CONSTRUCTION OF A NEW FACILITY

As an alternative to acquisition, entry into electronic media ownership may be achieved by construction of a new facility, or a start-up. Of the two possible means of ownership entry, this alternative is cheaper, riskier, and more difficult to finance. New builds also limit the range of choices as to the type of station and location. However, on the plus side, the entrepreneur is not paying an excessive price based upon the goodwill of an existing station.

357

Locating a Frequency or Franchise   To build a facility, one must first identify an open, or vacant, frequency or franchise. The procedure varies.

AM   In broadcast AM, the FCC does not assign frequencies to designated geographical areas. Instead, the prospective applicant must conduct a frequency search to identify what is available where, and when such an application may be filed. Most people are not in a position to do this unassisted, and the services of a consulting engineer must be obtained. Information on these consultants can be found in the "Technical Consultants" section of *Broadcasting & Cable Yearbook*. It is wise to obtain several quotes from these specialty firms on the cost of conducting a search.

FM   In the case of FM, there is information readily available on what frequencies are available and where. The FCC regularly updates this information, and it can be obtained from the agency directly. It may also be available through attorneys who specialize in FCC practice. Such data identify the frequency, power, and location. It had been FCC practice to set filing dates, known as *windows*, so that applicants could apply for new FM allocations. When there were multiple applicants for open frequencies, the commission employed comparative criteria to determine the best-qualified applicant. That process occasioned delay, expense, and litigation.

In 2004, the process was replaced by a simple auction to the highest bidder. The first auction of 288 FM frequencies was in November 2004 and the FCC was gathering additional FM frequencies for follow-on auctions (Figure 10.12).

The new process will expedite the new-build ownership option, but will favor those with ready resources. The FCC's comparative process favored those who had no other broadcast interests. It was perfect for first-time owners or minority applicants.

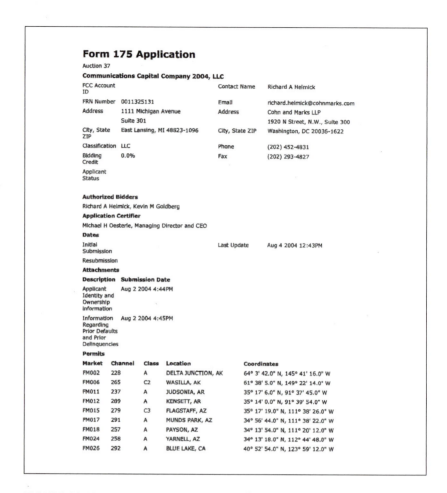

FIGURE 10.12 FCC Form 175 auction application. (Source: Communications Capital Company 2004, LLC. Used with permission.)

In its absence, those with ownership aspirations but without deep pockets might consider application for the low-power FM commercial stations as an alternative (see Chapter 9, "Public Broadcast Station Management").

TELEVISION   New television allocations are made by the FCC from time to time. However, as noted, all vacant broadcast spectrum available for licensing today is awarded by auction.

At some point, there will be a TV spectrum sale of analog channels being vacated by existing TV licensees. But the FCC has indicated that some, or all, of that retired spectrum may be reallocated to a use other than television.

CABLE   Cable systems are licensed by local governmental bodies, most often cities or counties, and such licenses are called franchises. In the case of a new service, the body usually authorizes the proposed new cable service by an ordinance that outlines the specifications an applicant will have to include in a proposal. Local governments have not been bashful in setting out their service and financial requirements. The list of items to be supplied spans the spectrum from local access channels to mandatory support of city services or donation of facilities. Inordinate franchising demands in no small way prompted passage of the Cable Communications Policy Act of 1984 and the prohibition on the award of exclusive franchises contained in the Cable Television Consumer Protection and Competition Act of 1992.[16] Following the ordinance, the local body will request proposals from interested parties. These proposal requests are called RFPs (requests for proposals). Existence of these new service opportunities can be found by reading cable trade publications, through cable brokers such as Communications Equity Associates, or by a review of legal notices in papers of general circulation in communities in which there is an interest. There are, of course, other methods. A call to a state cable television association, for example, may uncover a new-build opportunity.

New Service: Application, Construction, and License

Once the vacancy has been identified, an application must be filed with the appropriate governmental body, the new facility must be constructed, and a license or franchise must be obtained.

359

BROADCAST   For broadcasting, the procedure is to file an application with the FCC on FCC Form 301 (Figure 10.13). Note that the form is entitled Application for Construction Permit for Commercial Broadcast Station. This means that the prospective applicant must be qualified for, and receive, a construction permit prior to the issuance of a license for the proposed facility. Assistance of counsel in preparing this application is desirable, but not essential. Most successful applicants do use communications attorneys, a list of whom can be found in the "Professional Services" section of *Broadcasting & Cable Yearbook*. Many of these attorneys are located in Washington, DC, where the FCC has its offices.

The applicant must satisfy certain basic qualification requirements. Among these are legal, technical, financial, and character rules, as set out in the Communications Act of 1934.[17] For example, the act precludes ownership of licenses by aliens or persons who have had a previous license revoked for antitrust violations. In addition, the proposed new service must not interfere with any existing service. This means that the applicant must affix an engineering exhibit identifying the tower site, height, power, and coverage area. The assistance of a consulting engineer is normally required to prepare the exhibit. The height and location of the tower may necessitate the filing of an application with the Federal Aviation Administration (FAA). The consulting engineer who prepares the engineering exhibit will be able to advise how to satisfy this requirement.

The applicant must also demonstrate the financial ability to complete the project. This requires a showing that the prospective licensee can construct the station and operate for three months without any revenue.

The final area of examination is character. The FCC looks at three main character questions: (1) Has the prospective applicant engaged in conduct that violated the 1934 act or FCC rules? (2) Has the applicant been guilty of

Federal Communications Commission
Washington, D. C. 20554

Approved by OMB
3060-0027

FOR FCC USE ONLY

FCC 301

APPLICATION FOR CONSTRUCTION PERMIT FOR COMMERCIAL BROADCAST STATION

FOR COMMISSION USE ONLY
FILE NO.

Section I - General Information

1. Legal Name of the Applicant

Mailing Address			
City		State or Country (if foreign address)	ZIP Code
Telephone Number (include area code)		E-Mail Address (if available)	
FCC Registration Number	Call Sign	Facility ID Number	

2. Contact Representative (if other than applicant) | Firm or Company Name

Mailing Address		
City	State or Country (if foreign address)	ZIP Code
Telephone Number (include area code)	E-Mail Address (if available)	

3. If this application has been submitted without a fee, indicate reason for fee exemption (see 47 C.F.R. Section 1.1114):

☐ Governmental Entity ☐ Other ____________

4. **Application Purpose.**

☐ New station ☐ Major Modification of construction permit
☐ Major Change in licensed facility ☐ Minor Modification of construction permit
☐ Minor Change in licensed facility ☐ Major Amendment to pending application
☐ Minor Amendment to pending application

a. File number of original construction permit: ____________ ☐ N/A

b. Service Type: ☐ AM ☐ FM ☐ TV ☐ DTV

c. Community of License: City | State

d. Facility Type: ☐ Main ☐ Auxiliary

If an amendment, **submit as an Exhibit** a listing by Section and Question Number of the portions of the pending application that are being revised. Exhibit No.

FCC Form 301
September 2004

FIGURE 10.13 Excerpt from FCC Form 301: application for construction permit for commercial broadcast station.

misrepresentation or lack of candor before the FCC? (3) Has the applicant aired fraudulent programming? The FCC has broadened its character review to include certain applicant felony and misdemeanor convictions that are not broadcast-related. Drug convictions are a specific problem. All of these threshold basic qualifications must be satisfied.

When complete, the application is filed with the Media Bureau of the FCC. If the licensing requirements of the 1934 act have been met, the FCC issues a

NOTE: In addition to the information called for in this section, an explanatory exhibit providing full particulars must be submitted for each question for which a "No" response is provided.

Section II - Legal

1. **Certification.** Applicant certifies that it has answered each question in this application ☐ Yes ☐ No based on its review of the application instructions and worksheets. Applicant further certifies that where it has made an affirmative certification below, this certification constitutes its representation that the application satisfies each of the pertinent standards and criteria set forth in the application instructions and worksheets.

2. **Parties to the Application.**

   a. List the applicant, and, if other than a natural person, its officers, directors, stockholders and other entities with attributable interests, non-insulated partners and/or members. If a corporation or partnership holds an attributable interest in the applicant, list separately its officers, directors, stockholders and other entities with attributable interests, non-insulated partners and/or members. Create a separate row for each individual or entity. Attach additional pages if necessary.

   (1) Name and address of the applicant and each party to the application holding an attributable interest (if other than individual also show name, address and citizenship of natural person authorized to vote the stock or holding the attributable interest). List the applicant first, officers next, then directors and, thereafter, remaining stockholders and other entities with attributable interests, and partners.

   (2) Citizenship.
   (3) Positional Interest: Officer, director, general partner, limited partner, LLC member, investor/creditor attributable under the Commission's **equity/debt plus** standard, etc.
   (4) Percentage of votes.
   (5) Percentage of total assets (equity plus debt).

(1)	(2)	(3)	(4)	(5)

   b. Applicant certifies that equity and financial interests not set forth above are non-attributable.   ☐ Yes ☐ No   [See Explanation in Exhibit No.]   ☐ N/A   Exhibit No. ☐ N/A

3. **Other Authorizations.** List call signs, locations, and facility identifiers of all other broadcast stations in which applicant or any party to the application has an attributable interest.

4. **Multiple Ownership.**

   a. Is the applicant or any party to the application the holder of an attributable radio joint sales agreement or an attributable radio or television time brokerage agreement in the same market as the station subject to this application?   ☐ Yes ☐ No

   If "YES," radio applicants must submit as an Exhibit a copy of each such agreement for radio stations.   Exhibit No.

FCC Form 301 (Page 2)
September 2004

FIGURE 10.13 *Continued.*

construction permit, known as a CP. The new station then must be constructed within a designated period or the permit will lapse at the end of three years.

With the issuance of the construction permit and the construction of the station, the process is almost over. Once constructed, the new facility is tested to determine conformity with the technical outlines set forth in the applicant's FCC Form 301. Assuming the results are positive, the applicant now files an FCC Form 302 to obtain the license.

CABLE   The procedure for processing a cable application requires that the franchise proposals be submitted by a certain date. Multiple applications are compared for conformity with the bid requirements in the RFP. Additional consideration might be the extent of local ownership and the expertise and financial capability of each applicant. Public hearings may or may not be required. Legal appeals by dissatisfied applicants are possible, but at some point the franchise will be granted and construction will begin. Often the franchise grant contains specific requirements as to what parts of the system will be built when.

A final note on cable is necessary. It is a capital-intensive business. Everything, from the headend or origination source to miles of cable, is very costly. It is significantly more difficult to construct a new cable system than a new broadcast station. Coupled with the frontend capital costs is the likelihood that it will be years before revenue exceeds cost and debt service. Usually, it takes six years to break even on a cable start-up. For this reason, cable construction often falls to large companies already in the business that have adequate capital and that can realize the tax benefits accruing from interest and depreciation.

This is not an enterprise to be embarked upon with anything less than full knowledge and substantial funding. However, the financial markets tend to view cable very favorably, which enhances the prospects of successfully undertaking the new system project.

As discussed earlier, this construction alternative for ownership entry is generally much cheaper than the purchase of an existing property, even with the new FM auction rules.

WHAT'S AHEAD?

As a consequence of the station consolidation that followed the Telecommunications Act of 1996, the number of individual owners declined. So, too, did the number of opportunities for individuals with ownership aspirations. However, as noted earlier in the chapter, application of some of the FCC's June 2003 ownership rule changes and revision of market definition might actually stimulate new ownership opportunities.

For today's student, the road to ownership will be more difficult than in the past, but not impossible. The markets and the quality of available stations may not be as good as in the pre-1996 period. And financing for the single owner may be harder to obtain.

The best opportunities may now arise through competing for new allocations that the FCC will authorize or auction from time to time. However, even here there is a new reality. Competing applications will be decided by auction. Again, that puts an emphasis on financial resources.

Financing will depend on demonstrated success in earlier employment. Management experience and professional and financial acumen will be even more important than in past years.

There will still be ownership opportunities, institutions willing to finance, and even sellers willing to take seller paper. But it will be different from earlier years. And the reduced number of opportunities will go only to those who have demonstrated their command of the ownership prerequisites.

SUMMARY

Entry into the electronic media business can be achieved either by employment or ownership. Since experience may be required to secure financing to own, employment is often the first step. It is a necessary first step for those who aspire to management.

Typically, initial employment is in an entry-level position in a station or cable system. Small markets provide the greatest number of openings and offer opportunities to develop a depth of knowledge and breadth of experience. Advancement comes as a result of promotion within a station, system, or group, or through a move to another station or market. Job vacancies may be identified through trade and association publications. Clearinghouses and specialized employment firms also are used to locate positions.

Ownership is accomplished through buying or building. The purchase of a property begins with the identification of stations or systems for sale. This can be done directly or indirectly through a media broker. Once identified, the purchase candidate must be evaluated as to market, competition, and price. Price evaluation begins with standard multiples.

Prior to making an offer, the prospective purchaser must have a financing commitment to complete the transaction. There are seven traditional financing sources from which to select, depending upon circumstances: banks, venture capital, investment banks, funds for minority acquisition, seller financing, and governmental agencies, and nontraditional financing. Once the offer is accepted by the seller, contracts are prepared, and an application to transfer the license or franchise is made to the appropriate governmental authority. Subsequent to transfer approval, the transaction is completed when the buyer pays the seller.

Construction of a new station or cable system is an alternative to purchase. Information on available frequencies or franchises can be obtained in a variety of ways and may require the services of a consulting engineer. Once the opportunity has been located, application for the new service will have to be made to the FCC for broadcast or to the local governmental authority for cable. In some cases, the process will involve a spectrum auction. Once the application evaluation has been completed, the appropriate body will issue a construction permit or franchise. At this point, construction commences, and it must be completed in a timely manner. In broadcast, the licensing follows completion of construction and operational tests. A cable franchise precedes construction.

Construction of a new facility is a riskier venture than the purchase of an existing operation, though it is also less expensive.

363

CASE STUDY: ACQUISITION— NON-TRADITIONAL FINANCING

Penny Wise, a recent graduate in broadcast management, desperately wants to own her own radio station. Her problem is that she comes from humble origins. That means she has no money. Because she has bills to pay, including student loans, she takes a job as an assistant account executive at a large advertising agency in Chicago.

While it is a rewarding and much sought-after job, Penny continues to dream of owning a station. She calls brokers and station owners ad nauseam, but there is nothing in her price range, about $75.00.

Almost ready to give up, she hits on a plan. She convinces her parents to lend her $10,000 for the down payment on a run-down house in a fairly nice neighborhood. The seller takes back a note for the rest of the purchase price. Her parents are delighted because their daughter is finally settling down.

Little did they know about Penny's plan. She promptly began work on her fixer-upper. She ripped out carpets, finding hardwood floors underneath, which she refinished. She painted and redecorated. Almost everything she did was cosmetic. But the result was impressive. The house appraised for $75,000 more than the purchase price. She immediately took out a second mortgage for $75,000, which she banked as a down payment on the radio station.

Still, this is insufficient. She approaches one of her parents' wealthy friends and offers her the following opportunity: for a $100,000 investment, Penny will give her a note at 10 percent, plus 25 percent ownership of the profits of the station she buys.

This is not quite enough of an economic incentive to her angel investor. So Penny offers to sell her the prospective station's equipment and to have the station lease it back. This sale-leaseback will have no net cash consequence to the station, but will provide tax advantages to the angel in the form of depreciation deductions and investment tax credits.

Armed with $175,000 cash, Penny finds a decrepit AM/FM 20 miles from Lansing, Michigan, which she buys for $320,000. She puts $80,000 down. The remaining $240,000 is a note to the seller. The balance of Penny's available cash, $95,000, is dedicated to working capital and equipment.

Penny runs out of working capital. She cannot make the station profitable as quickly as she planned, but she increases the limits on her credit cards and uses the cash to meet payroll.

Then, she obtains a construction permit from the FCC to move the FM closer to Lansing. Since the proposed coverage blankets most of Lansing, a bank lends her the money to build a new facility, which she does.

She operates the FM in a niche format, taking audience from one of the market's group owners. Two years later, the group owner purchases Penny's FM station for $1.4 million.

EXERCISES

1. Name three types of financing used by Penny in her radio acquisition.

2. What percentage of the total purchase price was her down payment? According to market standards, was it adequate?

3. What form did Penny have to file with the FCC to obtain her construction permit?

4. How long did Penny have to build the upgrade once the construction permit was issued?

5. What form did Penny have to file with the FCC to transfer the license from the seller to her?

CASE STUDY: NEW BUILD

Penny had a classmate at Radio-TV University (RTU), whose name was Cash Galore. Ms. Galore, who hailed from Japan, also had a yen to own an FM station. Cash can buy the best ratings and profits available in any major market, which is where she wants to be.

You are a yesteryear graduate of RTU and now are a broker and investment adviser for aspiring broadcast owners like Cash.

365

EXERCISES

1. To satisfy her desire to become a stand-alone media mogul in a major metropolitan American city, what two principal ownership options can you advise the Japanese expatriate to consider?

2. What initial steps should Cash initiate to get either option under way?

3. Discuss the major advantages and disadvantages of each.

4. Ms. Galore may have a problem in achieving her goal and no amount of money can cure it. What is it?

NOTES

[1] National Association of Broadcasters, 1771 N Street, N.W., Washington, DC 20036, http://www.nab.org.

[2] Radio-Television News Directors Association, 1600 K Street, N.W., Suite 700, Washington, DC 20006, http://www.rtnda.org.

[3] http://www.MediaRecruiter.com.

[4] *Broadcasting & Cable Yearbook.* New Providence, NJ: R. R. Bowker.

[5] *BIA Financial Network*, 15120 Enterprise Court, Chantilly, VA 20151-1217, http://www.BIA.com.

[6] Relevant information may be found in *Broadcasting & Cable Yearbook.*

7 *Television and Cable Factbook.* Washington, DC: Warren Communications News.

8 http://www.nab.org and http://www.ncta.com.

9 "Station Sales Scorecard," *Broadcasting & Cable,* January 12, 2004, p. 50.

10 "Stations Sales Scorecard," *Broadcasting & Cable,* June 28, 2004, p. 51.

11 47 *CFR* 73.202.

12 "Commercial FM Filing Window is July 22–August 6," *Antenna,* Drinker, Biddle & Reath, July 2004, pp. 1, 8.

13 For a more complete listing of financial institutions with electronic media expertise, see the "Professional Services" section of *Broadcasting & Cable Yearbook.*

14 Available from the National Association of Broadcasters.

15 47 *USC* 537.

16 47 *USC* 541.

17 47 *USC* 308(b), 310(b), 313.

ADDITIONAL READINGS

Albarran, Alan B. *Media Economics: Understanding Markets, Industries and Concepts,* 2nd ed. Ames: Iowa State Press, 2002.

Alexander, Alison, James Owers, Rod Carveth, C. Ann Hollifield, and Albert N. Greco (eds.). *Media Economics: Theory and Practice,* 3rd ed. Mahwah, NJ: Lawrence Erlbaum, 2004.

Cable Yellow Pages: The Directory For and About The Cable Industry. Torrance, CA: Teton Media.

Dimmick, John W. *Media Competition and Coexistence: The Theory of the Niche.* Mahwah, NJ: Lawrence Erlbaum, 2003.

Einstein, Mara. *Media Diversity: Economics, Ownership, and the FCC. Mahwah,* NJ: Lawrence Erlbaum, 2004.

Krasnow, Erwin G., J. Geoffrey Bentley, and Robin Martin. *Buying or Building a Broadcast Station in the '90s,* 3rd ed. Washington, DC: National Association of Broadcasters, 1991.

Orlik, Peter B. *Career Perspectives in Electronic Media.* Ames, IA: Blackwell, 2004.

Understanding Broadcast and Cable Finance: A Handbook for the Non-Financial Manager. Northfield, IL: BCFM Press, 1994.

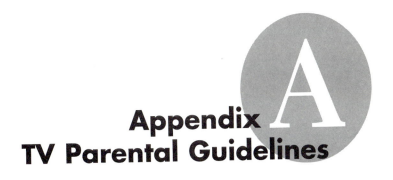

Appendix A
TV Parental Guidelines

TV-Y All Children This program is designed to be appropriate for all children. Whether animated or live-action, the themes and elements in this program are specifically designed for a very young audience, including children from aged 2 to 6. This program is not expected to frighten younger children.

TV-Y7 Directed to Older Children This program is designed for children aged 7 and above. It may be more appropriate for children who have acquired the developmental skills needed to distinguish between make-believe and reality. Themes and elements in this program may include mild fantasy violence or comedic violence, or may frighten children under the age of 7. Therefore, parents may wish to consider the suitability of this program for their very young children.

TV-Y7-FV Directed to Older Children—Fantasy Violence For those programs where fantasy violence may be more intense or more combative than other programs in this category, such programs will be designated TV-Y7-FV.

TV-G General Audience Most parents would find this program suitable for all ages. Although this rating does not signify a program designed specifically for children, most parents may let younger children watch this program unattended. It contains little or no violence, no strong language, and little or no sexual dialogue or situations.

TV-PG Parental Guidance Suggested This program contains material that parents may find unsuitable for younger children. Many parents may want to watch it with their younger children. The theme itself may call for parental guidance and/or the program contains one or more of the following: moderate violence (V), some sexual situations (S), infrequent coarse language (L), or some suggestive dialogue (D).

TV-14 Parents Strongly Cautioned This program contains some material that many parents would find unsuitable for children under 14 years of age. Parents are strongly urged to exercise greater care in monitoring this program and are cautioned against letting children under the age of 14 watch unattended. This program contains one or more of the following: intense violence (V), intense sexual situations (S), strong coarse language (L), or intensely suggestive dialogue (D).

TV-MA Mature Audience Only This program is specifically designed to be viewed by adults and therefore may be unsuitable for children under 17. This program contains one or more of the following: graphic violence (V), explicit sexual activity (S), or crude indecent language (L).

368

Appendix **B**
Excerpt from Membership
Drive Producer's Manual

Source: WWOZ-FM, New Orleans. Used with Permission.

WWOZ 2003 SPRING DRIVE Membership Levels:

$1500	**TIPITINA'S & MID-CITY LANES ROCK'N BOWL YEARLY PASSES (some restrictions) for Four** **ONE** Unlimited Entry New Orleans Jazz & Heritage Festival **BRASS PASS** WWOZ Sunbrella WWOZ Collector's CD #19 WWOZ Membership Card WWOZ Bumper Sticker One Second-Thursday JazzFest Ticket
$1000	**TIPITINA'S & MID-CITY LANES ROCK'N BOWL YEARLY PASSES (some restrictions) for Two** **ONE** Unlimited Entry New Orleans Jazz & Heritage Festival **BRASS PASS** WWOZ Sunbrella WWOZ Collector's CD #19 WWOZ Membership Card WWOZ Bumper Sticker One Second-Thursday JazzFest Ticket
$600	**TWO** Unlimited Entry New Orleans Jazz & Heritage Festival **BRASS PASSES** WWOZ Sunbrellas (TWO) WWOZ Collector's CDs #19 (TWO) WWOZ Membership Cards (TWO) WWOZ Bumper Stickers (TWO) Two Second-Thursday JazzFest Tickets
$450	**WWOZ JAZZFEST OVERPASS** *NEW!*
$300	**ONE** Unlimited Entry New Orleans Jazz & Heritage Festival **BRASS PASS** Your personal pass to all eight days of fairgrounds admission to the JazzFest including access to the exclusive WWOZ Hospitality Tent. Also includes: WWOZ Sunbrella WWOZ Collector's CD #19 WWOZ Membership Card WWOZ Bumper Sticker One Second-Thursday JazzFest Ticket
$125	WWOZ Party Pack WWOZ Collector's CD #19 WWOZ Membership Card WWOZ Bumper Sticker One Second-Thursday JazzFest Ticket
$60	WWOZ Collector's CD #19 WWOZ Membership Card WWOZ Bumper Sticker One Second-Thursday JazzFest Ticket
$40	WWOZ Membership Card WWOZ Bumper Sticker One Second-Thursday JazzFest Ticket

On-Air Checklist for WWOZ Fund Drives

Plan ahead: Immediately following a break, plan the next one. Don't ramble on and have listeners tune out.

A. *Key Point*: What are the reasons for asking for money?
B. *Break Length*: How long will the break be? Don't go over 7 minutes, preferably shorter. Spread information over your show.
C. *Business*: What business needs tending to? Goals, matching pledges, signing-up new donors, accurate recording of information on forms, etc.

Wear Headphones: Watch your voice levels

A. *Be Heard*: Speaking off mike or yelling from across the room does not work. If you have a guest make sure their mike is turned on and monitor the levels closely!
B. *Talk one at a time*: Be careful not to speak at the same time. Trying to say the phone numbers in unison does not work. It's hard for the listener to understand.

Watch what you say
A. *Keep Pledge Information Confidential*: Don't reveal the amount of the pledge, address or other personal info. over the air! **You may say their name *only* if they give permission.** (this is an FCC rule). You may mention the amount of the pledge only if no name is associated with the announcement. Let listeners know periodically that you won't mention their name on the air if they don't want.
B. *Delete "We need" from your vocabulary* (except when listing things we actually need: see section on "What Their Contributions Do"): It's not about what we need. It's about what *they need and want*. Our listeners love to listen to this station and we provide a service to them.
C. *Say phone numbers last*: Listeners will remember the very last thing they heard the easiest.
Say #s often and <u>Always</u> end your break with "

Call 504-568-1234
Other hints:
Come prepared, plan ahead and practice. Spend some time writing down the reasons you care about the station (see also "What Their Contributions Do").

Pay attention to the log and be sure to play all underwriting and other announcements on time. There are very few during the drive so it will be easy to work them in.

Map out what the main message will be, what business needs to be taken care of, who will say what and how long the break will be before your show begins.
Roughly plan the timing of your pitching for the entire program.
Keep pitches focused on one idea or concept. If you give too much information you will confuse the listener. **Long stories or lectures are a bore.**

To keep listeners attentive, avoid one person talking for too long, if you have two people in the studio, take turns giving information to the listeners or even better yet, converse with them. **Two voices on-air is good,** three is O.K. but four can be too confusing for the listener to follow. **Don't talk over each other**. It is nearly impossible for a listener to understand what is being said when people talk at the same time. Please do not try to say the phone numbers in unison!

HOW TO TIME YOUR PITCHES

Remember that listeners *need to be asked* to give many times (over half need to be asked five or more times), and it is important to vary the length of your pitching. Keep the following in mind:

Length Of Pitch Breaks: Allow your audience to build at the beginning of the program with more programming and less frequent, shorter pitch breaks. As you approach the midpoint of your program, mix in some longer pitch breaks with a little less programming. Towards the end of the program pitching should become more frequent and shorter. This method helps build a sense of urgency near the end. Type of music will also have an effect on your pitching. The longer cuts of Jazz or Blues may require lengthier pitches, while short funk or other cuts can be interspersed with more frequent but shorter pitches.

Topic Of Your Pitches: Pitching mixes two types of messages. Toward the beginning of your program focus on helping your listeners realize that they appreciate our high quality programming and that it's a good idea to contribute to the station. As you progress through your program increase the frequency that you ask your listeners to call with their pledge. The last part of your program should emphasize asking the listener to give now.

How Many Minutes?: Seven or eight minutes of pitching is about the maximum, four or five is better. Be responsive to your audience. If they are calling, you are doing something right. If they are not, something may need to change strategy.

What Doesn't Work: *Guilt, pessimism, lies, whining, begging, apologizing. haranguing, scolding or guilt tripping.*
01. If you come across in a negative way, people will tune out. Threatening, insulting or whining to the listener is not the way to stimulate the spirit of giving.

02. Blackmail doesn't work. It does not work to say you won't play any music until someone pledges. People will call with fake pledges.

03. Refrain from saying "we are going off the air if you don't pledge." **It's not true**.

372

04. **<u>Do not</u>** compare WWOZ to other radio stations directly.
It doesn't matter what others do, it only matters that we do what we do, the best we can.
Do discuss in general terms how radio has become homogenized and how WWOZ is true
radio with all the personality and flavor of New Orleans

OTHER REMINDERS FOR YOUR AUDIENCE

- **Encourage the use of credit cards**. Also encourage them to send or bring their
payment to us sooner rather than later. Both of these save the expense of billing for their
pledge, thus better using their hard-earned contribution.

- Most people listen to radio in small time blocks and may be doing something else at the
same time, so don't be afraid to repeat the essential information. There are always new
people listening.

- Mention that they should ask their personnel department if their company has a
matching gift policy. This can double or triple the value of their contribution.

- **Hold on to your audience**: Let them know what you'll be playing after your
membership message. Promote upcoming shows and special guests!

- Have Fun!

373

Pitch Ideas/Concepts

Spring 2003 Special Note:
<u>Under No Circumstances is anyone to condemn the war or the President</u>
Every message every pitch must come from a positive angle

1. **"Be Radio Active".** Ask the listener to be an "active" listener. Not everyone has the time or the ability to volunteer. Simply by picking up the phone and making that pledge your action makes a difference.

2. **WWOZ is not beholden to any corporation or outside interests** except our supporters. Most of our funding comes directly from our listeners (60%). As such the only interests we are beholden to are our listeners and members. Without them we would not exist.

3. **Every listener who becomes a member of WWOZ not only helps us by giving us their money, but also by giving us their name, and voice.** When WWOZ approaches other funding sources one of the main questions that is asked is "Are we supported by our listeners?" Each individual who joins gives us that much more clout and power.

4. **"Special Moments"** Think about a time when listening to WWOZ has played a special part in your life. Relay that personal experience to the listeners. Ask them to reflect on their WWOZ "Special Moments".

5. **WWOZ as a Resource.** Talk about the services WWOZ provides for it's listeners outside of the music. Community Notebooks, Livewire, Public Service Announcements. Ask the listener to reflect on how many times they have used these services as resources in their lives.

6. **Diversity.** WWOZ is diverse in both its people and in its music. The people who work and volunteer at the station come from all different races, religions, ethnic backgrounds, and walks of life. This is reflected in the diversity of the music we play. Our supporters are equally as diverse. It is in this diversity that we find our strength, and our unique voice.

7. **Jazz.** The Ken Burns Documentary has brought a lot of attention to Jazz since it was released. WWOZ has been dedicated to playing, promoting, and educating people about Jazz for over 20 years. 60% of our programs are Jazz oriented. After all the whoopla has passed with the documentary, **WWOZ continues to be dedicated to playing, preserving and nurturing Jazz.**

8. **Live Music.** WWOZ is your source for live music in New Orleans. List some of the live events WWOZ has broadcast over the years. Let listeners know that we will continue to expand our live coverage in the future. Let listeners know that we have the ability to do these events because their contributions allowed us to purchases our mobile broadcast studio, and all of the technology necessary to do remote broadcasts.

9. **WWOZ is programmed locally.** WWOZ is bucking the trend of homogenized radio. From city to city radio stations sound the same. WWOZ has it's own voice. We don't have play lists and never will. Our hosts decide what will be played.

10. **Internet listeners.** Even though many of our Internet listeners have community or public radio stations in their own towns, they tune in via WWOZ.ORG to hear our broadcast. We are their "voice of New Orleans". Did you know that our web site gets 2 million hits per month? People all over the planet are listening to us.

11. **"The Next guy will do it"** Many people don't bother to pledge because they figure the others will take care of it. If everybody thought this way, radio like WWOZ could not exist. Let people know that we need every listener to raise their voice and support the station.

12. **It's easy.** Pledging to WWOZ is an easy process. We accept credit cards so once you pledge all you have to do is sit back and wait for your membership package. (Turn around is approximately 3-4 weeks).

13. **"If not me...who? If not now...when?"** Ask people to make the commitment to WWOZ. There is no reason to wait. If you plan to pledge do it now. Many times listeners put it off or say they'll do it next week, but then forget or get busy. Go to the phone right now and take the two minutes.

14. **Can't turn the radio off.** Have you ever had the experience of listening to a song that was just so good that you just can't turn the radio off? Have you ever been driving in your car and reach your destination but won't get out because you can't bear to turn the radio off? Have you ever been late because the music is just that good?

15. **Exposing people to new music.** Think of all the musicians and groups that you love that you heard for the first time on OZ. WWOZ exposes you to music you might not ever have heard. How much of your music collection is a direct result of hearing songs or artists for the first time on OZ.

375

16. **WWOZ is dedicated to supporting local music and local musicians.** Think of all the local players you heard for the first time on OZ. WWOZ dedicates 15 hours a week exclusively to New Orleans Music and most programmers play local musicians material. WWOZ has an open door policy. Musicians and members of the art community are always invited to use WWOZ as a resource to promote their projects and gigs on the air.

17. **Free Tickets.** Have you ever won free tickets to go to a musical event? WWOZ gives away thousands of free tickets every year. Chances are you have won a pair. This is just one more reason your membership is such a great value.

18. **WWOZ is always there for you. 24 hrs a day, 365 days a year.** If you need to hear good music we are there for you. When you wake up in the morning till you go to bed at night.

19. **WWOZ provides a voice for the voiceless.** Advertising on traditional media, newspaper, television, commercial radio is very expensive. Most small businesses and organizations can't afford it. WWOZ provides an inexpensive and often free outlet for organizations to get the word out. Non-profits can use our community notebook. Small galleries and arts organizations can use the art line, and small businesses can purchase inexpensive underwriting time. WWOZ is there for those in the community who have no other outlet.

20. **WWOZ helps to keep New Orleans unique cultural traditions alive.** From Mardi gras Indians to Social Aid and Pleasure Clubs' Second Lines. From Brass bands to Creole Patios. From carnival to JazzFest WWOZ brings you everything New Orleans and through the website brings the traditions and culture of the Crescent City to the world.

21. Voted best radio station time and again locally, recognized in Rolling Stone Magazine, the New York Times to name a few. Recipient of the W.C Handy Blues Award. So respected that The Guadalupe Jazz Festival and Cuban Jazz Festival paid to OZ to come and record these outstanding events. Call now do your part to keep this station vibrant.

22. **By becoming a member of WWOZ you are becoming part of a winning team.** OZ is a healthy, thriving, growing organization that has big plans for the future. Talk about the new building and OZ's other goals for the future

23. **Talk about your personal experiences with WWOZ.** Ask the listener to reflect on their own. Bring a phone volunteer up to share there experience.

376

24. **WWOZ is an excellent investment.** OZ does not produce toxic chemicals. We do not pollute the environment. OZ is not political or controversial. You can feel good about your investment in the station. The only thing we manufacture is good music and your contribution helps keep it alive and thriving.

25. **Think back to the first time you heard the station.** Ask the listener to do the same. What was the first song you heard? What was your reaction?

26. **WWOZ is a volunteer powered station.** Over 150 dedicated volunteers make this station tick. All of the programmers volunteer their time and expertise. Volunteers do most of the day-to-day office work. WWOZ has only 10 paid staff; people who donate their time do everything else. The people who are answering the pledge drive phones are volunteers.

27. **Create a contest** – Internet vs. Locals. Jefferson vs. Orleans. etc.

28. **Call out neighborhoods and be specific.** People love to hear their neighborhoods on the radio, i.e. Treme, Marigny, French Quarter, Back o' Town, Irish Channel, Riverbend, Carrolton, Girttown, Jefferson, etc.

29. **WWOZ keeps roots music alive.** Jazz, Blues, R&B, African, Caribbean, Brazilian, Latin, Irish, Cajun, Zydeco. None of these are ever heard on commercial radio. We don't play music because it is popular, we play it because it is vital. We are not for everybody, but if you listen, we are for you.

30. On WWOZ not only do you get entertained with great music, but our **knowledgeable programmers also help to educate our listeners about the music.** Programmers always include interesting facts and information about the lives and music of the musicians heard.

31. **WWOZ is not commercial. OZ is all music all the time.** We only to pledge drives twice a year and even during those times you still hear more music in an hour than you do on most commercial stations. All of the other time is given to music or community info.

32. **Renew the commitment.** Perhaps it's been a couple of years since you last pledged. Perhaps you moved away from New Orleans and now listen on the internet. Now is a good time for you to renew your support for WWOZ and return to the family.

33. **A great way to meet people.** WWOZ makes for excellent conversation. Either as volunteer or as listeners who enjoy OZ at home on their own time.

377

34. **New in Town?** Appeal to people who are new in town and who have just recently discovered the Station. For many folks who come into town, we are an oasis on the dial.

35. **WWOZ is always first to bring you new music.** WWOZ gets new music from the biggest to the most obscure record labels often before the record is commercially available. Our programmers constantly update their collection of new music to keep their presentations fresh.

36. **The Classics.** From John Coltrane to Louis Armstrong. From Muddy Waters to Robert Johnson. From _____ to _____, WWOZ plays the classic artists and classic songs that you want to hear. Of course, we also throw in lots of obscure and rare material you may have never heard.

37. **Requests.** You know how there are some times you just gotta hear that one song you love. WWOZ's request line is always open. You can hear almost anything you need just by calling **568-1234**.

38. WWOZ live recordings have been added to the Library of Congress Archives. You continued support will allow for us to continue to record and preserve the great musical performances for generations to come.

39. With all the changes in the sound media landscape, that is how you hear your music, Internet in your car and satellite radio. Your continued support will keep WWOZ not just for today but able to prepare and be part of the future, bringing the sounds of New Orleans around the world. Call Now

378

Glossary

Acceptable Use Policy (AUP): policy to govern employee use of company computers.

Accounts payable ledger: an account book that reflects amounts owed to the providers of goods and services.

Accounts receivable ledger: an account book that records amounts owed to a broadcast station by its clients or to a cable system by its clients and subscribers.

Administrative management: a managerial approach emphasizing the effectiveness and efficiency of the total organization.

Affiliation contract: an agreement governing the relationship between a network and an affiliated station.

Age Discrimination in Employment Act: legislation that forbids employers with 20 or more employees from discriminating in employment practices against any person 40 years of age or older.

Americans with Disabilities Act: legislation that prohibits employers with 15 or more employees from discriminating in employment practices against qualified individuals with disabilities.

Amortization: the systematic reduction or writing off of an amount over a specific number of time periods, usually years.

Asset: an object, right, or claim that is expected to provide benefits to its owners.

Audience flow: the movement of an audience from one television program to another on the same channel.

Auditorium testing: a radio station research method that seeks reactions to short excerpts from recordings played to several dozen people gathered in a large room or auditorium.

Average quarter-hour (AQH) audience: average number of persons listening or viewing for at least five minutes in a 15-minute period.

Balance sheet: a periodic financial statement that reports a company's assets, liabilities, and net worth.

Barter: a transaction involving the exchange of advertising time for goods or services. Also called a *trade-out.*

Barter-plus-cash programming: a station acquires a syndicated program for a fee and also surrenders to the syndicator some of the commercial inventory.

Barter programming: a syndicator provides a program to a station at no cost, but retains for sale some of the commercial inventory.

Basic cable: the minimum number of cable channels a subscriber may receive for a monthly fee.

Behavioral school of management: a school of management thought that emphasizes employee needs and their role in motivation.

Block programming: scheduling several television programs of similar kind or with similar audience appeal back-to-back. Also called *vertical programming.*

Bonus spots: spots given to an advertiser at no cost as a consideration for buying other spots. Also called *spins.*

Budget: a financial plan showing estimated or planned revenues and expenses.

Bureaucratic management: an approach to management that pays special attention to the structure of the organization and its impact on efficiency.

Call-out research: a radio station research method that seeks reactions to recordings by playing over the telephone short excerpts or "hooks."

Cash disbursements journal: a transaction record of all funds disbursed by a company.

Cash flow: operating income before charges for depreciation, interest, amortization, and taxes.

Cash receipts journal: a transaction record of all funds received by a company from any source.

Checkerboard programming: scheduling a different TV program series in the same time period daily.

Churn: the turnover in cable television subscribers.

Civil Rights Act: legislation that prohibits discrimination in employment practices based on race, color, religion, sex, or national origin.

Classical school of management: a school of management thought that embraces administrative, bureaucratic, and scientific approaches to management.

Community Service Grant (CSG): a grant from the Corporation for Public Broadcasting to public radio and television stations for operating costs and program purchases.

Compact disc (CD): a recording whose content is encoded in digital form and read by a laser beam.

Contingency theory: a management approach that takes into account the particular circumstances in reaching decisions and undertaking actions.

Contract: a formal legal document containing all the terms of a proposed transaction between buyer and seller, and accompanied by exhibits reflecting details of all assets to be conveyed and all liabilities to be assumed.

Co-op advertising: the cost of the retailer's advertising is shared, usually between the retailer and the manufacturer. An abbreviation for *cooperative advertising*.

Core programming: FCC term to describe television programming designed primarily to meet the educational and informational needs of children 16 years old or younger.

Cost-per-rating point (CPP): the cost of a spot divided by the rating for the program or period in which it is broadcast.

Cost-per-thousand (CPM): the cost of reaching 1,000 targeted households or persons with a commercial.

Counter-programming: scheduling a TV program that appeals to a different audience from that sought by the competition in the same time period.

Cume: an abbreviation for *cumulative audience*—an estimate of the number of different households or persons viewing or listening for at least five minutes in a specified period.

Current asset: an asset expected to be sold, used, or converted into cash within one year.

Current liability: amounts, taxes, and commissions payable in the near future, usually within one year.

Current ratio: the relationship of total current assets to total current liabilities.

DAB: digital audio broadcasting.

Debt-equity ratio: the relationship of total long-term liabilities to stockholders' equity.

Depreciation: the systematic reduction in value of long-lived assets due to use or obsolescence.

Designated market area (DMA): Nielsen's term for the geographic area in which television stations in the survey market receive a preponderance of viewing.

Diary: an audience measurement method in which a sample of people record their listening or viewing activity in a small booklet.

381

Digital audio broadcasting (DAB): a technology that broadcasts audio programming in digital form.

Digital television (DTV): use of digital modulation and compression to broadcast video, audio, and data signals to television sets.

Digital video recorder (DVR): records TV content to a hard disk in digital format. Also called a *personal video recorder.*

Direct broadcast satellite (DBS): the transmission of a television signal by satellite to a small receiving dish.

Domain name: an Internet address.

Duopoly: a situation in which two radio stations in the same service (i.e., AM or FM) in the same market are licensed to a single person or entity.

DVD: optical disc that can be used for storing data with high video and sound quality.

EBITDA: earnings before interest, taxes, depreciation, and amortization.

Equal Employment Opportunity Commission (EEOC): the governmental agency that ensures compliance with laws prohibiting discrimination in employment practices.

Equal Pay Act: legislation that prohibits wage discrimination between male and female employees.

Expenses: costs of services and facilities used in the production of current revenue.

Fair Labor Standards Act: legislation that sets forth requirements for minimum wage and overtime compensation.

Family and Medical Leave Act: legislation that requires employers with 50 or more employees to make available to them up to 12 weeks of unpaid leave during any 12-month period for specified family or medical reasons.

Fiber optics: the conversion of electrical signals into light waves sent through glass fibers.

Financial interest and syndication rules: FCC rules that prohibited networks from ownership interest in, and syndication of, their prime-time entertainment programs. The rules were relaxed in the early 1990s to allow for network ownership interest in such programs.

First-run syndication: the sale to television stations or other outlets of programs produced expressly for syndication.

Fixed asset: an asset that will be held or used for a long term, usually more than one year.

Flipping: the use of a remote-control pad to switch from channel to channel within and between television programs.

Focus group: a research method in which a dozen or so people engage in a moderator-led discussion on a question of importance.

Format: a radio station's principal content element or sound.

Format search: a research method to determine if there is a need or place in a market for a radio format or for elements within a format.

Franchise: an agreement between a governmental body and a cable television company setting forth the conditions under which the company may operate.

Frequency: the number of times a home or person is exposed to a program or commercial.

General journal: an account book used to record "other" expenses, such as depreciation, amortization, and interest.

General ledger: the basic accounts book, in two sections: one records figures for assets, liabilities, and capital; the other, income and expense account figures.

Generic promo: a promotional announcement for a program series.

383

Goodwill: the term used to describe the intangible assets of a broadcast station, such as reputation, image in the market, and the value of the license.

Grazing: the continuous scanning of the TV dial with the use of a remote-control pad.

Grid card: reflects fluctuations in advertising rates according to supply and demand.

Gross impressions (GIs): the total number of exposures to a schedule of commercials.

Gross rating points (GRPs): the total of all rating points achieved for a schedule of commercials.

Hammocking: placing a new or untested television program between two popular programs.

Hawthorne Effect: despite a deterioration in working conditions, productivity is likely to increase when managers pay special attention to employees. Takes its name from Western Electric's plant in Hawthorne, IL, where the phenomenon was observed.

Head-to-head programming: a strategy whereby a television station competes directly against another station (or stations) by scheduling a similar program or one with similar audience appeal in the same time period.

Hierarchy of needs: Abraham Maslow's theory that human beings have certain basic needs that are organized in a hierarchy.

High-definition television (HDTV): a television system using more than 1,000 scan lines and an increased width-to-height ratio.

Hook: see *call-out research.*

Horizontal programming: see *strip programming.*

House accounts: accounts that require no selling or servicing and on which no commissions are paid.

Households using television (HUT): the percentage of all television households in a survey area with TV sets in operation at a particular time.

Hygiene factors: Frederick Herzberg's term to describe factors associated with conditions surrounding work, such as salary, benefits, and job security.

Image promotion: an attempt to establish, shift, or solidify public perceptions of a station.

Income statement: a periodic financial statement that reports a company's revenues, expenses, and resulting profit or loss. Also called an *operating statement* or *profit and loss (P and L) statement.*

Information superhighway: a term coined to describe the projected high-capacity networks and information services interconnecting every home and business in the country.

Internet: worldwide network of computer networks; also called *the Net.*

Internet Service Provider (ISP): a company that connects subscribers directly to the Internet. Also called *Internet Access Provider.*

Leased access channel: a cable television channel on which time may be purchased by individuals or groups for the transmission of programs.

Liability: an obligation to pay an amount or perform a service.

Local marketing agreement (LMA): a contractual agreement whereby a radio or a television station sells a block of air time to a third-party programmer, who uses the time to broadcast content, including commercials, over the station. May also be applied to a situation where the licensee sells only its commercial inventory to a third party and retains programming control.

Local origination channel: a cable television channel equipped and maintained by the cable system to provide locally originated programming.

Logo: a distinctive symbol that identifies a station and often incorporates its call letters and frequency or channel number.

Long-term liability: an obligation, such as bank debt, mortgages, and program contracts, to be paid over an extended period of time.

Loss: the excess of expenses over revenue.

Lottery: a contest containing the elements of prize, chance, and consideration.

Lower-level managers: those responsible for overseeing the day-to-day performance of employees.

Low-power television (LPTV): a television station that broadcasts to a limited geographical area, usually about 10 to 15 miles in radius.

Management: the process of planning, organizing, influencing, and controlling to accomplish organizational goals through the coordinated use of human and material resources.

Management by objectives (MBO): a management approach whereby all employees establish objectives designed to assist in the achievement of organizational goals, and the progress toward attaining them is reviewed periodically.

Management science: a school of management thought that uses mathematical models to simulate situations and to project the outcomes of different decisions.

Market perceptual study: a research method to determine target audience perceptions of a station.

Metro area: a geographical area generally corresponding to the metropolitan area defined by the U.S. Government's Office of Management and Budget.

Middle managers: those responsible for the coordination of activities designed to assist the organization in achieving its overall goals.

Motivators: the term coined by Frederick Herzberg to describe factors associated with job content, such as achievement, recognition, and advancement.

Multiple: a number by which the cash flow of a company is multiplied to determine the offering price.

385

Multiple system operator (MSO): a company that operates more than one cable television system.

Must carry: FCC rule providing that television stations may demand carriage on cable systems within their designated market area.

National Telecommunications and Information Administration (NTIA): the White House telecommunications policy office, located within the Department of Commerce.

Net loss: the excess of all expenses, including taxes, over revenue.

Net profit: the excess of revenue over all expenses, including taxes.

Net worth: the owners' equity in a company, reflecting the difference between total assets and total liabilities.

Nontraditional revenue (NTR): revenue from sources other than the sale of airtime.

NSI area: Nielsen's term for a market's metro and designated market area counties, plus other counties necessary to account for approximately 95 percent of the average quarter-hour audience of stations in the market.

Occupational Safety and Health Act: legislation that requires employers to ensure that the workplace is free of hazards that could cause illness, injury, or death.

Occupational Safety and Health Administration (OSHA): the governmental agency that administers the Occupational Safety and Health Act.

Off-network syndication: the sale to stations or other outlets of programs formerly aired on a television network.

Operating expense: the expense of performing normal business activities as opposed to the expense of financing the business.

Operating loss: the excess of operating expenses over revenue.

Operating profit: the excess of revenue over operating expenses, excluding depreciation, amortization, interest, and taxes.

Operating statement: see *income statement.*

Orientation: the process whereby new employees are introduced to other employees and the station.

"Other" expenses: nonoperating cash and noncash costs of a business, usually including depreciation, amortization, and interest.

Pay cable: channels added to basic cable offerings for which an extra subscriber fee is required.

Payola: the practice whereby recording company representatives secretly reward disc jockeys for playing or plugging certain recordings.

Pay-per-view (PPV): cable programming for which the subscriber pays on a per-program or per-event basis.

PEG channel: cable television channel allocated for public, educational, and governmental use.

People meter: electronic metering system used by Nielsen to measure audiences for broadcast and cable networks and nationally distributed barter-syndicated programs.

Per-inquiry advertising: an advertiser pays a commercial rate based on the number of responses generated by the advertising.

Personal video recorder (PVR): see *digital video recorder.*

Piracy: the unauthorized reception of a cable television signal.

Playlist: the list of recordings played by a radio station.

Plugola: the on-air promotion of goods and services in which someone responsible for selecting the material broadcast has a financial interest, without disclosing that fact to the audience.

Policy book: contains the philosophy and policies of a broadcast station and sets forth the responsibilities of individuals and departments.

Pregnancy Discrimination Act: legislation that forbids discrimination in employment practices based on pregnancy, childbirth, or related medical conditions.

Prepaid expense: an expense paid in advance of its occurrence.

Pretax loss: the excess of expenses, including depreciation, amortization, and interest, but excluding taxes, over revenue.

Pretax profit: the excess of revenue over expenses, including depreciation, amortization, and interest, but excluding taxes.

Prime-time access rule (PTAR): discontinued rule generally forbidding network-affiliated television stations in the top-50 markets from airing more than three hours of network or off-network programming between 7:00 P.M. and 11:00 P.M. (ET).

Profit: the excess of revenue over expenses.

Profit and loss (P and L) statement: see *income statement*.

Program promotion: the promotion of a station's content.

Promo: an announcement promoting a station and/or its content. An abbreviation for *promotional announcement*.

Public access channel: a cable television channel for which individual members of the public or groups provide content.

Rating: in television, the percentage of all television households or persons in a survey area viewing a particular station. In radio, the percentage of all persons in a survey area listening to a particular station.

Reach: the number of different homes or persons exposed to a program or commercial.

Request for proposals (RFP): an invitation from a governmental body to submit a proposal for the establishment of a cable television system.

Retransmission consent: legislation that permits a station to waive its "must-carry" right in return for the right to require its consent before a cable system may carry its signal.

Revenue: the inflow of resources to a broadcast or cable business from the sale of time or the provision of services.

Rotation: the frequency with which a recording is played by a radio station.

Sales journal: a transaction record of billings to clients for commercials run over a certain period of time, usually a month.

Saturation schedule: a heavy commercial load aired when targeted homes or persons are tuned in.

Scientific management: a systematic approach to management with an emphasis on productivity.

SDARS: satellite digital audio radio services.

Share (of audience): in television, the percentage of households or persons using television tuned to a particular station. In radio, the percentage of all listeners tuned to a particular station.

Specific promo: a promotional announcement for one program in a series.

Spectrum plan: a moderate number of spots scheduled throughout the day.

Spins: see *bonus spots*.

Spot schedule: a series of commercials aired in only one or two periods of the day.

Station rep: a company that represents a radio or television station in the sale of time to national advertisers and advises the station on the purchase, scheduling, and promotion of programs.

Strip programming: scheduling a TV program series at the same time each day, usually Monday through Friday. Also called *horizontal programming*.

Superduopoly: a situation in which three or more radio stations in the same service (i.e., AM or FM) and in the same market are licensed to the same person or entity.

Syndicated program exclusivity rule (syndex): a rule protecting a local television station's syndicated programs against duplication from signals imported by a cable television system.

Syndicators: companies that sell programs or features to radio and television stations and other outlets.

Systems theory: a management approach that views an organization as a system of parts related to each other and to the external environment.

Telco: an abbreviation for a telephone company.

Television network: the FCC defines it as an entity providing more than fifteen hours per week of prime-time entertainment programming to interconnected affiliates on a regular basis. Such programming must reach at least 75 percent of the nation's television households.

Theory X: a philosophy of human nature, advanced by Douglas McGregor, suggesting that managers must coerce, control, and even threaten to motivate employees.

Theory Y: a philosophy of human nature, advanced by Douglas McGregor, suggesting that employees are capable of accepting responsibility and exercising self-direction.

Tier: a level of service offered by a cable television company.

Time spent listening (TSL): the time a person listens to a radio station during a specific period of the day.

Top managers: those who coordinate an organization's activities and provide its overall direction.

Total quality management (TQM): a management approach that focuses on the customer and emphasizes quality in everything the organization undertakes.

Trade-out: see *barter.*

Trailing cash flow: a company's cash flow for the most recent 12-month period, which may or may not correspond with the fiscal year.

Underwriting: the provision of funds by businesses for the production and airing of programs on public radio and television stations in exchange for announcements in the programs.

Union contract: an agreement governing relations between an employer and unionized employees.

Vendor support program: a method whereby a retailer obtains manufacturer dollars to cover advertising costs.

Venture capital: financing in which the company providing the funds receives an ownership interest in the facility to be acquired, as well as interest on the funds advanced.

Vertical programming: see *block programming.*

Webcasting: carriage of a station's signal on the World Wide Web.

Web page: units of information on one or more computer screens, often with links to other pages or graphics.

389

Web site: location of a computer called a server that contains the home pages for a company.

World Wide Web (WWW): a portion of the Internet formatted with hypertext links.

Zapping: using a remote-control pad to change TV channels to avoid commercials.

Zipping: the fast-forwarding of videocassette recorders through commercials in recorded programs.

Bibliography

The first part of the bibliography lists works cited in the text and others that a student of electronic media management may find useful. The second part consists of selected periodicals.

WORKS CONSULTED

Accounting Manual for Radio Stations. Washington, DC: National Association of Broadcasters, 1981.

Albarran, Alan B. *Media Economics: Understanding Markets, Industries and Concepts,* 2nd ed. Ames: Iowa State Press, 2002.

Albarran, Alan B., and Angel Arrese (eds.). *Time and Media Markets.* Mahwah, NJ: Lawrence Erlbaum, 2003.

Albarran, Alan B., and David H. Goff (eds.). *Understanding the Web: Social, Political, and Economic Dimensions of the Internet.* Ames: Iowa State Press, 2000.

Albarran, Alan B., and Gregory G. Pitts. *The Radio Broadcasting Industry.* Boston: Allyn and Bacon, 2001.

Alexander, Alison, James Owers, Rod Carveth, C. Ann Hollifield, and Albert N. Greco (eds.). *Media Economics: Theory and Practice,* 3rd ed. Mahwah, NJ: Lawrence Erlbaum, 2004.

Bagdikian, Ben H. *The New Media Monopoly, 20th Anniversary Ed.* Boston: Beacon Press, 2004.

Bartlett, Eugene. *Cable Communications: Building the Information Infrastructure.* New York: McGraw-Hill, 1995.

Berkman, Robert I., and Christopher A. Shumway. *Digital Dilemmas: Ethical Issues for Online Media Professionals*. Ames, IA: Blackwell, 2003.

BIB Television Programming Source Books. Philadelphia: North American Publishing, published annually.

Bobeck, Ann. *Casinos, Lotteries & Contests*, 2nd ed. Washington, DC: National Association of Broadcasters, 2003.

Book, Constance Ledoux. *Digital Television: DTV and the Consumer*. Ames, IA: Blackwell, 2004.

Brady, Frank R., and J. Angel Vasquez. *Direct Response Television: The Authoritative Guide*. Lincolnwood, IL: NTC Publishing Group, 1995.

Brinkley, Joel. *Defining Vision: The Battle for the Future of Television*. New York: Harcourt Brace, 1997.

Broadcast Accounting Guidelines. Northfield, IL: Broadcast Cable Financial Management Association, 1996.

Broadcasting & Cable Yearbook. New Providence, NJ: R.R. Bowker, published annually.

Brown, James A., and Ward L. Quaal. *Radio-Television-Cable Management*, 3rd ed. New York: McGraw-Hill, 1998.

Buckingham, Marcus, and Curt Coffman. *First, Break All the Rules: What the World's Greatest Managers Do Differently*. New York: Simon and Schuster, 1999.

Cable Yellow Pages: The Directory For and About the Cable Industry. Torrance, CA: Teton Media, published annually.

Carlisle, Howard M. *Management Essentials: Concepts for Productivity and Innovation*, 2nd ed. Chicago: Science Research Associates, 1987.

Carter, T. Barton, Marc A. Franklin, and Jay B. Wright. *The First Amendment and the Fifth Estate: Regulation of Electronic Mass Media*, 3rd ed. Westbury, NY: Foundation Press, 1993.

Certo, Samuel C., and S. Trevis Certo. *Modern Management*, 10th ed. Upper Saddle River, NJ: Prentice Hall, 2005.

Christians, Clifford G., Kim B. Rotzoll, Mark B. Fackler, Kathy Brittain McKee, and Robert H. Woods, Jr. *Media Ethics: Cases and Moral Reasoning*, 7th ed. Boston: Allyn and Bacon, 2005.

Compaine, Benjamin M., and Douglas Gomery. *Who Owns the Media? Competition and Concentration in the Mass Media Industry*, 3rd ed. Mahwah, NJ: Lawrence Erlbaum, 2000.

Covington, William G., Jr. *Creativity in TV & Cable Managing and Producing*. Lanham, MD: University Press of America, 1999.

Covington, William G., Jr. *Systems Theory Applied to Television Station Management: In the Competitive Marketplace*. Lanham, MD: University Press of America, 1997.

Crandall, Robert W., and Harold Furchgott-Roth. *Cable TV: Regulation or Competition?* Washington, DC: Brookings Institution, 1996.

Creech, Kenneth C. *Electronic Media Law and Regulation*, 4th ed. Boston: Focal Press, 2003.

Daft, Richard L. *Management*, 7th ed. Mason, OH: South-Western, 2004.

Davie, William R., and James R. Upshaw. *Principles of Electronic Media.* Boston: Allyn and Bacon, 2003.

Day, Louis A. *Ethics in Media Communications: Cases and Controversies*, 5th ed. Belmont, CA: Thomson Wadsworth, 2006.

The DBS Revolution: Emerging Markets Bring New Competition. Washington, DC: National Association of Broadcasters, 1997.

Dimmick, John W. *Media Competition and Coexistence: The Theory of the Niche.* Mahwah, NJ: Lawrence Erlbaum, 2003.

Ditingo, Vincent M. *The Remaking of Radio.* Boston: Focal Press, 1995.

Drucker, Peter F. *Management Challenges for the 21st Century.* New York: HarperBusiness, 2001.

Drucker, Peter F. *Management: Tasks, Responsibilities, Practices.* New York: Harper and Row, 1974.

Drucker, Peter F. *Managing in a Time of Great Change.* New York: Truman Talley Books/Dutton, 1995.

Drucker, Peter F. *The Practice of Management.* New York: Harper and Row, 1954.

Dupagne, Michel, and Peter B. Seel. *High-Definition Television: A Global Perspective.* Ames: Iowa State University Press, 1998.

Eastman, Susan Tyler (ed.). *Research in Media Promotion.* Mahwah, NJ: Lawrence Erlbaum, 2000.

Eastman, Susan Tyler, and Douglas A. Ferguson. *Media Programming: Strategies and Practices*, 7th ed. Belmont, CA: Thomson Wadsworth, 2005.

Eastman, Susan Tyler, Douglas A. Ferguson, and Robert Klein (eds.). *Promotion and Marketing for Broadcasting, Cable & the Web*, 4th ed. Boston: Focal Press, 2001.

Eicoff, Alvin, and Anne Knudsen. *Direct Marketing through Broadcast Media: TV, Radio, Cable, Infomercials, Home Shopping and More.* Lincolnwood, IL: NTC Publishing Group, 1995.

Einstein, Mara. *Media Diversity: Economics, Ownership, and the FCC.* Mahwah, NJ: Lawrence Erlbaum, 2004.

Fayol, Henri. *General and Industrial Management.* Translated by Constance Storrs. London, England: Sir Isaac Pitman and Sons, 1965.

Fidler, Roger. *Mediamorphosis: Understanding New Media.* Thousand Oaks, CA: Pine Forge Press, 1997.

Forrester, Chris. *The Business of Digital Television.* Boston: Focal Press, 2000.

393

Franklin, Marc A., David A. Anderson, and Fred H. Cate. *Cases and Materials on Mass Media Law,* 6th ed. New York: Foundation Press, 2000.

Gershon, Richard A. *Telecommunications Management: Industry Structures and Planning Strategies.* Mahwah, NJ: Lawrence Erlbaum, 2001.

Gillmor, Donald M., Jerome A. Barron, and Todd F. Simon. *Mass Communication Law: Cases and Comment,* 6th ed. Belmont, CA: Wadsworth, 1998.

Grant, August E., and Jennifer H. Meadows. *Communication Technology Update,* 9th ed. Boston: Focal Press, 2004.

Green, Bill. *NAB Legal Guide to Broadcast Law and Regulation Update.* Washington, DC: National Association of Broadcasters, 1998.

Greenwood, Ken. *High Performance Selling.* West Palm Beach, FL: Streamline Press, 1995.

A Guide to Disability Rights Laws. Washington, DC: U.S. Department of Justice Civil Rights Division, 1996.

Hausman, Carl, Philip Benoit, Frank Messere, and Lewis O'Donnell. *Modern Radio Production: Production, Programming, and Performance,* 6th ed. Belmont, CA: Thomson Wadsworth, 2004.

Hersey, Paul, Kenneth H. Blanchard, and Dewey E. Johnson. *Management of Organizational Behavior: Leading Human Resources,* 8th ed. Englewood Cliffs, NJ: Prentice Hall, 2001.

Herweg, Ashley, and Godfrey Herweg. *Recruiting, Interviewing, Hiring and Developing Superior Salespeople,* 4th ed. Washington, DC: National Association of Broadcasters, 1993.

Herweg, Godfrey, and Ashley Herweg. *Making More Money: Selling Radio Advertising Without Numbers,* 2nd ed. Washington, DC: National Association of Broadcasters, 1995.

Herzberg, Frederick. *Work and the Nature of Man.* Cleveland, OH: World, 1967.

Herzberg, Frederick, Bernard Mausner, and Barbara Bloch Snyderman. *The Motivation to Work,* 2nd ed. New York: John Wiley, 1959.

Hilliard, Robert L., and Michael C. Keith. *Dirty Discourse: Sex and Indecency in American Radio.* Ames: Iowa State Press, 2003.

Hilliard, Robert L., and Michael C. Keith. *The Hidden Screen: Low-Power Television in America.* Armonk, NY: M. E Sharpe, 1999.

Huff, W. A. Kelly. *Regulating the Future: Broadcasting Technology and Governmental Control.* Westport, CT: Greenwood Press, 2001.

Internet and Multimedia 12: The Value of Internet Broadcast Advertising. New York: Arbitron, 2004.

Internet and Multimedia 2005: The On-Demand Media Consumer. Arbitron, and Somerville, NJ: Edison Media Research, 2005.

394

Jablonsky, Stephen F., and Noah P. Barsky. *The Manager's Guide to Financial Statement Analysis*, 2nd ed. Hoboken, NJ: John Wiley & Sons, 2001.

Keith, Michael C. *The Radio Station*, 6th ed. Boston: Focal Press, 2003.

Killebrew, Kenneth C. *Managing Media Convergence: Pathways to Journalistic Cooperation*. Ames, IA: Blackwell, 2004.

Krasnow, Erwin G., J. Geoffrey Bentley, and Robin Martin. *Buying or Building a Broadcast Station in the '90s*, 3rd ed. Washington, DC: National Association of Broadcasters, 1991.

Langevin, Michael J. *Basic Radio Programming Manual*. Washington, DC: National Association of Broadcasters, 1996.

Leslie, Larry Z. *Mass Communication Ethics: Decision Making in Postmodern Culture*, 2nd ed. Boston: Houghton Mifflin, 2004.

Lynch, Joanna R., and Greg Gillispie. *Process and Practice of Radio Programming*. Lanham, MD: University Press of America, 1998.

MacFarland, David T. *Future Radio Programming Strategies: Cultivating Listenership in the Digital Age*, 2nd ed. Mahwah, NJ: Lawrence Erlbaum, 1997.

Maslow, Abraham H. *Motivation and Personality*, 2nd ed. New York: Harper and Row, 1970.

McCauley, Michael P., Eric E. Peterson, B. Lee Artz, and DeeDee Halleck (eds.). *Public Broadcasting and the Public Interest*. Armonk, NY: M. E. Sharpe, 2003.

McGregor, Douglas. *The Human Side of Enterprise*. New York: McGraw-Hill, 1960.

Metcalf, Henry C., and L. Urwick (eds.). *Dynamic Administration: The Collected Papers of Mary Parker Follett*. London: Harper and Brothers, 1942.

Middleton, Kent R., William E. Lee, and Bill F. Chamberlin. *The Law of Public Communication*, 7th ed. Boston: Allyn and Bacon, 2005.

Miles, Peggy. *Internet World Guide to Webcasting: The Complete Guide to Broadcasting on the Web*. New York: John Wiley, 1998.

Mintzberg, Henry. *The Nature of Managerial Work*. Englewood Cliffs, NJ: Prentice Hall, 1980.

Mirabito, Michael M. A., and Barbara Morgenstern. *The New Communications Technologies: Applications, Policy, and Impact*, 5th ed. Boston: Focal Press, 2004.

Mondy, R. Wayne, Robert E. Holmes, and Edwin B. Flippo. *Management: Concepts and Practices*, 2nd ed. Boston: Allyn and Bacon, 1983.

Money Makers II: Sales Promotions from the Hundred Plus Television Markets, 2nd ed. Washington, DC: National Association of Broadcasters, 1996.

Moore, Roy L. *Mass Communication Law and Ethics*, 2nd ed. Mahwah, NJ: Lawrence Erlbaum, 1999.

NAB/BCFM Television Employee Compensation & Fringe Benefits Report. Washington, DC: National Association of Broadcasters, published biennially.

NAB/BCFM 2004 Television Financial Report. Washington, DC: National Association of Broadcasters, 2004.

1998 Report on Television. New York: Nielsen Media Research, 1998.

Noam, Eli, Jo Groebel, and Darcy Gerbarg (eds.). *Internet Television.* Mahwah, NJ: Lawrence Erlbaum, 2004.

Norberg, Eric G. *Radio Programming: Tactics and Strategy.* Boston: Focal Press, 1996.

Orlik, Peter B. *Career Perspectives in Electronic Media.* Ames, IA: Blackwell, 2004.

Ouchi, William G. *Theory Z: How American Business Can Meet the Japanese Challenge.* Reading, MA: Addison-Wesley, 1981.

Overbeck, Wayne G. *Major Principles of Media Law,* 2006 Edition. Belmont, CA: Thomson Wadsworth, 2006.

Owen, Bruce M. *The Internet Challenge to Television.* Cambridge, MA: Harvard University Press, 1999.

Parsons, Patrick R., and Robert M. Frieden. *The Cable and Satellite Television Industries.* Boston: Allyn and Bacon, 1998.

Patterson, Philip, and Lee C. Wilkins. *Media Ethics: Issues and Cases,* 5th ed. New York: McGraw-Hill, 2005.

Pavlik, John V. *New Media Technology: Cultural and Commercial Perspectives,* 2nd ed. Boston: Allyn and Bacon, 1998.

Pember, Don R. *Mass Media Law,* 3rd ed. Dubuque, IA: William C. Brown, 1984.

Perebinossoff, Philippe, Brian Gross, and Lynne S. Gross. *Programming for TV, Radio and the Internet: Strategy, Development and Evaluation,* 2nd ed. Boston: Focal Press, 2005.

Phillips, John B., Jr. *Employment Law Desk Book.* Nashville, TN: M. Lee Smith, 1989.

Picard, Robert G. (ed.). *Media Firms: Structures, Operations, and Performance.* Mahwah, NJ: Lawrence Erlbaum, 2002.

Plum, Shyrl L. *Underwriting 101: Selling College Radio.* Mahwah, NJ: Lawrence Erlbaum, 2000.

Plummer, Deborah L. (ed.). *Handbook of Diversity Management: Beyond Awareness to Competency Based Learning.* Lanham, MD: University Press of America, 2003.

Poindexter, Paula M., and Maxwell E. McCombs. *Research in Mass Communication: A Practical Guide.* Boston: Bedford/St. Martin's, 2000.

Pringle, Charles D., Daniel F. Jennings, and Justin G. Longenecker. *Managing Organizations: Functions and Behaviors.* Columbus, OH: Merrill, 1988.

Public Television, a Program For Action: The Report and Recommendations of the Carnegie Commission on Educational Television. New York: Harper & Row, 1967.

A Public Trust: The Report of the Carnegie Commission on the Future of Public Broadcasting. New York: Bantam Books, 1979.

Radio Marketing Guide & Fact Book, 2004–2005 Edition. Irving, TX: Radio Advertising Bureau, 2004.

Radio Station Web Site Content: An In-Depth Look. Somerville, NJ: Edison Media Research and New York: The Arbitron Company, 2000.

Radio Today: How America Listens to Radio, 2005 Edition. New York: Arbitron, 2005.

Rauscher, David Grant. *The Broadcaster's Guide to the Internet and the World Wide Web.* Washington, DC: National Association of Broadcasters, 1996.

Reinsch, J. Leonard, and E. I. Ellis. *Radio Station Management*, 2nd ed. revised. New York: Harper and Brothers, 1960.

Robbins, Stephen P., and Mary Coulter. *Management*, 8th ed. Upper Saddle River, NJ: Prentice Hall, 2005.

Sadler, Roger L. *Electronic Media Law.* Thousand Oaks, CA: Sage, 2005.

Sashkin, Marshall, and Kenneth J. Kiser. *Putting Total Quality Management to Work: What TQM Means, How to Use It, and How to Sustain It over the Long Run.* San Francisco: Berrett-Koehler, 1993.

Sauls, Samuel J. *The Culture of the American College Radio.* Ames: Iowa State Press, 2000.

Schoderbek, Peter P., Charles D. Schoderbek, and Asterios G. Kefalas. *Management Systems: Conceptual Considerations*, 3rd ed., revised. Plano, TX: Business Publications, 1985.

Schoderbek, Peter P., Richard A. Cosier, and John C. Aplin. *Management.* San Diego, CA: Harcourt Brace Jovanovich, 1988.

Schulberg, Pete. *Radio Advertising: The Authoritative Handbook*, 2nd ed. Lincolnwood, IL: NTC Publishing Group, 1996.

Seel, Peter B., and August E. Grant (eds.). *Broadcast Technology Update.* Boston: Focal Press, 1997.

Seguin, James. *Media Career Guide: Preparing for Jobs in the 21st Century*, 4th ed. Boston: Bedford/St. Martin's, 2004.

Senge, Peter M. *The Fifth Discipline: The Art & Practice of the Learning Organization.* New York: Doubleday, 1990.

Shane, Ed. *Selling Electronic Media.* Boston: Focal Press, 1999.

Sherman, Barry L. *Telecommunications Management: Broadcasting/Cable and the New Technologies*, 2nd ed. New York: McGraw-Hill, 1995.

Siegel, Paul. *Communication Law in America.* Boston: Allyn and Bacon, 2002.

Teeter, Dwight L., Jr., and Bill Loving. *Law of Mass Communications: Freedom and Con-trol of Print and Broadcast Media*, 11th ed. Westbury, NY: Foundation Press, 2004.

Television and Cable Factbook. Washington, DC: Warren Communications News, published annually.

Todreas, Timothy M. *Value Creation and Branding in Television's Digital Age.* Westport, CT: Quorum Books, 1999.

Tracy, John A. *How to Read a Financial Report: Wringing Vital Signs Out of the Numbers*, 6th ed. Hoboken, NJ: John Wiley & Sons, 2004.

Understanding Broadcast and Cable Finance: A Handbook for the Non-Financial Manager. Northfield, IL: BCFM Press, 1994.

Walker, James R., and Douglas A. Ferguson. *The Broadcast Television Industry.* Boston: Allyn and Bacon, 1998.

Warner, Charles, and Joseph Buchman. *Media Selling: Broadcast, Cable, Print and Interactive*, 3rd ed. Ames, IA: Blackwell, 2003.

Warren, Steve. *Radio: The Book*, 4th ed. Boston: Focal Press, 2004.

Weber, Max. *The Theory of Social and Economic Organization.* Translated by A. M. Henderson and Talcott Parsons. Edited with an introduction by Talcott Parsons. New York: The Free Press, 1947.

Webster, James G., and Patricia F. Phalen. *The Mass Audience: Rediscovering the Dominant Model.* Mahwah, NJ: Lawrence Erlbaum, 1997.

Webster, James G., Patricia F. Phalen, and Lawrence W. Lichty. *Ratings Analysis: The Theory and Practice of Audience Research*, 2nd ed. Mahwah, NJ: Lawrence Erlbaum, 2000.

Wicks, Jan LeBlanc, George Sylvie, C. Ann Hollifield, Stephen Lacy, Ardyth Broadrick Sohn, and Angela Powers. *Media Management: A Casebook Approach*, 3rd ed. Hillsdale, NJ: Lawrence Erlbaum, 2004.

Wimmer, Roger D., and Joseph R. Dominick. *Mass Media Research: An Introduction*, 8th ed. Belmont, CA: Thomson Wadsworth, 2006.

Witherspoon, John, Roselle Kovitz, Robert K. Avery, and Alan G. Stavitsky. *A History of Public Broadcasting*, revised ed. Washington, DC: Educational Broadcasting Corp., 2000.

Zelezny, John D. *Cases in Communications Law: Liberties, Restraints, and the Modern Media*, 4th ed. Belmont, CA: Thomson Wadsworth, 2004.

PERIODICALS

Advertising Age. Crain Communications. Weekly.

B&C Broadcasting & Cable. Reed Business Information. Weekly.

Billboard. VNU. Weekly.

Broadband Advertising. Kagan World Media. Monthly.

Broadband Technology. Kagan Research. Monthly.

Broadcast Engineering. Primedia Business Magazines & Media. Monthly.

Broadcast Investor. Kagan Research. Monthly.

Broadcasting and the Law. Monthly.

Cable Fax's Cable WORLD. Access Intelligence. Biweekly.

Cable TV Investor. Kagan Research. Broadcasting and the Law. Monthly.

Columbia Journalism Review. Columbia University, Graduate School of Journalism. Bimonthly.

Communications and the Law. William S. Hein & Co. Quarterly.

Communications Daily. Warren Communications News. Weekdays.

Communicator. Radio-Television News Directors Association. Monthly.

Community Media Review. Alliance for Community Media. Quarterly.

Daily Variety. Reed Business Information. Weekdays.

The DBS Report. Kagan Research. Monthly.

Emmy. Academy of Television Arts & Sciences. Bimonthly.

Entertainment Employment Journal. Studiolot Publishing. Monthly.

Feedback. Broadcast Education Association. Quarterly.

Inside Radio. Inside Radio. Weekdays.

Journal of Broadcasting & Electronic Media. Lawrence Erlbaum. Quarterly.

Journal of Popular Film and Television. Heldref Publications. Quarterly.

Journalism and Mass Communication Quarterly. Association for Education in Journalism and Mass Communication. Quarterly.

Multichannel News. Reed Business Information. Weekly.

NRB Magazine. National Religious Broadcasters. Monthly.

Promax International. Promotion & Marketing Executives in the Electronic Media. Quarterly.

Public Broadcasting Report. Warren Communications News. Biweekly.

R&R. Radio & Records. Weekly.

Radio & Television Business Report. Radio & Television Business Report. Monthly.

Satellite Direct. Vogel Communications. Monthly.

SMPTE Motion Imaging Journal. Society of Motion Picture and Television Engineers. Monthly.

Television Digest with Consumer Electronics. Warren Communications News. Weekly.

Television Quarterly. National Television Academy. Quarterly.

TelevisionWeek. Crain Communications. Weekly.

399

TFM: The Financial Manager. Broadcast Cable Financial Management Association. Bimonthly.

TV Guide. Gemstar/TV Guide International. Weekly.

TV Technology. IMAS Publishing Group. Biweekly.

Variety. Reed Business Information. Weekly.

Wireless Satellite and Broadcasting Telecommunications. Information Gatekeepers. Monthly.

400

Index

402

405

407